lot of sense to a Generation X kid like me . . . At first glance I ...... to be a bit of a ch............ nd it hard to put the book down . . . You just keep getting drawn further and further in, and saying more and more "yeah, that's right!" Iconoclastic, insightful, intriguing, ten out of ten for Mark Davis' *Gangland*', Sandie van der Stolk, *Opus* ¶ 'Deserves to become a manifesto for a disenfranchised generation', *Australian Financial Review* ¶ 'The most significant book I've read for a long time . . . buy it, read it, fight back if you have to. But whatever you do don't ignore it', Ian Syson, *Overland* ¶ 'One of those rare books that prise open a space for revaluation of the direction of a culture . . . exposes tentacular networks of chummy patronage, mutual puffery, and cultural power', John Docker, *Australian Book Review* ¶ 'In the best traditions of the neglected art of

gangland

Mark Davis was born in Geelong, Victoria. He has worked as a clerk, factory hand, surveyor's chainman, storeman, ski-lodge manager, musician and graphic designer. He is married and lives in Melbourne, where he is completing a PhD in the English department at the University of Melbourne. *Gangland* received an honourable mention for 'an outstanding contribution to Australian culture' in the Centre for Australian Cultural Studies 1997 National Awards and was short-listed for the Gleebooks prize in the 1999 New South Wales Premier's Literary Awards.

gangland

cultural elites and the new generationalism

mark davis

second edition

ALLEN & UNWIN

To Foong Ling,
my family,
and in memory of my father

Copyright © Mark Davis 1997, 1999

All rights reserved. No part of this book may be reproduced or transmitted in any form or by any means, electronic or mechanical, including photocopying, recording or by any information storage and retrieval system, without prior permission in writing from the publisher.

This edition published in 1999
First published in 1997 by
Allen & Unwin
9 Atchison Street
St Leonards NSW 1590 Australia
Phone: (61 2) 8425 0100
Fax: (61 2) 9906 2218
E-mail: frontdesk@allen-unwin.com.au
Web: http://www.allen-unwin.com.au

National Library of Australia
Cataloguing-in-Publication data:

Davis, Mark R., 1959– .
  Gangland: cultural elites and the new generationalism.

  Rev. ed.
  Includes index.
  ISBN 1 86508 106 X.

  1. Conflict of generations — Social aspects — Australia. 2. Generation X — Australia — Public opinion. 3. Social classes — Australia. 4. Elite (Social sciences) — Australia. 5. Culture diffusion — Australia. I. Title.

305.50994

Designed and typeset by text-art
Printed by Australian Print Group, Maryborough, Vic.
10 9 8 7 6 5 4 3 2 1

Mark Davis on the web: www.renewal.org.au/markdavis/

Contents

Preface to the second edition. . . . . *ix*
Introduction . . . . *xi*

1 Playing the generation game: insiders, outsiders and the new generationalism *1*
2 The New Establishment: on now at a media outlet near you *21*
3 Running scared: 'political correctness', boomer-whinge and the big panic *45*
4 Stoned again: the 'victim feminism' scare *75*
5 Lockout: 'legislated nostalgia' and 'dumbing-down'. *99*
6 The culture racket: making a literature *113*
7 Growing old gracefully: publishing the 'generation of '68'. *140*
8 An illiberal education: liberals versus the 'postmodern' *155*
9 Canned goods and culture wars: the Metropolis comes to town *184*
10 All hands on deck in the 'Year of the Helens' *208*
11 Dark underbelly: youth, culture, policy. *232*
12 Theory, death and me: a Realpolitik of generationalism *255*
13 Ringing in the changes: life after liberalism *270*

14 Who is at the centre? *302*
15 Damning the torpedoes: politics after punk *326*

   Notes *352*
   Index *383*

Preface to the second edition

It is by extraordinary luck that I have the opportunity here to write a brief preface for a second edition of *Gangland*. Never did I expect the book would be such a success.

This new edition takes up where the first left off. The first twelve chapters and the introduction remain the same here as in the first edition, down to the page numbers. Three new chapters have been added at the end of the book to flesh out and complete its original arguments, as well as to cover events since late 1997.

I was staggered by the amount of coverage the first edition of *Gangland* received. Most was favourable, but the book also created 'controversy', especially among sections of the literati, who seemed to think it was simply about them. The way some of these critics carried on, you'd think I'd said things that were untrue. Having read and listened carefully to these comments, in general I've decided not to deal with those criticisms here. Rather than discuss the issues the book raised in good faith, much of the negative criticism of the book turned out to be disappointingly self-serving and harping.[1] Some of these critics, too, verged on self-parody, underlining the book's argument about gangs and gatekeepers. To write about the Australian cultural establishment is to discover how many of your targets have friends, lovers and ex-lovers who review books.

Gangland

Where appropriate, the new chapters address some of the more relevant issues raised in discussion of the book. Again, as in the first edition, I hope it's understood that the criticisms of individuals' work found here aren't intended to smear reputations or create personal injury. They are intended as commentary on the nature of contemporary Australian debate.

There are, as in any new edition, new people to thank. In addition to all those people I thanked in the first edition who, again, were of enormous assistance, I'd like to thank Stephen Banham, Daniel Batt, Elisa Berg, Rachel Berger, Paul Best, Bec Carey, Geoff Danaher, Simone Ford, John Frow, Craig Garrett, Georgia Gould, Chris Gregory, Alisha Hall, Felicity Holland, Nathan Hollier, Dean Kiley, Mary-Rose MacColl, Peter Milne, Shane Paxton, Sue-Anne Post, Melita Rogowski, silverchair, Ian Syson, Kathryn Tuckwell, Kerry Watson, Marcus Westbury and Drew Williamson. The preparation of this new edition was marred by the untimely death of David McComb, whom I was just getting to know at the time. This new edition, I hope, in some small way serves his memory. I'd also like to thank Stephen Muecke, R. J. Stove and Boris Frankel, who pointed out minor errors in the first edition. These have been corrected in this edition.

I was heartened by the gracious response of many whose work is criticised in this book. Phillip Adams, Louise Adler, Peter Ellingsen, Shelley Gare, Simon Hughes, Rosemary Sorensen, David Williamson, and a number of others displayed a humbling generosity. Others, such as Helen Garner, maintained a dignified silence, which I also admire.

Finally, thanks to all those who wrote letters and sent emails, and all the people I've spoken to while researching both editions of this book. I continue to owe you an enormous debt for the information and suggestions you generously passed on.

> Mark Davis
> Melbourne, May 1999

Introduction

Is there a backlash against young people and the way they think? Has an older generation of cultural apparatchiks, used to being at the centre and having a strong media presence, more or less systematically set out to discredit young people and their ideas, even progressive opinion generally?

Often it seems this is the case. When we see the Paxtons being abused as typical young 'dole bludgers', or the editors of a student newspaper being prosecuted for publishing an article on shoplifting, or young people being described as if they were a different species, it is hard to escape the conclusion that some people have it in for the rising generation. At the same time, younger people are underrepresented in the mainstream media. Where, for example, are the young political commentators and radio talkback hosts? Where are the 'serious' journalists under forty with columns of their own? There are a few, but not many. The field is dominated by opinion-makers who have been around for ten or twenty years, the 'usual suspects' who have nominated themselves as guardians of the nation's moral fibre.

Where are the young feminists? Everywhere, of course. But the old guard still dominates mainstream coverage, as if nothing worthwhile has happened in feminism since 1975. And when young feminists do get published, the old guard tends to pick favourites and jump on the rest.

What's happening in cultural politics? All we find out is filtered through the eyes and ears of people whose formative experiences occurred at least twenty years ago. They seem to have grown conservative and dull, and are frightened of new ideas. A gulf has opened between what they are saying and what younger people are thinking.

Old news, you say? Perhaps; talk of 'generation gaps' has been around for thirty years or so as well. But this time there's a difference.

Behind the hype and trivialisation that has accompanied the much-loathed moniker 'Generation X', young people are suffering. They have the highest suicide rates in the country. They are most likely to be long-term unemployed. The numbers of homeless young people have risen rapidly. They have been among the main losers in cuts to government services. In Australia's new 'flexible' labour market, young people have little prospect of the job security that their parents took for granted.

At the same time, youth and their preoccupations are being discredited, even demonised, in the media. A spate of media stories has focused on youth gangs and youth crime. Young people are caught on the wrong side of an increasing gap between 'official' sanctioned culture and renegade culture. They seem to be drowning in a sea of sixties revivals, while their pleasures — be they dance parties or so-called 'grunge' fiction — are denigrated, ghettoised or ignored.

This book sketches links between these issues. Much of its argument takes place in the context of the 'culture wars' over so-called political correctness, victim feminism, censorship and literary theory. While race and gender politics are at the forefront of the 'culture wars', youth issues are also involved. The fears about declines of ethics, historical memory and old-style politics and aesthetics that are at the heart of the 'culture wars' are often played out across a generation gap. This is especially clear in media debates over Helen Garner's *The First Stone*, or

Introduction

David Williamson's top-grossing play, *Dead White Males*, or Robert Manne's book about the Darville-Demidenko affair, *The Culture of Forgetting*. In a wider sense, the local cultural elite's agonising over the 'culture wars' provides a window on how such elites work, and reveals the imaginary fears and powerful networks that sustain them.

While only a relatively small proportion of the Australian population has attended university — where the 'culture wars' supposedly originate — universities function as a metaphor for wider cultural changes. The shift from mainstream politics to 'identity politics' in the universities registers more widely in young people's disenchantment with party politics and disengagement from the official culture espoused by the print media, where their pleasures are being disregarded or discounted as exotica or esoterica.

Cultural establishments dominate many areas of life — in music there is the old breed of 'oz-rock' record-company executive who signs dance acts because they sell, but secretly longs for the old days of pub-rock; in the visual arts a closed system of gallery patronage militates against younger artists — but in this book I have chosen to concentrate on literature, the arts and the media, especially the broadsheet press. I chose these fields for a number of reasons. First, they are what I know. Secondly, as I was researching this book, I got the feeling that if I looked for generational inequities across the board I could go on for ever, and I had a deadline. Finally, these are the areas of culture that are deemed to have 'intellectual' content. They are where ideas get made and brokered. Where wisdoms, received and otherwise, about current issues are sheltered, nursed and adopted, consciously or unconsciously. Where power plays are made and opinion massaged. Politics and religion, according to the cultural critic Meaghan Morris, have ceased to be the arenas where social ideas are discussed; in the past twenty years they have been displaced by culture. To which I would add, especially by journalistic writing, given the storms that erupted over *The First Stone* or Helen Darville's *The Hand that Signed the Paper*, and the status these events have been accorded in the media as social barometers.

In various ways, every such event over the past few years, obliquely or directly, has involved an attack on youth.

But before I go on, in order to head off some misconceptions and to save myself some hot air later, it's worth talking about what this book is *not* about.

First, despite the possible implications of its title, and of what I have said above, this is not a book that sets out to attack baby-boomers. Rather, it is about those cultural and political elites who have adopted as their own the stereotypical privileges associated with baby-boomers. They are used to being at the centre, used to being listened to. Perhaps twenty-five years ago they were singing 'hope I die before I get old', but now they look forward to an extended economic twilight at the expense of those who follow, and a lifelong tenure at the centre of public commentary on issues and ideas. As it happens, some were born at the height of the baby boom, especially the 1940s, just as some were born before it, but it is their assumption of privilege, not their dates of birth, that will be held against them here.

Nor is this a book about 'generation X'. Frankly, I don't think many so-called Gen-Xers give a shit about generationalism, except when they are victims of it. I take this as a healthy sign. The idea of generationalism is more generally taken up by stereotypical baby-boomers or those who write editorial about them, perpetuating the myth that their generation brought with it a sea-change, a shift in the *Zeitgeist*. But how is such a thing possible? How can anyone deal in such general, even universal concepts now that everything is so heterogeneous — as indeed it was then? Those who volunteered to go to Vietnam are often forgotten in the mythologising about the Woodstock generation. In the context of this book, 'generationalism' isn't a claim I will be making, but is more

Introduction

often a furphy used by the figures I discuss, who lash out on generational grounds at the ideas of those under thirty-five in the same way they perhaps once lashed out on generational grounds at those over thirty-five, as if this might cover for their lack of thinking about new ideas, or their inability to keep up to date. Something, incidentally, that many others of a similar age, who are not prominent in the mainstream media and the 'culture industry', have had little trouble doing.

Nor, on a personal note, is this a book about me. Technically I'm a baby-boomer, albeit a very late one, who got sick of hearing how unlucky I was to have 'just missed out'. Very luckily, I was rescued by a gang of similarly pissed-off late baby-boomers, to 'come of age' in the spirit of punk, not the summer of love. A remarkable thing I find speaking to people of my age (though this book is written around younger people, especially those from their late teens to early thirties) is the extent to which they too feel excluded by the current cultural mafia. It's hard to be continually made to feel 'too young' and 'not up to it' when you're pushing forty. So if I've been forced to use a rather uncomfortable array of third-person terms such as 'youth' and 'younger people' instead of 'we', now you know why. Read this as a kind of inside job.

Finally, this book is not about scrapheaps. I don't think *anyone* should be put on one. I'm not in the business of playing one group or idea off against another — a currently fashionable populist sport — but of insisting that many types of writing and thinking should be able to exist side by side, in a relatively paranoia-free manner. Attempting to demystify something is not the same as tearing it down. What I offer here is a critique, not of specific ideas so much as of the intolerance that currently seems to go with them — a critique of cultural monopoly. This critique is made with what might seem an old-fashioned objective in mind: that is, with a view to opening up new ideas about spaces for public debate and policy-making. This is important, especially given the declining availability of public spaces generally, and especially to the young — swamped, like everything else, by the 'more of the same' mentality espoused by those used to having their hands on the levers of opinion.

Gangland is also in part about the refusal of a certain cultural establishment to let go. In their determination to hang on to a virtual monopoly (gerrymander, shut-down, lockout, call it what you will) on the ideas market, its members refuse to acknowledge that paradigms are clashing, changing, in almost every area of life, and they scapegoat a younger generation for the shifts. There is an unwillingness to admit that ideas can no longer pretend to cut across all times and places.

'Boomer-whinge' — a term that appears several times in this book — describes the particular set of values that underpins that refusal to let go. Here the panics over the 'culture wars', 'political correctness' and 'victim feminism', over rap music, Ecstasy and piercings, meet up with the endless newspaper features mythologising Hendrix, reinventing the 1960s, revisiting the Vietnam war and telling people about the difficulties of 'living in the nineties'. Our cultural landscape is currently peppered with examples of a desperate, backward-looking stasis, a fearful hanging on, manifested as a long, slow, unproductive whinge.

This book is also about youth policy, and a certain culture of generationalism it has fostered in relation to young people, again in the wake of anti-youth scaremongering. The spectre of the 'teen gang' is a media cliché that can be linked to a new harshness in law-making and sentencing. Another worry is the growing legislative attention to censorship of music, videos and the Internet, all aimed at restricting youth access. At the same time, young people have borne much of the burden of the major political parties' bipartisan commitment to economic rationalism. Policies to alleviate youth unemployment, homelessness and suicide have been neglected, schools have been

Introduction

closed down, fees imposed in higher education, youth wages reduced and access to the dole tightened.

What follows is a series of interlinked chapters that do not attempt to move towards a conclusion so much as span a range of concerns. Sometimes these concerns overlap; there are strong similarities between the forces driving the vilification of the so-called 'politically correct' and 'victim feminists', for example, but I treat them as separate issues here. Others are sequential. The chapter on how writers are published, for example, flows from the one on how literatures are made. None of these chapters pretends to be conclusive. Instead they are a series of sketches, even snapshots, of particular moments in particular sections of the 'culture industry' and the 'policy industry'. They name names, map networks, show who is who, and point to patterns of ideas that drive the whole machine, linking what might appear to be an unstructured mass of random events to an extent that I failed to anticipate when I started researching. These chapters, I must point out, also exist to be differed with; I hope I am offering up topics for discussion. What they don't do is attempt a deep theoretical analysis. For all my own involvement with cultural theory, what I offer here is largely an old-fashioned, empirical account of events; a scholarly account, interested in specific dates and places, and facts. Not that I regard such facts as absolute or final. But they offer a better basis for debate than some of the skewed and anecdotal versions that have been passed off as debate on many of these issues so far.

Given that this book is at least in part about the hidden allegiances and clubbishness that shape our intellectual and cultural lives, I would like to declare mine at the outset. Nothing happens in a vacuum, and I, like many I take to task here, have been fortunate to have influential friends, even if they don't run national cultural agendas. Without them this book would never have been published. But in the main my support has come from the much less influential, and I would like to thank them first. In particular, my thanks go to Foong Ling Kong for her intellectual rigour and shared enjoyment of philosophy-in-the-kitchen. Thanks too to the many friends, peers, associates and interviewees I pestered throughout this project, especially Penny D, Annie M, Stuart H, Linda F, Gary G, Alex T, Christos T, Wayne V der S, Mel T, Kaz C and Neil J, even if I know they'll find much to disagree with here. I would like to thank my family for their support and ribbing. Special thanks go to Katrina Tannock, who contributed so much to the enthusiastic genesis of this book, but tragically didn't live to see it published.

I am also grateful to Philip, Jenna and Sylvia Mead, who were the try-out audience for the very first glimmerings of an idea in their lounge room many years ago, and to Jenna, especially, for putting up with my questions about the Ormond affair and *The First Stone*. The publication of that book, though torturous for her, proved useful for me. Deepest thanks also to Jenny Lee, who, as editor of *Meanjin*, gave me my first encouragement as a writer, and for her continuing friendship, as well as for all her work on the manuscript. Thanks also to K.K. Ruthven, Meaghan Morris, Teresa O'Sullivan, Stephen Muecke, George Papaellinas, John Bangsund and Moira Rayner. None of which is to say that any of the above endorse what follows. Other thanks go to my many friends among the staff at Melbourne University, and the postgrads down at the pub. No apologies for snippets of conversation you might find in here.

Thanks too to my agent, Fiona Inglis, whose friendship, enthusiasm and support helped me survive the writing, and to my publishers Allen & Unwin, especially Sophie Cunningham, Patrick Gallagher, and Monica Joyce for showing the same faith in me as a writer as they have shown in our long previous association as client and book designer.

Introduction

This is an unashamedly provocative book, but I had no intention of writing a hateful book. So small is Australia's literary and arts culture that in the process of researching it I have run into many of the people whose ideas I attack here. With rare exceptions, I have found them likeable and humorous. I would like to thank them too.

In her book *Bad Manners*, Kate Jennings describes how an earlier book of hers was 'bazooka-ed' by the critics.[1] Jennings often trots out precisely the sort of unflappable stock-seventies orthodoxies that I'm critical of, and I've quoted her accordingly. Yet in places I've also quoted her *for* my argument. The borderlines that spring up in debates like this are rarely as clear-cut as they seem, and the rules of engagement are often misunderstood. To quote Jennings:

> I was hung, drawn and quartered by reviewers for my last book of essays. My crime: I generalised, particularly about Australia and Australians. Yet generalisations are the stock in trade of essayists. I was also charged with palming off opinion as fact, when essays are notorious for being exploratory in spirit, but unequivocal in tone. Qualifying words and phrases, such as 'perhaps', 'maybe', 'in my experience', and 'I think' are routinely dropped; it is a convention of the genre. If essayists hedged their bets, you wouldn't enjoy reading them; their essays would be lumpy with appeasement.[2]

What follows is not intended as a personal attack, which isn't to say debate should lack passion. If, as I argue, we need forums for debate that allow sophisticated positions, then I hope I have granted sufficient credit to the sophistications of those whose work I discuss here.

Finally, one of the best things about writing this book was the instant support the idea received from a myriad of people I hardly knew, whom I met at parties, through mutual friends, through work, in interviews, or in the process of researching.

Gangland

Thanks for your enthusiasm, which I have shamelessly fed off and used to endure the slog. I hope what follows encapsulates some of the frustration you expressed and justifies the hopes you vested in it.

> Mark Davis
> Melbourne, May 1997

Playing the generation game: insiders, outsiders and the new generationalism

> *Just imagine what will happen when your classic baby boomers get over 50 and start to feel ignored because they're supposed to be past it.*
>
> Don Porritt of the research group AMR: Quantum[1]

> *no one was ever supposed to be younger than we are.*
>
> Michael Kinsley, US writer, on baby-boomers

Have you seen that ad for the Yellow Pages? The one where a woman takes her kids shopping when she could have used the phone instead? She's in the shop trying to talk to the salesperson and there they are, the two kids, in the foreground, unruly, unpleasant little shits, fighting, hell-bent on destruction. True, kids aren't necessarily angels. And it's nice to see a little truth in advertising. But what's the bigger picture?

The most prized generation of kids, of course, were the baby-boomers, born between 1945 and 1960. Arriving in the aftermath of a world war, they signified new hope and new beginnings, and grew up in an era of unprecedented prosperity. These days most baby-boomers, like the woman in the ad, have had kids. And are they trouble!

Don't want to get out of bed on Christmas morning? asks an ad for the newly inaugurated Christmas Day edition of a newspaper. Get it delivered. Let the kids have their fun while you lie in bed and read the paper. What, open the presents with them? Forget it. If you live in a house built since the mid-1970s, chances are you won't hear them anyway. They'll be down the other end of the house, in the area zoned for their use, while you'll be in your 'parents' retreat', a hideaway separated from theirs by the kitchen and formal living areas, complete with its own adjoining bathroom and study.

This physical distance is lately cultural. Signalling disdain for younger people and their culture is now a media sport. When Nirvana lead singer Kurt Cobain committed suicide, the columnist Bill Wyndham wrote:

> The greater tragedy is not that Cobain is dead. After all, just how many brown and sonorous chord cacophonies does the world need? No, the real pity is that his demise has temporarily overshadowed another native of Seattle who also burned out at the tender age of 27: Jimi Hendrix.[2]

This columnist's line (common throughout the media), that Cobain and his generation lacked 1960s-style cool, prompted a storm of letters:

> Wyndham is typical of the survivors of the summer of love. They now grapple with mid-life crises and deify the heroes of their adolescence — Hendrix, Morrison, Joplin — while denigrating the very special place artists such as Kurt Cobain and Nirvana have in expressing the anger, cynicism and intelligence of *their* generation.
>
> It is folks like Wyndham who have given us the scourge of classic rock on our radio, and the endless misty-eyed reminiscences of the carefree '60s on our screens. It is also this same tribe of burnt-out hippies that told us that greed was good as they rampaged through the free market in the '80s, and then asked us to pay the price with chronic unemployment in its aftermath.[3]

Playing the generation game

Or:

> Cobain was no Jim Morrison; he didn't suffer for his art specifically: in a world full of AIDS, environmental destruction, rampant drug addiction, basic disillusionment, etc, he just suffered . . . The greater tragedy is not that the culturally smothering baby boomers don't want us to have heroes of our own . . . No, the real pity is that they trashed the place and left us to clean up.[4]

Those who disparaged Cobain weren't alone in representing young people as a bunch of spoilt whingers who buckle when the going gets tough. As a *Newsweek* columnist put it:

> As a baby boomer, I'm fed up with the ceaseless carping of a handful of spoiled, self-indulgent, overgrown adolescents. Generation Xers may like to call themselves the 'Why Me' generation, but they should be called the 'Whiny' generation . . . [T]he twenty-somethings were indulged with every toy, game and electronic device available. They didn't even have to learn how to amuse themselves since Mom and Dad were always there to ferry them from one organized activity to another . . . Now, when they finally face adulthood, they expect the gift-giving to continue.[5]

Deirdre Macken, writing in the Fairfax colour freebie *Good Weekend*, claims 'Gen X-ers', as she calls them, aren't so much whining as plain repellent:

> There is a new genre of literature on the streets called 'grunge lit' . . . these books have heaps of sex, drugs, sex with men, drinking, sex with women, violence, sex with nose rings . . . guys, you're writing about stuff we've never imagined. Hell, we wouldn't have owned up to those thoughts if we were on an LSD trip with Mick Jagger. I can feel the chasm of a generation gap opening up and, frankly, I'm glad to put a bit of distance between us [. . .] I saw an

advertisement for body piercing in a 'youth magazine' (sounds benign, doesn't it). It was a close-up photograph of a ring piercing what I presumed was a bellybutton . . . On closer inspection it wasn't a navel. It was a . . . let's just say that the Nursing Mother's Association is going to have a tough job dispensing advice to breastfeeding mothers in a few years [. . .] When we Baby Boomers face the children, we only have to explain why we thought floral flares and towering cork shoes were attractive [. . .] But when these X-ers have kids, they're going to have to answer queries like [. . .] 'When I grow up will I grow a hole in my nose too?'[6]

Her tone is familiar. Some readers will recognise it in federal education minister Amanda Vanstone's accusation that university students complaining about fee rises are 'the ugly face of self-interest' and 'selfish little brutes . . . squealing like stuck pigs'.[7] They might recognise it in Helen Garner's assertion in her book *The First Stone* that the complainants in a university sexual harassment case were punitive, 'priggish' and 'pitiless'.[8]

Younger people just can't get it right. They're either full of piercings or complete prudes. Whatever the case, they just aren't *it*. No matter what the commentators' complaint, the rhetorical strategy remains the same, which is to put a distance between their own self-consciously invoked generation and those who follow.

Meanwhile, as if to reinforce the sense of disparity between one era and another — the metaphorical distance from parents' retreat to kid's bedroom — newspaper feature articles with titles like 'Trapped in the Nineties'[9] and 'The Nervous Nineties', complaining about the perils of living in a new, unfamiliar age, have become a genre in themselves. They're full of anxiety:

> The recession struck harder than anyone had prepared us for and the gap between income groups began to yawn as the

middle class felt its grip on the Nice Life slipping inexorably. The class which accounted for 70 per cent of the population in the early '80s comprised barely 40 per cent in 1992, using income as a measure.[10]

Daunting statistics, but note the assumption about readership. Who is the 'us' mentioned in the first line? One assumption is that readers are old enough to compare this decade to others of their adulthood. Another is that they feel out of sorts living in an era that isn't 'theirs'. The illustration accompanying this particular article featured a man developing in stages, from caveman to bearded hippy, complete with peace medallion, to a sharp 1970s businessman in a suit with mile-wide lapels, then a 1980s shyster with Gordon Gecko slicked-back hair, and finally as ageing house-husband, carrying a child. It's the classic born-in-the-1940s time-line: male-centred, complete with early idealism, a thirty-something flush of wealth, late child-rearing and fear of change, with anxiety represented as the feminisation of men. The overwhelming rhetoric is one of loss: look at all those things being *taken away*.

Another recent line in newspaper journalism is the feature designed to 'explain' developments in youth culture. Again, the assumption is that those who might be party to these cultures aren't part of the reading audience. It's as if, having set themselves up as the generation to end all generations, feature writers are keeping a sort of watching brief on any youth culture that might intrude to remind them of their age. These features function like spotters' guides, designed to translate lifestyles that might otherwise seem incomprehensible into comforting, familiar prose, with anthropologising titles like 'Kids These Days',[11] or 'Melbourne's Tribes',[12] or even 'What Teen is That?'[13] The last-mentioned identifies nine different types, from 'genus hippie to 'genus Christian', and is illustrated by an unflattering portrayal of various misfits. In 'Melbourne's Tribes', Surfers, Punks and Skaters are listed as major 'tribes', with Ferals, Goths, Homeboys, Rastafarians, Mods, Metal Fans and Grungers listed as minor categories, each with its own neat little description, like a bird-spotters' handbook. Another piece entitled 'Just Don't Call us Ferals' purports to explain the strange lifestyles of environmental activists, describing them as 'children who had grown up comfortable, gone native, gone tribal, gone feral, whatever. But most certainly gone'.[14]

There is little attempt to engage with the ideas that underpin these cultures. Instead it's all about reassimilating and repackaging their most superficial aspects for general 'understanding'. The effect is one of youth being offered up for consumption — or at least titillation. Another article, 'What to Wear Out When You Want to Fit In', laments the complexity of today's 'sub-cultures' and gives fashion tips on how to look like 'The Grunger', 'The Gothic', 'The Skater' and 'The Homeboy'.[15] Journalist Susan Kurosawa has even put together a book on youth subcultures in which she claims there are 'at least 10 distinct species of teenagers'.[16]

Even when the press tries to go beyond superficial physical appearances, it still tends to ghettoise younger people. Well-meaning special features designed to give young people a chance to tell their stories 'in their own words', such as an 8-page 'Teen Spirit' liftout in the *Sunday Age* based on interviews with a range of teenagers, or a series 'Generation S' in the *Sydney Morning Herald*, nevertheless reinforce the impression that young people are a different race.[17] Why should such articles be necessary? Who is representing whom here, and for whom? If there was any real 'cross-generational' inclusiveness in these newspapers, such articles could hardly justify their existence.

Never has a 'generation' looked over its shoulder so constantly and with such fear. The early baby-boomers are now turning fifty. Magazines and newspapers have celebrated the event with a fit of self-indulgence that is almost a parody of the stereotypes of white, liberal privilege associated with that age group. A 1996 special issue of *Life* magazine, for example, was entirely devoted to celebrating the 'birthday' (its centrespread was a full-colour photo of the JFK assassination). As always, chinks of uncomfortable light are provided by the non-baby-boomer party-poopers — cited in that issue of *Life* as 'a couple of token Gen-Xers' who helped to produce the issue, and to 'keep us in check'.[18]

From Mickey Mouse Club to Frequent Flier Club, baby-boomers have traditionally led a clubbish life organised around happenings and trends, from the twist to hula hoops to frisbees to disco to aerobics to line dancing. They give the impression that baby-boomerdom itself is a club, an exclusive gang, with everyone else on the outer. As a way of understanding, the anthropologisation that goes with such clubbishness is doomed to failure. But that hasn't stopped feature writers pretending that the generation following them can be dismissed, not so much as a generation as an object of curiosity. 'Gen X', for them, is also a club. A bad one. Not so much a generation as a retrograde 'trend'.

Like *Life* magazine, many newspapers cater predominantly to the 35-plus demographic. In line with this, other taste-makers have done their best to ensure that older cultures are everywhere, replicated according to some sort of idealised model of what life was like during the 1950s, 1960s and even 1970s. If it's not newspaper columnists lamenting Kurt Cobain's lack of baby-boomer cachet, then it's conservative radio-station playlist managers prescribing a never-ending diet of 'classic rock'. Or television programmers and film-makers rehashing old shows from the 1950s and 1960s. Or theatre repertoire managers dishing up ever more recycled relics imported from some long-lost golden era of stage and song. Or literary gatekeepers disparaging young writers who depart from a certain style of realist descriptive prose.

Gangland

Even the personages have remained the same. Many of the same columnists have been writing the same newspaper columns for more than twenty years, and 'chatting' about the same issues to the same radio hosts who have been there for as long. In the major political parties, even elected representatives have stayed more or less the same, at least at the senior level, with a familiar procession of party hacks swapping portfolios endlessly among themselves, having run the gauntlet of — or just plain run — labyrinthine systems of entrenched, matesy patronage.

Entertainment and sport industries aside, where in the cultural 'mainstream' are the hordes of new young voices? In television there is a generation that monopolises current-affairs reporting, and in theatre another that keeps a firm hand on repertoire and casting. Those who work in advertising will be familiar with the 'bushy moustache' generation of the 1970s and 1980s still calling the shots. In the music industry new young acts and hip middle managers come and go, looking for ever-elusive job satisfaction, while senior management lingers on. The story is much the same in other business sectors: many people under the age of thirty-five or so feel stuck in a never-ending 'apprenticeship', constantly being told they are 'not ready'.

Given the preponderance of 'classic hits' formats and talk shows, it doesn't take a genius to figure out the mean age of radio stations' target listeners. As comedian Tony Martin says, 'I listen into those shows and it's like I'm listening to my parents having a conversation'.[19] But alternatives to the status quo often get short shrift. When the volunteer youth radio station HITZ FM was granted a trial licence in Melbourne in 1994, playing predominantly techno, trance, hip-hop, rap and independently produced Australian music by artists then seldom heard on commercial radio such as Kulcha and Rebekah Ryan, it immediately gathered a sizeable audience. As word of mouth spread, the ratings of the 'classics hits' stations began to take a

Playing the generation game

beating, and this small station, with no paid announcers, was able to top the ratings among the under-30s, with 15.1 per cent of the 10–17 age group and 12.8 per cent of the 18–24 age group.[20] Fox FM fell from first to fourth. After lobbying from within the industry, HITZ FM's licence was not renewed, and Australian Broadcasting Authority rules were changed so that trial broadcasters were limited to one month rather than three, denying them the opportunity to generate a following. Two years later, when three bidders competed for a single licence for a 'youth station', HITZ FM's application was fiercely contested by established radio stations on the grounds that they had yet to show community support.[21]

Even as young bands like silverchair, Spiderbait and Savage Garden have given inspiration, confidence and heart to a new generation of young fans and musicians, governments have lost interest in sponsoring distinctive local work that reflects the aspirations of a teen and twenty-something generation. The government support that local music enjoyed during the 1970s and 1980s has fallen away, with subsidies for under-age gigs and funding for organisations like Ausmusic and the Push in steep decline. More bands battle it out for fewer gigs, as the appealingly down-at-heel pubs of the 1980s are reborn as steel, glass and blond-wood bars or gambling venues. All this has happened at the same time as music shows have fallen off prime-time TV schedules.

Now that it's no longer the baby-boomers' cultural artefacts that are pushing boundaries, and no longer them doing the shocking, censorship is suddenly on the agenda — often supported by the very people who lobbied so hard for the relaxation of controls in the first place. In 1995 the Labor government put the music industry on notice to institute a code of self-censorship dealing with explicit and potentially offensive lyrics, or have a mandatory code imposed on it. The pressure for censorship intensified after the Port Arthur massacre. The new Howard government sought to toughen up the requirements of the code, despite the fact that public submissions from the music-listening community had reflected broad and substantial rejection of the previous proposals — concerns that were summarily swept aside by the Labor Attorney-General. After Port Arthur the State Attorneys-General, backed by the federal government, unanimously demanded that an over-18 category be instituted, as well as a refusal-of-classification category, and that a hotline be established for 'concerned citizens' to dob in retailers they found selling 'offensive' material. In late 1996, rather than have a mandatory scheme imposed on it, the industry adopted a voluntary code of conduct on a twelve-month trial, in which warnings would appear on CDs and cassettes with offensive lyrics, and those with lyrics advocating extreme violence or crime would be banned.[22] That's you, Death Metal and Gangsta fans.

Rave parties are another target of the culture brokers. Newspapers had a field day following the death of 15-year-old Anna Wood after a dance party, apparently due to Ecstasy use. 'Anna's Deadly Party', screamed the headline on the Sydney *Daily Telegraph Mirror*, followed by a sub-head that read: 'On Saturday night, Anna Wood, 15, took a $70 ecstasy tab and went to a dance party. At 3.55 pm yesterday she died.'[23] As stories went, it had all the elements — youth, youth drug, dance party, death — wrapped up in a neat little package. Most comments on Wood's death demonised the dance scene and Ecstasy as the youth drug of choice. Her friends too were demonised as uncaring and callous. Yet no direct link has been established between Wood's death and Ecstasy. Her friends, it was later revealed, were not so much callous as lacking information. In the press there was little mention of the dehydration that many Ecstasy users suffer and how to avoid it, or of the free liquids provided at most dance parties. In May 1997 the New South Wales government announced tighter controls on dance parties, preventing their being advertised as 'raves'.

Playing the generation game

Things are different when the drug of choice is not one exclusively associated with youth. According to Paul Dillon of the University of New South Wales' Drug and Alcohol Research Centre, the same weekend that Anna Wood died, six teenage boys died as a result of alcoholic poisoning, without mention in the press.[24] The *Telegraph Mirror* hasn't exactly been helping on the drugs information front since then, either. In early 1996 the paper campaigned against the 'check yourself before you wreck yourself' harm minimisation campaign on the grounds that it promoted drug abuse.

Younger people, it seems, are some kind of trouble. Their dress doesn't fit the paradigms. Their music doesn't fit the paradigms. Their art doesn't fit the paradigms. Their behaviour doesn't fit the paradigms. Everything from dance parties to youth gatherings ('gangs') to recent new fiction is reported in a climate of chronic social difference, fear, moral decline and scandal. The party's over. Man the barricades. Pull up the bridges. It's all downhill from here on.

The pattern keeps repeating. At the invitation of a road construction firm, art students in 1996 put up Barbara Kruger-like posters on Melbourne construction hoardings, with the messages 'You know your superiority is an illusion', 'Why are you afraid of your vulnerability?' and 'Why do you control?' The posters were covered up after direct intervention from the Kennett government. As it happens, Kruger herself was in Melbourne shortly afterwards. 'Don't be a jerk' was her message, plastered on large billboards over town. They stayed.

Censorship had already been on the Victorian government's mind. In 1994 it passed the Tertiary Education Amendment Act, forbidding student organisations from publishing student newspapers out of their own members' funds. As a result several student newspapers were forced to close down, or to rely on patronage from university administrations and the federal government. The media gave remarkably little coverage to the protests against these changes, and the important free-speech issues they raised have barely entered any national political agenda.

Student newspapers were again in the news when the editors of the La Trobe University student newspaper, *Rabelais*, published an article on shoplifting. Politicians, business figures and a range of 'community leaders' spoke out against the article. Amid all the moral outrage, there was no serious discussion about why students might need to shoplift, or what issues are raised when politicians curtail freedom of speech. Simon Crean, then Labor's Minister for Higher Education, personally intervened to ensure that any student publication republishing the article as a gesture of solidarity would have its funding curtailed. Crean promised John Laws on his 2UE radio show that 'if there's something that can be done about this by us, the Federal Government, it will be done'.[25] The following day Crean reportedly notified the Victorian Attorney-General, Jan Wade, of legal avenues under which the students could be prosecuted, and wrote to Laws to confirm he would be cutting *Rabelais*' funding. The four students were subsequently charged under the Victorian *Classification of Films and Publications Act 1990*. At around the same time two major women's magazines, *She* and *Australian Women's Forum*, published articles in which they revealed shoplifting techniques, attracting no adverse commentary. The *Rabelais* article had previously been published on eleven separate occasions between late 1991 and 1995, without any legal action being taken.[26]

Then there was the rant of talkback shock-jock Alan Jones, also on 2UE, launching a broadside at the band Regurgitator and their song 'I Sucked a Lot of Cock to Get Where I Am' for what Jones claimed was its rampant, youth-destroying obscenity. Or that of John Laws, who reportedly embarked on a five-minute tirade against the students — 'those feminist bitches' — at the centre of the Ormond College sexual harassment case partially described in *The First Stone*.[27]

Playing the generation game

In 1996 the Howard Liberal government massively increased the university fees scale introduced by the previous Labor government, providing the spectacle of a generation of politicians who received free university educations in effect legislating away the careers of many poorer young people. The education minister, Amanda Vanstone, advised students to consider apprenticeships, and suggested that they needed to 'take a reality check'.[28]

Soon afterwards the federal government announced a proposal to restrict Medicare provider numbers, limiting new medical graduates' ability to practise and denying them access to the same professional privileges as their peers. The proposal was watered down only after doctors went on strike.

Then there was the case of the three young adults from the Paxton family who were vilified after they refused to accept jobs at a Queensland tourist resort in a set-up situation organised by *A Current Affair*. The resort owner later conceded that he had offered the Paxtons jobs to get publicity, and had gone into receivership six days earlier. John Laws called the Paxtons 'putrid' on his 2UE programme, and they were publicly attacked as 'bludgers' by the prime minister, John Howard. The original segment on *A Current Affair* didn't mention that the jobs were offered on the basis that all three Paxtons had to take them, and that they had to cut their hair (from one generation to the next, the cry remains the same: 'get a haircut'), or that it was within the Paxtons' rights to refuse these conditions. The Paxton affair was a ratings coup for *A Current Affair*, which ran seven stories on the family, attracting over two million viewers each time. Meanwhile, the Department of Social Security cut off the Paxtons' benefits, and they were deluged with hate mail. Soon afterwards the government introduced a diary-surveillance system for the unemployed and announced a 'dob in a dole bludger' campaign.[29]

Nor did *A Current Affair* make an effort to explain that there are many more unemployed youth than jobs available.

Gangland

Younger people have suffered disproportionately as a result of recent economic policies. Of the total pool of unemployed, 40 per cent are aged 15 to 24.[30] The number of full-time job vacancies for young people in 1995 was half that of 1960. According to Professor Ann Harding of the University of Canberra's National Centre for Social and Economic Modelling, of the 11 per cent of Australians living in poverty as of May 1995, 31 per cent were aged under 14.[31]

When young writers have addressed these new realities, their work has been ghettoised and dismissed under the tag 'grunge', as if all they offered was a pale Antipodean reflection of the 'authentic' American 'grunge' literary tradition made famous by Raymond Carver. Typical of the misunderstanding that goes on was an interview with Justine Ettler, author of *The River Ophelia*, by Andrea Stretton on SBS's *Bookmark* show. Stretton asked time and time again, with disbelief, how Ettler faced the anguish and despair that are the themes of her fiction without caving in to them. Ettler's response — that this is what many young people do every day — was almost incomprehensible to Stretton. It seemed a shock to her that some of the themes of this fiction drew not so much on an American fashion as on a current Australian urban reality for many younger people finding ways to live with high suicide rates, high unemployment rates, reduced access to education and high rates of infection with HIV/AIDS. Or that writing now might be alienated by the failures of soft, fuzzy liberalism. As the writer Christos Tsiolkas puts it: 'there seems to be no hope in any social movement'.[32]

Mainstream commentators complain that there is little room for metaphor or experimentation in recent culture; meanwhile, its contexts and subtleties remain unread. Novels such as Bret Easton Ellis's *Less Than Zero* and *American Psycho*, which attempted to be satires as well as social documents, have been treated as literal prescriptions for moral decline. Films with cult cachet among the under-30s such as Quentin Tarantino's

Playing the generation game

Pulp Fiction are judged along similar literal-minded lines, in ways that 'authorised culture' isn't.

Lately the moral panic about youth culture has given rise to repressive legislation as well. The trend began in Western Australia during the early 1990s. After a series of deaths resulting from high-speed police chases involving young people in stolen cars, the Labor government, led by Carmen Lawrence, passed the draconian *Crime (Serious and Repeat Offenders Sentencing Act) 1992*. The Act put quite a few kids in jail — especially Aboriginal kids — and deprived the rest of some fundamental human rights, but it didn't stop the chases. The Labor government's legislate-the-problem-away approach nevertheless found imitators elsewhere. Since then pressure to introduce youth curfews, wider police powers and mandatory sentencing for juvenile crime has built up in several States. Meanwhile, back in the West, the Court Liberal government continued the crackdown, introducing military-style boot camps for young offenders.

But if this argument so far has seemed to be embracing the idea of generationalism, that isn't quite the case. The taunt of generationalism here generally comes from above. 'Generation X' isn't an expression used by anyone in the age group it refers to. Generationalism itself, as a marker of intrinsic difference, is an idea distinctly out of fashion except, it seems, among those who like to think of themselves as *the* generation, and who use the idea to keep a little distance between themselves and whoever follows.

This book, then, isn't so much an argument for generationalism as an argument against it, even if the word will inevitably be used in a more positive sense where there is progressive social change and exuberant defiance. As I see it, generationalism, like gender or race, is one of the major 'regulatory categories' around which Western culture is organised, though it's often overlooked as such. Discourses of generationalism manifest themselves in many ways. They are used to signify a group of similar age or background, or to signify change and differentiate between 'eras' according to a familial logic. Or, in a more sinister way, to inscribe social divides, with one group to one side and one on the other, according to some kind of essentialist logic. I want to discuss generationalism here primarily in terms of the way the idea is used to single out social groups, apportioning tastes and ideologies according to age, to set up young people, even demonise them, as 'outsiders'. This 'new generationalism' is currently acting as a kind of cultural gatekeeping, and is underpinned by a specific political economy.

The present outbreak of generationalism is unlike previous outbreaks, in that it takes place against the background of the rise of economic rationalism, the increase in particular forms of youth demonisation in the wake of the US 'culture wars', and the sheer numbers of baby-boomers in the population. Younger people have grown up in the shadow of a giant demographic bulge, which foreshadows certain social problems. In other respects too, they've grown up in a distinctive 'era' that they take as 'theirs', even as others question whether it can produce authentic cultures of its own. Work patterns have changed: casual work has taken over from full-time work as the main area of employment growth. Families have changed: this is an age of single parents and 'blended' families. Younger people have grown up in an era marked by HIV/AIDS and a decline in health services. Even the food people eat is different, with takeaway becoming the norm. The dominant belief systems of the early to mid-twentieth century have changed. This is an age of discredited philosophies and institutions: the church, state, family and even the sciences no longer have the authority they once did.

At the same time, economic insecurity has become endemic in most Western countries, producing its own kind of social nostalgia. The growth in real wages peaked in the mid-1970s, as most Western economies ended a remarkable period of expansion. Geopolitical balances have also shifted with the end of the Cold War; the global political is operating in new ways, and the sorts of struggles that take place within it have changed. The idea of public culture has dwindled, with public institutions being privatised or corporatised and media ownership being concentrated in fewer and fewer hands. Economies have become globalised, markets rationalised and corporations downsized, making this quite a different world from that of even twenty years ago. Such shifts, as I suggest throughout this book, are liable to produce their own kinds of ideas, solutions and art.

There have been technological shifts too. The advent of cheap digital technology has affected all the standard technologies of mid-twentieth-century modernity, from photography to international stock trading to marketing, surveillance, communications, inventory-keeping, medicine, scientific modelling, (on-line) information provision and urban planning, altering the way information is collected, stored, processed and reproduced, changing the relationship between cultural production and cultural consumption. A book, for example, can be written, edited, designed and laid out on a home computer — as this one was — without recourse to typesetters and production houses; this has made publishing technology more widely available, yet has spelt the death of entire trades such as typesetting, colour-combining and plate-making, all of which are in rapid decline.

On the face of it, fragmentation is a handy word to describe it all. Trades and industries, even nations, are fragmenting, and perhaps realigning according to different principles, much as digital technology fragments information into discrete particles that have no readily apparent 'natural' relationship with each other. If analogue information is physically discrete, involves linearity and is relatively difficult to manipulate or duplicate, then digital information is organised primarily according to mathematical principles, is otherwise non-linear, and is almost infinitely malleable.

A link between technology and culture can be seen in the way the ready propagation of digital information over networks such as the Internet problematises ideas such as the notion of sacred intellectual property. It hardly seems possible to describe the way cultures are organised now without taking these developments into account. Pastiche and eclecticism now rule in fashion, in music, in design and in film, even in what was once haute cuisine, with styles melded together, ever shifting, never stable. 'Linear' classicism is everywhere in retreat, except when it is rejuvenated to take part in pastiche. Witness acid jazz, hip-hop sampling and sound borrowing, 'genre mining' in contemporary film, multi-tasking in jobs, and even the inability of couturiers to find a new definitive 'look'. In the process, the boundaries between 'high' and 'low' cultures are blurring as new, hybrid forms come to the fore.

In graphic design new digital typefaces such as 'Dead History', 'Illiterate' and 'Template Gothic' satirise the traditional type virtues of classicism and legibility. According to its designer Barry Deck, Template Gothic is designed to look 'as if it had suffered the distortive ravages of photomechanical reproduction': everything has already been done, and now can only be endlessly reproduced. Compared with traditional typefaces, it 'reflects more truly the imperfect language of an imperfect world inhabited by imperfect beings'.[33] Template Gothic is a typeface that does seem to say 'now'; it is used in the credits of Channel Ten's nightly news bulletin.

At the same time, there has been a shift in the familiar ground rules of the great political and social struggles of the last hundred years. Activists are asking whether rights advocacy necessarily involves 'essentialism', and what notion of inherent 'identity' is needed to maintain political solidarity. Which isn't to say the old headings are no longer seen as important —

there has probably never been greater emotional or conceptual investment in them as vehicles for change — but the old liberal idea of authenticity, like the liberal idea of universalism, has morphed and is itself open to debate, according to changed ideas about how cultures and the subjects that inhabit them are made.

Impatience with old orthodoxies could be seen, for example, in the bitter power struggle that went on in the Society of St Vincent de Paul in 1995, where a traditionalist conservative bloc mobilised to resist a youthful challenge to the society's policy of refusing to become involved in advocacy on social justice issues, to address the underlying causes of poverty. For the old guard, the society exists purely as a charitable organisation, and shouldn't be politicised, while the younger challengers took for granted the idea that everything is already political. Ironically, the eventually successful old guard were reportedly backed by B. A. Santamaria's National Civic Council, itself a political organisation.

Shifts that are more clearly global, yet nevertheless fragmenting, have made themselves felt on other fronts too. The great liberal social reforming zeal of the first three-quarters of the century has suffered a failure of nerve, transmogrifying into quite a different set of philosophies. Markets alone, we are told, can make people's lives better — whatever the consequences for government service provision and the 'social fabric'. In most Western democracies this has signalled a lurch to the political right, often articulated in the form of skirmishes over different forms of cultural knowledge and cultural investments. The battle over 'political correctness', and recent controversies in feminism and the arts, have raised issues of generationalism against a background of broad social change where one thing that hasn't changed has been the cultural incumbency of a range of figures who first gained prominence in the 1960s and 1970s, or who take these as their formative intellectual eras.

Gangland

Generationalism, lately, *has* become a way of lashing out. But, against a background where the politics of generationalism are now routinely deployed at many different levels, it is in the highly public arenas of the arts and media that the backlash against youth culture is given its most vicious spin.

2
The New Establishment: on now at a media outlet near you

The times they are a changing back.

Tim Robbins, in *Bob Roberts*

If we are to have any serious engagement with culture and ideas in this country, the next generation must start wrestling for that baton.

Barrie Kosky[1]

'Do you think this is a generation thing', Helen Garner asks in *The First Stone*, 'are we on the scrapheap?'[2] It's an old anxiety for her. Nearly ten years earlier, in an interview with the writer Candida Baker, commenting on being questioned by young journalists about why she writes such 'traditional' books, she said, 'there I am on the scrap-heap and I'm only forty-two!'[3]

She's not alone. Talk of scrapheaps, of living in a 'fin de siècle age', of witnessing the death of literature, the death of the novel,[4] the decline of 'truth and beauty' as touchstones in art, the end of the great humanist quest to 'know thyself',[5] are currently rife among a certain cultural elite. And through all these ruminations about the 'world we had lost'[6] runs another vein of discussion to do with cultural and moral decline, and the importance of keeping certain values and practices in place.

Gangland

In *The First Stone* Garner argues that a kind of moral decline has taken place in feminism, which she suggests has embraced a cult of punitive victimism. She figures the difference as generational, playing out the rift between what she sees as two quite different brands of feminism — 'forgiving' on the one hand and 'punitive' on the other — as a possible difference between mothers and daughters. She's not alone in doing that, either. Ethical and aesthetic declines are increasingly represented as having something to do with the present 'younger generation'. *The First Stone* is an important book, not because it signals the appearance of 'victim-feminism' in its supposed local guise, but because it exemplifies the way a climate of defensive orthodoxy has taken hold in a certain community of artists, writers and commentators.

But first some background.

There is a group of figures, born somewhere between the late 1930s and early 1950s, who now dominate the media, who set the tone of debate on popular social issues from feminism to education to multiculturalism. Over and above the sameness of the voices and faces who dominate the general run of popular commentary, they are institutions. Their names are well known. They form a familiar parade in the 'what's inside' banners above the headlines on page one of the newspapers, and most of them have done so for many years. As television current-affairs journalists they have hosted the majority of shows from *This Day Tonight* onwards. As talkback hosts, all much the same age, all the same sex, they are the radio 'names'. They are the same women who have somehow become the authorised voices of feminism. The same political commentators who for decades have repeated the same political orthodoxies. The same economics commentators, forever pushing *their* orthodoxy. The same book reviewers, pushing the same writers' barrows. The 'usual suspects' who get wheeled out whenever there is an 'issue' to be discussed or a controversy that needs to be presided over, and can be relied on to say pretty much what you expect them to.

When I was gathering material for this book, it struck me how few spaces there are in Australian media for people under the age of forty, or even fifty, to speak. Sure, there is plenty of room for the comical etiquette column or the lifestyle column in a weekend colour supplement, but there are very few places where younger people are allowed to have a serious opinion on anything other than a 'youth' issue or, if they are female, a 'women's issue' or, if they have an ethnic background, an 'ethnic' issue, articulated in a manner that isn't anecdotal, comic or 'personal'. It's as if people under the age of forty don't have credible opinions, such is their general invisibility in the media and their lack of access to a wide 'public'.

Hard to believe? Try flicking through the pages of the papers, or across the TV channels, or around the radio dial. Leafing through the pages of the *Sydney Morning Herald* one morning, I came across an article canvassing opinion on race issues, complete with a vox pop of thirteen 'prominent people'. The 'usual suspects' were well in evidence, and the average age was well over fifty; the only under-40 person interviewed was Poppy King. Call me cynical, but is she included because she is financially successful — and therefore rates where younger people, who generally feature in bad-news stories, otherwise don't?[7]

A casual read of a column by Michael Gawenda in the Melbourne *Age* about Baz Luhrmann's film *William Shakespeare's Romeo and Juliet* shows up another familiar trend. Gawenda says that the film threatens to overwhelm the 'magic of the words' with visual pyrotechnics, yet succeeds almost in spite of itself because 'Luhrmann has managed somehow to retain something of the magic and power of the original play in a film that seems designed to subvert it'. Whether or not you agree with this, the young people in the film's audience certainly aren't construed as part of the possible audience for

Gawenda's column. The column instead comes off as a piece of gatekeeping, of passing judgement on this 'youth art', to see if it comes up to scratch.[8] Luhrmann, according to Gawenda, is saved from producing 'just another example of popular culture's technical brilliance . . . its life-denying nihilism', only by 'Shakespeare's genius' — unlike the similarly pyrotechnic, Tarantino-influenced *From Dusk to Dawn*, which Gawenda implies, against his better judgement, is a possible argument for censorship.

Perhaps it's unfair to single Gawenda out. A recent returnee to high-profile newspaper column-writing after a stint at *Time*, he operates alongside a generation of columnists, from Phillip Adams to Bettina Arndt to P. P. McGuinness, who have dominated broadsheet opinion pages for far longer. Rather than blood new columnists, lately the major dailies have concentrated on trading the old ones for large sums, reportedly $250 000 in one case. McGuinness moved from the *Australian* to the *Age* and the *Sydney Morning Herald*. Robert Manne left the Fairfax papers to join the Murdoch stable; Bettina Arndt and Gerard Henderson went the other way. Rather than taking on a young, fresh art critic, the *Australian* imported a conservative, middle-aged one from England to judge local art with a quietly superior eye.

Serious commentary on TV is more or less dominated by the *This Day Tonight* generation, a bevy of journalists from Ray Martin to Stuart Littlemore, to George Negus, Richard Carleton, Peter Luck, Paul Lyneham, Mike Munro, Paul Murphy and Mike Willesee. Littlemore at least had the gall to ask the head of ABC news, on air, why another of the *TDT* alumni, Kerry O'Brien, did all the interviewing on the ABC's *7.30 Report*. Where was the next generation of ABC interviewers coming from, he asked; was the art of interviewing in danger of being lost at the ABC?[9]

The same could be said of other current-affairs television. Younger people are much less likely to present a segment in

The New Establishment

TV current-affairs land than to be made its objects, in one of the regular features on youth crime, truancy, drug-taking or welfare cheating. Even when the *TDT* alumni aren't in evidence, the pattern is familiar. Surfing through the channels late one night, I came across *The Last Shout*, a programme featuring what was supposed to be a more or less representative panel of journalists and 'prominent figures' discussing issues of the day. Anne Summers sat it out with ex-senator and ex-Treasury head John Stone and ex-newspaper editor Piers Akerman. The sole younger face was that of journalist Malcolm McGregor, who functioned as a sort of humorous diversion and whipping boy for the rest of the panel, and had to battle to get a word in edgeways.

By now everyone is familiar with the generation of talkback radio hosts, from Alan Jones to Ron Casey to John Laws. There, too, the same 'personalities' go from one station to another, or from radio to TV and back to radio, while younger voices are only ever heard on 'youth' stations, most of which, apart from subscription stations, trial licensees and JJJ, play the type of music their parents would have first heard at around the same age.

Not that the syndrome is confined to the media. On my desk as I write is a leaflet I received in the mail, advertising a conference entitled 'Authors, authenticity and appropriation: who owns the text?' The question itself seems interesting enough, though preoccupied with a certain type of old-fashioned anxiety about authorial 'authenticity' in response to the Darville-Demidenko literary hoax. More interesting is the list of speakers. Of the fourteen listed on the flier, the vast majority are over forty, and are cultural institutions — Louise Adler, Robert Dessaix, Beatrice Faust, Morag Fraser, Gerard Henderson, Frank Moorhouse — the sort of figures who often crop up as keepers of authorised culture: that is, culture to do with politics, policy-making, high art and 'mainstream' social issues. These figures apparently embody something that younger people cannot. They are the anointed spokespeople, the ones with their hands on the levers of the cultural machine, who have been appointed to speak on issues affecting the national moral fibre.

Younger people, when they do get a gig in the mass media, more often than not are employed as 'translators'. During the life of the *Independent Monthly* one of the few regular young columnists was John Birmingham, author of the hilarious novel *He Died With a Felafel in His Hand*. His subject in the *Independent*? The Internet and new technologies. In the debate surrounding *The First Stone*, some newspapers fell over themselves to interview young women about feminism for a week or two (others had to be badgered into it). But this soon died off, and the issue ended up as grist for the media mill.

The debate over *The First Stone* fomented another trend: that younger people *are* permitted a voice if they talk specifically under the heading of generationalism. This has been the case for feminist writers in particular. In the USA, conservative anti-feminist writers such as Katie Roiphe and Rene Denfeld seemed to have been given licence to attack feminism in, respectively, *The Morning After* and *The New Victorians*, provided they did so on generational grounds. Generationalism was also a major — and somewhat limiting — theme in two of the young-feminist-writes-back books that appeared in Australia in response to *The First Stone*. Generationalism, as Garner's book showed, is a saleable commodity, providing the sort of 'us versus them' spectacle that is the bread and butter of marketeers and conservative sectors of the media.

This rush to commodification affects the way stories are handled. Would the Ormond affair have been of such import if the sexual mores of younger women weren't placed at the centre of *The First Stone*? Would the Darville-Demidenko affair have played out the same way if Helen Darville hadn't been a young, photogenic woman? It's surprising (and a little sad) that the physical appearance and sexual presence of the Ormond complainants were made issues not only in *The First Stone*, but also in two of the counter-tracts, Virginia Trioli's *Generation F* and Kathy Bail's *DIY Feminism*. Both Trioli and Bail took time out to observe one of the Ormond complainants in her role as a singer in a band. Why? Must those who seek to defend younger people against generationalism start by anthropologising their subjects in much the same way as those they claim to be critiquing?

Topics weren't allocated on the basis of age in the same way when the present group of cultural and media incumbents came to the fore. Many were in their twenties when they first found themselves taken seriously as having something to say that was of general import. The *This Day Tonight* team, and a raft of commentators from Laurie Oakes to Bob Ellis to Anne Summers to Richard Neville to Germaine Greer, all got a toehold in the national consciousness before they turned thirty. Now they seem to have permanent tenure — which isn't to say they should retire, or have nothing more to offer — while many younger writers, journalists and commentators suffer a prolonged, enforced adolescence. At the same time the conceptual frameworks that govern the way news and current affairs are presented, the way novels are received, the way social issues are discussed, stay resolutely in more or less the same place.

An article in the *Sydney Morning Herald* introducing the 'best young Australian novelists' for 1997 in terms of the 'cult of youth in Australian publishing' summed up the extended adolescence syndrome. Not only did it present the authors as a 'youth ghetto', but the average age of the writers interviewed was well over thirty.[10] This is now 'young'? It's certainly too old to continue to be pushed aside by the sort of literary establishment that sets itself up to make judgements about who is and isn't deemed a 'proper' writer. What of those novelists, and there are plenty of them (good ones, too), in their early to mid-twenties or even late teens?

Gangland

★

Put it down to an ageing population, but demographics alone don't seem enough to explain the incumbency of the present range of commentators. They're more entrenched than that. Not only do they discuss news, they *are* news. Not only do they discuss ideas, they *are* the idea. When they speak it is as much a media event as whatever debate they have joined, or started.

On a day-to-day basis this gives them enormous power. Debates are manicured. Barrows are pushed. Barely so much as a book review appears in a Saturday broadsheet without some orchestration of cultural space having taken place. Certain causes are systematically promoted and others systematically ignored. Crusades are undertaken. The commentator's 'name' automatically gives him or her the right to be invasive and to pick over targets. The 'public figure' gets to decide what is and isn't in the 'public interest' or the 'public domain'.

The personal and philosophical connections between such figures are often close. Over the years they have found allies at arts festivals and conferences and in the corridors of the academy. They have published in the same places. They have used parallel systems of patronage. They share similar dislikes, especially of upstarts. They act as advocates or opponents of each other's works; either way, they *notice* each other's works. In a Rolodex culture, they have ready access to particular publishers, journalists, publicists, editors, agents and each other.

During the Darville-Demidenko affair, one prominent figure apparently spent days on the phone, currying favour where it mattered, stirring up the issue, lobbying a range of media outlets to carry certain views, organising the right figures to present those views, and even reportedly orchestrating an embargo on any pro-Darville commentary in one of the metropolitan newspapers. These are the sorts of calls that only a certain cultural elite can easily make. Which isn't to suggest

The New Establishment

that any of this is planned, or that a conspiracy exists; rather, it is a matter of a group of people of a similar age sharing similar concerns and a similar way of thinking.

They share similar backgrounds too. Take the remnants of the 1970s scene based around the Pram Factory and La Mama theatres in Melbourne, and put it with the leftovers of the Sydney Push and associates, and from David Williamson to Helen Garner, from Frank Moorhouse to Germaine Greer, from P. P. McGuinness to Robert Hughes, you have a surprising proportion of the cultural figures setting mainstream agendas today. Throw in a few stray 1970s activists who came to prominence during the post-Whitlam institutionalisation of feminism, add a range of recipients from the inaugural rounds of Australia Council grants, a few journalists and a strong Adelaide contingent, and, without wanting to homogenise or wallpaper over the differences between them, from Beatrice Faust to Les Murray, you more or less have the full set of icons usually taken to embody the national cultural consciousness.

This loose-knit group forms a well-entrenched New Establishment that presides over the culture industry in the same way as the old establishment continues to dominate commerce and industry. Their ascendancy dovetails neatly into the rise of the culture industry itself. Their power lies not so much in boardrooms or political corridors (though there are connections) but in the increasingly important — and prominent — industries of the arts and media, where tastes are made and public opinion presided over. Many were early beneficiaries of the 1970s ascendancy of the arts, as part of what the journalist Paul Kelly calls 'Whitlam's coalition' of 'women, migrants, environmentalists, Aborigines, public servants, artists and nationalists' — he might have added journalists.[11] But if they remain keen nationalists (and often prominent republicans) they are now as likely to speak out against multiculturalism as for it, or to number themselves against feminism as with it.

Gangland

Their ascendancy has to do with another phenomenon of the past twenty years. Culture, as Meaghan Morris describes it, has supplanted politics and religion as the dominant heading under which the social and moral issues of the day are played out.[12] This can be seen in the prominence given the controversies that took place over *The First Stone* or the Darville-Demidenko affair. Or in the debates over 'political correctness' and 'identity politics' that took place in the context of plays like *Dead White Males* before they made it onto newspaper front pages as party politics.

In recent years this New Establishment has produced a spate of books, speeches and plays on similar themes, backward-looking, shrouded in rage and gloom. Put Garner's *The First Stone* together with Williamson's troika of conservative plays — *Brilliant Lies*, *Dead White Males* and *Heretic* — plus books such as Peter Coleman's *Doubletake*, Robert Manne's *The Culture of Forgetting*, Robert Hughes' *Culture of Complaint*, Keith Windschuttle's *The Killing of History*, Kate Jennings' *Bad Manners*, Don Anderson's *Real Opinions* and *Sex and Text*, Terry Lane's *Hobbyhorses*, and even *John Laws' Book of Irreverent Logic* and *John Laws' Book of Uncommon Sense*, and a picture starts to emerge. Add to these Anne Summers' patronising 'Letter to the Next Generation', which appears as the final chapter in the updated edition of her *Damned Whores and God's Police*. Add to that a series of articles published by Christopher Pearson's *Adelaide Review*. Add to that a series of speeches, such as Garner's to the Sydney Institute in the wake of the reception of *The First Stone*, Christopher Koch's 1996 speech on winning the Miles Franklin Award, Pierre Ryckmans' 1996 Boyer lectures and Robert Dessaix's speech to the 1995 Victorian Premier's Literary Awards dinner, along with a series of newspaper articles and media appearances by various figures such as P. P. McGuinness, Barry Oakley, Luke Slattery, Susan Mitchell, Peter Craven, Les Murray, Frank Moorhouse, Richard Neville and Beatrice Faust, and despite the differences between the members of this loose-knit gang, the common themes are striking.

None looks forward except with gloom. They all seem to long for the good old days when feminists burned bras, queer meant strange, literature meant Shakespeare, when divisions between high culture and low, critic and object, were unambiguous, and ethnicity meant nothing more complex than eating out. Since their heyday the world has become a strange, fearful place. To them, young feminists are no longer representatives of a social movement, but act out of retribution. Literary critics are no longer experimenters who think about what makes literature tick, but are actively setting out to destroy culture. Shakespeare is 'dead'. The literary 'canon' of great and universally important works is under grave threat from 'cultural relativists'. Grand social movements have been hijacked by people hell-bent on acting out victimhood. Race politics, once a cause for middlebrow liberal concern, is barely mentionable any more without risk of saying something 'offensive'.

What these figures have tended to offer lately isn't so much creative energy as backlash politics. It's as if the North American 'culture wars' of the late 1980s, which took the form of attacks on minority groups and those who promoted their causes, have finally seeped through and licensed a sort of road rage among the local cultural elite.

Having grown up in the 1970s myself, I remember many of these figures as, if not radical, then somewhere to the left. With parents who were keen ABC listeners, I remember Terry Lane as the progressive voice of radio, just as I recall Garner as a writer who challenged staid ideas about what could be written in Australian fiction. Richard Neville was the libertarian anti-censorship campaigner of the *Oz* trials. And it was a triumph that successful movies like *Stork* or *Don's Party* could be made from equally successful, distinctively local, satirical plays. But something has happened. Individually and collectively, many of the figures who led Australian culture out of the wilderness in the 1970s seem to have lurched into a sort of Endgameism, a high modernist cosmopolitanism gone wrong.

In the late 1960s and early 1970s it seemed a truism that the left had the moral upper hand in debates on social issues. A self-fashioned generation of poets, novelists, playwrights, academics, film-makers and journalists spoke to an equally self-fashioned new audience about new political causes — class conflict, feminism, race relations, Vietnam. Two decades later the right came into the ascendancy, and suddenly books, plays and newspaper columns were dominated by feminist-baiters, anti-multiculturalism campaigners and complainers about academic theorists and leftie 'political correctness'. Thing is, they were much the same people.

Terry Lane's *Hobbyhorses* is an interesting book, full of memorable moments, but beset by a profound sense of insecurity. Lane seems to take feminism personally, as if this social movement could have no greater purpose than to affront his masculinity. According to the reductive version he offers in *Hobbyhorses*, feminism is little more than a collection of 'cardinal myths', not real knowledges that deserve to be taken seriously, or that serve some wider purpose other than attacking men.[13] If not for feminism, he suggests, everything would be fine. It's not too far from the set of ideas offered in *Dead White Males*, where the feminist wife secretly wants nothing more than to recant, to find her 'Petruchio'. Or, for that matter, from John Laws' suggestion that 'most real women care more about the economic welfare of themselves and their families than they do about feminazi claptrap'.[14] Laws, though, was never a progressive in the same way as Lane and Williamson. Meanwhile, Richard Neville has railed against films like *Romper Stomper* and *The Cook, the Thief, his Wife and her Lover*, broadly recanting the views he took on censorship during the *Oz* trials.[15] He was by no means the first. As early as 1974 Peter Coleman had come to believe that his own earlier libertarian views on censorship had gone too far.[16]

The New Establishment

When asked if she is still a feminist, Helen Garner has stated 'that is a question I'm sick of thinking about',[17] and poet Les Murray (who admittedly was never a radical) has gone from being a long-time recipient of government grant money to arch-crusader against the grants system.

Reading, watching and listening to this recent spate of books, essays and speeches is like listening to a glum conversation about shared prejudices carried out in an airless room, a gangland hideout. These mythologies have developed a family likeness; they've been breathing each other's air too long. Things get out of hand. Masculinity, according to Les Murray, is 'now underground; it's carried on between men in a kind of private conversation, it's not allowed to be published or broadcast'.[18] This is news to anyone who has recently gone to a motor-sport event or a cricket match, spent an afternoon at the football, laughed along with *The Footy Show*, or noted the preponderance of men's sports in television news bulletins and the hero-worship of the stars.

Even the political elites are getting into the act. Former Governor-General and Labor Party leader Bill Hayden has warned against the 'new agenda setters' in Australian politics who would promote affirmative action, environmentalism, anti-discrimination and minority rights.[19] He joins other retired Labor politicians and commentators such as Peter Walsh and Barry Cohen, who lament the transformation of one-time left causes into 'political correctness' and 'victim cults'. Cohen writes: 'As one whose prime motivation to enter politics was a passionate hatred of prejudice in all its forms, I wonder why it is that whenever I hear the words discrimination, racism or multiculturalism these days, I feel an attack of the ague coming on.'[20]

Like holier-than-thou reformed smokers, these figures dish the dirt, playing the part of 'native informant', setting themselves up as authentic reporters of what's wrong with the position they left behind. Such is their ascendancy that sometimes it seems as if the only views we hear on certain issues are those of people who no longer subscribe: disenchanted feminists on feminism, former lefties on the left, once-were-activists on activism, once-anti-censorship campaigners arguing for censorship, all with the familiar cry that things have 'gone too far'.

These commentators like to portray themselves as under siege, as 'dissenters' swimming bravely against the tyrannical imposts of marauding feminists, multiculturalists and 'organised opinion', as if their networks and hierarchies of patronage are neither organised nor entrenched. Every new play and every new book must have its controversy and be besieged by unreasonable zealots who supposedly want to scuttle it. Garner made headlines claiming *The First Stone* was the victim of an ideologically driven 'girlcott' because some chose not to read it, even if the book was a best-seller.[21] Peter Coleman, in the preface to *Doubletake*, speaks of 'the *fatwa* on Les Murray, Christopher Koch, Geoffrey Blainey, the late David Stove, Kate Jennings and other non-conformists'.[22] Yet all remain prominent figures, apparently under no death threats or in the Gulag.

If this is 'dissent', then it's a stage-managed affair indeed — a diversion designed to make tame orthodoxies look brave. A conceit that is soon exposed when something or someone comes along to disrupt the smooth, orderly surfaces of cultural life. Theatre director Barrie Kosky caused such a kerfuffle merely by asking why the artistic community was 'so quiet, so controlled, so calm, so collected, so sensible', and theatre so safe.[23] He was met with a wave of genteel put-downs from the established arts community — a drawing-room community that abhors aesthetic adventurousness and warns against everything but their own art. It's not hard to tell the difference between Kosky's sort of dissent and the institutionalised sort mentioned above. The latter, apart from offering the spectacle of the iconic cultural figure as wounded martyr, raises no real issues. Rather, it tends to distract from them. What Kosky showed, whether you agreed with him or not, was an appetite for ideas, offering the spectacle of someone genuinely mad, bad and dangerous to know.

★

Ideas, though, aren't the currency of this New Establishment. On the contrary, most of the views articulated in the loose corpus outlined above are shaped by a failure to foresee the possibility of new knowledges, or else a failure to take them seriously. The elite never foresaw that their brand of libertarianism might come under threat. That new categories like race and ethnicity would impose themselves. That there would be new models for cultural and political activism. That ideas about literature and reading, producer and audience, highbrow and lowbrow, might change. That the cultural authority of mainstream media, or the idea of the mainstream itself, or the idea of a unified 'public sphere', might be destabilised by other forms of media and a sheer proliferation of cultures, information and images.

Instead, they have resolutely stayed in the same place, clinging to past paradigms. An example was Robert Dessaix's keynote speech at the 1995 Premier's Literary Awards dinner in Melbourne. Dessaix took the standard swipes at feminism and multiculturalism, and expressed an anxiety that young readers (he mentioned a young woman) don't read him as he wants to be read. It all reeked of nostalgia for the old liberal-arts climate of the 1950s, where middle-class young women, with an education but not too much of an education, curled up with middlebrow books written by more educated writers, just as the eighteenth-century aesthetic prescribed, and dutifully read them as their authors desired.

Christopher Koch explored similar ideas in his acceptance speech for the 1996 Miles Franklin Award. His theme was literary theorists: 'I appeal to young writers in particular to heed a simple plea: take any risks you like, but never listen to a deconstructionist.'[24] Such speeches became something of a fashion. At the 1996 Warana Writers' Week in Brisbane, Frank Moorhouse gave vent to a similar diatribe against 'postmodern terrorists', 'gender supremacists' and 'Asianists',[25] and broadcaster Louise Adler issued an anti-'theory' broadside at the conference on authenticity mentioned above. But, much as each of these speeches pretended to be against programmatic reading, each in its way was a set of pedagogical directives about how to read, as well as an attempt to (re)organise cultural space, backwards.

I mention literary theory and university arts curricula as fashionable targets because universities, as the essayist McKenzie Wark has pointed out, are where the 'negotiation of the inter-generational takes place'.[26] Almost all the recent controversies occupying the present cultural elite are at least to some extent sited in universities and oriented around the morality of students, taken as representative of their generation. Obviously there are broader constituencies to be invoked when questions about feminism, ethnicity or queerness are raised, but all the recent debates about gender politics, victim-feminism, the teaching of literary theory in universities, political correctness, literary authenticity and even multiculturalism in one way or another converge on the questions of youth and generationalism. Helen Garner worries about young feminists. Dessaix worries about younger readers. Christopher Koch issues a warning to young writers. Robert Manne worries about 'postmodernism' erasing 'historical memory' among the young. All focus on students. In all three of David Williamson's plays, *Brilliant Lies, Dead White Males* and *Heretic*, the plot and resultant moral crisis hinge on the shonky veracity or gullibility of a young woman. From Susy in *Brilliant Lies* through Angela in *Dead White Males* to the caricature of the young Margaret Mead in *Heretic*, all these characters suffer from a susceptibility to new ideas that needs putting back in its box.

Pervading these anxieties is a logic of 'moral panic', as if the ethical stuff of society were in danger of being fatally destabilised. The language used invokes images of conspiracy, siege, loss and moral decline. Young feminists are 'taking over'. 'Deconstructionists' are 'taking over'. Underpinning the urgency of debate over *The First Stone* was the implication that there is some sort of feminist conspiracy going on — which, since the complainants in the Ormond case didn't wish to talk to her, Garner 'proved' by setting herself up as its final victim. In *The Culture of Forgetting*, Robert Manne amplified and pathologised Helen Darville's anti-Semitism into a general malaise.[27] Dessaix, tilting against multiculturalism, feminism and young 'grunge' writers, says 'I do feel we've lost something'.[28] The moral impetus of *Dead White Males* is generated by the idea that academics brainwash students rather than teach them, just as Koch thinks students are prey to deconstructionists and Coleman argues that certain writers are victims of 'politically correct' *fatwas*. Armies of the night, it seems, are on the move, even if the 'conspirators' are forever on the sidelines, their voices oddly absent, while their supposed 'victims' monopolise the field.

Academics, feminism, race. These are often the stuff of moral panics. The scapegoats for the latest moral malaise are almost invariably drawn from the ranks of those who can be characterised as disruptive intruders from some 'other' place. Academics, famously, are supposed to inhabit ivory towers. Feminists are supposed to go around in self-contained gangs, promoting 'alien' non-sexist languages. And other races, well, they just come from 'elsewhere'. Recently younger people too have been figured as coming from 'elsewhere'. Bouts of hysteria about youth 'gangs', Ecstasy, the rave scene and so on have been played out in the rhetoric of moral panic as much as controversies about victim-feminism, literary theory, 'political correctness' or campus speech codes.[29] All have included a sidebar anxiety about the continued cultural incumbency of those doing the complaining, expressed as a desire to claim, or maintain, superior knowledge, articulated in a language suggesting that a return to some phantasmic past — a mythical era of 'free speech' and 'direct action', or pre-technology, pre-'ideology', or just plain pre-anything — will reinvigorate that old, looking-a-bit-tired knowledge and make it relevant again.

When the figures who write or speak these controversies issue forth, it is often to express outrage at hoax authors, hoax feminists, hoax theorists and the mother of all hoaxes — 'political correctness' — and to lay the blame on a hoax generation. Younger people, the clichés go, don't know how to party, don't know how to protest, don't know how to think. They have no sense of humour, no self-discipline and take no pleasure in anything. 'If only the whole gang of them hadn't been so afraid of life', writes Garner at the end of *The First Stone* — now isn't that one of the great platitudes of the current generationalism?[30]

Younger people, according to Anne Summers, don't even know themselves, not having 'come forward' in the proper way, as prescribed by her 'Letter to the Next Generation'. The implication is that if you don't occupy public space in a certain accepted way, according to paradigms set by the arbiters of culture, you're barely breathing.

It's as if there's a looking-glass culture that wants to see itself endlessly reflected back in terms of its own aesthetic, its own politics, its own values.

'Sisters, if you don't want to help me, get out of my light', wrote Beatrice Faust in a column criticising Kathy Bail's *DIY Feminism*. While Faust made some telling comments about Bail's highly individuated and somewhat conservative form of feminism, her condescending title, 'Time You Grew Up Little Sister', was of a piece with the implication that younger feminists in general were blocking her light, preventing *her* from getting on with the proper business of feminism.[31] Later she wrote that 'many young women are so naive that if you spit in their face they'll say it's raining'. The inference is that younger feminists don't know how to mix it with the big girls and boys when it comes to lobbying governments and defending the gains made by Faust's generation, and that young feminists' proper role is to serve and support those older feminists who have a mortgage on the facts and figures of feminism.[32]

A popular theme here is that a particular generation functions as the 'proper' repository of authentic cultural memory. According to Robert Hughes:

> Millions of Americans, especially young ones, imagine that the 'truth' about the Kennedy assassination resides in Oliver Stone's vivid lying film *JFK* . . . How many of them saw anything wrong with Stone's frequent claim that he was 'creating a counter-myth' to the Warren Commission's findings, as though one's knowledge of the past equated with the propagation of myth?[33]

Hughes' rhetoric, like so much else here, seems designed to rearticulate his own generation's claims to the role of cultural gatekeepers. Implicitly, they are *the* knowers of the cultural real. Young people are cast as blank slates waiting to be filled (presumably by evil 'deconstructionists'). But are younger people any more or less taken in by Stone's propaganda than anyone else? After all, they're generally media-savvy, and have grown up watching endless re-runs of *that* footage.

This kind of logic has had a big run lately. Robert Dessaix explored a similar theme in his speech: 'What disappoints me, for example, in the current trend for grunge naturalism is the memory seems to be blank. The reader who remembers Boccaccio . . . can't help finding these fumblings in a flat in Brunswick rather weary, stale and flat — but of course, as we know, not necessarily unprofitable'.[34] In the wake of the Darville-Demidenko affair, John McLaren, then editor of the literary journal *Overland*, voiced his fear that Christos Tsiolkas's *Loaded*, 'by presenting a hero who asserts that life holds nothing but music, films and sex' might be 'demolishing the sense of common obligation that alone stands between human society and fascism, with all its attendant evils'.[35] The critic Peter Craven took another tack when he used the Darville-Demidenko affair to attack young writers. According to him, what made the affair possible was 'the arts organisations' obsessions with youth and ethnicity'.[36]

Another typical piece was an article by Susan Mitchell, academic, arts identity, author of such popular books as *Tall Poppies*, and a regular columnist in the *Australian*. Anger was on Mitchell's agenda too, when she described how she'd found a flier stuck to the back of a campus toilet door telling students who to complain to 'if your lecturers and/or tutors use racist or sexist language'. She was especially angry about a line that followed: 'Whether you want to have them brought down, or would like to make an informal complaint, come and see us. You need never be identified.'[37] What most offended Mitchell were the words 'brought down'. Here is evidence, she thunders, of a new punitive mentality among students, and younger people generally, who are being 'guided by the dictums of the so-called politically correct', having 'absorbed the culture of complaint along with Big Macs, KFC and wearing a baseball cap backwards'.[38] (The spectre of the baseball cap worn backwards haunts many a journalistic piece centring on youth.)

As it happened, the flier in question was already out of date; most of the copies had been voluntarily withdrawn from circulation because its content had been judged inflammatory. But Mitchell did not mention this until near the end of the article, and in the interim she commanded a full-page lead article in a newspaper features section damning an entire generation because of something she chanced to see on a toilet door. The only other source of information Mitchell mentioned was a single phone call to the student named in the flier as the contact point — a call for which he was entirely unprepared. When he didn't come up with immediate answers to her no doubt prepared questions on sexual harassment, Mitchell cited this as further evidence of a malaise. The student would have been easily identifiable, as the article gave his title and where he worked, even if it did not name him. Against this the student, presumably lacking Mitchell's media access, would have had little right of reply.

The context Mitchell cited for her feature was *The First Stone*, in which Garner maintained that a college master was similarly 'brought down'. In Mitchell's case, however, no such resignation was mentioned. No-one lost a job — in fact, the poster was withdrawn. Yet on the basis of those two words, 'brought down', Mitchell sees the germ of a dreadful future:

> This young man [who was cited in the flier], consciously or unconsciously, is a future professional helper of victims, guided by the dictums of the so-called politically correct, his language a direct import from American universities, where students have been known to witch-hunt and hound lecturers out of their jobs. The culture of complaint is with us.

Mitchell's piece is full of the standard rhetorical strategies of the New Establishment, including hyperbole and selectivity. She approvingly cites Faust's dictum that 'social work . . . is a profession in search of problems', and attacks the flier's offer of anonymity as an 'incitement to go behind the back of the alleged perpetrator', without mentioning that anonymity is a legitimate protocol of institutional complaints procedure, as otherwise many legitimate complaints go unvoiced because of intimidation and fear of retribution. In criticising the leaflet's use of vernacular, she is apparently unaware that such posters risk alienating possible respondents if they address them using 'bureaucratese' of the kind also used by the institution where the intimidation took place.

But what 'culture of complaint' are we talking of here? Is it one recently imported by students from American universities, as Mitchell implies, or a culture of complaint and whingeing hyperbole among older journalists and writers who interpret every new social detail through a very specific, equally imported lens? When have student leaflets *not* been a little over the top? The expression 'culture of complaint', used by Mitchell in her subtitle and regularly throughout her piece, is from Robert Hughes' book *Culture of Complaint: The Fraying of America* (173 pages, and he complains on every one of them). Where Mitchell writes 'complaint gives power', so Hughes writes 'complaint gives you power'.[39] The expression 'culture of complaint' has become part of the elite's vernacular. Virginia Trioli is a 'one-woman culture of complaint', writes the journalist Rosemary Neill in a review of Bail's and Trioli's books. Neill suggests that sexual harassment procedure is something that involves jailing guilty men (fathers, husbands — shock, horror! — boyfriends, brothers), evidently taking Garner's *The First Stone* as a reliable guide to complaints procedure as well as to the machinations of the Ormond case. Despite Neill's misgivings (at 34, she claims she 'straddles the generational divide'), most of the fire here also takes place across crudely orchestrated generational lines. Young feminists just don't cut it, Neill concludes, having homogenised Trioli's and Bail's very different books and ignored the perhaps unpleasantly cogent definition of sexual harassment in Trioli's.[40]

★

Who is, and who isn't, the *genuine* speaking voice of culture is a hotly contested question these days. Not only because this cultural elite, with their cult of obsolescence, are worried about the durability of their own power base, but also in a broader sense. Since 'Whitlam's coalition' first gained ascendancy, there have been real shifts in social power. Globalisation, in the forms of easy, speedy communication, economic systematisation and participation in common global events and cultures, has tended to make societies more porous and cosmopolitan. At the same time feminism and immigration, the two most significant social movements of the past half-century, have opened up questions about how to organise increasingly disparate societies in which regimes of knowledge, identity and speaking position are no longer so clear-cut as they once seemed to be. A sustained refusal of questions about speaking position, for example, is at the heart of the 'political correctness' debate — 'political correctness' can be understood as one of the ways globalisation negotiates with the local, even at the simple level of an awareness that 'we're not alone'.

The New Establishment seems surprised that questions about speaking position are a problem at all. Rather than engaging with new categories, the elite has characteristically adopted a stance of denial. Its attacks on feminism, multiculturalism and 'theory' are framed in terms of a desire to put certain cultural institutions (literature, for example) beyond criticism.

You can see tensions about speaking position in the whole idea of a conference on authenticity. If questions of authenticity often involve a question about race, so it was at the conference in question, where what began as a discussion about writing ended up as a series of disclosures about the misrepresented or mistaken racial origins of writers such as Darville-Demidenko, Mudrooroo and Gordon Matthews. While most speakers at the conference were sympathetic to the plight of the last two, who inadvertently claimed to be of Aboriginal origin, the whole event raises the question: just who decides what is authentic? The scope of the conference itself suggested a closeted nostalgia for the idea that *they*, the delegates, were the ones entitled to ask such questions. The conference was also notable for its tirades from the usual suspects against — you guessed it — newer forms of knowledge, especially those that grapple with problems of authenticity and speaking position.

Anxieties about cultural succession. Paradigms clashing. Crises of cultural authority. Much of the sting in recent cultural debates comes from elites who could once take their position for granted, but are now required to grapple with new ideas and articulate a position. Many of the New Establishment are too old to be baby-boomers, but their nostalgia nevertheless manifests itself in a kind of 'boomer-whinge' — a longing for an authentic 1950s past that cherishes the stereotypical baby-boomer privileges. So, given the air of crisis, what else has this New Establishment been doing lately?

③ Running scared: 'political correctness', boomer-whinge and the big panic

It was like, everywhere you looked Glenfield was in your face. Wogs, nips, Maoris and skips strolled the streets, and on rare occasions there'd be an Abo, but not very often. I had nothing against wogs or nips, but used these words as frequently as hello. We were wogs . . .

Daniella Petkovic, Maria Kokokiris, Monica Kalinowska, *Livin' Large*[1]

The world has gotten too big — way beyond our capacity to tell stories about it.

Douglas Coupland, *Generation X*[2]

It all started with campus speech codes and course outlines. But not many people heard about that. It was a debate of sporadic pot-shots across no-man's land in an ideological trench warfare that took place mainly among specialists. A couple of old fogeys and rising young-fogey journalists on one side, and a bunch of concerned leftie academics on the other, penning the odd letter, column and essay in newspaper sidebars and literary journals about some strange thing called 'political correctness'. What the fogeys said was that a kind of leftist orthodoxy had infected the mainstream, somehow censoring everyday speech. The leftie academics pointed out that a double standard was being applied. Have you noticed, they said, that when somebody attacks the right they're being 'politically correct', but when someone attacks the left it's 'common sense'?

That was all before the 1996 federal election campaign. In the lead-up to that election, John Howard, soon to be prime minister, campaigned strongly on an anti-'political correctness' platform. As Aboriginal activist Noel Pearson pointed out, even the Liberal Party's apparently benign campaign slogan — 'For all of us' — sought to exploit a perception among voters that the previous government had pandered to minority groups, especially Aborigines, given that native title legislation was its landmark achievement. Fringe elements in the Liberal–National Coalition only underlined Pearson's observation. Candidates such as Pauline Hanson, Bob Katter and Wilson Tuckey all complained about Labor's bias towards 'politically correct' pro-Aboriginal policies at the expense of the average voter. Joining their chorus, Labor renegade Graeme Campbell said he had a message for all parties about 'political correctness', and that 'people are sick of the guilt and grievance industry, the Aboriginal industry and the femi-nazis'.[3] Howard distanced himself from his candidates, withdrew Hanson's endorsement and rebuked Katter, but still kept on complaining about 'political correctness'. It was an ugly, racially divisive campaign.

Perhaps Noel Pearson knew something many 'expert' political commentators of a certain age didn't. Hanson went on to win her seat handsomely as an independent, as did Campbell. Katter increased his majority, and Tuckey received the biggest two-party preferred vote in the entire country. One of the first acts of the new Howard government was to attack the Aboriginal and Torres Strait Islander Commission (ATSIC), undermining its funding and compromising its independence with a threatened return to old-style white overseeing. Soon after, the Coalition backbench and State premiers started agitating for changes to the Native Title Act. Complaints of racist abuse to the New South Wales anti-discrimination board skyrocketed after the election.[4] Formal complaints to the federal Race Discrimination Commission doubled.[5] Mary Kalantzis, an academic who had argued against 'political correctness' scaremongering, said that after the election she was hit by an unprecedented wave of hate mail and obscene phone calls.[6]

It would be rash to blame this on the advent of a new government alone. The racism had evidently long been simmering. What it had found was a powerful new legitimating language. As historian Henry Reynolds put it, the challenge for the Liberal Party, in attracting traditional Labor voters disenchanted with the previous government's approaches to immigration, indigenous rights and engagement with Asia, 'was to craft a message that spoke to their dissatisfaction without appearing to sanction the particular views that gave it birth'.[7]

Nor did Howard pull the anti-'PC', anti-'minority politics' rhetoric out of a hat. Within the Coalition, Tim Fischer, leader of the National Party, had been complaining about 'politically correct agenda setters' for six months before the campaign.[8] And in intellectual circles the above-mentioned phoney war had been under way since early 1991, when the *Australian* published the first internationally syndicated articles about 'PC' by US writers Dinesh D'Souza and David Segal. Before that, some might remember, Australian lefties used to talk about being 'ideologically sound', which, being for the most part self-directed, had an irony the accusation of 'political correctness' usually lacks.

After the publication of the syndicated American pieces, the story was initially slow to seep through the media. In mid-1991 Michael Barnard, veteran conservative columnist for the *Age*, took a few pot-shots at supposed 'political correctness' on campus, targeting feminist and deconstructionist courses and claiming that they 'denigrated and degraded' the Western cultural tradition.[9] Luke Slattery and Peter Ellingsen, then education writers for the *Age*, joined him a few months later with a tirade against the vandalising of 'the traditional canon of great works'[10] by university courses that claimed racial bias, class and patriarchy to be central to literary production.

What started off as a trickle began to grow into a veritable flood, catching up every second journalist looking to put a little lifestyle-oriented spin on a bit of otherwise unpromising copy. 'Political correctness is about to claim another victim', claimed the headline to an article about the renaming of lolly cigarettes 'Fags' as 'Fads'.[11] 'Girls just want to have a ball' ran the headline to an article that claimed 'It's supposed to be politically incorrect but, due to popular demand, some schools are bringing back the debutante ball'.[12] Others whinged that political correctness had led to the demise of the *Benny Hill Show*, failing to mention that Hill died rich and with a fresh contract in his hands, or that the show had been a cult item among many 'politically correct' tertiary students, feminists included.[13]

Complaining about 'political correctness' soon became an orthodoxy more clichéd than the supposed 'political correctness' itself. It had an irresistible allure for many middle-aged patrician opinion-makers. The rules were simple, the targets predictable. John Hyde, a former politician and regular contributor to the *Australian*, claimed 'multiculturalism has come to be associated with political correctness' and 'has gone wrong',[14] derailed by ideologues — of whose influence he was strangely in awe, given his past tenure as executive director of the Institute of Public Affairs. Dame Leonie Kramer claimed that 'ideologies are limiting our language',[15] but didn't say where unlimited language might be found. Barry Cohen, a politician turned columnist, complained about the 'politically correct' agenda that had taken over an exhibition on multiculturalism — just because it dared confront the fact that every new wave of immigrants met racism.[16] Columnist and sports writer Les Carlyon said 'The politically correct are a boring lot who murder the language and pretend to be liberal',[17] selling short his own credentials. P. P. McGuinness complained that the 'PC movement' suppressed 'serious discussion',[18] without actually managing to explain how, if freedom of speech was so limited, he had his own column published.

Rarely mentioned in other media, the 'PC' scare is tailor-made for the newspaper feature or the radio rant, in lieu of discussion of more important issues. It ties in neatly with what the critic Adrian Martin calls the vicious anti-intellectualism of Australian life:

> the more common journalistic pose is to scoff loudly at any concept that seems even mildly esoteric, all the while pretending to speak for the common person who, it is presumed, knows nothing of this highbrow stuff . . . the chief prerequisite for becoming a mass-media loudmouth in this country is the curious ability to appear smart, but never intellectual, even (or especially) if you once were intellectual in a previous life. The guardian of public opinion knows only as much as he or she needs to know of the new lingo in order to furiously, wittily denounce it.[19]

As Martin forecast, few of the tirades against 'PC' were designed to focus on burning local issues. In fact, they merely reiterated the themes of D'Souza's original piece. Instead there was a certain pompous defensiveness in the air, and, underneath all the grandiose certainty and journalistic dick-swinging, more than a little insecurity. As if the whole lot of them were running scared, caught up in a Big Panic. But scared of what?

First in the firing line were the universities. Slattery, having transferred to the *Australian*, wrote an infamous piece entitled 'I Think, Therefore I Think', lambasting theoretical courses oriented around 'identity politics' for their lack of vocational, 'real-world' use, blaming them for the demise of an 'older Socratic tradition' of 'knowledge and truth'.[20] Robert Manne claimed that academics were guilty of a new ideological totalitarianism, citing the reaction to Geoffrey Blainey's remarks about Asian immigration — as if Blainey's comments hadn't sparked more widespread concern.[21] Really, Manne was just following an age-old tradition in which conservatives are presented as a set-upon minority. P. P. McGuinness, deploying a more emotive rhetoric, complained about attempts to 'brainwash' students in the name of 'compulsory units of gender or feminist studies'.[22]

Universities are often seen as a breeding ground for 'identity politics' — the crucible of 'PC' — and for 'deconstructionists' hell-bent on destroying the fabric of society. It's hardly a new line of argument. Conservative movements have a long history of targeting intellectuals and universities. And in a society where the broad left lacks institutional focus, perhaps arts faculties *have* started to look like hotbeds of dissent, even if they aren't in quite as strong a position to storm the barricades of high culture and everyday life as their populist opponents like to imply. British feminist Toril Moi once remarked that, far from regretting the academisation of feminism, she was grateful for the refuge the liberal academy had given it in increasingly hostile times, given that the left had been in retreat for twenty years.[23] But attacks on the liberal academy, even for 'harbouring' feminism, have also tended to function as a way of avoiding having to think about other things. In focusing on campus speech codes and course designs, conservative critics have overlooked the social forces driving what they call 'political correctness'.

Demographics, someone once said, are destiny. Whether or not this is true in the case of the 'PC' debate, demographics count for a lot. When National Party leader Tim Fischer started criticising 'PC' as an attack on the family, claiming that modern society was 'downgrading the role of the male, the father',[24] and that values were being corrupted by gay minority interests who sought to 'undermine the family', in a way he hit the nail on the head. Like many of the other complainers about 'PC', Fischer harks back to outdated stereotypes of home, hearth and happy, heterosexual white nuclear family, all held sacrosanct, sealed off as if in some glass bell.

Most of those complaining about 'PC' are in fact white, middle-class males who seem to be worrying about their own declining proprietorial role in society as other groups come to the fore. In the USA, crucible of the 'PC' scare, non-whites will number 47 per cent of the population by 2050, up from 26 per cent in 1996.[25] As the writer Hanif Kureishi puts it, 'The immigrant is the Everyman of the twentieth century'.[26] At one level, 'political correctness' is nothing more than a courtesy to these changes, even an acknowledgement that they are partly a legacy of Western colonialism. If once it was possible to pretend that differences could be overlooked and accommodated according to a universal liberal model, these days aggrieved groups resist being dissolved into one great cultural mass on someone else's terms, universalist or otherwise. Changes in social manners are an inevitable consequence. Locally, it hardly seems an accident that the charge of 'political correctness' has come to the fore in the context of a backlash against native title and 'Asian' immigration.

Similar social forces have produced feminism. Despite the fact that the term 'straight white male' has become something of a rhetorical cliché, studies nevertheless show that poverty is inextricably related to gender as well as race, with white males, on average, getting the best deal. In 1994 Australian women were still earning an average of $150 per week less than their male counterparts.[27] A Bureau of Statistics study in 1991 showed that fewer than 10 per cent of top private-sector managers were women, and women occupied 74 per cent of clerical and sales jobs.[28] If such patterns of injustice are to change, and to be registered as socially important, new ways of speaking are called for. As the writer Christos Tsiolkas says:

> I no longer wish to use the term 'political correctness' because I do not want to align myself with the homophobes,

misogynists, and polite racists who can't stop whingeing about the number of poofters, dykes, abos, wogs and chinks getting published. Any perusal of any Australian section of a bookshop in this city will show that the dead white males, and might I add, the dead white females, are still writing and getting published. I wish there were more faggots, dykes, wogs, blackfellas, trannies, punks, ferals, surrealists and Ukrainians getting published.[29]

Given the 'conservatively correct' codes that have generally been used to keep 'black writers', 'women writers', 'gay and lesbian writers' or 'Asian writers' in their place, it's perhaps no surprise that 'white males' dislike having their sub-group status signalled at the expense of their hitherto assumed universality.

But if recent social movements have tended to be caricatured as 'organised opinion' by self-styled 'dissenters', it is difficult to see what such so-called 'dissenters' stand for but more of the same. The entrenched, even if lately challenged, *whiteness* of local culture remains in place across the range of middle-brow journalism, irrespective of positions on 'PC'. Fifties-style assumptions about the homogeneous whiteness of Australian society abound when Ray Martin, for example, asks his audience how they feel about Asian immigration and Asians living next door. What about his Asian viewers? Columnist Hugh Mackay quips that many Australians 'remain deeply suspicious of the concept of multiculturalism, simply because it seems to imply a fragmentation of *our* cultural identity' (my italics).[30] Do the 25 per cent of the population born overseas, not to mention the indigenous population, not read?[31] A similar assumption was projected in John Howard's assertion that under his government speech was a little freer. Freer for whom? Certainly not for many non-white Australians, who found themselves suffering a renewed climate of everyday vilification.

The prospect of these social changes and an acknowledgement of diversity have hit the established cultural order like a dose of B-grade movie hysteria. David Williamson, admittedly in a jokey mood, has said he thinks heterosexuality has a future, 'a rather daring thing to think these days, wouldn't you say?'[32] Even if he doesn't seriously think this to be the case, his remark nevertheless dramatised an insecurity about social primacy. Les Murray, launching Liberal parliamentarian Tony Abbott's book on the monarchy, claimed that free speech is dead in Australia, and that people 'are going to be punished with extreme social opprobrium if they express certain opinions which are not on the social agenda'.[33] Really? By whom? Luke Slattery, who is young enough to know better, thinks that, because of multiculturalism and 'postmodern detachment', Australia has forgotten its 'home-grown heroes' and is literally a 'nation without a past'.[34] Really? Shortly after Slattery made his remark, the evening news bulletins were full of the story that some new Henry Lawson poems had been found.[35]

The crude either/or logic of these remarks, according to which new forms of knowledge can only make themselves heard by suppressing the old, seems calculated to produce a certain effect, as if some great national disaster is just around the corner. And always there is that same rhetoric of loss.

★

Perhaps because younger people are seen as embodying social change, attacks on 'PC' often directly target the young. This was also a feature of the American 'PC' debate. Without wanting to overstate things, it's not surprising that attacks on freedom of speech — including censorship and funding cuts to student newspapers (and funding cuts to universities generally) — should be taking place in a climate where old-guard culture racketeers have done their best to demonise universities and cast aspersions on students. In *The First Stone*, for example, Garner complained about campus newspapers run by 'puritan feminists'.[36] Robert Manne too regards political correctness as a cancer that, having taken hold in universities, is infecting 'a new generation of students', spreading from there into mainstream life.[37] In *The Culture of Forgetting* he implies that Helen Darville's actions can be attributed to her youth, her ahistorical anti-Semitism, her university education and her supposed embrace of fashionable causes.

Other commentators reveal their generational bias more plainly. According to Beatrice Faust:

> Political correctness . . . is strongest among the first generation tertiary educated who suffer the stresses of upward mobility. Which is more tragic? That a gaggle of noisy first-generation-educated social-change merchants appropriated just causes and made them odious by doctrinaire and stubborn refusal to consult, or the fact that a large number of averagely decent and politically engaged intellectuals let them hijack the debate?[38]

Terry Lane too thinks 'PC' has something to do with younger people. He claims that white racism cannot be the central obstacle to Aboriginal reconciliation because 90.8 per cent of people voted 'Yes' in the 1967 referendum on Aboriginal rights. According to Lane, the extent of white support is 'underreported by the kiddies who run the news and current affairs programs' because of their desire to tell a certain story about the oppression of Aboriginals at the hands of whites. As Lane puts it:

> Once a chap passes a certain age — I put it at around 55 — he starts to read what purports to be records of events in which he personally participated. And he laughs. The next thing to do is to check the bona fides of the author. Ah well, there it is then. He/she is 30 years old. He/she was not even born when I, as a young adult, was participating in the events that he/she is describing with such careless disregard for the truth.[39]

Running scared

In *Dead White Males*, David Williamson plays out a fantasy in which Angela, the young woman at the centre of the play, on the brink of becoming 'politically correct' under the influence of her feminist mother and evil literary theorist lecturer Swain, discovers her grandfather's working-class self-sacrifice, and is at the same time propelled from Swain's arms into Shakespeare's, from feminism into a happy heterosexual relationship.

The emphasis on universities and student activism follows on from the US 'PC' scare, which got going on the back of a number of lurid anecdotes that have taken on the status of folklore since they were publicised in Dinesh D'Souza's book on 'PC', *Illiberal Education*. One was that a professor at Harvard could no longer give his course on slavery because students had hounded him for using the word 'Indians' instead of 'Native Americans'. In fact, as John Wilson shows in *The Myth of Political Correctness*, only a small number of students complained, the professor was never punished, and it was his own decision to stop teaching the class despite the wishes of everyone involved. In another widely repeated anecdote a group of students supposedly marched around Stanford chanting 'Hey, hey, ho, ho, Western culture has got to go'. As Wilson points out, the students were actually berating a course entitled 'Western culture', contrary to D'Souza's suggestion that the apocalypse was nigh.[40] Such myths, and there are many, are repeated from one conservative columnist to the next, up to 35 times in some cases, seeding the 'PC' mythology over and over again. The pattern is similar in Australia, with celebrated instances, such as the depiction of the Ormond case in *The First Stone*, following precisely the generic pattern of the US 'cases', taking on a life of their own through partial accounts and top-spin bias.

There was the spectacle of generationalism too in the *60 Minutes* television report that showed Pauline Hanson standing in the street and berating a group of Aboriginal teenagers,

Gangland

screaming 'I have just as much right to be here as you'.[41] And in the charges laid against two young Aborigines who were jailed for allegedly spitting on her. Not only did both incidents provide a vignette of an old white Australia against the new, but the former also said a lot about the rhetorical strategies of anti-'PC' campaigners. No-one had accused Hanson of having no right to be there. But 'straw man' arguments and paranoid misrepresentations of opponents' positions are precisely how the 'PC' debate gets going.

Old and new Australia? It would be a mistake to map some kind of crude generational model on to any difference, just as it would be a mistake to label all youth politically progressive. Conservatism is widespread now, as can be seen in the extensive youth support for the Kennett and Howard governments. The present unfashionability of 'political correctness' crosses all boundaries. Nevertheless, feminism, cultural mixes or queerness aren't a threat so much as part of life for those who have grown up with cultural diversity, or who *are* first-generation immigrants, or their offspring, or feminists, or queer. These so-called 'issues' simply don't carry the same sort of baggage they once did. They are to be defended, or celebrated, as an intrinsic part of the social landscape.

It is a media sport, though — even an article of faith — to pretend that the young aren't engaged in politics. They are a dowdy, apathetic lot, characterised by their lack of engagement in *anything*. Again, this is symptomatic of a failure to recognise alternative cultures and a tendency to write off paradigms other than one's own. It's a cliché designed to pretend that the current generation of commentators are the only possible producers of authentic politics, and to obscure the lack of mainstream media opportunities available to the young.

In fact, young people today are perhaps more politically engaged than their parents' generation. Students were among the first to rally against Pauline Hanson and her opinions on immigration.[42] Throughout 1996 and 1997 there were large rallies in most capital cities and numerous smaller actions against cuts to education spending and the introduction of tertiary fees. In October 1996 students jostled the prime minister in a protest at the University of Sydney. In May 1997 students occupied administration buildings at Melbourne University and Deakin University in protest against the introduction of places for local full-fee-paying students. As anyone involved in voluntary work for needle exchanges, women's refuges, refuges for the homeless, HIV/AIDS work, alternative and community radio or youth outwork will know, the idea of apolitical, apathetic youth is a myth. In the US, where comfortable and often self-serving myths about apolitical students also prevail (somewhat paradoxically, since students are often accused of being both 'PC' and antipolitical), a higher proportion of students than ever before is actively involved in campus politics. Volunteer rates for the Peace Corps are up. Participation rates in volunteer activities are at an all-time high, whether it be in Greenpeace, Amnesty International or local organisations such as feminist groups and organised charities. According to a survey at the University of California at Los Angeles, a record 40 per cent of students took part in demonstrations in 1992, twice the level of the late 1960s. In this same survey one-third of students said that becoming a leader in the community was important or essential — double the 1972 figure.[43]

The idea that young people are empty of politics is bound up with the idea that they are empty, period. That is, empty vessels waiting to be filled, which is the assumption routinely made in many of the tirades against 'political correctness' that resolutely presume the young to be their ideal audience. Plays such as *Dead White Males* are pedagogical as much as theatrical acts, designed to function as a powerful alternative to what Williamson evidently imagines is being taught in universities. It is no accident that Williamson (William's son?) exhorts his audience to forsake the 'theory' supposedly being foisted on them by charlatan lecturers and go 'back to Shakespeare', the paradigmatic monocultural Englishman. Williamson's later play *Heretic* does a similar thing, warning against new-fangled ideas and casting those who renounce them as intellectual heroes. Disturbingly, both imply that students are impressionable targets for brainwashing, and that they enrol in 'theoretical' courses not of their own volition, but because they are at the mercy of unscrupulous staff. This is pure wishful thinking. What Williamson forgets is that, if there are enforced campus speech codes (in my own time at university I have yet to encounter any), or an emphasis on 'ideologically based' courses, such things came into existence not because of sudden benevolence on the part of vice-chancellors and faculty heads, but because of pressure from students.

★

Another of the persistent jokes of the anti-'PC' campaign is the idea that 'PC' is some form of censorship. This mythology overlooks the fact that everyone is to a degree self-censoring; the notion that some Utopia exists where there is absolute freedom from manners is surely the last great liberal fantasy. Are we to return to the days when whites unselfconsciously called non-whites 'boongs' and Aboriginal children 'piccaninnies'?

Phillip Adams has claimed that self-censorship is the most insidious form of censorship.[44] This is a gesture typical of the (orthodox) distaste for orthodoxy that bled through some strands of 1970s progressive politics. As the writer Drusilla Modjeska has said, those of her generation often take up 'a very '70s position . . . which is sometimes called anarchist, or is suspicious of the State, which is about personal empowerment, which really has a deep, deep, deep-seated antagonism to the notion that personal life can be regulated'.[45] While Adams is one of the least conservative of the old-guard commentators, his logic is typical of tirades against 'PC', whether they come from remnants of the 1970s left or the resurgent 1980s and 1990s right (it gets harder to tell the difference). There is a refusal to acknowledge that everyone is in some way self-censoring, and always has been, much as the pretence that this is a new thing has the effect of dressing up diatribes against 'political correctness' as crusades for freedom and openness.

Many local campaigners against 'PC' have complex links to earlier intellectual movements. Peter Coleman's attacks on 'PC', for example, contain an echo of the self-conscious dissent and unconstrained libertarian freedom espoused by the arch-individualist John Anderson, professor of philosophy at Sydney University from 1927 to 1958. Anderson, whose own political position underwent a series of shifts, had a complicated relationship with the Sydney Push, a loose-knit and heterogeneous group of thinkers and activists who were influential in the 1940s, '50s and '60s. Various movements were associated with the Push, including the Freethought Society and Libertarianism, often in reaction against each other, though their members often socialised in the same places. After a split in the 1950s over attitudes to the Cold War, the rump of the Freethought Society promoted a more conservative, anti-Marxist strand of Andersonianism (initiated by Anderson himself). This influenced the new Australian right into the early 1960s. The fortnightly *Observer* (later to merge with the *Bulletin*), edited by Donald Horne, with Peter Coleman as his assistant, was a driving force behind an emerging liberal anti-communist orthodoxy, also represented by magazines such as *Quadrant*, founded by James McAuley, co-edited by Horne through the mid-1960s and edited by Coleman into the 1980s.[46] Robert Manne became editor in 1989, with David Armstrong, another Push figure, as an editorial adviser.

The attitudes of the Push freethinkers, according to the critic John Docker, were consistent with a broader Sydney tradition characterised by an anti-collectivist, anti-welfarist, anti-egalitarian idealism and a desire to transcend history and the social. Adherents of this tradition 'consciously or unconsciously cling to the romantic idea of the natural as real in life, and the social as accidental'.[47] But for all its pluralism and belief in unconstrained freedom, Docker suggests, this creed did not preclude a secret masculinist conformism. A similar point is made by writer and 1960s radical Kate Jennings: while the Push 'professed to be the enemies of conformity, they demanded a high degree of compliance among their members. They hated moralisers, moralising all the while themselves.'[48] Anne Coombs, biographer of the Push, agrees. Even if the Push seemed radical, she says, they were actually socially conservative, and although they embraced nonconformism, 'they stymied any latent activists in their midst'.[49]

Whether or not the Push has anything to do with it, the idea that 'dissenters' would be free but for the censorship imposed by politics junkies is rife throughout the 'PC' debate. The so-called 'censorship', however, tends to amount to little more than normal informed criticism. This form of self-martyrdom pervades *The First Stone*, where Garner casts herself as chief victim of an imaginary feminist conspiracy, and the monologues of *Dead White Males* and *Heretic*, and trickles through to the columns of P. P. McGuinness. Every criticism, it seems, is evidence of an 'industry'. When John Herron was criticised as having mishandled his Aboriginal affairs portfolio, for example, John Howard retaliated by claiming that the minister had been targeted by 'thought police' and was the victim of an 'Aboriginal industry'.[50]

To compound the joke, any progressive political organisation would kill for the media coverage enjoyed by most of the poor suffering victims of this supposed censorship. If 'political correctness' is so censoring, then how do its most vocal opponents remain at the centre of wide-ranging and powerful networks, with close links to both government and the press? Peter Coleman, for example, whose book *Doubletake* exists as a forum for complaints about 'PC' (interestingly, his previous book was called *Memoirs of a Slow Learner*), has been a State parliamentarian, as well as editor of *Quadrant* and the *Bulletin*.

Christopher Pearson, a vociferous anti-'PC' campaigner and contributor to *Doubletake*, is editor of the *Adelaide Review*, and worked as a Howard speech-writer in the lead-up to the 1996 election. He is also a defender of Chris Kenny, a journalist and *Adelaide Review* columnist, and has edited Kenny's book on the 'secret women's business' that initially blocked the construction of the Hindmarsh Island bridge. Kenny, you might remember, conducted the famous TV interview in which Doug Milperra claimed the 'women's business' was fabricated, sparking a Royal Commission.

The circle of influence extends to *Doubletake*'s reception. It was gushingly reviewed in Pearson's *Adelaide Review*,[51] as well as by Andrew Riemer, another veteran campaigner against 'PC', in the *Sydney Morning Herald*,[52] and Kenneth Minogue in the *Australian*.[53] Minogue, a crusty British-based anti-'PC' campaigner who was on a lecture tour at the time, thinks it's a man's job to be manly and a woman's to nurture, and that 'feminists . . . are the clinging vines of institutions'.[54] According to an article he wrote for the *Adelaide Review*, 'Feminism . . . is certainly the most serious threat to Western civilisation since, by setting women against men as competitors for benefits, it weakens the entire range of activities in civil society'.[55]

Along with Minogue, Pearson regularly publishes notables such as novelist Frank Moorhouse, another contributor to the Coleman book, who, like Coleman and other notable anti-'PC'-ites P. P. McGuinness, Don Anderson, Bob Ellis and Robert Hughes, is a one-time associate of the Push, a group hardly known for their lack of influence or media infiltration; Clive James, Germaine Greer, Eva Cox and Richard Neville are other alumni. Other contributors to the Coleman book, such as Beatrice Faust and Les Murray, have a similarly strong media presence. Both, in fact, seem to have had something of a renaissance because of the 'PC' scare. Faust is ever dragged on board as your non-card-carrying, non-ideological feminist, and Murray has become something of a media pet, along with other arts notables of the Whitlam era such as Bob Ellis and David Williamson, as well as prominent neo-conservatives such as John Stone and former Alexander Downer adviser Stephen Rimmer. For months on end in 1995 and 1996 these few were authoritatively cited in every second article on 'PC' — with barely a countervailing quote.[56]

In an article that profiled eighteen so-called 'dissenters', the journalist Roy Eccleston asked 'What chance has the lone voice against organised opinion?'[57] Every chance, it would seem, given that his article took up eight pages in a weekend magazine distributed free in the country's only national broadsheet. Yet Eccleston claimed they had been silenced by opposition, 'particularly from the politically correct'.[58] As an authority for this insight he cited — you guessed it — Peter Coleman. All those featured in the article were establishment figures with high media profiles and successful careers, including Pearson, ex-senator Peter Walsh, Geoffrey Blainey and Bruce Ruxton.

It was an influential article, deemed worthy of an editorial in the main body of the paper.[59] The problem was that the closer you looked at the piece the more its central thesis looked like wishful thinking. Only a scant few of the interviewees actually mentioned 'PC' (or anything like it) as a problem, and one, Pat O'Shane, later went on television to argue *for* 'political correctness'. As if to confirm what it takes to be any kind of personage in political commentary, all of Eccleston's eighteen 'dissenters' were aged between 43 and 69, the average age being 58, a fact Eccleston tries to cover by talking about young people's supposed lack of interest in politics. Similarly, all the contributors to Coleman's book, he admits, 'are either representative figures of the 1960s/1970s generation or its heirs'.[60] Frankly, I couldn't spot the heirs.

Also among the heavily 'censored' on the anti-'PC' hustings are radio talkback jocks such as John Laws, Alan Jones and Stan Zemanek, all of whom preside over high-rating populist shows and don't seem to be short of access to those in power. It's hard to take their rantings seriously — at least the print commentators cling to a semblance of reason and follow print journalism's unwritten ethic of not directly encouraging the lunatic fringe. Laws, for example, has claimed that 'The thought police will go to *any* lengths to make any point, because they convince themselves that they know better. They will distort, manipulate, misrepresent and even prevent the truth if they believe the cause is good.'[61] Alan Jones has attacked political parties that 'indulge minorities' and claimed that Australians have been brainwashed by 'political correctness'.[62] Stan Zemanek, another 2UE host, talks of a similar kind of tyranny: 'The perception in society today in Australia is that the minority groups get more than the majority . . . and that's what the Australian taxpayer gets sick and tired of and all he seems to hear is the minority groups going out there and protecting the bludgers of our society and keeping people on the gravy train.'[63] Never has such an elite had so much space made available for them to complain about how censored they feel.

But is the anti-'PC' campaigner the real voice of 'dissent' — the loner battling it out against 'organised opinion'? What of those who campaign against 'conservative correctness'? At about the time Eccleston's piece was published, and Coleman was whingeing about un-'PC' writers being 'bazooka'd' — a triumph of paranoid emotiveness, considering that all that had happened was that people had disagreed with them — a columnist for a major daily told me, on the condition that I not mention any names, that it took six months of heavy lobbying to get a column attempting to debunk the myth of 'PC' published, and then in heavily truncated form.

While some critics have described the anti-'PC' panickers as a 'straight male voting and lobbying bloc',[64] from the way popular campaigners against so-called 'political correctness' speak, you'd think there were lynch mobs out in the street waiting every time they uttered an opinion — as if the left had won the great political battles of our time and 'femi-nazi' media proprietors had gathered under the banners of global socialism, ready to deny them their weekly ration of hundreds of column inches or hours of air-time. Perhaps they confuse freedom of speech with immunity from criticism.

Indeed, if freedom of speech was really the issue here, there would be less chest- and brow-beating about so-called 'PC', and more about the treatment of the 'boat people' detained in Port Hedland, who have even been denied the right to be informed of their human rights, including free speech. Or the systematic dismantling of common-law rights to legal redress against actions of the Victorian State government. Or the restrictions imposed on Freedom of Information laws in the name of 'commercial confidentiality'. Or even the legislated closure of student newspapers, no matter how much our prominent 'dissenters' may dislike their left-wing slant.

And why is it that, with a couple of notable exceptions, those old war-horses who would disguise their arch-conservatism as a panegyric to intellectual openness get to be the ones who tell us what politics is now? As Phillip Adams, to his credit, has pointed out, 'overwhelmingly, Australia's newspaper columnists are pro-conservative' by contrast with the mid-1970s, when he recalls 'talking to the late Graham Perkin, then editor of the *Age*, about the urgent need to recruit at least one conservative columnist'.[65] Even Gerard Henderson, former Howard adviser and executive director of the Sydney Institute, says 'the non-left have never had a better run in the mainstream Australian media'.[66] And why is it that, again with a few notable exceptions, younger commentators get 'safe' space to crack jokes or talk about the Internet, but they don't get space to talk about politics of any hue, unless they're Bill O'Chee, or are being set up as 'young feminists'?

It's a strange pass when almost all the information in the mainstream press about politics — even progressive politics — is filtered through the rhetoric of a conservative, mainly patrician elite. Some are disenchanted members of the 1970s left who use their credentials as proof of the virtues of recanting, even as they swamp other progressive commentary. Others are old Cold Warriors who nearly found themselves out of a job with the fall of the Berlin Wall, but swapped the Red Menace for the 'PC' Menace with barely a missed rhetorical beat and hardly a day's retraining: like the Reds, 'PC'-ers are supposedly censorious; both are conspiracies run by the left; both are 'enemies of the West' and 'natural enemies' of freedom and liberty; and both are cast as the overarching bogey of the times. The old 'fellow-traveller' metaphor still has its uses, too. It's just like the good old days.

★

Is it possible, then, that the Liberal Party, with its 1996 campaign rhetoric, did little more than substitute one political demon for another? In some ways the John Howard who stood at a lectern mouthing certainties about 'political correctness' seemed little different from the Liberal treasurer who stood at a lectern fifteen years earlier mouthing similar certainties about Labor 'socialists'. Perhaps one major difference is that since then there has been a renaissance in right-wing politics with the emergence of privately funded policy think-tanks and the development of economic rationalist policies, and a hyper-tuned 'individualist' rhetoric to go with them. Forget 'free love' and Woodstock: the enduring legacy of the baby-boomers is economic rationalism. Certainly, one of the triumphs of the new right is the extent to which politicians, the press and even ordinary people have begun to parrot its rhetoric. Look at the way we have all learned to 'recognise' 'PC' as an infringement on our own free speech. As prominent US neo-conservative Irving Kristol said, commenting on the conservative resurgence of the 1980s, 'neoconservatism today is an integral part of the language of conservative politics . . . the merger of neoconservatism and traditional conservatism under way since the election of Ronald Reagan is largely complete'.[67]

The attack on 'PC' is entirely consistent with economic rationalist agendas. Its advocacy of the privatisation of ethics, for example, is no less an attack on collectivism than the neo-conservative assault on the trade unions. As the gap between rich and poor widens, with real wages having fallen by between 13 and 15 per cent since 1975,[68] and with both major parties having adopted economic rationalist policies, it isn't surprising that we should see the emergence of a discourse that seeks to apportion the social costs elsewhere, with an ever more sophisticated way of discrediting the victim as a mere 'complainer'. Howard tried to exploit this new disfranchisement in his 1996 campaign, courting the 'battler', even if his tune changed soon after the election with his assault on the Paxtons — typical victims of economic rationalism — as 'bludgers'. Nor is it surprising, given that many of the policies of economic rationalism have impacted squarely on youth, that attacks on 'PC' often take the young as their audience and universities as their targets. As the writer and academic David Bennett says, the attack on education works 'in the interests of producing a "flexible" or compliant workforce, a homogeneous national identity, and a technocratic taming of fractious difference'.[69]

Here we revisit D'Souza, who was responsible for one of the articles on 'PC' originally syndicated in the *Australian*. The rise of the Reagan right during the 1980s played no small part in the publication of his much-cited book *Illiberal Education*. It was written with the assistance of $150 000 from the Olin Foundation plus $100 000 from the American Enterprise Institute, both of which are US neo-conservative think-tanks. The conservative Institute for Educational Affairs and the Madison Centre also chipped in $30 000 and $20 000 respectively.[70] At the time D'Souza was also a Reagan staffer. The buzz among the US right then, as now, was against the Equal

Rights Amendment, multiculturalism and affirmative action. In particular, they wanted to see the dismantling of affirmative action legislation (this was achieved in California in 1996, with the passing of Proposition 209). The talk among US think-tanks then was about finding mechanisms for implementing (rather than just formulating) their programmes. This produced the electoral strategy of identifying 'wedge' issues to split the Democrat vote by appealing to its less educated, working-class proportion and playing them off against the tertiary-educated 'bleeding heart' liberals. The strategy was underpinned by 'attack politics' as employed by radio 'shock-jocks' such as Rush Limbaugh, who were happy to home in on the liberal Democrat involvement with minority politics, sending a message to white working-class Democrat voters that they were losing out: the real demons here weren't the wealthy and powerful, but the 'politically correct'.

Locally, neo-conservative think-tanks such as the Tasman Institute and the Centre for Independent Studies have also prospered over the past twenty years, forging close ties to governments and acting as a haven for conservative politicians on the way up, and down. The Institute of Public Affairs (IPA) has direct links to the Liberal Party through its former director, Rod Kemp, now a Liberal senator. Other prominent conservative politicians who have spoken out strongly about 'PC', such as John Stone (former Treasury head and National Party senator) and John Hyde (former WA Liberal parliamentarian and *Australian* columnist), are also closely associated with the IPA. Hyde was its director for many years, as well as a member of the influential 'crossroads' group, originally formed to promote economic rationalism within the Liberal Party. Another prominent IPA member, Hugh Morgan of Western Mining (known for his disparaging remarks about the 'chattering classes', an early version of anti-'PC' rhetoric), is also a member of the 'crossroads' group and co-founder, with federal treasurer Peter Costello, of the conservative H. R. Nicholls

Society. In recent years, under a new director, the Institute of Public Affairs has acknowledged that its earlier aim of promoting economic rationalism has largely been achieved, and has broadened its agenda to Aboriginal and immigration matters. It has produced discussion papers claiming that multiculturalism is of benefit mainly to a 'multicultural mafia' (ATSIC, come on down!), and leads to ethnic segregation and special interest feather-bedding, as well as the creation of 'political power bases'.[71]

The IPA, of course, is yet to explain in what way it isn't a 'political power base', just as the major political parties, for that matter, are yet to explain in what way they (or the mining business) aren't an 'industry'. The messy business of 'organised opinion', it would seem, is always elsewhere.

With this proviso firmly in mind, it's worth mentioning further associations that underscore what's at stake in the local version of the 'PC' debate. The political elites were out in force, for example, in June 1996, when the Minister for Aboriginal Affairs, John Herron, launched Geoffrey Partington's book *Hasluck versus Coombs*. This occasion not only provided the spectacle of a government minister launching a pro-assimilation book at Parliament House, but also prompted Howard's remarks about the minister being a victim of the 'thought police'.[72] Partington, who has been associated with a range of right-wing think-tanks, is an important figure in mining industry opposition to the Mabo judgment and a prolific writer of papers for right-wing causes. When Herron was criticised for remarking that the 'stolen generation' of Aboriginal children had benefited from their forced assimilation, Christopher Pearson was quick to leap into print in his defence.[73]

At around the same time Howard found himself tacitly (but not directly or instinctively) trying to distance himself from another speech, the infamous maiden speech of independent MP Pauline Hanson, in which she claimed that

Aborigines were the best-off people in Australia and that the country was in danger of being swamped by Asians. For all of Howard's disavowals of similarities between himself and Hanson, their rhetoric on 'political correctness' and 'free speech' was the same.

Robert Manne has commented that Hanson's populist speeches 'demonstrated more clearly than any episode in our recent national life the political explosiveness of the cultural divide between the views of ordinary people and the views of the intelligentsia'.[74] On the contrary. While most of the cultural elite were horrified by Hanson's extremism, the great unsayable of that debate was that they themselves had been complaining about multiculturalism, feminism, affirmative action, 'political correctness', special interest groups, identity politics and minority rights, albeit less stridently and in different contexts, long before Pauline Hanson arrived on the scene. Most, with a few honourable exceptions (and some dishonourable ones), went very quiet after the Hanson affair broke, reformulating just where they were coming from on multiculturalism and 'political correctness'.

At the level of party politics the priorities were slightly different. As Henry Reynolds has pointed out:

> The Coalition's use of race, however subtle, represents an important departure for mainstream Australian politics. Until recently there has been a broad consensus among politicians that while they would compete across a wide terrain on many issues, they would leave aside questions of race.[75]

The Coalition's powerful anti-'PC' rhetoric and Howard's comments that when it comes to minority politics he has obligations to 'the whole Australian community, not just particular communities'[76] were an attack on the concept of minority rights and the principle of supporting the disfranchised and underprivileged through the mechanism of the whole — a principle that many argue is itself central to the concept of democracy. Howard's failure to repudiate Hanson's speech or to defend those she attacked created the impression that, for the first time in living memory, Australians were represented by a government whose first instinct wasn't to defend the rights of all its citizens.

Looking at the way the Labor vote went in the 1996 election, it would seem that the Liberals' attack on Labor's supposedly 'politically correct' policy-making worked at least a little 'wedge issue' magic. According to the Australian Electoral Commission, the biggest swings against Labor were in its safe seats (6.1 per cent, compared with 4.5 per cent in fairly safe seats), especially blue-collar seats. The biggest swings came in Queensland (16.1 per cent), especially in formerly safe seats such as Oxley, now held by Pauline Hanson (18.3 per cent). As Phillip Adams has pointed out, citing political journalist Alan Ramsey, of the 40 electorates with the highest Aboriginal population, before the election Labor held 21, of which it lost 14. Of the ten electorates with the highest Aboriginal population, Labor now holds none, as against five before the election.[77] The Liberal campaign was reportedly devised with the help of US Republican Party strategists.[78]

At the level of wider policy, the targets of the anti-'PC' campaign were remarkably consistent with Republican Party strategy. This is also true of the commentators. The coalition of US government agencies and institutions mentioned by D'Souza in his original research parallels the Australian institutions singled out by Coleman for admonition as repositories of 'organised opinion': 'the universities, the media, the Australia Council, the cultural organisations, the ABC'.[79] Manne in *Quadrant* does the same, situating 'PC' in 'the bailiwicks inhabited by the intelligentsia — the universities, the quality media, the teaching profession and the public service'.[80] Discounting the privately owned media, these sectors — along with ATSIC — were in the front line of the Howard government's first major round of funding cuts. The attack on affirmative action was more subtle, involving a downgrading of the Office of the Status of Women that led to the resignation of its head, Sue Walpole. Defence, meanwhile, was quarantined from cuts, a trend foreshadowed in the above-mentioned IPA discussion paper.

D'Souza, meanwhile, has taken his rhetoric of social division and hate a step further. In his latest book, *The End of Racism: Principles For a Multicultural Society*, with its deceptively moderate-sounding title, he argues, among other things, that racism is justified because it is rational for white people to worry about being in close proximity to black people, given the higher involvement of black people in violent crime. In this there is an echo of the presently 'correct' economic rationalist thinking that insists the only way to break the welfare cycle is to eliminate welfare altogether. The local press are only too willing to play ball. P. P. McGuinness, while dissociating himself from D'Souza's book, has nevertheless continued to argue that 'affirmative action programs have for the most part promoted separatism and hatred between the races'[81] — one implication being that the possible benefits of such programmes should be ignored for so long as there is a chance that their existence will offend those who least need them. This sort of logic, like the Liberal Party's 'for all of us', is designed to put the 'mainstream' at the centre, and to perpetuate a climate of resentment against the margins — more 'wedge issue' magic. Or, as Hanson has summarised it, 'racism is starting in this country because the government is looking after the Aborigines too much'.[82]

All this overlapping rhetoric pretends to be about one thing (the collective welfare?), but is actually about something else: the maintenance of a status quo. And what better way to stifle real dissent than an all-purpose pejorative such as 'political correctness', which amounts to little more than a blanket way of discrediting anything that looks remotely like a progressive idea, without having to resort to argument? Such an aim would be complicit with the 'equity' campaigns run by the right over recent years, even if it turns out that such 'equity' is available only to the already strong, just as those with the greatest opportunity to prosper in a world without 'minority politics' or 'ideology' turn out to be the already privileged.

★

In the wake of these policy changes, the debate on 'PC' has also begun to change. On the one hand, for a year after the 1996 election the hate industry had a field day, spurred on by the government, squealing 'PC' at every turn. On the other, some of the louder 'PC' complainers, especially those with links to the 1970s left, have apparently roused, as if from a long sleep, and realised just who is in the same bed. It must have been disquieting to watch the Liberal Party come to power on a platform at least partly to do with bashing the 'politically correct', and immediately start attacking Aboriginal organisations and newly arrived immigrants. As it must have been disturbing to hear the gun lobby use anti-'PC' rhetoric to campaign against new gun laws following the Port Arthur massacre (Ian McNiven, who gave the famous pro-guns 'Gympie address', praised his own political incorrectness and thanked Pauline Hanson, 'that courageous little lady', for getting the ball rolling).[83]

Perhaps another milestone was a panel debate on the ABC's *7.30 Report* in April 1996, in which the arch-conservative monarchist Liberal parliamentarian (and former Howard press secretary and *Adelaide Review* columnist) Tony Abbott and radio shock-jock Stan Zemanek rolled out anti-'PC' rhetoric with a surly cockiness that was as alienating as it was fascinating. Their grandiose claims struggled in the cold hard light of debate, and they were trounced by Pat O'Shane and Mary Kalantzis on the pro-'PC' side. Kalantzis, in particular, convincingly showed that, if there is any such thing as 'PC', then there is perhaps a little 'PC' courtesy in all of us, even in the

Coalition's campaign for government — if not in its rhetoric and policies thereafter.[84]

There was disquiet among conservatives too. Having initially attempted to read Hansonism as a sign that the cultural elites are out of touch, Robert Manne has since conceded that many members of the 'conservative intelligentsia' would find 'their own ideas — on the new class, political correctness, Mabo, multiculturalism, Asian migration, the High Court — absorbed, simplified, systematised and radicalised' in Hanson's rhetoric.[85] It was telling that Manne spoke of this 'intelligentsia' in the third person, without directly implicating himself. It was as if those who had propagated the disease now wanted to offer the cure, while taking up media space in both instances.

A few months earlier, opening the paper on my breakfast table, I found an article by Williamson about political correctness, not attacking it vociferously, as he had earlier, but calling for a laying down of arms, a rethinking of the focus on 'identity politics', in order to remember who the 'real enemies' are, so as to facilitate a rejuvenation of the left. In some ways it seemed all he wanted to do was turn the clock back to the 1970s, when everything was obvious and politics were readable to his eye. His call for the 'laying down of arms' would be viable only if 'political correctness' was what he thought it was. 'Political correctness' — if it can be said to exist as such — is not driven by academic puppet-masters (Williamson, sadly, had not got over his obsession with Foucault) or trenchant ideologues of any variety, but by social change. Those involved with queer activism, for example, know that the focus on identity is not because of any course to do with Foucault or anyone else, but for reasons such as the political coalition-making that has become necessary in order to wring AIDS education funding out of extremely conservative governments.

It seems many commentators of Williamson's generation don't see any of this as legitimate and necessary politics. They look for a single issue that will define the left, as the Vietnam war did in the 1960s. While there have been signs that something of the kind is happening again, with the emergence of a broad coalition of interests under the anti-racism banner, there is a range of issues that broadly speak the left now: Aboriginal rights, AIDS funding, youth homelessness, urban poverty, feminisms, the rights of people with disabilities, prisoners' rights, environmental protection, refugees' rights and mental health activism. 'Identity categories', for better or worse — in a play of the politics of 'authenticity' against the improvised contingencies of political organisation — have become necessary to Realpolitik. From my own experience talking to a wide range of activists working in these fields, they are comfortable with this hybridity and diversity. Certainly there is a lot going on, even if little of it aspires to the sort of left monoculture (did it ever really exist?) often invoked by those superannuated remnants of the 1970s left (and right) who dominate mainstream media discussion about what progressive politics is now.

4
Stoned again: the 'victim feminism' scare

one needs perspective, not attitudes; context, not anecdotes; analyses, not postures.

Toni Morrison[1]

I think people underestimate their own nasty motives.

Helen Garner[2]

Lately, touching base with feminist commentators in the media has been like listening to a bad commercial radio station. I keep hearing the same old song over and over again, like a 1970s 'classic rock' hit repeated *ad nauseam*. It's either a tune about 'victim feminism' or 'puritan feminism', and it's played mainly by feminists who were around then. Beatrice Faust, for example, talks of 'wimp feminism', and says: 'Wimp victims believe that they will be victims for the rest of their lives.' For Faust wimp feminism is 'revolutionary feminism gone to seed'.[3] Susan Mitchell asks 'was it for this that feminists had fought so hard?', lamenting what she sees as the new scourge of 'victimhood' among young feminists on campus.[4] Bettina Arndt worries that sexual harassment legislation and amendments to the Victorian Domestic Violence Act might usher in a new era of punitiveness and retribution by feminist ideologues with a victim mentality and a taste for 'vengeance'.[5] And Helen Garner speaks of 'this determination to cling to victimhood at any cost, which seems to have become the loudest voice of feminism today'.[6]

There's nothing new here. Like 'classic rock' radio, the formula had its genesis in the USA. Compare the above statements, for example, with those of the self-styled renegade academic, Camille Paglia, who has specialised in exposing 'the creeping fascism of the date-rape and sexual harassment hysteria' among young American feminists.[7] Naomi Wolf, a young feminist herself, has written:

> Over the last twenty years the old belief in a tolerant assertiveness, a claim to human participation and human rights — power feminism — was embattled by the rise of a set of beliefs that cast women as beleaguered, fragile, intuitive angels: victim feminism.[8]

According to Rene Denfeld, a 'power feminism' campaigner who likes to be photographed wearing boxing gloves and squaring off to the camera, 'feminists focus heavily on victimization and assault . . . This is victim mythology.'[9] Katie Roiphe, who publicised 'date-rape' hysteria in her book *The Morning After: Sex, Fear and Feminism on Campus*, says the 'inflamed rhetoric against [sexual] harassment implies that all women are potential victims'.[10] Even art critic Robert Hughes weighs in: 'The new orthodoxy of feminism is abandoning the image of the independent, existentially responsible woman in favor of woman as helpless victim of male oppression — treat her as equal before the law and you are compounding her victimization.'[11]

Anyone who has heard these tunes often enough will be familiar with their common refrain: there's a new type of feminism abroad — a negative, doctrinaire, punitive feminism that can focus on only one thing at the expense of all else: the idea that women are victims. According to its critics, this is a feminism that allows no possibility for fun, sex or female power, and it has reached plague proportions among young women.

Stoned again

The big crossover hit in the local charts was Helen Garner's *The First Stone*. This book is presented as an account of events that took place at a prestigious residential college of Melbourne University, where five female students filed complaints about the behaviour of their college master at a dance following a valedictory dinner in October 1991. The incidents eventually ended up with the police laying charges and cases going before the courts. One student alleged that while she was dancing with the master, he squeezed her breast. Another alleged that while they were together in his study he locked the door, touched her breasts and made suggestive remarks about 'having indecent thoughts about her'.[12] Garner's assertion is that these women played the role of victim by not taking direct action against the master (by, say, slapping him in the face), and compounded this by adopting a punitive, legislative approach in going to the police and participating in an ideologically driven feminist cabal designed to orchestrate the master's dismissal.

The problem with *The First Stone*, as with most victim-panic tracts, is that its propositions are too simple by half. Far from going directly to the police, the complainants embarked on six months of informal negotiations in good faith (as the college itself has since agreed), enduring at the same time, according to the Equal Opportunity Commission ruling on the case, a sustained campaign by the college to discredit them. But the book doesn't give these facts the same prominence as those that are unfavourable to the complainants. Also obscured are the networks of patronage brought to bear by the college in its handling of the case, and details of the legalistic requirements the college hierarchy forced on the complainants in attempting to close the matter. The college committee finally set up to deal with the charges had no brief to investigate them, or to test the veracity of the complainants' accounts, but nevertheless formally closed the matter so far as the college was concerned. The complainants were also warned by the college that accepting the committee's 'findings' would leave them open to litigation. They were eventually advised to go to the police, not by an ideologically driven feminist cabal but by a hired lawyer, who suggested this course of action as an independent and on-the-record means of verifying their stories where no other was available. Garner has since explained that to avoid litigation one character was split into several, adding to the impression of a cabal.

Defenders of Garner's narrative strategy have suggested that it relies on teasing out ambiguities,[13] but the underlying structure of *The First Stone* follows the ground rules of the victim-panic genre almost to the letter. Bursts of strong polemic distract attention from muddied accounts of fact. The book reverses the underlying power dynamic of the situation to suggest that it is women who have unleashed incredible power in getting the 'Ormond blokes on the run'.[14] It underplays the fact that it was the college hierarchy who closed ranks and first sought legalistic solutions. As the feminist critic bell hooks has written, one strategy of Roiphe's *The Morning After* is 'to construct and attack a monolithic young "feminist" group that shares a common response to feminist thinking, most particularly around issues of sexuality and physical assault'.[15] *The First Stone* also constructs precisely this kind of scenario on the assumption that feminism is no longer a social movement, but operates according to a logic of conspiracy.

It makes for a good sound-bite. 'Victim feminists' take their place among all those other armies of the night — Asian crime waves, youth gangs and the rest — rarely seen, yet always real, a silent bogey whose existence is somehow proved by speaking of their invisibility. Like most victim-panic tracts, *The First Stone* expedites its argument by endlessly repeating tantalising possibilities. The book makes repeated mention of a supposed leaking of information to the press at the time of the initial college investigation into the matter, although there is no evidence of a link between any such leak and the complainants' supporters. Another claim, that a leaflet calling for the master's

Stoned again

sacking was circulated throughout the university, is also linked to the complainants' supporters through association, though no concrete evidence is supplied. The complainants' supporters specifically dissociated themselves from the leaks and the leaflet, both in print and formally before the college council, but in a narrative twist Garner uses this against them, taking at face value a college council member's query as to why they would mention the leaflet if they didn't have anything to do with it. Never is the possibility entertained that they were acting in good faith or that, like all involved in the case, they had a vested interest in not escalating it.

The language of conspiracy is everywhere in *The First Stone*, to a level that is almost hilarious, despite Garner's claims to the contrary.[16] Garner mysteriously mentions 'a certain nexus of forces', or speaks of 'several other university feminists who had supported the complainants', of a 'faceless group of women', of 'radical feminists' and 'ideological passions . . . on the rampage', of 'puritan feminists' who exerted a 'certain influence', of 'faceless supporters', 'feminist ideologues', and 'the politically correct gang', who as a group 'maintained facelessness and voicelessness'. 'What sort of feminists are these?' she asks. 'What kind of thought-police, of saboteurs?'[17] In a triumphant moment of unsubstantiated certainty, Garner even speaks of 'the feminist group in Ormond which had organised against Colin Shepherd' (Garner's name for the college master).[18] There are silent advisers who ensure that Garner's 'path to Elizabeth Rosen and Nicole Stewart [her names for the two complainants mentioned in the book] was plainly not only blocked but mined and ambushed',[19] and who maintain a '*cordon sanitaire*'[20] around them — implying that the complainants are mindless dupes who can't decide anything for themselves. Even the complainants' refusal to speak with Garner (who had earlier written the master a letter of support) becomes evidence, not only of a feminist cabal at Ormond, but also of a failure among some feminists to want to engage

79

in debate generally, as if Garner might be the only available interlocutor.

The First Stone is full of flashes of empathy for the complainants, but Garner never uses them as a basis from which to advance the narrative. As with most victim-panic texts, it's the men here who do the 'truth-telling'. When the college master says 'I think there was a conspiracy, very well orchestrated and organised',[21] Garner doesn't editorialise, but slips it into the text at face value. When he offers the view that the complainants are 'at the root of all my problems',[22] this too is reported almost unremarked. On the other hand, when the women's solicitor is quoted as saying that 'the girls' aim was not to destroy Shepherd',[23] the narrator intervenes straight away: 'So Dr Shepherd was only caught in the crossfire between the girls and the college? I found this hard to swallow.'[24]

If, as many columnists writing on the matter were eager to claim, *The First Stone* sparked a debate about running to the law and excessive social legislation, then it arguably did so, not because the book was candid, but because it played straight into fashionable mythologies about living in a landslide of so-called 'political correctness'. Contemporary anxieties about social legislation, with their parallel anxiety about the loss of long-enjoyed privileges among those already in powerful positions (namely, powerful men), are writ large throughout *The First Stone* and the ensuing debate. P. P. McGuinness took *The First Stone* at face value, claiming that the 'persecution and destruction of the Master . . . is reminiscent of the way German universities in the '30s submitted to the pressures of the Nazi students and forced out Jewish teachers'.[25] *Eureka Street* editor Morag Fraser claimed the book was 'premised on the belief that truth is more important than feminist party solidarity'.[26] Terry Lane compared the Ormond case to 'Salem witch-hunts'.[27] An editorial writer in the *Sydney Morning Herald* claimed the book's account of the master's dismissal had resulted in a strong critique of feminism.[28]

Stoned again

★

Of the many feminists I know, none speaks of 'victim feminism' with any seriousness. None behaves like the 'victims' described in the victim-panic books, especially not those with the institutional credentials that perpetrators of the 'victim cultures' are supposed to have. Stereotypical notions that younger feminists have a 'fear of sex' or a 'fear of life', or are hell-bent on 'retribution', sit uneasily with the iconic status of Madonna, Penny Arcade, Annie Sprinkle and the Harley-riding k. d. lang, or the wide general acceptance of make-up, tattoos, piercings and even S&M among many young feminists.

So where does the anti-victim scare come from?

From Roiphe's *The Morning After* to Christina Hoff Sommers' *Who Stole Feminism?* to Denfeld's *The New Victorians* to Wolf's *Fire with Fire* to *The First Stone*, the truth, it seems, is mainly in the telling. These aren't books about anyone's lives so much as they have a 'typical' story to tell — after a little narrative nip and tuck, that is. Their composers, eager to contribute to a certain popular narrative about feminism, commonly bend events, imposing a template on stories to make them fit a pattern. But you rarely encounter a balanced, substantiated account. Roiphe's depiction of Take Back the Night marches in *The Morning After* portrays every woman who ever put up a hand to tell her story about sexual harassment as thinking of herself only as a victim, and as therefore symptomatic of everything that's wrong with feminism. Other possibilities simply don't get mentioned. Rene Denfeld expounds a similar anti-'wowser' line of thinking when, criticising a rape-avoidance pamphlet, she says 'Rarely is it acknowledged that women might want to have sex. In victim mythology, the idea alone is an affront. The assumption is that they don't.'[29] But is it really so surprising, in the context of a rape-avoidance pamphlet, not to find material rhapsodising the pleasures of sex?

The First Stone makes use of similar strategies. While it claims to ask 'some questions about sex and power', the book fails to mention that sexual harassment, by definition, usually occurs in situations where one party seeks to exercise power associated with their formal position. The book also fails to differentiate between such abuse of position and the normal sexual friction that occurs between people — 'Eros', as Garner calls it. In wanting to tell a certain 'typical' story about young women being reluctant to use their personal power, *The First Stone* neglects the fact that the complainants were in an institutional relationship with the master, who had a duty of fiduciary care toward them, as well as access to their academic and personal records, say-so over their college bursaries and, as master of a college with close links to the legal fraternity, influence over their future legal careers. Having failed in its philosophical promise, the book also fails as journalism. Important incidents are split into fragments that are spread throughout the book in such a way that a casual reader can hardly grasp their relevance. Other incidents with little relevance to the case, such as a sexual harassment officer's use of the word 'retribution' in a conversation with Garner, are linked to the case by innuendo.

Victim-panic tales are compelling, though, not because they claim to provide factual information about 'victim feminism', but because they aspire to tell a certain story about feminism — namely, of contemporary feminism's supposed corruption and decline. Being a self-professed feminist heretic is big business these days. It's certainly where the kudos is in mainstream journalistic writing about feminism. As the successes of writers such as Garner and Roiphe have shown, it's possible to maintain a strong media presence through attacking feminisms. In Australia there are several other prominent 'white-knight' feminists who like to play the renegade. Bettina Arndt heads up many of her articles in the mainstream press with claims about their 'feminist heresy', while Beatrice Faust's self-professed rebel status is a continuing theme in her regular column for the *Weekend Australian*.[30] It's a calling-card that inadvertently says much about the public spaces available for feminism — and, more generally, for women. Faust's contribution to Peter Coleman's *Doubletake* is self-consciously entitled 'Reflections of a Sceptical Feminist'. She is the only woman among the contributors.

The future-of-feminism story is so noisy that it tends to drown out any meaningful discussion about processes for countering sexual harassment. Such stories tend to portray responses to sexual harassment as a problem within feminism, rather than as a wider social problem. In the debate over *The First Stone* there was almost no discussion about sexual harassment, the irony being that one reason the case escalated at Ormond was a similar lack of discussion. While controversy about the future of feminism raged, there was little commentary on the fact that many university colleges, including Ormond, had introduced new procedures for handling harassment, as a result of which a similar case at Ormond was resolved relatively painlessly after being put in the hands of an independent arbitrator. There were exceptions to the orthodoxy. John O'Neill, writing in the *Independent Monthly* on a similar case at the Australian National University, suggested it might be the 'system of investigation, rather than puritanical feminism, which drives students with complaints — and who want disciplinary action — to outside organisations'.[31] But these sorts of stories got lost in the shadow of the bigger story about a grand movement betrayed.

And who might the betrayers be? In part victim panics are a story about young women fucking up and getting it wrong, again, and feminists with a certain media presence making themselves available to blow the whistle. A favourite tactic of several local media feminists is to dichotomise between their feminisms and what follows by casting themselves as the movement's mothers, presenting feminism as something over which they have ownership, often with scant regard to the contributions of other older feminists. Anne Summers does it in her gently patronising 'Letter to the Next Generation' and in feature articles she has written since, telling young feminists that they 'have yet to map out the feminism they think is worth fighting for',[32] as if *her* apparent lack of engagement is a satisfactory marker of *their* inaction. Faust does it when she asks, speaking of so-called 'victim feminism', 'did a generation of feminists work so hard for this? Is this the way that feminism ends — not with a bang but a whimper?'[33] Susan Mitchell suggests that older feminists have been wasting their time, since they are evidently handing the baton to an unworthy generation.[34] The inference is that they are the *real* feminists.

Garner uses a similar generational mother/daughter ploy throughout *The First Stone*. Readers hear about her 'twenty years of involvement with feminist rhetoric',[35] and are told that, so far as one young feminist is concerned, 'I was her political mother'.[36] 'Feminism', Garner says, 'is not the exclusive property of a priggish, literal-minded vengeance squad that gets Eros in its sights, gives him both barrels, and marches away in its Blundstones, leaving the gods' messenger sprawled in the mud with his wings all bloody and torn.'[37]

But who sought proprietorship over feminism? No-one, actually. Like so much else on these airwaves, it's a straw (wo)man argument, designed to articulate the unsuitability of young women as heirs to the feminist tradition.

★

Like so many shoddy goods bought wholesale off the international journalistic racks, the victim-panic formula turns out to be mostly imported. As a media product it rides on the tail of the US 'culture wars'. Camille Paglia was almost invisible — a washed-up academic (she said it herself) — until she started attacking feminism in the media. As Naomi Wolf says, 'Paglia

Stoned again

was fêted in the very press that had, over the course of the decade, assiduously neglected to present to the public the currents of thought she had indicted'.[38] Her inflammatory remarks against feminism launched her career as a public figure and, according to bell hooks, those of Roiphe and Wolf as well:

> Without Paglia as trailblazer and symbolic mentor, there would be no cultural limelight for white girls such as Katie Roiphe and Naomi Wolf. And no matter how hard they work to put that Oedipal distance between their writing and hers, they are singing the same tune on way too many things. And (dare I say it) that tune always seems to be a jazzed up version of 'The Way We Were' — you know, the good old days before feminism and multiculturalism and the unbiased curriculum fucked everything up.[39]

As hooks points out, it's no accident that these women have made a career from criticising feminism in the media while implying at the same time that they are the only ones doing so. This is the pattern in Australia as well. The contributions of feminist auto-critics such as Wendy Bacon, Eva Cox, Elizabeth Grosz, Sneja Gunew, Sylvia Lawson, Catharine Lumby and Meaghan Morris tend to be forgotten, or ignored, by those pushing highly publicised attacks on feminism.

The rhetoric has been imported along with the controversy. Where Garner likes to criticise 'priggish' young feminists in their Blundstones, Paglia also likes to attack young feminists with their so-called 'dress codes'. In her essay, 'No Law in the Arena', she says:

> Ambitious young women today are taught to ignore or suppress every natural instinct, if it conflicts with the feminist agenda imposed on them . . . Today, with the callow new brand of yuppie feminist with her simpering prom-queen manner, we have regressed to the Fifties era of cashmere

Gangland

sweaters and pearls . . . Victorian spinsters, shrieking at a mouse.[40]

Where Paglia says 'It is woman, as mistress of birth, who has the real power',[41] Garner asks: 'has a girl like Elizabeth Rosen even the faintest idea what a powerful anima figure she is to the men she encounters in her life?'[42] Paglia says, 'If you advertise, you'd better be ready to sell . . . In America one sees overprotected white girls . . . conspicuously and bouncingly braless, a sight guaranteed to invite unwanted attention',[43] and complains that:

> Today, these young women want the freedom that we won, but they don't want to acknowledge the risk. That's the problem. The minute you go out with a man, the minute you go to a bar and have a drink, there is a risk. You have to accept the fact that part of the sizzle of sex comes from the danger of sex. You can be overpowered.[44]

Garner says:

> It is an article of faith amongst some young feminists that a woman can go about the world dressed in any way she pleases. They think that for a man to respond to . . . what he sees as a statement of her sexuality, and her own attitude to it, is some sort of outrage . . . Sexy clothes are part of the wonderful game of life, but to dress to display your body, and then to project all the sexuality of the situation onto men and then blame them for it just so you can continue to be innocent and put upon, is not at all responsible.[45]

It seems odd that, twenty-five years after the second wave of feminism, we are still hearing that women should take responsibility for men's desire and are misbehaving if they don't. Where Garner asks 'Why did they go to the police?',[46] Paglia

Stoned again

says 'Running to Mommy and Daddy on the campus grievance committee is unworthy of strong women'.[47] Where Paglia says 'Don't slink off to whimper and simper with the campus shrinking violets. Deal with it. On the spot',[48] Garner recommends a heel to instep. Where Paglia calls sexual harassment complainants 'stupid, shrewish, puritanical, sermonizing, hysterical',[49] Garner calls them 'grim and dull and wowserish and self-righteous'.[50] Paglia says:

> Men strike women . . . because physical superiority is their only weapon against a being far more powerful than they. The blow does not subordinate; it equalises . . . the violence came not from his sense of power but from its opposite, his wounded desperation and helplessness.[51]

Garner speaks of 'the terrible fragility of men's egos',[52] remarking that 'blokes who behave as Colin Shepherd was accused of doing aren't scary or powerful. They're just poor bastards.'[53]

Garner isn't the only member of the local cultural establishment seeking to downplay the imperatives of gender politics through such rhetoric. Its echoes reverberate through many other establishment writers' works. So, in Drusilla Modjeska's *The Orchard*, we read that:

> Alec says women make the mistake of thinking men are powerful. He says we think that because they exercise a warped sort of sexual agency they are powerful in themselves. On the contrary, he says, men are driven, poor sops.[54]

The two big targets of US anti-feminism are Andrea Dworkin and Catharine MacKinnon, who made their names as virulent anti-pornography campaigners and were advocates of Anita Hill (belatedly in MacKinnon's case) in the Hill–Clarence Thomas hearings. Hill's allegations of sexual harassment by Thomas shook the US Senate; this case is where much of the

US rhetoric against 'victim feminism' gathered momentum. Paglia, Roiphe, Denfeld and Robert Hughes have all taken part in bashing Dworkin and MacKinnon. An exception is Wolf, who points out that the media versions of many of Dworkin and MacKinnon's supposed slogans, such as 'all sex is rape', rely on quoting them out of context and using other 'sleights of hand' in order to demonise them as extremists.[55]

In Australia Dworkin and MacKinnon have almost no mainstream media profile, and there is no parallel to the Hill–Thomas sexual harassment scandal or the parallel anti-affirmative action campaign, in which Thomas played an important role. But local media feminists have learnt to parrot anti-Dworkin–MacKinnon rhetoric without mentioning the names, and to use anti-anti-harassment rhetoric without canvassing the issues. When Paglia concludes an essay with the statement that 'MacKinnon and Dworkin, peddling their diseased rhetoric, are in denial, and what they are blocking is life itself, in all its grandeur and messiness',[56] the conclusion of *The First Stone* comes to mind — 'If only the whole gang of them hadn't been so afraid of life'.[57]

For anyone with a passing knowledge of recent feminisms it seems strange to see the US anti-pornography debate, dominated by two crusading liberals, held up as a warning about contemporary Australian feminisms, which are mostly critical of liberalism. As Anne Summers has astutely commented, 'Either we are dealing with a serious time-lag problem, or the US experience — and the books that emanate from it — have little relevance to Australian women. (I opt for the latter explanation myself.)'[58]

★

Taken together, victim-panic narratives form a recognisable genre because they address a specific contemporary anxiety. They all make mention of sexual harassment legislation (twenty years after the fact in the Australian case!) and dutifully try to anticipate possible male responses to it. Not for nothing are the vast majority of victims of injustice in victim-panic narratives naive, middle-aged men, cut down by attractive and knowing young women with a grasp of recent feminist knowledge. The same tableau is rehearsed obsessively, from David Williamson's *Brilliant Lies* to David Mamet's play *Oleanna*; from *The Morning After* to *The First Stone* to the Kennedy–Miller movie *Gross Misconduct* (shot at Ormond!), based on a play based on the infamous Sydney Sparkes Orr sexual harassment case in Tasmania. This tableau always has the same closely scripted narrative elements — a young woman, a student or junior employee, who destroys or attempts to destroy the career of an older man, her boss or a professor, via a charge of sexual harassment. Her archetypal features are unreasonableness and a hint of dishonesty, while his are innocence and surprise.

Like so many cover versions, these stories follow the underlying structure of *femme fatale* narratives, made famous by hard-boiled detective fiction (and resurrected in recent films such as *Basic Instinct* and *Fatal Attraction*), where a woman of ambiguous, possibly 'dysfunctional' sexuality (she doesn't want him/is she gay/an incest victim?) 'leads on', annihilates and emasculates a man who desires her, leaving him in tatters as a form of retribution against the 'crime' of his desire, or for some other crime that is depicted as being at least half in her imagination.

One strategy of victim-panic narratives is to try and normalise such masculine desire. In *Brilliant Lies* the long-suffering father of the complainant in a sexual harassment case talks of 'profound mysteries in the dance of the sexes'.[59] In *The First Stone*, Garner talks of the dance of 'Eros'. If to speak of 'Eros' is to suggest that society is heterogeneous, no law is universal, the sum of desire is too complex to map comprehensively, then this, strangely, is not so far from the later Foucault, or from discussions taking place in some recent feminisms. Unfortunately 'Eros' in *The First Stone* serves a simpler function, as the white hooray-word to the black boo-words, 'sexual harassment legislation'. 'Eros' here doesn't suggest a Foucault-style matrix where power and desire are multi-dimensional; rather it valorises a crude opposition that puts the social and 'ideological' on one side and the spiritual on the other. Paglia tries a similar thing with her use of 'paganism' in *Sexual Personae*. Both are attempts to sidestep politics; to represent the 'human' as outside political power.

But the trouble with attempts to get outside politics is that to talk about things as being outside the social is to draw them back into the social, and therefore the political, through the very act of speaking. If 'Eros' is a comfort zone that Garner wants to leave pure, virginally untouched by ideology, then ultimately 'Eros' is just a version of masculine desire. Worse, 'Eros' has feet of clay. As Garner wants to imagine it, 'Eros' is a beautiful dream; but the places where desire gets played out, in the end, are always specific and involve actual people. Garner never mentions whether or not she thinks 'Eros' should be a two-way street, but unless 'Eros' cuts both ways, 'the spark that ignites and connects' is just a wank.[60]

Another rhetorical strategy that victim-panic tracts use to sidestep the political is to veer off into affirmational anecdotes. Their discussions of sexual harassment tend to slide very quickly from being about due process, power or institutional context to being about individual mores. Usually the anecdotes are about someone who slapped a wrist or pushed away a hand in a circumstance where there was little consequence, or who was stridently brave enough to resist an advance where there was, and who should therefore serve as an example to the rest, as proof of everyone else's cowardice, and as a sign that the purveyors of bigger-picture politics have got it wrong. *The Morning After*, *The New Victorians*, *Fire with Fire* and many media feminist columns are full of such stories. In *The First Stone* they muddy the waters, as if Garner's own failure to chastise a masseur who molested her, or her own consenting dalliance with a tutor, might shed light on the Ormond case.

What these anecdotes deny is the institutional nature of sexual harassment. They elide the fact that such matters involve formal as well as informal power. 'Equity' feminism of the sort broadly implied by most anti-'victim' crusaders will always be blind to this at one level or another, because it lacks a theoretical apparatus capable of analysing deeper sexisms. It seeks to make women equal, but only within the existing social system, which it seeks to validate.

I'm not the first to notice this problem. Many recent feminist writers have suggested that the liberal contract of individualism that underpins the existing social system is itself masculinist, and that, according to the equity model, women are defined by default according to a male archetype. They point out that 'equity' feminism not only aspires to a middle-class version of white masculine citizenship, but tends to be espoused by white, middle-class feminists who can afford to take their 'individualist' privileges for granted. What 'equity' feminists tend to laud as the freedom of equality and freedom from ideology, more recent feminisms see as the logic of the status quo. They argue that to aspire to this kind of equity is to buy into a whole new set of (patriarchal) ideologies, even if no-one speaks of them as such.

It's here that the victim-panic narrative gets going. If 'equity' feminisms seem almost allergic to critical insights about the masculinism of the status quo and tend to fling the label 'victim mentality' about accordingly, it's because the logic they privilege is one of individuation. The central idea behind most 'equity' feminisms is that the individual functions as a node of inherent truth who is defined by making autonomous choices. Seen in this light, gender politics tends to involve private and personal matters of choice, as opposed to public or institutional matters of power. Such feminisms tend to read more recent, institutionally oriented approaches to gender politics as promoting a stance of de-individuated powerlessness. When Garner talks about how much she hates 'this constant stress on passivity and weakness — this creation of a political position based on the virtue of helplessness',[61] her formulation seems to stem partly from a refusal to acknowledge the underlying politics that govern gender relations. She shares with others a tendency to see any mention of such systems as a form of victimism or, to put it another way, a lack of proper individualism.

Consistent with this, for all their self-professed concern about feminism as an issue, media feminists rarely discuss gender politics in depth. Rather than engaging with newer feminist knowledges, the writings of media feminists tend to collude with a quiet misogyny.

So, in an article on a new domestic violence component of divorce legislation, Bettina Arndt establishes her feminist credentials early on, opening with a pro-feminist flourish about the potential of the new legislation. But what follows is a diatribe about 'punitive laws' and the possibility that some aggrieved women might use the legislation as a means of 'retribution'. While she gives a lot of space to the possible disadvantages of the legislation for men, based on extreme hypothetical cases, there are no equivalent paragraphs dealing any more than peripherally with possible benefits or drawbacks for women. Over and over again, the article raises the spectre of rampant feminist ideologues and mentions the possibility of 'significant payouts' by men suffering at the hands of unscrupulous women, with scant mention of any inbuilt checks and balances.[62]

For practitioners of recent feminisms it makes sense that the media should sponsor this sort of rhetoric at the expense of others. One implication of the victim-panic genre is that women's sexual complaints shouldn't enter the masculinised public spaces of the media or the law.

The language of *The First Stone* is similarly revealing. The book is populated by the most agreeable bunch of men you could ever meet. They are variously 'pleasantly spoken' and 'smiling', or possess a 'tough posture ... softened by a smile and a warm expression', or are 'decent' and 'open', and exude 'warmth and energy'. That is, when they are not being 'commanding' or 'straight-shooting'.[63] Throughout the book these men are routinely taken at their word, and their dialogue is quoted without narrative intervention. Garner is sometimes sceptical about their authority, but never seriously challenges it. The Christ-like, biblically pure Shepherd, especially, is described as an innocent. He's a pure, good, 'agreeable looking' man; welcoming, dog-loving, with hands like a pianist and a 'soft' face with 'bright blue'[64] eyes, who welcomes Garner into a large, pleasant reception room full of light.

The women, on the other hand, are described in almost entirely negative terms. When Garner is faced with the possibility of the 'head-on smash' between her feminism and her ethics, she always veers the same way.[65] Left to these women, 'Eros' would be dead, poor angel, and the pleasantness of the master's reception room would almost certainly be replaced by the anarchy of the young feminist's room, which 'could have been beautiful', but was 'amazingly disordered'.[66] Elizabeth Rosen's room was also in 'a disgusting state ... There were cigarette butts, broken glass, cigarette ash, obviously spilt alcohol in the carpet ... drawings on the walls and furniture'. Worse, she 'didn't perform any of the functions expected'. 'She never went to uni. She played loud music very late', and 'her three aims in life were to own a Ferrari, a diamond necklace, and for someone to have her name tattooed on them'.[67] Against the meek Shepherd, Rosen is 'elated by her own careless authority and power'. Likewise, Nicky Stewart, the other complainant described in Garner's book, 'never fitted in'.[68] Neither is once taken at her word. Together they are described as 'priggish, disingenuous, unforgiving', 'over the top', 'two college misfits' in the grip of 'an absurd, hysterical tantrum', and 'wimps who ran to the law to whinge'. They are 'noisy, talkative, opinionated' ideologues, with a 'mingy, whining, cringeing terror of sex'.[69]

A similar contrast is seen in *The Morning After*. Roiphe also takes men at their word while determinedly doubting women. For example, after a 'big jock' pins a freshman woman to a wall at a crowded party by putting his hands on either side of her head without touching her, then whispers in her ear 'So baby, when are we going out?', Roiphe chastises not him, but the woman, for carrying this incident 'around in her head for six years' as an overblown instance of 'sexual harassment' and thinking it symbolic of campus sexual politics.[70] Refusal of unwanted advances, for Roiphe, equates with puritan sexlessness. She equates women's liberation with sexual liberation and, lacking a framework for deeper analysis, is doomed to characterise its 'opposite' as prudery and repression. Throughout *The Morning After* Roiphe always excuses the aggressor, not the aggrieved, inverting the underlying power relationship. It's the woman, cast in the traditional female role of the hysteric for refusing unwanted sex, who is the real problem.

Again, as is typical of victim-panic tracts, this deft flip short-circuits the argument, reducing the problem to one not of community standards, but of undecidables about private mores, avoiding the possibility of a deeper politics while upholding the contract that many 'equity' feminists, especially those prominent in the media, apparently enter into. This contract is seemingly that, having championed at every turn a gender system that accepts them as 'equals', they are allowed popular forums in which to police its boundaries, gatekeeping — as Paglia does so expertly — what henceforth is and isn't acceptable feminism.

Given that some of the strongest challenges to equity feminism have come from within universities, it's no coincidence that many victim-panic fables are set there. Again, this is the pattern with the US version of the scare. Both Garner's and

Stoned again

Roiphe's books focus on campus life and portray universities as being full of rampant young feminists. Both talk of sourpuss feminists destroying male academic careers. Both are centred on a college dorm — Garner has Ormond, Roiphe Adams House. Both portray a vulnerable and naive college professor beset by young feminists. Both recommend a good slap in the face as a solution to harassment. Both even focus on the supposed slovenly housekeeping of young 'victim feminists', with their messy dorm rooms.

Victim-panic fables and attacks on the so-called excesses of feminism are often vehemently anti-intellectual. Many of Beatrice Faust's columns, or David Williamson's *Dead White Males*, are cases in point. Garner too has accused academic feminists of 'being stuck in the university with their heads up their own arses'.[71] Here another parallel emerges between local attacks on 'victim feminism' and the North American debate about the Hill–Thomas incident. As the Nobel prize-winning writer Toni Morrison commented: 'Anita Hill's witnesses, credible and persuasive as they were, could be dismissed, as one "reporter" said, apparently without shame, because they were too intellectual to be believed (!).'[72]

Far from being the long-awaited corrective they aggressively advertise themselves to be, recent attacks on feminism have a more conservative end. They suggest we are witnessing a 'dumbing-down' of approaches to sexual harassment.

★

The accusation of 'victim mentality' is currently doing good business, and not just among high-profile feminists working in the media. It's one of several tracks getting 'thrashed' on contemporary playlists, all telling people that their problems have nothing to do with systemic ills or fundamental social inequities, but are failures of their own volition. Behind it all is the jangly rhythm of a deregulated economic 'Eros'. Like the emergence of anti-'victim feminism' rhetoric from second-wave 'equity' feminism, the rise of economic rationalism has marked a shift. Moderate liberal rhetorics about creating social change have become radical, neo-liberal, neo-conservative rhetorics about social correction. The shift from liberalism to neo-liberalism, in both feminisms and economics, is marked by a collective crisis of belief, especially in the possibility of achieving social justice. The once moderate idea of 'equity' is no longer a goal to be accomplished by regulatory means, but has become an excuse for not undertaking such redistribution. The presumption is that people are always already equal, and that further redistributive measures will make them less so. This theme can be heard in recent cries that affirmative action campaigns are themselves sexist or racist — never mind that they seek to counteract a greater sexism or racism.

Victim-panic rhetorics have much in common with those of economic rationalism. Both discredit the idea of the public self in favour of the idea of the privatised self. Both seek to discredit the idea of community and collective action. Both prescribe sole agency and striking individual contracts. Both laud the old Reaganesque 'can-do' attitude — 'go the extra mile', *The First Stone* suggests.[73] Both upend underlying power dynamics to suggest that social inequities can be reduced to questions of individual choice and decision. Both adopt the classic liberal model of negative liberty (where 'freedom' is envisaged in negative terms as 'freedom *from*'), and imagine humans as centres of inherent, essential 'truth' who become more 'true' and humane as they are freed from social regulation to make unconstrained choices. Both enjoy the patronage of a recently globalised media industry that has itself been one of the major beneficiaries of deregulation. Both have hardened from a relatively tolerant liberalism to a neo-conservative intolerance of social difference, while using increasingly strident and vitriolic rhetorics to defame their critics. Both segue from attacks on perceived system 'abusers' to attacks on welfare and advocacy systems. Both espouse philosophies that facilitate a

Stoned again

winding back of welfare. As I write, supporting parents' pensions are under attack on the grounds that they encourage a 'victim' mentality. In the USA the anti-'victim' campaign has dovetailed into the Republican Party's anti-'affirmative-action' campaign, feeding off the Hill–Thomas case. Its local counterpart is an *Age* editorial published during the debate over *The First Stone*, calling for a watering down of sexual harassment legislation.[74]

Anti-intellectualism and anti-academicism are much-played tunes in both worlds. In 1993 sociologist Michael Pusey predicted that economic rationalism, having successfully widened the gap between rich and poor, would

> pull up the ladders and cover the tracks. Since the strategies are simple adaptations of Thatcherism and Republican 'attack politics' the third predictable prong of the strategy will be an assault on the quality press, public broadcasting, the remains of the liberal university, and on other constituents of critical debate in a 'public sphere'.[75]

Sound familiar?

One complaint often made by those who whinge about recent feminisms is that the university courses in which these things are supposedly 'taught' are no use in the 'real world'. Just as neo-conservatives draw a dichotomy between the academy and the real world to discredit non-vocational education, older-style feminists do so to discredit recent feminisms. Summers, for example, has said that for young feminists, 'years on campus, arguing theories and being cosseted by a comfortable set of shared assumptions among most of their colleagues, had in no way prepared them for the real world'.[76]

This kind of thing doesn't reflect the experiences of my own feminist friends with university educations, few of whom have had the problems that Summers describes. Most work in their chosen professions as writers, editors, lawyers, filmmakers, journalists and activists, just as many feminists of

Gangland

Summers' generation did at the same age (though under less favourable conditions). More than two decades after International Women's Year, during which my own daughterless mother (who I'm proud to say has moved with the times) decided she had a duty to introduce her sons to feminism through 'academic' texts such as *The Female Eunuch* and *Damned Whores and God's Police*, it's sobering to hear a feminist with Summers' credentials being critical of feminist courses of any kind. Or to observe how neatly her comments, with their high-handed tone, their hyperbole and fear of new approaches, their quiet pandering to conventional wisdom and louder cross-generational paranoia, so neatly embellish what the loudest voices here — middle-aged male columnists and self-styled feminist heretics — have insisted on calling a thoroughgoing 'debate'.

5 Lockout: 'legislated nostalgia' and 'dumbing-down'

My generation is turning 50. If the people of this generation were defined by anything, it was their youth . . . the baby boomers came along and made getting older a sort of crime . . . this generation may not know how to grow old.

Michael Gawenda[1]

there is nothing so loathsome as a young politician.

P. P. McGuinness[2]

So what is it about the past? The present certainly doesn't seem to be the place where anybody wants to be lately. The latest pretence is that it's been evacuated of ideas and new cultural forms. We seem doomed to live in wave after wave of 1950s, 1960s and 1970s, even 1980s revivals (Gordon Gecko hair, anyone?). And young people just aren't sexy any more. Well, they are, but mainly if they work in (and are readily commodifiable by) the entertainment or fashion industries. They aren't generally exciting in the way that young people were once considered exciting. Once being young was a romantic adventure. Not one that ended in the popular stereotypes of the dole queue, the teen gang, the single mother, or the feminist daughter.

Young people once had the world at their feet. The Future tumbled out to greet them, with a capital 'F'. In the 1950s and 1960s new things were happening. Bands like the Beatles and actors like James Dean embellished an era to the point where they seemed to shape it. When a young Dean, full of a sullen bravado, swaggered down the sidewalk in Times Square, it was clear that something new was afoot. When the Beatles first topped the charts, it seemed there was nothing four fresh-faced working-class boys couldn't do.

These day being young is not such a romantic experience. Youthfulness is no longer clearly equated with hope. And the charts are dominated by, well, the Beatles, who had the best-selling release of the past decade. It's middle age that is now romanticised, as jaundiced baby-boomers, frowning on the strange pursuits of the young and looking backwards for their values, rush out in their millions (at least 9.5 million) to buy a copy of *The Bridges of Madison County*, or to watch Clint Eastwood in the film of it.[3]

It might be that this folksy tale of a middle-aged philanderer sums up a world of lost values for many members of a certain generation. It harks back to an age when men were men, more or less happily inhabiting places 'back along the stems of Darwin's logic', without having had to go out into the woods as part of some new-age clan to howl, Robert Bly-style, at a waxing moon.[4] The heroine of *Bridges* reassuringly knows her place. She's prepared to sacrifice all for family. She's 'lived a little', and doesn't have the vast permutations of recent 'identity politics' to overstimulate her discontents.

Not that I have anything against middle-aged people — nor, by the way, do I think they have anything in particular against the young. But the Beatles' rebirth, the *Bridges* phenomenon and all the resurrections of 1950s, 1960s and 1970s culture all suggest that this is an age that doesn't generally celebrate the contemporary. Young people, according to the writer Douglas Coupland, are subject to a kind of 'legislated nostalgia', being forced 'to have memories they do not actually possess'.[5] Or, as a daily broadsheet put it, 'Close your eyes, readers, and remember 1966, when the Beatles played their last concert . . . It seems like only yesterday.'[6]

The metropolitan dailies aren't alone. The 1950s, 1960s and 1970s are back, without irony, on television too. Popular programmes from twenty or thirty years ago such as *In Melbourne Tonight*, *Blankety Blanks* and *This is Your Life* have been resurrected, repeating their original formulas down to the finest detail. Then there was the mini-series *Kangaroo Palace*, set in 1965, the same year as *The Bridges of Madison County*. In their appeal to nostalgia, these series continue a tradition established by programmes such as *Heartbeat*, *The Wonder Years* or even *Happy Days*, and movies such as *The Big Chill*. That is, they appeal to an audience that comprises the single largest demographic group: those born between 1945 and 1960, who perhaps remember these programmes or these times from their teens and twenties — or at least are being asked to behave as if they do.

Serious attempts to engage with youth culture are few and far between in the mainstream media, even though they are largely run by people of a generation who voiced similar complaints twenty or thirty years ago. It's barely possible to open a newspaper now, or to watch a TV show, or listen to radio, without coming across some paean to a misremembered past. It is even possible, as Richard Neville has shown, to make a small industry out of being a rememberer. Neville's book, *Hippie Hippie Shake*, a memoir of his time as an *Oz* editor in the 1960s and early 1970s, was surely one of the big hits of recent years on the media circuit, where it generated wall-to-wall coverage.

I don't begrudge Neville his success or his past, but what process of memorialisation is going on here? What role is the past being asked to play? At around the same time the *1968* exhibition was being run at the National Gallery in Canberra, to generally approving reviews. The photographer Bob Whitaker, who took some of *Oz*'s more famous photos, was also in town with a touring exhibition. His famous photo of Mick Jagger in a broad-brimmed hat appeared in almost every major newspaper. Most young bands, or photographers, can only dream of such coverage.

The past has lately become *the* place of possibility, not only for TV programmers looking for a low-risk mass audience, but also for highbrow novelists. It is a phenomenon, lately, that middle-aged male novelists are hard at work on novels set in some previous century that bespeak a certain nostalgia for lost professions and simpler times, whether it be Robert Drewe's *The Drowner* or Melvyn Bragg's *Credo*.

Les Murray, meanwhile, has declared the twentieth century over — or at least, the latter part of it.[7] Recovering from a life-threatening illness, Murray has noted a return to old-fashioned values with the demise of 'political correctness'; he claims that there has been a catharsis, leading to a 'nice kind of a hiatus', similar, he says, to the 1950s.

Journalists too have taken to renovating the past to make it look good. Like so many inner-city terraces, it is being gentrified and made habitable. 'Thank God for the Atom Bomb' was one headline, fronting an article in the *Independent Monthly* on the eve of the fiftieth anniversary of the nuclear bombing of Nagasaki and Hiroshima, which the article claimed, somewhat distastefully, had shortened the war and saved a million American lives — at what psychic cost to the West, or at what cost to the people of Japan, the author did not say.[8] 'Why the Vietnam War was Just and Winnable' went another headline, this time in the *Australian*.[9] Columnists are at it too. Feminists in the old days, P. P. McGuinness has argued, were much more palatable, not like the 'wimminists' of today.[10] Terry Lane sees history as a grim trajectory. In the 1950s, he complains, it was possible to use perfectly satisfactory words such as 'assimilation' to describe migrant policy, and in the 1970s there was 'integration', whereas in the 1980s we got stuck with the dread word 'multiculturalism', which he takes as a measure of a decline in national confidence.[11] We no longer have the courage to ask migrants to be like us, he says, and have instead resorted to an 'ugly word which produces an uneasy, slightly nauseous feeling'.[12]

Crude nationalism marries well with the desire for a return to the past, expressed through the notion that contemporary ideas about social justice not only haven't worked, but are proving a disadvantage. Two characters in David Williamson's play *Brilliant Lies*, sum up:

> GARY: Listen to Radio National some time . . . Sexual harassment, land rights, Affirmative Action and Multiculturalism. Our moral agenda is being dictated by Gay Armenians and Lesbian Turks. It's been open season on Anglo Celtic males for the last twenty years . . . It's Australia in the nineties. The thought police have won. You don't have to have evidence, you just have to be able to lie. We're white wealthy males. Forget the fact that my parents were dirt poor, that I went to a lousy school, that I worked as a barman and studied until two o'clock in the morning to get my diploma. Forget all that. I'm a white middle class male, so I had it easy, so I'm fair game. It's Australia in the nineties.
> VINCE: It's very, very sad. This used to be the greatest country in the world. What happened?
> GARY: We blinked, the trendies took over, and goodbye Australia.[13]

Odes to the past can take other, more subtle forms. Take, for example, the *This Day Tonight* generation, which has dominated the on-camera face of television journalism since the 1970s. *This Day Tonight* was a brave venture, famous for the derring-do of its on-camera staff, who dared to ask politicians tough questions — a practice unheard-of before then. Since that time most of the shows fronted by these anchors have maintained the same adversarial format, which now seems outdated and simplistic. As is usual when a given culture and a certain aesthetic dominate a field, certain ideas are considered natural, others impossible, and important questions don't get asked.

This Day Tonight also marked the emergence of the journalist as star, a formula since perfected by shows such as *60 Minutes* and *A Current Affair*. A good example is *Foreign Correspondent*, created when George Negus, an alumnus of *TDT* and *60 Minutes*, was given the opportunity to return to the ABC with an open brief. Probably among the best of the current crop, the show nevertheless serves up yet another version of the journalist-as-hero, often perpetuating the myth of danger and an old-fashioned notion of the exotic foreignness of far-off places. A piece on Zaire, for example, had plenty about the murderous regime of President Mobutu, and how the first bribe was solicited even before one had crossed the tarmac from plane to terminal, and the danger to citizens and travellers alike posed by ever-present armed militias (pan from 'innocent villagers' to journalist on jeep, careering through dangerous outback), but precious little on the legacy of Belgian colonialism. A report on the Rwanda massacres was similar. Such massacres, audiences were told, were the product of two warring tribes; there was scant mention of the uneven colonial patronage or arbitrary partitioning of lands that set them at loggerheads. Instead, according to a logic that is itself crudely colonial, Africa, which is non-Western, and therefore 'exotic', was presented as being therefore 'chaotic'. What could be more natural than for its tribes to be irrationally warlike?

Shows that don't fit the Hemingway paradigm, or don't sport the familiar faces, don't last long in TV current-affairs land. One of the casualties was *Attitude*, a show that looked at youth affairs in a fresh-faced, contemporary format, and seemed destined to begin the careers of some excellent journalists and presenters. ABC management shunted the show from timeslot to timeslot and from format to format — not because it was unsuccessful; apparently it was too successful in its first, hour-long, lateish-night format, and management decided to do more with it. When it failed to do as they hoped in a new timeslot they lost faith, shortening the programme to half an hour and moving it about until its demise became inevitable.

In the mainstream current-affairs shows, cartoonish oppositions dominate: rich–poor, corrupt–honest, East–West, battler–tycoon, crook–innocent, despot–democrat; whether these orthodoxies are imposed by the medium or reflect the orthodoxies of the incumbent generation it is hard to tell. The press, too, likes a simple adversarial formula. Kerry versus Rupert, old feminists versus young, Keynesianism versus economic rationalism, Camille Paglia versus Julie Burchill, Germaine Greer versus Suzanne Moore, Coke versus Pepsi, even snow-boarders versus skiers — the preponderance of this sort of mock battle makes more sophisticated debates difficult.

But when it comes to cultural nostalgia, nothing matches talkback radio. Like current-affairs TV, talkback radio is in the business of nationalism. How many times an hour do announcers such as Ron Casey, Alan Jones, Stan Zemanek or John Laws, or Ray Martin for that matter, use the words 'Australia' or 'Aussie'? Talkback callers and announcers alike often seem to be having a sort of shared conversation about a mythological past and place: Australia before 'Gay Armenians and Lesbian Turks' fucked everything up. Over to John Laws:

> If the civil libertarians and do-gooders of today were asked to assess the pioneers of this country, they would have to conclude that they were politically incorrect . . . They were certainly sexist, they were certainly homophobic, they were certainly openly religious and they were absolutely elitist. You could never say they were friendly to the Aborigines, they trapped animals and they could never be described as vegetarian. And yet it's to the people who pioneered this country that the do-gooders, the doom boosters, the

politically correct, the feminazis, the gays, the civil libertarians, the uncivil vegetarians . . . all the rest, owe their very existence.[14]

Nationalist appeals on talkback radio and current-affairs television act to form a sense of imagined community, mainly white. The ratings of such programmes depend on generating a heady mix of fear and nostalgia, and they need enemies to do it. The resultant spectacle is always one of the audience, positioned as 'middle Australia', at war with a range of marginal figures who are positioned as alien and alterior, whether they be shonky plumbers, 'femi-nazis' or members of the Greek community supposedly ripping off the social welfare system. The battles are always played out with reference to an ideal moment in a privileged, golden past when such things didn't happen.

Talkback radio generates an imagined 'back fence' community straight out of the 1950s. One of the reasons that talkback rhetorics about youth crime (which are discussed at length in chapter 11) have been so powerful is that they pretend that it is precisely this community that is 'under siege'. No longer is it possible to chat over the back fence, and the fact that everyone is on the phone seems to confirm the truism. Both talkback radio and current-affairs TV are famous for their ageing demographic. The listening audience of most talkback radio, like that of shows such as *A Current Affair* and *Today Tonight*, is predominantly over fifty, and this is reflected in the topics covered. As one radio programme director said, attributing an announcer's success to his appeal among the over-50s, 'we were tending to program more to the 35-to-45 age group and maybe ignoring our core audience of the 50-plusses'.[15]

Radio programmes such as the ABC's *Australia All Over* don't ask listeners to engage with the present either, but instead indulge their nostalgia about Australia as it supposedly once was: a place where anecdotes about stockmen, country hotels and the difficulties of climbing barbed-wire fences could unproblematically be taken as a metaphor for the nation as a whole. This sort of cultural nostalgia, as the Pauline Hanson phenomenon shows, isn't so much temporal as spatial. It plays out the ancient dichotomy between the city and the bush that has been at the heart of many Australian political and cultural controversies. As the Queensland Premier Rob Borbidge showed in his fierce anti-Mabo, anti-Wik posturing, the past is rural, and has everything to do with race.

Cities, in the present conservative imagination, are 'cosmopolitan', where 'cosmopolitan' figures as a code-word for 'full of immigrants'. Cosmopolitan intellectuals, according to the book produced by Pauline Hanson's One Nation Party, *Pauline Hanson: The Truth*, are behind the present social corruption that is blighting contemporary Australia with crime, drug-taking and immigration, leading to a future where, by the year 2050, the national capital is called Vuo Wah and the country is presided over by a lesbian president named Poona Li Hung. The trouble is, these dichotomies are a myth. Looking to an idealised past in rural Australia overlooks a long history of rural immigration. The 'rural past' was a place of wide ethnic and political diversity with its own intelligentsias and its own power elites.

★

But the past, circulating around cultural reference points from the 1950s, 1960s and 1970s, nevertheless remains a generous theme park, one that proffers all sorts of benefits as long as its underlying heterogeneity is overlooked. Perhaps the ideal narrative of this cultural nostalgia is played out in the film *Forrest Gump*. Gump, the central character in this top-grossing, multi-Oscar-winning movie, leads a life that skips from one iconographic thirty-year-old cultural reference point to another, all to a soundtrack provided by signature tunes from the era. It's a simple life, played out by a simple character with homespun panache. Life was easier then, the film seems to say, and it should be so easy now. The dark side of *Forrest Gump*, as the writers Kathy Laster and Kirsten Deane argue, is that Gump, with his affability and reliance on folk wisdoms for his considerable financial success, nevertheless remains a spectator to the turbulence of recent American history. Given that Gump is an all-American hero, the implication is that white folk like him don't need to think of themselves as part of the problem, or as sharing responsibility for solving it.[16]

Forrest Gump sparked a controversy about the 'dumbing-down' of American culture. Critics of the film argued that it implicitly advocated a reversion to simple, homespun individualism. Most recent forms of Australian cultural nostalgia do the same thing. In particular, they are marked by the idea that it is no longer possible for governments to redistribute wealth and power to minority groups. The social apparatus put in place to aid such a redistribution should therefore be dismantled in the name of ceding wealth and power back to the long-suffering white Anglo-Saxons. For all their differences, Williamson, Murray, Lane, Laws and Hanson have all thematised Anglo-Saxons, especially Anglo-Saxon males, as a neglected group in contemporary society.

The particular cultural nostalgia evoked here is not only for the fifties, but for a certain cultural formation. Henry Reynolds points out that postcolonialism has left a legacy of uncertainty among those who

> recall a world of European Empires. Maps in their primary school classrooms were one-third red, denoting the British empire on which the sun never set. People identified as being British. Asia was there to be feared, pitied or patronised. The White Australia policy was still a sacred text and few questioned the centrality of race as a means to understand the world. If the Aborigines entered public consciousness it was as a Stone Age people, interesting but inferior and destined to die out.[17]

Lockout

Many Hanson supporters, Reynolds adds, are in precisely this over-50 age group — the same group appealed to by the cultural nostalgias of talkback and prime-time current affairs. Hanson's platform makes a largely emotional appeal to this audience on the basis that the clock can somehow be wound back. In many ways her message is similar to that of *Forrest Gump*. As the blurb on the *Gump* video box says: 'Forrest is the embodiment of an era, an innocent at large in an America that is losing its innocence. His heart knows what his limited IQ cannot.'[18] Current-affairs television and talkback radio, with their large over-50s audiences, tend to play the emotional card. Their brand of cultural nostalgia is one that turns away from the rational. David Williamson and John Laws have lately come out against Hanson, showing an understanding of what sort of damage to the wider polity attacks on minority groups can do.[19] But it is doubtful that radio generally or current-affairs TV can do the same, given their strong commercial vested interest in the politics of emotion and their leaning to the sizeable 50-plus audience.

The logic of this kind of populism and dumbing-down is to play the centre off against the margins. The logic of margins and mainstream is presently a familiar one in other circles too. It is recognisable as the populist catch-cry of the Howard government, which successfully evoked the mythological homogeneity of an earlier era in its 1996 election campaign. 'The handing over of Australia to the "mainstream"', as the journalist Shaun Carney put it, 'is the triumph of the talkback radio kings.'[20] This government has about it the tinge of 1950s cultural reference points, epitomised when Janette Howard wore white gloves to greet Hillary Clinton. As the humorist Tony Martin put it, impersonating Howard: 'What am I supposed to do today? Announce my bold visionary plan to return Australia to the Menzies era?'[21]

There was a flashback to the past too in Coalition responses to the High Court's Wik decision, which affirmed native title

Gangland

holders' access rights to pastoral leaseholds. The federal government immediately set about finding a way of nullifying the effect of the ruling without rendering itself liable to Aboriginal compensation claims. When Aboriginal activists threatened to take their protests to the international arena, deputy prime minister Tim Fischer was appalled. 'Wik is an Australian set of problems,' Fischer said. 'Australia and Australians all need to work together to solve these problems on Australian soil and not through the misuse of international organisations and forums.'[22] Fischer's remark seemed to spring almost whole from an earlier era. Change the national references and it could easily have been any one of a dozen white South African politicians trying to brush off the international outcry against apartheid during the 1970s.

Fischer implicitly suggested a dumbing-down of Aboriginal protests, advising against the use of remedies and resources available under international law. The similarities between the Howard government and the US Republican Party don't end with the Coalition's use of Reagan-style 'divide and rule' attack politics in the 1996 election campaign. As Robert Hughes has said, 'With somnambulistic efficiency, Reagan educated America down to his level. He left his country a little stupider in 1988 than it had been in 1980.'[23] Under Howard and Fischer, Australia is being nudged in the same direction.

Talkback radio has a part to play here too. Government and talkback radio share a similar *modus operandi*: both create phantom, often youthful enemies for a 'mainstream' that is figured as middle-aged and white. As Laws has said:

> When are you people going to realise the parks — out of which you and your children have been driven because they are unsafe, the streets that you can't walk at night because they're unsafe, the public transport on which you can't travel alone because it's unsafe — are all paid for by you. And those who have driven you out of the parks, the

streets, the public transport and taken possession themselves are gangs of slothful youths, criminals, drug addicts, and one way or another, you are paying for them too. Don't you think it's time you stopped paying for one or the other?[24]

More to the point, when talkback speaks, governments listen. The appeal of talkback radio to a late-middle-aged audience tends to produce a climate in which governments are tempted to engage in hit-and-run initiatives to please an unrepresentative, noisy minority whose fears have already been pandered to by talkback radio itself.

Perhaps the most insidious dumbing-down in recent years has come in the form of attacks on freedom of speech. While the cultural, political and media elites have been bleating about supposed censorship by the 'politically correct', all the recent examples of *real* censorship have come from moral majority-type lobbies and the conservative side of politics. Two Victorian instances are the banning of Roger McGough's satirical poem 'The Lesson' from schools and the City of Port Phillip's refusal to make a venue available for the play *The Essentials*, which criticised Victorian government policies. In New South Wales Gillian Mears' *Fineflour* and Caryl Churchill's *Top Girls* were removed from school reading lists because they didn't 'meet the requirements' of the literature course. Several State governments have also legislated to impose heavy penalties on teachers, public servants and even local councillors who make unauthorised public statements.

Meanwhile, the State governments have shown little inclination to reform their archaic defamation laws, which are a significant obstacle to freedom of speech. A certain amount of liberalisation was achieved in 1994 as a result of the High Court's Theophanous decision, which restricted the use of defamation laws to silence press criticism of public figures. In 1996, however, governments of all political persuasions united to try and persuade the High Court to reconsider this decision.

It's also getting harder to make a living out of writing. The concentration of media ownership and the closure of many newspapers have placed journalists under pressure. With job cuts and less choice of potential employers, there is a strong incentive to toe the line. Administrative changes such as cutbacks to public libraries and the introduction of more stringent eligibility criteria for Australia Council support have all reduced writers' potential sources of income, and hence the incentive to write. At the same time there have been savage cuts to education budgets, raising questions about where a diversity of future critique might come from. The 1950s are back, not only in the form of 'legislated nostalgia', as Douglas Coupland put it, but just plain legislated.

The great lie of cultural nostalgia is that, if there is to be a return to some imaginary past, with columnists, TV programmers, talkback jocks and politicians all taking turns to hold up the mirror to it, the benefits must nevertheless accrue in the present. Above this, one question remains the same. Who then will benefit? Whose interests will be served? As it stands, one answer to that question *can* be found in the various wildernesses of *Madison County*, *Forrest Gump* and urban paranoia, just as it *can* be found in the bunkers occupied by the cultural, political and media elites. But it's not a just, equitable answer. One thing is for sure: if the benefits of cultural nostalgia nevertheless accrue in the present, the arguments against such nostalgia will by necessity be found in the present too.

6
The culture racket: making a literature

> *There is, let's face it, a male critical establishment in this country and it would be stupid of anybody to deny that. If you're a good girl they'll let you in, but they're not going to let you off lightly. If you turn your back you can expect to hear a twanging sound behind you.*
>
> Helen Garner[1]

> *Went to the library of the Australian Consulate on Fifth Avenue in New York City and read through everything I could find in that line, and after an hour or two, I felt I had swum fifty laps in warm porridge. If you knew nothing about the place, you would get the impression from these reviewers that Australia is teeming with superlative writers; they outdazzle the sun.*
>
> Kate Jennings[2]

The weather on the final day of Writers' Week at the 1995 Melbourne Festival was dismal. It hadn't stopped raining for twenty-four hours, and the Malthouse Theatre was packed. Long queues stretched from the box office and fanned out from the doors of the two theatres where the panel sessions were being held. The foyer was jammed. It was an avuncular crowd. Strangers chatted, and writers who were going to sit on the panels mingled with prospective listeners. Standing in the queue for the final session of the festival — a panel discussion on the moral responsibilities of fiction writing — I glanced across and saw Helen Garner in the crowd. She was chatting to someone who I could only see from the back, but who was the same height and had exactly the same grey, bobbed hair as a friend of mine. I wondered if Garner knew her. While I speculated on possible connections, Garner glanced up and caught my eye, surprising me with a look of such piercing indignation that I glanced away.

I tried to catch her eye again after that because I wanted to make it clear I bore her no personal ill-will. I knew she'd had a difficult time at the festival. The previous evening, leaving the Malthouse, my partner and I had been standing in the street waiting for a taxi. At the head of the queue was a Writers' Week official cradling a large cardboard box in his arms. He seemed agitated. A smallish, dark-haired woman darted up to him and said 'It's all right, I've got her out the back way.' As she spoke a taxi pulled up and he climbed in, saying, 'Right, I'm going straight to the hotel. I should get there first and stop him getting in.' Someone had evidently got personal in the debate over *The First Stone*. I wanted to dissociate myself from that sort of personal attack with a friendly glance as I tried to catch her eye.

The person Garner was talking to turned out not to be my friend. I had been fooled by the shock of grey hair. As we entered the theatre I noticed a sizeable proportion of the crowd had grey hair. 'Mrs Knox', one publisher calls them, referring to a middle-class eastern suburb. They are the passionate reading classes who belong to book clubs, love the opportunity to brush by writers in a crowd, and don't mind queuing for ages at book-signing sessions. They like the way festivals are planned around daytime sessions, and they put their names on mailing lists so they can purchase tickets in advance.

Young people buy books too, but they are not festival stalwarts. At an earlier festival event — a launch to celebrate the

The culture racket

reprint of a first novel — a publisher turned to me and said, 'much younger crowd, thank Christ'. Publishers love younger readers. They see them as an untapped audience and as proof that publishing has a future. But the way most festivals are organised means that young people are thin on the ground. 'Let's get out of here. This place reminds me too much of Camberwell on a Sunday afternoon,' my friend Wayne said, as he and a bunch of others left for the pub.

The stand-out panel of the 1995 festival was for these readers. It was called 'Grunge', and took place on the morning of that rainy Sunday. A capacity crowd cheered and clapped all the speakers, especially Christos Tsiolkas who, like the others, disowned the tag 'grunge', but extrapolated its marketeering logic into a passionate speech about the economics of publishing, and then economic rationalism and politics generally. It was the only speech I heard at the festival that provoked a standing ovation, or got beyond the narcissistic navel-gazing of the writing and publishing world. But afterwards the young crowd evaporated. Those who remained found themselves teleported back into the world of publishing professionals, who as usual were flat out rubbing shoulders, making deals and schmoozing each other's authors, and the rest, who were enjoying the festival's careful stage management and leisurely *frisson*.

That final session on moral responsibility, once we had finally shuffled into the room, turned out to be a contrived, complacent affair. Along with Garner there were Carmel Bird, Frank Moorhouse and Kate Grenville, all writers of a similar hue, and Morag Fraser in the chair seemed all too ready to ask tame, leading questions. What followed was a series of cosy chats about the sanctified otherworldliness of art. There were no surprises when it came to the issue of authorial responsibility. Grenville talked about how life tended to imitate art in any case; Bird talked about how pure art veered from life so as to leave its subjects untouched; Moorhouse wittily preached art for art's sake; Garner reckoned that most people secretly like being portrayed by famous writers, even unsympathetically, and welcome a chance to learn about themselves. All talked about themselves more than about writing. Yes, they all concluded, art is more important than responsibility. It was like listening to auditors eulogising taxation.

The funny thing was that in the previous session, in that very same room, another set-piece panel had come to precisely the opposite conclusion, albeit with similar cosiness. This panel, chaired by Helen Daniel and comprising Michael Heyward, Robert Manne and David Brooks, had decided that, in the wake of the Darville-Demidenko affair, responsibility is much more important than art. According to them, fiction has limits, especially when it touches on the lives of real people. At the final session a few members of the audience who'd been to both sessions pointed to the disparity between the two, and even to the similar self-satisfaction with which opposite conclusions were drawn. The panel met these comments with mute incomprehension.

This incident says a lot about literary festivals. At festivals a little magic takes place, a little belief is given over. People seem to want to believe writers, even if writers are probably the last people they should believe. As Joan Didion says, 'writers are always selling somebody out'.[3] Festivals are highly organised, hierarchical events, carefully designed to appear casual and democratic. The strings are always hidden. Most people aren't to know that the person 'conversing' so fluently with the writer on the stage is an old friend and long-time supporter who has lobbied for months to get her on the programme. Or that the reviewer chatting casually to the guest of honour has been his foremost advocate in the press for any number of years, has helped make his reputation, and is now on the committee of the present festival. Or that festivals are two-tier events, serving the needs of a close-knit publishing community as much as the public. Instead, everything is designed to look completely natural, as if the writer who steps up to the lectern in a given forum has wound up there entirely on merit.

But festivals are only a microcosm of the literary world. When contributors are sought for an arts supplement, or reviewers for a books section, it's also a case of rounding up the 'usual suspects'. The same thing tends to happen among publishers. When a publisher is soliciting manuscripts or floating a project in need of an author, the same old names, or 'hot' new names, are brought up time and time again. Most publishers, as a senior editor once said to me, are only interested in what already glitters. Gerard Henderson once said the literary publishing establishment 'exudes the seven veils of mateship'.[4] At the time he was writing about the Darville-Demidenko affair. His idea was that the literati closed ranks to defend her. Whether or not this is the case — I think precisely the opposite happened — his basic point remains true. The usual claims about the 'fractious' literary scene, the shark pool 'riddled with rage and revenge', or the 'two-horse town . . . poisoned by feuds of biblical proportions'[5] might make for good copy, but the underlying culture is more of insider trading than infighting. It's just that the fights sometimes happen in public, while the deeper networks of patronage stay well hidden.

★

If there's one thing that all the various literary (and intellectual) tribes share, it's the idea that nothing can ever be left to chance, especially those things that are most apt to seem 'natural', such as the gathering of literary reputation. These things are too important to be left up to something so random as nature, even if it is essential that they look natural. When it comes to setting agendas or making literatures, which is what literary coteries are all about, the tribes are constantly at work trying to organise public space to suit their own ends. Talent may or may not be a naturally occurring thing, but reputations are no more 'natural' than eating with a knife and fork. They are to do with accumulated cultural capital and commercial power, and building them requires a lot of careful work by the writers and their advocates. The accumulation of *cultural* capital is never about something so crude as *nature*.

The traditional constructors of canons are the universities, and this remains the case, despite what you might have heard about literary theory and 'decanonisation'. Few people outside academe have the sort of institutional clout and access to research funds required to bring particular writers to notice and facilitate serious debate about their works. Ostensibly literary academics are paid to do just that. Before the Dawkins reforms of the late 1980s imposed economic rationalism on the universities they even had time to do it, but even now a sustained campaign by an academic can make a writer's career, and those who fail to attract the right sort of academic attention are likely to be overlooked as 'serious' or 'literary' writers. Also at work is the Australia Council, which funds writers directly, keeping mainly the established old guard of local writing in the money, with a dash of token youth bias and state-sponsored ethnic egalitarianism. Somewhere in between are the journals and broadsheet dailies.

Journals, in particular, play an important part in stoking the fires of the canon-making machine. In most cases they have such limited circulation that they are deemed insignificant. They appear dull and are easily missed on crammed bookshop shelves. They seem dense, arcane and a step behind the issues due to their long lead-times. Yet journals like *Meanjin*, *Overland*, *Southerly*, *Quadrant* and lately *Heat*, as relatively cheap, low-risk publishing, provide rallying points for like voices, and their collective contribution to local cultural life has been immense. Many an intellectual or literary campaign has made a start there. To take one alone, Arthur Phillips' now-famous expression, the 'cultural cringe', was first published in *Meanjin*, and Marjorie Barnard first championed the almost unknown Patrick White there. Xavier Herbert, A. D. Hope,

The culture racket

James McAuley, Nettie Palmer, Judith Wright, Kylie Tennant and Manning Clark were all active in its pages. In the early 1990s an important cultural policy debate was played out there, unnoticed by the mainstream media.

Journals foster coteries, supplying them with a forum to guarantee reproduction of their work and introduce it to new readers. Critical articles establish a familial relationship, identifying bloodlines of influence between the coterie's favoured writers and already canonical writers outside the circle. The formula is simple: take up space. According to cultural critic John Docker, writing in 1974, this has been a Melbourne tradition:

> In its social and aesthetic attitudes it develops the thinking of Arnold, Eliot, Pound and Leavis, in seeing literature and knowledge as central to society. It is a tradition which goes back to Coleridge's social thinking, and his idea that 'cultural values' are embodied in a 'clerisy', a central educated group, which stands as an ideal for the rest of society.[6]

The coterie sponsored by the now defunct highbrow journal *Scripsi* is a case in point. From its beginnings in the English department at Melbourne University to its final home in the halls of Ormond College (yes, *that* Ormond College), *Scripsi* staged itself as an internationalist intervention in parochial local literary life. Although it published erratically and lasted only a decade or so, from the early 1980s to the early 1990s, *Scripsi* established a bastion of liberal humanism in the literary scene when elsewhere it looked as if liberal humanism might be on the wane. It championed the work of Australian writers such as Elizabeth Jolley, David Malouf and Helen Garner, who are now the core of the living Australian canon, alongside the expatriate Robert Hughes and overseas thinkers such as Susan Sontag.

These days former *Scripsi* staff are prolific reviewers and columnists but remain connected. Peter Craven, a founding editor, writes regularly for the books pages in the *Age*, the *Australian* and the *Sunday Age*, as well as for journals such as *Australian Book Review*, and is probably Australia's most prolific and self-consciously literary book reviewer. Craven has also been influential in his role as a columnist in the *Australian Higher Education Supplement*, commissioned under Luke Slattery's editorship. Slattery was a protégé of *Overland* founder Stephen Murray-Smith, and is one of the few journalists to use words like 'cognate' and 'adumbrate'. He once wrote: 'Hovering above the autobiographical genre is a whiff of withdrawal, even termination; it's a summation from the far side of the life span, the recapitulation that caps the concerto.'[7]

Craven's columns in the *HES* also tend to the plummy, and often go over and over the same concerns: James Joyce, Robert Musil, Drusilla Modjeska, Robert Hughes, Helen Garner, David Malouf and Text Publishing authors such as Linda Jaivin, Gideon Haigh, John Button and Robert Manne. *Scripsi*'s later editors, Andrew Rutherford and Owen Richardson, write less regularly for the major broadsheets. Other members of the circle are also influential. Michael Heyward, the other founding editor, works as publisher at Text Publishing, alongside Di Gribble, co-founder with Hilary McPhee of the publishing house McPhee Gribble. Former *Scripsi* associates Rosemary Sorensen and Christina Thompson went on to edit *Australian Book Review* and *Meanjin* respectively.

Most coteries operate according to a principle of circularity. The formula is straightforward enough. Talk about something long and hard enough, and sooner or later someone — preferably someone influential — will sit up and take notice. In coteries the effect is magnified: everyone is talking about everyone else. A 1997 issue of *Meanjin* sums up the syndrome. This issue, entitled 'The Next Generation', featured a ten-page interview with Craven, as well as articles by Richardson (writing on Garner) and Rutherford (on the ins and outs of a classical education). The other essays were by writers over thirty, and were predominantly instructional in tone, including an article on why teenagers should read Shakespeare. Despite the implied promise of the title, and the possibility of a forum, the voices of younger essayists from outside the circle were entirely absent.

During a minor kerfuffle over the ethics of book reviewing, Craven defended his right to review books published under the Text imprint, stating that:

> I have no difficulty, in principle, with reviewing a book published by Heyward at Text. It would be grossly insulting to me for anyone to imagine that anything I wrote as a critic about any particular book published by that company had the slightest relation to my former association with him or my personal regard.[8]

Whatever the case, the circles of reviewing do seem to be limited. For example, when Robert Manne's *The Culture of Forgetting* was published by Text, Craven wrote the review for the *Australian*[9] and Rutherford for the *Sunday Age*.[10] There was a mild stir when Text published John Stephenson's novel *The Optimist*, a fictional biography of the poet Christopher Brennan, complete with cover endorsements from Tim Winton and Helen Garner, who had recently published *True Stories* with Text. Christopher Pearson, speaking at the 1996 Melbourne Writers' Festival, commented that, contrary to the impression given by the publicity generated by former *Scripsi* staff and associates, *The Optimist* need not have 'detained us for more than four paragraphs'.[11] Craven staunchly defended himself against the charge, stating that he hadn't mentioned the book except in his column, thinking it 'newsworthy'.[12] Slattery gave the book a warm reception with a 5-page feature in the *Weekend Australian* colour supplement,[13] then wrote a less warm review for the books pages.[14] Owen Richardson wrote a damning review for the *Sunday Age*.[15] Favourable or unfavourable, the result is that other reviewers don't get public space to discuss the books in question.

Controversy has never been too far from this group. A minor kerfuffle involving the *HES* took place under Slattery's editorship when the paper chose to run a profile on one of the three candidates for a professorial chair in English at Melbourne University — predictably the only one of the three who was a practising poet. Craven vigorously defended the column against a charge of favouritism made by former department head Terry Collits, saying that 'It is a dodgy procedure to assume that the public expression of enthusiasm is tantamount to the public expression of aversion for another'.[16] But aren't sins of omission often the most telling?

Limited circles of advocacy work in other arenas too. Perhaps one of the reasons the panel on the Demidenko affair at the 1995 Melbourne Writers' Festival seemed so staid was that, as well as Manne, it included Heyward, his publisher, and *Australian Book Review* editor Helen Daniel, who had published anti-Darville pieces by both. Daniel was prominent in calling for the resignation of the judges of the 1995 Miles Franklin Award after it was won by Darville.

So successful was *Scripsi* that much of the structure of the present literary canon is mirrored in that journal's pages. This brings to mind the final strategy coteries must deploy if any of this is to be of use, which is to make the right links to already canonical writers.

An example: Craven's essay 'Of War and Needlework' was an early and influential retrospective look at the first part of Garner's career, and signalled her international importance: 'Helen Garner can sometimes seem a bit like Christina Stead . . . Chekhov . . . Katherine Mansfield'.[17] Craven has reviewed all of Garner's books since 1992 for the *Australian*, and has written a number of features for other papers.[18] He often compares her work with that of famous European and American writers. In an article on Garner's screenplay for *The Last Days*

The culture racket

of Chez Nous he invokes Chekhov and Harold Pinter.[19] Elsewhere he calls down Raymond Carver, Virginia Woolf and Katherine Mansfield.[20] In another review her work is compared to that of Virginia Woolf and 'the Katherine Mansfield of the mature stories'.[21] In another, she is compared to Janet Malcolm.[22] Another talks of Jane Austen.[23] Garner, Craven has written, 'is the woman who shows us how we speak'.[24]

Strangely, Craven has sometimes nominated himself to do Garner's speaking and thinking for her. Worried that some critics denied Garner a place in the sun because she hadn't yet produced enough, in a review of Garner's *Cosmo Cosmolino* he wrote: 'Helen Garner is perhaps the most visible writer in the country and her visibility has made her chary of committing herself to paper too often.'[25] The rest of the review was a masterpiece of self-conscious salvage, seemingly dogged by the reviewer's fear that the book wasn't up to scratch. By the review's end, the book emerges as a collection of things the reviewer apparently finds fault in ('restless in its experimentation', 'an attempt to stretch the form of fiction', 'God-mad', 'more purple prose than Garner has allowed herself before', 'a remarkably game book'), which are excused because the faults are themselves found satisfying: 'The writing is cross-textured, with different parts of it more vivid than others, though it is convincing at each point.' It's a tough day in the life of a humble reviewer.

Other members of this circle are Drusilla Modjeska, David Malouf and Elizabeth Jolley, as well as the other *Scripsi* editors and, since the demise of *Scripsi*, figures such as Helen Daniel, editor of *ABR*, and Morag Fraser, editor of *Eureka Street*. Comparison is the pattern here too. Former *Scripsi* editor Owen Richardson, reviewing *Cosmo Cosmolino*, compared Garner's work to that of Dostoyevsky and Genet.[26] Writing on Modjeska, Craven invoked Susan Sontag and Joan Didion as suitable company.[27] In the same column he compared David Malouf to André Gide. In a piece for *Scripsi* he suggested

123

Tolstoy, Dostoyevsky and D. H. Lawrence as possible travelling companions for Malouf, finally settling the issue by announcing 'David Malouf is our Turgenev'.[28] Malouf wrote a gushing tribute to *Scripsi* that for a time was run in the magazine's opening pages as an epigraph.

Writing on Elizabeth Jolley, Craven compares her to William Blake, Patrick White and Barry Humphries.[29] In another review she is compared to F. Scott Fitzgerald.[30] Morag Fraser, writing on Jolley's *The Orchard Thieves*, noted the similarities between Jolley and Chekhov.[31] Writing on Garner in *Scripsi*, Jolley compares her work to that of Goethe, Jane Austen and Virginia Woolf.[32] Garner returns the compliment; she praises Jolley's work as being like Old Testament wisdom, and invokes the ghosts of Emerson and Stendhal.[33] Asked by the *Australian* what books she would recommend for Christmas, Garner recommends Jolley's *The Orchard Thieves*.[34] The same day, in the equivalent feature in the *Age*, Jolley recommends Garner's *The First Stone*.[35]

The grand opening flourish is standard form in this kind of literary journalism. A piece on Jolley by Craven in *ABR* begins: 'It's been apparent for some time that Elizabeth Jolley is one of the more significant writers we have and one of the very few writing on a large scale.'[36] In a separate review of Jolley's trilogy, *My Father's Moon*, *Cabin Fever* and *The George's Wife*, on the page facing Craven's, Modjeska writes:

> Just occasionally you read something of your own time and culture and know that when we're all dead and gone it will be the work that will illuminate to those who come after the times we only glimpse as we pass through them ... A few reviewers — Elizabeth Webby, Helen Daniel and Peter Craven among them — have alerted us to [the novels'] significance one by one, but the question I want to ask is why this trilogy, completed for a year now, has not been recommended to us ... from the cover of *Time* magazine and

every colour supplement in the country? To say nothing of the literary pages of our newspapers.[37]

It is true that Jolley's admirable trilogy never made it to the cover of *Time*. But if the trilogy received insufficient notice, it's not the fault of Craven and Daniel, nor of Modjeska. Between them they have penned nearly half the reviews of Jolley published in the country's three major broadsheets — the *Age*, *Australian* and *Sydney Morning Herald* — for the eight novels Jolley has published since *Mr Scobie's Riddle*. Daniel and Craven have accounted for all but one of the reviews of Jolley's books in the *Age* since then, as well as a number of feature articles in the *Age* and a series of essays and reviews in *ABR*.[38] Daniel, with Heyward, was also on the committee for the 1995 Melbourne Writers' Festival at which a tribute was made to Jolley.

Given that this business is to do with aspiring to national canons, it's important to tend the places of predecessors such as Christina Stead and Patrick White, with their large international reputations. 'I could die of envy for her hard eye,' Garner wrote of Stead in *Scripsi*. 'She writes without politeness, as brutally as a scientist.'[39] When Hazel Rowley's biography of Stead appeared in 1993, Craven interviewed Rowley for the *Age* as well as reviewing the book. Modjeska did the review for the *Sydney Morning Herald* and Garner for the *Sunday Age*.[40] Two years earlier, when David Marr's biography of White came out, Craven wrote a review for the *Age*, Malouf wrote a review for *ABR*, Jolley penned some impressions for *Scripsi*, and Modjeska wrote a review for *Australian Society*.[41]

In 1996, when Simon During (the successful applicant for the Melbourne University English chair, but not the one profiled in the *Australian*) published a critical monograph on the canonisation of White, Craven rushed into print in the *Australian* with a rebuttal that opened by querying the process by which professorial chairs are appointed.[42] It was written,

Craven implied, without his having read During's book. Craven later wrote a long article for *ABR*, in the course of which he compared White to Byron, Keats, D. H. Lawrence, Graham Greene, Evelyn Waugh, Kingsley Amis, Stendhal, William Golding, Dylan Thomas and Dostoyevsky. Because canons work by association, Craven also shielded David Marr, whom he compared to Richard Ellmann, George Painter and Brian Boyd, biographers of James Joyce, Marcel Proust and Nabokov respectively.[43] Craven claimed that the reason for his 'rage and shame' about the White book was a desire to protect the series of which During's book was a part, since 'I had some influence in persuading Oxford to initiate this critical series'.[44] Geoffrey Dutton later pointed out that the series was originated by Lloyd O'Neil at Lansdowne Press in 1961, when Craven would have been aged about ten.[45] Craven replied that he was thinking of the second series.

This sort of shepherding of literary reputations isn't an easy business. It requires constant husbandry, tending the flock, rounding up stragglers, cutting out the ring-ins, making sure everything is in tip-top condition. A team effort works best. The controversy surrounding the publication of *The First Stone*, for example, alarmed some of Garner's long-standing allies, who seemed afraid that Garner's place in the canon might have inadvertently been put under threat. Craven reviewed the book for the *Australian*. Andrew Rutherford reviewed it for the *Sunday Age*, with a wry commentary on the male traditions of Ormond College. Luke Slattery wrote a feature for the *Australian Magazine*, and Morag Fraser, a long-time Garner fan, did the review for the *Age*. In a later review for *ABR* of Garner's *True Stories*, Fraser compared Garner's work to that of E. Annie Proulx and Johann Sebastian Bach.[46]

There is, of course, nothing wrong with any of this. Such closeness has long been a feature of Australian literary and cultural life. As I write, Kristin Williamson is on the radio, on the Margaret Throsby show, singing the praises of *The First*

The culture racket

Stone.[47] Before me is a press clipping where Williamson cites the book as her favourite (comparing Garner to Janet Malcolm) and describes it as 'a tremendous breakthrough between fiction and non-fiction'.[48] Fair enough, too. Garner and the Williamsons go back a long way, and it's only natural to pay extra attention to books by people you know; I do the same myself. Yet such cosiness, and the set agendas and intellectual clubbiness that go with it, are rarely open to question. The allegiances and rules of the insider-trading game are rarely revealed. Nor are the publicity supply lines that mean, for example, that it is Williamson on the radio and not some 'young feminist' firebrand. Instead, it all takes place in the name of 'open debate'.

★

The Saturday book pages are important because they are the writing and publishing world's public face. Opening the *Age* one morning, more or less at random, I turned to the books section. There they were: three pages adorned with all-too-familiar names. There were three long lead reviews, all by men, about books by men. These reviewers were all members of the literary establishment, with an average age over 50. Sure, they write well. Yes, age should be no barrier. But where are the others? The one younger male reviewer had been allocated a few hundred words at the bottom of a page to review three books, all by men. The reviews by women appeared as secondary collections of mini-reviews assigned to the traditional women's place — the margins — and were predominantly about books written by women, and books for teenagers and children. The exception was a regular column by a woman, easy to miss at the bottom of the first page. This scant privilege was perhaps allowed because she, like the three male lead reviewers, is a denizen of the literary establishment.[49]

Or take the *Australian*'s offerings over a four-week period. In the first week the reviews kicked off with a feature review of an autobiography by a male writer, accompanied by a review of some male childhood reminiscences. The following week the books pages were dominated by three feature reviews of biographies of prominent men. The next week these same pages opened with another feature review of a biography of a prominent man. Inside were two long reviews, one of a biography of a prominent man and another of an autobiography of a prominent man. The following week's pages also opened with a full-page feature review of a biography of a prominent man. Most of the reviews over a two-month period were also by middle-aged men, the overwhelming majority reviewing books by men. If feature reviews alone are counted, the pro-male bias is much higher. So much for the supposed silencing of the 'straight white male'! The unwritten rule that women only review books by women, and that those with ethnic backgrounds only get to review ethnic books, applies here too.[50]

It was entertaining to look over another broadsheet's annual round-up of the best books for the year. Of the 30 'well-read Australians' whose opinions were solicited, two-thirds were from the generation of '68 — the generation the poet John Tranter described in 1978 as growing old gracefully on the fat of the literary land. They still are. Only one of the contributors was under thirty-five.[51] Of the 27 'critics' asked to comment on the 'reads that had the most impact' on them in the annual Christmas retrospective in another paper, none was under thirty-five.[52] As you might imagine, the books recommended in these articles follow much the same pattern. Some bookshops are publishing their own newsletters with a more balanced spread of books and reviewers, partly out of disenchantment with the newspaper review pages.

Given the chance to break the pattern with a substantial government grant and an editor from outside the literary scene, *The Australian's Review of Books* could only manage more of the same. According to its editor, Shelley Gare, the new journal's funding of $176 000 was justified because it would go straight to the writers, who were to be paid handsomely.[53] But which writers are these? Rather than strike out as the unique journal of a culture of letters, broadly defined, the *Review* has tended to sponsor the usual suspects (along with a few imported dinosaurs), granting them a new arena in which to write about each other, playing out agendas that sometimes go back decades. The effect is that a large slab of money that might have been used to sponsor newer, younger writers has been funnelled to an elite that is already relatively well-funded and gets plenty of airplay. According to Shelley Gare, younger writers are underrepresented in the *Review* because 'rarely do essayists hit their stride before their 30s and some of the best essayists are over 70'.[54]

The inbuilt biases of those who run the literary pages and write in them were nowhere more obvious than when it came to reviewing the latest wave of young writers, especially the so-called 'grunge' writers, who were evaluated almost entirely in terms of that caricaturing label. Admittedly some of these books were underdone. Some contrived to shock, but ended up looking more like moral tableaux designed to impress a middle-class liberal audience than the product of a writer with something to say. There was a lot of hype too, which tended to create the impression that older writers were being displaced. But there was never the largesse, the murky salvage work, the bending over backwards to make the best of a bad lot, that characterises the usual matesy review.

Few reviewers of 'grunge' paused to consider the contingencies of literary fashion, or to analyse why these books were so under-edited and over-hyped. There was almost no speculation on why publishers didn't seem interested in nurturing young writers to get a couple of books under their belts before trying for something 'big'. Or on how this might have denied some of these writers a medium or long-term future. Instead, most reviewers fell for the hype.

The reviews tended to ghettoise the books, leaving their non-'grunge' credentials largely unread, overlooking the possibility that they might have something else to offer. No mainstream reviewer noticed the obvious continuities between Christos Tsiolkas's *Loaded*, a second-generation immigrant book, and Rosa Cappiello's first-generation immigrant book, *Oh Lucky Country*. They missed the fact that almost every plot development in *Loaded* is obliquely or directly driven by the question of what it means to be a Greek, or a wog, or queer in Australia, when authenticity always seems to be elsewhere. Typical was a review which described *Loaded* as 'Australian grunge' engaged in 'a drab little competition with Justine Ettler (*The River Ophelia*) to see who can say f... the most times on one page'.[55] This is precisely the sort of comment *Oh Lucky Country* received when it was first published in English translation in 1984. Maybe, as *Loaded* implies, little has changed in attitudes to ethnicity since then.

Jamie Grant, writing on Edward Berridge's *Lives of the Saints*, pursued a similar theme, remarking that 'connoisseurs of pornography will find this familiar and no doubt stimulating'.[56] It evidently didn't occur to Grant that one of Berridge's themes was the impact of media, including pornography, on the way people speak and behave, and the forms of writing-in-good-faith this makes possible. Another form of ghettoisation was reviewing the books in tandem. Writing on Andrew McGahan's *1988* and Gaby Naher's *The Underwharf*, Kate Veitch said 'It's tremendously difficult for me, at 40, to hike through these two longish novels about a boy and a girl (respectively) stumbling through their twentieth year . . . I want to snarl "For God's sake, grow up!"'[57] But why is Veitch reviewing two books with which she feels so much at odds? In this situation many reviewers pass, knowing that being too far from a review title is as counterproductive as being too close.

Reviews of 'grunge' followed a pattern only too familiar in a literary culture that tends to grant hagiographies to 'approved culture' and damn everything else. Almost all the reviewers of 'grunge' were Veitch's age and older, as are the vast majority of reviewers, period. Why not younger reviewers, more adept at spotting the books' themes — not to construct an alternative hagiography, but to mount an informed critique? No reviewer spoke of any of the 'grunge' books as literatures of cultural dispossession. Nor were they likely to, as they manifestly lacked the apparatus to contextualise the books even in terms of obvious things, such as the social realities younger people face. Instead the books were spoken of in terms of a 1970s paradigm, as existential, individual rites of passage. And in these terms, naturally, they failed.

The smug, morally superior approach, pitched at a certain white-bread reader profile, is a staple of local literary culture. By the middlebrow, for the middlebrow, seems to be the motto. The same sort of sentiments were expressed even in Mandy Sayer's review of Irvine Welsh's *Trainspotting*: 'I can't help thinking . . . of dirty realism and deconstruction as two parallel tracks taking us on a hurtling train ride into nothingness,' she wrote. 'Sure, we're all travelling in the same direction, but I think I'd rather walk.'[58] What impressed me most about this line is that Sayer not only managed to ignore the chord the mega-selling *Trainspotting* struck among many younger readers, but in a single sentence pandered to both of the literary establishment's currently fashionable prejudices, lambasting both 'dirty realism' and deconstruction. Similarly Kate Veitch, having missed the thematic import of McGahan's book (personally, I think the deadpan and hilarious Gordon is one of the stand-out characters of recent fiction), instead came on like a schoolteacher, calling for 'more imaginative daring, greater projection of character'.

If 'grunge' writers were to be damned, literary columnist and former *ABR* editor Rosemary Sorensen was more openly dismissive than most. 'There is grunge and there is good writing,' she wrote, 'and the fad for teenybopper stuff that exploits the hype about the sex-and-violence in down-and-out settings will pass, leaving a few publishers with piles of unread junk.'[59] Reading this, I could only wonder where she got her information. It is well known that all the 'grunge' books sold well — over 10 000 copies in most cases, which, to put it in perspective, is somewhat better than the average novel written by one of your up-on-high literary establishment. All reprinted respectably, and some had sold over 30 000 copies when Sorensen's column appeared. Or is that the problem? These were books that, despite their variable quality, seemed to fill a need for something different in Australian writing. Sorensen's gesture, lumping them together as a way of taking *nothing* seriously, seemed to articulate, more clearly than most, the unspoken hopes of the literary establishment — not only is this stuff no good, but nobody wants it.

Peter Craven archly expressed similar sentiments in an approving review of Catherine Ford's *Dirt and Other Stories*, published by Text (Owen Richardson did the review for the the *Sunday Age*[60]), warning readers not to compare the 'grunge sensationalism' of 'generation Xers who appropriated the label' with the original 'dirty realists', Raymond Carver and Richard Ford.[61] Catherine Ford is Helen Garner's sister, a fact that Craven couldn't let his readers forget. Garner's name appeared seven times in the review, only a few times less than Ford's. It's almost as if Garner wrote the book by proxy, through the medium of the critic. Craven praised *Dirt* and compared it to Garner's *Monkey Grip* (and Christina Stead) in a way that cast them as the *proper* Australian heirs of the 'dirty realist' tradition. It was a complex canonical move, designed to rescue Ford from the company of those who might otherwise be seen as her peers. They, by contrast, were cast as mere copyists who can never equal any sort of US 'original', which somehow was supposed to serve as yet another reminder that they're not the *real* Australian writing. Ironically, Craven's dismissiveness reminded me of the early reception suffered by Garner's

Honour and Other People's Children. 'Helen Garner talks dirty and passes it off as realism', Peter Pierce wrote, provoking the comment from Garner that I've used as my epigraph for this chapter.[62]

But work by younger writers needn't masquerade under the moniker 'grunge' to be so disdained. Speaking on the announcement that Paul Radley, winner of the 1980 Vogel Prize for literature, had not written his own books, Craven wrote, 'the Radley revelation should serve as one more reminder that obsessions with youth, gender and multiculturalism — however necessary they may be in real politics — have real dangers when it comes to the world of books'.[63]

★

There is plenty at stake when it comes to funding younger writers. The present literary establishment has grown up, not only with the rise of the arts that began in the 1970s, but also with the Literature Board of the Australia Council, founded in 1973. A quick glance at Thomas Shapcott's history of the board shows that the recipients of the first few rounds of grants have been disproportionate recipients of money since. Most of the senior creative writing fellowships awarded in the mid-1990s (the 'Keatings') went to the Whitlam generation of writers. According to Hilary McPhee, former head of the Australia Council, artists under thirty receive less than 10 per cent of Australia Council individual grants.[64] There was a reminder of this in the reaction to a public speech on peer assessment in arts funding given by McPhee in 1995. Even the way newspaper reports on the speech were formulated tended to confirm the hegemony of a certain generation. Asked to comment on McPhee's speech in the *Age* were Roger Woodward, Thomas Keneally, George Fairfax, Les Murray, David Williamson and Jack Hibberd. All white, all male, all over fifty.[65] In a similar piece in the *Australian*, the existence of women artists was at least acknowledged, although the writers interviewed were all middle-aged and in mid-career.[66] None of those reporting on the speech sought comment from younger artists or writers, which was odd given that McPhee had raised the issue, saying:

> The baby-boom generation, who received free education and much else that no other generation ever had, has gone on receiving the lion's share of the funds available for their creative development . . . we have a couple of generations of artists for whom direct subsidies have been a boon and a lifeline. We have new generations coming up who deserve part of the cake — and we urgently need to share it with them.[67]

These words took on a hollow ring shortly afterwards, when the Australia Council announced a shake-up in the system of grants allocation, including a proposal for a mentor system for sponsoring young writers. This seemed an excellent method of giving patronage free rein and shutting down any new forms of writing and new ideas that might challenge the older formulas. Imagine interviews with the first of the young writers to come off the production line: 'How did X influence your work?' 'Your novel seems to differ from X's in some ways, but is similar in others. Can you explain further?' In effect, a mentor system looks like another way to perpetuate the hegemony of the old guard; the young writers act as their cipher, a filter through which we might gain access to yet another version of the 'master's' work. This isn't to say that older writers have nothing to offer, or that young writers would always succumb. But why be naive? What is mentorship, if not influence? The paternalism of such a scheme would be distasteful to the more adventurous writers, old and young, just as the 'safe' would be more likely to be chosen. Is the Australia Council suggesting that young writers can't be trusted on their own, or aren't deserving of grants in their own right? For struggling young writers (and isn't that almost everyone?) such schemes are a poor substitute for direct funding.

★

But if there are differences between types of literary culture, they don't necessarily have much to do with age. Rather, they have to do with incumbency. Mary Fallon's *Working Hot*, for example, has been in print continuously for many years, without registering on the mainstream canonical map. Fallon, like many younger writers, isn't the *right* sort of writer. Her work has been dismissed as 'subcultural' as a way of ricocheting her concerns back into the margins. But *Working Hot*, like Leonie Stevens' *Nature Strip* or Tsiolkas's *Loaded*, has appeal for a certain type of reader disenchanted with the mainstream of local literary fiction, and is being read accordingly. *None* of my own friends voluntarily reads Elizabeth Jolley or Helen Garner or Barry Hill or Robert Drewe or Rodney Hall or David Malouf, all no doubt excellent writers. But many have a treasured and dog-eared copy of *Working Hot* or similar lurking beside the bed, while the pristine copy of the latest up-on-high literary sensation lingers unhappily on the shelf and is praised from one end of the country to the other.

One difference has to do with aesthetics. Literary critic Jenna Mead argues that, if literature is often about failure, there is a strand of local fiction for which failure is always ethical and the way to mend the breach is to re-examine lax ethical standards and make a corrective return to a rebalanced, revitalised humanism. Garner's fictional works, from *Monkey Grip* to *Cosmo Cosmolino*, follow this pattern. The two novels written so far by Drusilla Modjeska and Robert Dessaix do the same, as do Tim Winton's works. Often the central metaphor is one of a breach in the family, especially to do with a missing mother. Modjeska's *Poppy* and essays in *The Orchard*, Winton's *The Riders*, Dessaix's autobiography, *A Mother's Disgrace*, and even Garner's *The First Stone* ('I wondered who was looking after them, or advising them. I asked myself what advice *I* would have given them')[68] are all to do with absent mothers and subsequent ethical problems.

For other strands of writing, failure isn't so much to do with lax ethical standards as with a failure of humanity, humanism and even the family itself. For them the whole idea of ethics is suspect. Distrusting humanism, they tend to undermine rather than comfort the expectations of readers, reviewers and publishers. Books like Ruby Langford Ginibi's *Don't Take Your Love to Town* or Cappiello's *Oh Lucky Country* encompass a range of experiences outside the frame of stereotypical white middle-class experience, and find themselves, at the same time, outside the high literary canon.

Robert Dessaix spoke on the sort of values he would like to see inhabit local writing in his keynote address to the 1995 Victorian Premier's Literary Awards dinner. His topic was 'enchantment'. It was an odd speech, implicitly attacking multiculturalism and 'postmodern' academics for undermining 'enchantment', which, according to Dessaix, is both a state and a value people have lost. These are common themes throughout literary and intellectual life: that someone or something ('postmodernism', 'deconstruction', technology, politics, 'private greed', modern life, lack of time) has robbed people of their finer sensibilities, diminished their historical knowledge, and left them with no appreciation of art, literature and finer things. But it is complacent to think that 'enchantment', like 'truth and beauty', is central to art. Even the best of humanist art, judged by its own standards, seems to be about doubt, ugliness and despair. Dostoyevsky, Flaubert, Tolstoy, Woolf, Stendhal, Mansfield, Gide — very little enchantment there. Much 'great art', from David's *Death of Marat* to Picasso's *Guernica* to Dostoyevsky's *The Devils*, is in fact deeply political.

It seems all too obvious why there is next to no 'enchantment' in Cappiello or Langford Ginibi. Neither plays out the triumph of form over content that Kate Jennings has called

The culture racket

'*nice* writing'[69] or indulges in what a friend refers to as the 'beautiful unmeaning' that dominates local fiction. Local literary culture, to its detriment, seems obsessed with the business of 'being a writer' rather than with the business of having something to say. This is one of the reasons why the high canon of local fiction often seems so self-conscious and contrived. Younger writers who master the style — a sort of manneredness that labours in the shadow of Patrick White's brilliant metaphors — sometimes find themselves invited to sit at the big table. One of the interesting things about Dessaix's speech and others of its kind is that those who tell us these things manage to present themselves as singularly unaffected by the maladies they describe. It's as if, again, in the authorial presence, a little magic happens, a little belief is given over. But was it just a trick? Even as an advocate of much of what Dessaix complains about, I quite regularly feel enchanted, often in surprising ways. Obviously his speech had many contexts, and I sympathise with some of them. But what else do such speeches say about the position granted their speakers? What literatures do such pronouncements seek to keep at arm's length?

Another speaker at the 1995 Melbourne Writers' Festival was Robert Hughes. He'd been invited by festival director Leo Schofield, who met him in New York. Schofield recalls asking Hughes over lunch what his speech was going to be about. 'The muses as equal opportunity employers,' Hughes replied.[70] Funny line, but it seemed a joke from an era of Latin educations, shared ideals and common prejudices — a closed, clerical world that somehow thinks itself universal. In a way that joke was a microcosm of the festival, and of the literary world at large.

Dissenting voices outside the cliques of mutual admiration tend to get short shrift. If 'being a writer' is more important than having something to say, then protecting literary reputation is more important than debating content. At the same festival, the journalist and novelist Fiona Capp gave an account of what she found wrong with *The First Stone* as journalism, a piece later published in *ABR*.[71] Soon afterwards, in a review of Garner's *True Stories*, Morag Fraser suggested that some unnamed 'journalists' who had criticised *The First Stone* were 'defending territorial as well as ethical imperatives'.[72] This seemed a gratuitous piece of border-patrolling. Too often what passes for debate in Australian literary culture is no more than an attempt to discredit motives and credentials.

Is there any hope for the Melbourne Writers' Festival, or for the other festivals that follow much the same format (complete with obligatory 'grunge' and 'ethnic' ghettos), or for the blinkered, gatekeeping literary culture associated with them? Fat chance if the organisers of the Melbourne Writers' Festival have their way. Around the time of the 1996 festival a flier arrived through the mail inviting me to become a member of 'Chapter One'. The front featured an illustration of William Shakespeare, with the accompanying text done in an Elizabethan script. The typeface used in the body of the flier was a Bible script. The leaflet offered members the chance to invest $95 in purchasing the right to participate in members-only surveys 'designed to ascertain what you, as the festival's most loyal supporters, would like to see at future festivals'.[73] The impression given was that the festival is not looking beyond the preferences of its existing subscribers.

Some sort of alternative was offered by the 1996 Sydney Writers' Festival. Among the guests was the poet Ko Un, who has sold an astounding 70 million books in his native Korea. In search of an audience, organisers promoted both the session and the festival heavily to Sydney's Korean community. The move was a resounding success, and Ko Un's sessions generated a cross-cultural dynamic that is rarely encountered at such events. Wanting to draw younger people to the festival, organisers programmed a number of sessions at 11.00 p.m. They were also a success. Hopefully there is a trend emerging here. While certain older writers and critics complain about the

The culture racket

ascendancy of 'sexy' young writers, the real picture here isn't one of young writers having taken over. In fact, such complaints tend to point to the continuing incumbency of those who make them. Their dominance of commentary about writing is itself an argument for the continued publication of young writers who sell to new audiences in large numbers. Hopefully, for the sake of all concerned, they might disrupt the stifling business of 'literature as usual', where the loudest noises are the barely audible squeaks of barrows being pushed and the quiet hiss of urine entering pockets.

7. Growing old gracefully: publishing the 'generation of '68'

My generation was brought up being promised so much. Advertising promised so much. The lucky country promised so much. We reached adulthood and found it wasn't there.

Richard King, 1995 *Australian*/Vogel literary award winner

Myth can mesmerise reason.

Brian Castro[1]

As long ago as 1978, in his prescient essay 'Growing Old Gracefully: The Generation of '68', the poet John Tranter wrote about the continuing importance of this generation to Australian culture. Little has changed. Tranter was talking about writing, and this chapter will again deal with writing as a form of cultural production, taking a slightly different tack from chapter 6. But many younger people who have worked (or not worked) across a range of industries will recognise the syndromes I'm going to talk about here. As companies have shrunk, so a given generation has tightened its hold on the upper echelon of jobs. Ironically, the economic good times came and went with the generation that was supposed to have turned on, tuned in and dropped out from capitalism. The corporate 'downsizings' and public service 'rationalisations' of the late 1980s and 1990s have left a whole generation in limbo,

Growing old gracefully

stalled near the bottom of the career ladder, if they have jobs at all.

What follows is about the publishing industry, not only because it's an industry I know, having spent more than a decade working there as a book designer, but because it's a typical sort of industry in the present economic and management climate — an era when electronic data processing, Total Quality Management and Just in Time delivery routines have been overlaid on older corporate structures. In some respects, this is a double-edged chapter. The work practices and job prospects in publishing are similar to those in many other industries, but publishing has a particular importance because it plays a part in the culture industry, and because of its relationship with cultural elites. What I want to talk about, then, is the relationship between economic rationalism, the opportunities available for younger people, and the types of cultures that are currently being produced.

Barrie Kosky, in his famous 1996 speech, described theatre as priding itself on a kind of fake authenticity, manufactured and exploited by self-styled arts gurus. Publishing is little different. Like the arts industry as a whole, it's run mainly by self-styled gurus, and has enjoyed a remarkable ascendancy since the Whitlam era. It's also an industry that in some ways has radically changed. The mantle of soulfulness, which publishing was happier to wear than most industries, has slipped, pushed aside by 1990s managerialism.

It's now the market (and often the marketing manager) that leads. The integrity and quality of the product are declining, not in appearance — books have never looked better — but in standards of writing and editing, which are often conspicuously poor. The rise of the arts guru and the economic rationalisation of the theatre and festival industry, according to Kosky, have resulted in rank populism, diminishing the theatre as a forum for ideas. Publishers have lately shown a similar compulsion to produce spectacle and 'events'.

Gangland

Underpinning the culture of the spectacle is a Hollywood-style star system, a culture of nameism. As publishing has become big business, this culture has become entrenched as a byword for success. Despite the rumour going around Australian publishing at the moment that publishers are crawling over each other to sign up new names, this hasn't been my own experience. When I first sat down to discuss my idea for this book with a literary agent, a major concern was that I had no 'name'. There was little thought about the possibility of establishing a name, or even about the techniques that might be used to do such a thing. Nor, strangely, was it conceivable that my lack of a 'name' might be in keeping with the general themes of a book such as this. Now, the agent in question is a pragmatist, who, like most agents, makes not a cent on the basis of idealistic principle. But this culture of nameism proved a problem at every stage.

Once I had another agent, the book had to run the gauntlet of publishers, with similar concerns. I heard a story about a marketing manager in one company who never says a word in meetings on new projects, but nevertheless has the final word. He simply puts a thumb up in the air, or down, depending on the marketability of the idea or persona involved. Given the present emphasis on marketing 'front-list' titles (as opposed to 'backlist' reprints of previously published titles, which were once the backbone of publishers' marketing strategies), the question most frequently asked about new authors isn't whether or not they are capable of producing a decent work, but whether they're promotable — the assumption being that existing 'name' authors are. Publishing Australian writers is hard enough in a small market, so the conventional wisdom goes, let alone trying to break new writers, unless they are exceptionally photogenic. Younger writers tend to be signed up because they have accrued some sort of 'vibe' (i.e. they have a canny agent), or because they can be hitched to fashionable bandwagons that have their own logic of spectacle.

Growing old gracefully

With a few very honourable exceptions, local publishers aren't very original. The big sport in Australian publishing isn't hunting down new writers — though an occasional chase is fun — but poaching existing big names for their next book. The publishers nurture a tight little club of those who know each other, who lunch, who have a certain recognition factor when they go out in public or on TV. Those who, most importantly, are regarded as having the veins through which the *real* cultural blood of the nation flows.

Finally, publishers generally are averse to risk. Some of the publishers who showed an interest in my book were lobbied by real 'names' who had got a whiff of what might be in it. At every step during the preparation of the manuscript, I was reminded of the danger of offending these 'names', as if criticism were tantamount to contempt, and as if there might be no possible alternative version of local culture to the one they sponsor. Some publishers actually seemed to be *afraid*. Such 'names' are important, of course, because signing up any one of them brings prestige to a publisher's imprint, and they have a propensity to hunt in packs. The culture of nameism can have a strangling effect, especially when 'name writers' are intervening on the same side in various public controversies, as they have been in recent years. In each case there have been whispers about publishers' rejecting countervailing books for fear of alienating certain of the big industry 'names'.

The growing practice of offering large advances to 'name' writers also causes problems. Ten new young authors could have been signed up on respectable advances for the amount one old-guard celebrity was said to have been offered recently, for a book everyone knows has little chance of recouping the investment made in it. Another publishing house proposed spending a good proportion of its annual budget to poach a 'name' as a prestigious figurehead for their various imprints. Nameism works in the mass market as well. In May 1997 Penguin Books signed up Bryce Courtenay for a two-book deal, rumoured to be worth $2 million, 'largely contingent on the implementation of a dynamic marketing and distribution plan' that would put books on supermarket shelves.[2]

Nameism, in its recent incarnations, is interesting because it straddles two cultures. On the one hand it reflects a new marketing-led interest in quick-fix methods of adding value to an imprint. On the other hand, the names mentioned inevitably date from the 1970s, the golden era in Australian publishing when the present crop of senior publishing execs cut their teeth. In the 1970s cheap offshore colour printing and typesetting became readily available for the first time, mostly in Hong Kong, launching an avalanche of pictorial books into the local marketplace. Riding on a wave of nationalism — the anniversary of Captain Cook's first landing had been celebrated in 1970 — illustrated Australiana became the biggest single category on many publishers' lists. (It's all but dead now.) The Whitlam Labor government revamped arts funding, several new local publishing ventures started up, and publishers began showing a new enthusiasm for seeking out local writers.

Though publishing has adopted modern-day marketeering, it also aspires to the highbrow. The value of the names publishers seek to promote comes almost entirely from their status as producers of 'literature'. Despite its new marketing edge, publishing remains a business fraught with highbrow prejudices. Yet publishers, and many of the names themselves, lately seem intent on a kind of populism. The tensions between highbrow and lowbrow that drive many recent cultural controversies are at work in publishing too. They mirror the way the industry is structured and influence what is being published.

But if this seems in line with the general blurring of divisions between high and low cultures, it doesn't mean that publishers have wholeheartedly embraced popular culture. They want to sell books and be relevant to 'middle Australia', and are fiercely populist in what they think is publishable, but, like

Growing old gracefully

the cultural elite, they secretly claim superior knowledge. This is particularly the case when it comes to putting complex ideas, or even complex designs, before their audiences. 'They won't understand that' is the chorus at every second production meeting, from a crowd of publishers, editors and designers, all of whom have immediately understood the proposal at hand, and who are probably a lot more like the average reader than they imagine. The received wisdom in many publishing companies seems to be that those who enter the building possess moral and intellectual insights denied their audiences.

Like populist politicians, publishers are prepared to offer 'what people want', but actually operate from up on high. One of the results is a dumbing-down of publishing. Books are being emptied of their content — of long words and difficult concepts — in the name of easy marketing and instant audience appeal. It's fun and fascinating to have close 'insider' ties to the book trade (though I probably won't for much longer). You not only get to hear about what has been published, but what *hasn't* been published, which, as it turns out, is far more interesting. Let's get the obvious 'unpublishables' out of the way. Anything with big words. Anything about cultural theory or recent 'isms' (old, familiar and safely neutered 'isms' are OK). Anything with a little depth of analysis that the publishing companies fear will tax the reader unduly. Beset by a new populist mood, worried by the proliferation of new visual media, publishers seem to be increasingly afraid of words.

The trouble is that, with its rush to bottom-line publishing, the industry has arguably sacrificed one of its traditional strengths. Ideas are perhaps the one unique thing publishing has to sell. To canvass an issue, or furnish a set of instructions and a philosophy about anything from cooking to interior design, or play out a series of fictional events in detail and at length, are things TV, newspapers, magazines or even the movies simply can't do. But publishing now strives to be as much like TV, newspapers, magazines and the movies as possible — again, false populism. The loudest sound in publishing first thing on a Monday morning isn't that of desks being cleared for the coming week's innovative and original thinking. It's the sound of pages turning on a thousand copies of *Who Weekly*.

The rise of managerialism alongside crude attempts at populism that don't really understand the popular is a feature of many industries and marketing pitches. The creativity and discrimination that were once routinely brought to bear on developing the inside of the book are now being brought to bear on the author publicity tour. The new science in publishing now is maximising 'facings', that is, the titles displayed face-out in the shops. Increasingly, books are beautiful objects that are designed not so much to be read as to nourish the dream of reading for consumers who would like to read, but who are short on time. Cover design budgets have increased as editorial budgets have been reduced, and the design process is now so fraught with publisher anxiety as to become a complete pain in the arse for the designer (but that's another story). Facings, author tours and, ahem, design all have an important place, but the irony of the embrace of marketeering is that the Unique Selling Proposition of books, the qualities that drive publishing as an industry and underpin its very viability as a business, are 'intangibles' that don't show up in ready-to-wear graduate-school-of-management marketing plans. The value of books and imprints — cultural and monetary, highbrow and low — resides in the fact that books are an iconographic cultural item to which people attach a unique value. But some larger publishers seem to be losing interest in protecting the 'added value' of their imprints, their writers, and their products as a set of ideas. Short-changing readers with over-hyped books that leave them feeling duped is not a long-term recipe for success, either for writer or publisher. Already the market is showing signs of saturation.

Ironically, some publishing companies have recognised the blurring that has taken place between high culture and low, and have done well out of it, using much the same practices that established publishing as a popular medium in the first place. Former *Scripsi* editor Michael Heyward has been conspicuously successful as a publisher at Text. While not notable for signing up many under-35s, Heyward has published a string of books that others would reject as 'too hard' — and, at a time when publishers at some of the multinationals barely read the books they commission, Heyward edits them himself. The Text imprint *stands* for something at a time when many other imprints seem to be being milked of any sense of intrinsic value. Heyward also defied the colonial ethic that dominates publishing to pull off the 'impossible', selling overseas rights for a first-time author — Linda Jaivin — for a six-figure sum. Most larger publishing companies tend to be buyers from overseas markets rather than sellers to them. Another independent that has ignored the traditional high culture–low culture divide to good effect is Hyland House. Against the industry orthodoxy that 'poetry doesn't sell', they made a best-seller out of Dorothy Porter's *The Monkey's Mask*.

One problem is that in large bureaucratic companies where the person who initiated the project tends to lose touch with it once the contract is signed, publishing tends to become a rule-bound process. To map this back on to the general themes of this book for a moment, this is an era when knowledges have professionalised. Much of the reaction of the 1970s cultural elite against sexual harassment legislation, 'Asianists' and so on seems a reaction against professionalisation by a culture where (informed) amateurism was the norm. In the publishing industry, this professionalisation hasn't been well executed. Instead, largely untrained though often highly experienced staff have been expected to behave as if they have professional knowledge, often without any serious market research. The result is that self-fulfilling orthodoxies develop about what the market will and won't tolerate, and publishers tend to concentrate on what they 'know' will work. In such circumstances it's difficult to explore new forms and carve out new readerships and markets.

Historically, in Australia the larger publishing companies' standard response to this problem has been to buy up energetic smaller imprints, fillet their lists and, after a suitably polite delay, ditch the local imprint. This too tends to reduce cultural diversity. Only the bravest independents can resist this process; publishing local writing in a relatively small market is hardly the most profitable exercise at the best of times, and even the liveliest independent publishers are vulnerable to any economic downturn or management hiccup.

During the 1960s and 1970s, and even into the 1980s, the trend went the other way. There were remarkable success stories that bucked the colonialist trend, as when Geoffrey Dutton, Max Harris and Brian Stonier bailed out of Penguin and set up Sun Books. Or when John Currey joined Lloyd O'Neil to form Currey O'Neil. Or when Sally Milner set up Greenhouse. Or when Hilary McPhee and Di Gribble set up McPhee Gribble. Or when a management buy-out established Allen & Unwin as the largest of the local independents. But globalisation has swung the pendulum back again. Sun Books was absorbed by Pan Macmillan. Currey O'Neil, Greenhouse and McPhee Gribble were absorbed by Penguin. The largest of the local imprints, Angus & Robertson, is now owned by Rupert Murdoch's HarperCollins. All of these companies have some great staff and a strong commitment to local writing, but are tied to head offices elsewhere. Text Publishing was taken under the umbrella of the multinational Reed Books trade division (itself since broken up and largely absorbed by Random House), but later bucked the trend and regained its independence.

★

If publishing for the most part remains secretly wedded to an old-fashioned low culture–high culture split, this stratification is reflected in its structure. Similar splits occur at other levels. Publishing is an overwhelmingly white, middle-class business. Almost every single board member of a local publishing company is Anglo, and the same is true of the middle echelons. A mere handful of production staff are of non-Anglo backgrounds. The pattern only starts to change in the warehouse. There are relatively few Greeks, Italians or Asians, and I've never met an Aboriginal person working in mainstream publishing — in sharp contrast with other branches of the culture industry.

One reason for the whiteness of publishing is the industry's colonial background. The industry remains basically overseas-owned, through lately the local companies have acted less as outposts of empire than as nodes in globalised cartels. The educational publishers Rigby Heinemann, Oxford University Press, Cambridge University Press and Macmillan are all British-owned, Thomas Nelson is Canadian-owned, Longman is US-owned, and HarperCollins is owned by Murdoch. Local imprints such as Cheshire, Dove and Rigby have been absorbed along the way. HarperCollins is also a large trade publisher, along with Penguin and Hodder Headline, both UK-owned, Pan Macmillan and Transworld, both German-owned, and the US-based Random House. Between them they dominate the market. Colonialised or globalised, the effect is more or less the same. Australian branches of some overseas publishers are expected to repatriate funds 'home' on request. One large imprint even sources all its ISBNs from 'home' — even those for local titles — ignoring the local service. Most local branches have to put up with staffing levels and budgets, as well as ownership, being decided overseas. (Anyone who has worked in the local branch of an overseas company will be familiar with the annual ritual: when the big-wig from head office turns up, the normally authoritative MD goes to water and meekly shows him around the building, company figures tucked under arm. As an aside, in one company where the big-wig was a British peer, the staff were expected to stand whenever he entered the room.)

There is a similar split at the level of gender. Most Australian publishers are notoriously places where the majority of staff are women, but a gang of men (the 'suits') hold all the top jobs and the overwhelming majority of boardroom seats, their appointments often being either made or vetted from overseas. The big generational and gender schism in publishing is between upper management and those who actually publish, promote and sell the books. When it comes to finding the contemporary market, the suits' approach is usually to draft editors or publishers who happen to be young, and plug them into the existing corporate culture. There is little understanding that to capture new markets publishing culture itself needs to change, and to participate fully in the changes in the wider culture.

Recently there has been a lot of hype about the new generation of young women publishers — the so called 'black pack' — as if that shift was finally taking place. 'Young Women Now Have the Last Word' announced a headline on the young female publishers 'taking over the Australian book industry'.[3] Nice idea. But many of these women feel frustrated. Far from having taken over, what they want to talk about, off the record, is the suits. With some notable exceptions, local publishers maintain hierarchical, 'top-down' systems of management, based on the old British model. Most of the men at the top in publishing are highly experienced and widely liked and respected — generally more so than in many other industries. But they nevertheless control the purse-strings, and are good at making sure *they* still have the last word. Thirty-something female executives, especially those working in the media industries, tend to function as the companies' attractive 'public face' without being granted a full measure of power and responsibility. Often these women are doubly scrutinised and must doubly prove themselves. Although they are sometimes wooed as a source of new ideas and inspiration, they're seldom given an opportunity to change the corporate culture, but are tested to see how they adapt to it.

Because of the high proportion of female staff (except in warehousing and distribution), in some respects publishing is ahead of other industries on gender issues. But the industry is in some trouble when it comes to younger women. 'I've got to get out of publishing' are the words on many lips (young and old). And many have. Young editors are leaving the industry in worrying numbers. Many of them went into publishing in the first place because the abysmally low salaries were offset by 'intangibles' such as the pleasures of working in an industry that had a certain amount of integrity. Now the charms have largely gone. Many former editors and soon-to-be-former editors express more or less the same sentiment, which is that if publishing is going to become an 'ordinary' industry, they might as well find an alternative career with a decent salary while they're still young. Yet the relevance and therefore the future of publishing is largely in their hands. According to Laurie Muller, director of University of Queensland Press:

> The unknown writer has to be championed by the young editor. She has to argue for the writer firstly among peers and colleagues. It's the editor who actually gets books over the line. She has to have the confidence within an organisation that has some tradition, feel she can also be a tradition maker . . . It comes down to appointing some very young editors. If we want to be part of cultural change, of cultural renewal, it has to come from younger viewpoints.[4]

Many industries have a similar cross-generational stratification. And many have a stratum of young disenchanted staff. The risk is that a generation of energy and ideas, and especially the sort of 'breaking the mould' ideas that most industries need to outgrow hidebound orthodoxies, is being lost. One young local designer, tired of pitching book ideas to local publishers and having them rejected, got on a plane to the US, and returned with contracts for several projects, including one with a six-figure advance. The question he was asked over and over again was 'Why don't they want these great ideas at home?'

Training in publishing, more so than in most other industries, used to operate on an informal mentor system. But the industry has grown too big, job turnover is too high, and there are too many new people to train. Apart from a handful of postgraduate diploma courses with limited enrolments, nothing has evolved to take the place of the mentor system. By contrast, in the American system, editors do the commissioning and act as mentors to younger editors, who learn all aspects of the production process. Alarmingly, even some of the new breed of female middle managers in Australia seem reluctant to pass skills on or divest power down the line. Virginia Trioli has described the syndrome where older women get into positions of power then 'kick out the ladder'.[5] In publishing too, young editors often complain that they have learnt little more than how to edit basic copy and book the boss's plane tickets.

★

One of the difficulties of adopting economic rationalist-inspired production and marketing regimes in publishing is that books don't lend themselves to standardisation. Every project is different, with its own lead-times, development costs and scheduling requirements, and most involve close one-to-one work between writer and editor. The development time of books is often longer than their shelf life, but is extremely difficult to estimate accurately. Yet publishing has attempted to adopt market-led, just-in-time delivery practices. No longer do publishers expect to make their profits from their backlist with second printings of books that have already returned their initial fixed-cost investments in editing, design and layout. The front-list of readily promotable hopefully big sellers is all-important. In part this is a response to a less intelligent bookshop culture, but it is also because most publishing companies are no longer privately owned, but globally owned. Stockholders expect predictable results.

Marketing departments have grown in size and importance in order to try and deliver such results. The global cartels also tend to set budgets that necessitate quick and sizeable profits, further engendering a 'blockbuster' culture in which risks are minimised by linking books to existing names, fads, topical events and other media such as TV and movies. More books are being published, and limited editing resources spread over more titles. The importance of meeting sales schedules means that books increasingly tend to be edited to a given time-frame and a limited budget, rather than to the requirements of a given job. Editing tends to be under-resourced because, in the lexicon of economic newspeak, editorial departments aren't deemed to be 'profit centres'. As such, they're early targets for 'downsizing' in corporate efficiency drives. As a result, like many other industries, the Australian publishing industry is losing skills, and costs usually rise as a result, not least because more mistakes are made. Editorial budgets and time-frames are now such that few books get the attention they need. Leaving aside the spelling and grammatical errors that so often attract comment from the more pedantic reviewers, it is commonplace to read second-rate books, by both new and older writers, that with a little work could have been great books (though older writers tend to be insulated from such editorial neglect because of their greater clout). Often the marketing department does double duty here, being expected to take up the slack for underdone books.

The adoption of economic rationalist strategies in publishing has not, in fact, been rational. It has been piecemeal, and has ignored publishing's traditional centres of value. Nor has it addressed publishing's traditional weaknesses in training and research. Economic rationalism tends to focus on the visible, the superficial and the easily marketable, which are not publishing's main profit centre. Smaller companies outside this circuit have a different problem: distribution. My first job in publishing, twenty years ago, was in a small independent distribution company set up to try and solve this problem. It's still a problem now. But there is a bright future given the role independent companies continue to play in bringing the most innovative books to local audiences, staying one step ahead in understanding the implications of the melding of high and low cultures, and resisting the trend towards beautiful, content-free books.

As for the generation of '68, as I've perhaps unfairly caricatured them, the 'literati' still basks in that most anachronistic of all local publishing mythologies: that publishing mainly means novels. Non-fiction books comprise the vast majority of all trade books published, but, to the chagrin of most publishers, they don't rate much of a mention in the books pages, nor in the minds of the funding bodies, nor even in the activities of some formal industry organisations. The literati don't seem to have noticed that the new stars of publishing aren't novelists but cookbook writers. It is they who are being fêted at all-star launches attended by the cream of 'high society'. And cookbooks are constantly at the top of the best-seller lists. Given publishers' propensity to lash out on the occasional big lunch, even in these straitened times, and the literati's tendency not to recoup the investments made in them, maybe it's just a case of cutting out the middleman.

8. An illiberal education: liberals versus the 'postmodern'

Neither artists nor journalists can hold themselves out as universal experts on public issues in the way that was common twenty years ago and still provide regular amusement in the opinion columns.

McKenzie Wark[1]

2 girls on a dead man's chest
Doing what they like to do best
Pecking at a dead alphabet

Kathy Acker

Somewhere out the back there must be a big scrapheap. That's where all the 'dead white males' are. It's where all the lovers of literature are too. And the authors. Even the Bard himself, complete with nasty gunshot wound. History is out there — stone cold dead, its fans left with nothing to do but pick over a carcass. Memory, we're told, has literally been assassinated, so it must be out there too. Science is there, corpse distorted beyond recognition. In this palace of dead icons, truth and beauty have pride of place, alongside the old-fashioned humanities, and any possibility of normal relations between men and women.

Or so they say, that bevy of prominent social commentators, writers, reviewers and critics who make it their business to

Gangland

pass on messages from beyond this grave. Oddly, and here is a twist, they've also been busily consigning themselves to it, howling with anguish about what they've identified as the scandals of the day — the hijacking of literature by 'deconstructionism'; the mixed receptions of David Williamson's play *Dead White Males* and Helen Garner's book *The First Stone*; the strange triumphs of Helen Darville-Demidenko; and the publication of a myth-busting book on Patrick White.

And who's behind all this?

Like a class of dutiful primary-school children, we're all supposed to know by now: the 'big, bad wolf' — of cultural studies practitioners, poststructuralists, feminists and postmodernists.

These are the people who killed the author and reduced truth and meaning to a crude 'textual relativism', who replaced literary appreciation with deconstruction, English Literature with Cultural Studies and Shakespeare with Mickey Mouse. Along the way, they planted the seeds of amoral postmodernism in Helen Darville's head and mistook the Holocaust for mere text. They corrupted feminism, brainwashed the Ormond complainants, tried to say there was no reality, and ushered in the end of Western civilisation.

They also started a war. Keith Windschuttle thinks history is under 'mortal attack' from literary and social theorists who have made a 'general frontal assault' on traditional history and 'entrenched themselves behind the lines' of the debate.[2] Mark Allinson, writing in *Quadrant*, thinks the 'universities of the Western world are in the process of being commandeered'.[3] Luke Slattery, writing about the rise of critical theory in universities, talks of 'the battlefields on which these intellectual disputes are being fought'.[4] According to David Williamson, critics were 'passionately divided' in their reactions to *Dead White Males* because of the battle going on between the 'liberal humanist view' and the 'cultural determinist view'.[5] Literary editor and columnist Barry Oakley thinks 'the Marxists, the

An illiberal education

feminists, the blacks, the gays, the one-text-is-as-good-as-another deconstructionists have all declared war' on the traditions of literary excellence.[6] Don Anderson, paraphrasing Hermann Göring, says 'When I hear anyone talk of Cultural Studies, I reach for my revolver.'[7] And Helen Garner says of the relationship between young academic feminists and older feminists: 'It's not a dialogue . . . It's a fucking *war*.'[8]

I don't know any of these people — maybe I've been in my own little trench too long? Sure, I've met a few of them in passing. I brushed past Don Anderson once at a launch, and was introduced to Keith Windschuttle at a party. I spoke to Luke Slattery once at another party. All very pleasant it was too, as far as it went. But I think I've been missing something. Evidently I've never been there when the shots were ringing out. So, having failed to move in the right circles, and failed to hear the right first-person accounts of this war, would it be unfair of me to call these hawkish cultural apparatchiks blind?

One of the amazing things about these critics' attitude to that strange and bewildering thing, postmodernism, is that they seem to think it's to do with university arts faculties. Having attempted to shoot the messenger, they miss the message when it comes to thinking about the complex, even postmodern, contingencies of present life. For them there is no genetic science, working from mere code to reproduce life-forms that lack originals. There are no smart cards or global money markets, raising economic exchanges to a further power of intertextual, conventionalised abstraction. There is no *Simpsons*, no *Pulp Fiction* or Kathy Acker, all reliant on intertextual pastiche for meaning. They evidently don't listen to the cut-up, sampled sounds of rap, hip-hop or house, or else don't think them relevant. The out-takes at the end of Jackie Chan movies and episodes of *Roseanne*, impossible in the era of *Leave it to Beaver*, apparently have no cultural significance. Nor the vast, unhierarchically labyrinthine hypertextuality of the Internet. Nor the tag-line that bills *Frontline* as 'The story behind the story . . .

behind the stories', setting it up as classic 'hall of mirrors' postmodernism. Eurocentric culture, for them, isn't suffering an identity crisis as a result of deep social shifts and the failure of the traditional 'metanarratives' of church, family and state. Nor is it worth trying to find a language for the sheer difficulty of narrativising relentless global flows of information, and the way they tend to undermine the authority of overarching knowledge systems. None of these things, apparently, is evidence of the sort of cultural shifts that academic theorists loosely bracket under the heading 'postmodernity'.

Missed conversations, it seems, are typical of local cultural life. In a climate of excessive coterie familiarity, some things get discussed too much and others not at all. Some stories are endlessly retold, while others are ignored. What is lore among a certain set remains irrelevant to others.

Missed conversations of another kind are endemic as well. Robert Manne, in writing *The Culture of Forgetting*, his book about the Darville-Demidenko affair, never met Helen Darville, though he tried, as he admits in his preface. Helen Garner, famously, never met the two women she writes of as being at the centre of the Ormond case in *The First Stone*. So, having missed a few meetings myself, having not talked to these people, and not even having tried, perhaps I write in a tradition. But I'm not trying to find out anything about my quarry's personal lives. I quote them from their public lives, as public figures, in so far as the broad spectrum of their remarks makes a pattern. For me, this is enough — everything I have to say here takes place in a public arena of ideas and debate, not the private arenas of motivations, home truths, personalities and speculation about private mores.

Manne's and Garner's books are attempts to get into the private lives of young people, to find out what makes them tick. 'Are they postmodern?' is the question that they both seek to ask, in differently inflected ways. The bodies of Darville and the two Ormond complainants are like laboratory

An illiberal education

specimens; through the proper rituals of dissection, Manne and Garner hope to find out something about the age — to stumble, perhaps, on an essence of postmodernity, manifested as a breakdown of manners or ethics. But what they seek to find out about postmodernism is coloured by their own prejudices about what postmodernism is; it is limited by their own refusals of knowledge, their own blindnesses.

In one important sense it is difficult to take issue with *The Culture of Forgetting*. Like Manne, I found *The Hand that Signed the Paper* anti-Semitic and was worried by Darville's rhetoric in the media. But Manne wants to set himself up as a cultural arbiter on the basis that those who disagree with him have missed a signal truth about the book, whereas I don't think that sort of judgement is mine to make. So far as *The Culture of Forgetting* goes, there are plenty of faults in Manne's detail. Everything proceeds through amateur psychology ('By this transformation she returned, psychologically, to her earlier high school fascination with Ukrainian war criminals'[9]) and through the lens of Manne's own dismissive cynicism about left politics ('she was an environmentalist, a multiculturalist, an anti-racist and an anti-homophobe . . . She had fashioned for herself the necessary disadvantages'[10]). I might agree with Manne that *The Hand that Signed the Paper* is anti-Semitic, but it's hard not to notice that anti-Semitism is the only 'ism' Manne takes seriously. And, like the Miles Franklin Award judges who praised the book as a first-person account, Manne chronically confuses the book's narrators with Darville, collapsing them together. He must, otherwise there would be much less to say about what makes Darville tick.

Bigger problems arise when Manne tries to extrapolate his theme to the corpus of Australian society as evidence of a 'culture of forgetting'. Two words haunt this amplification: 'postmodernism' and 'youth'. Darville, we are constantly told, not only lacked the necessary *parental guidance*, but was guided by academics who, like wicked step-parents, practise that most dubious of disciplines, 'postmodernism'. As Manne puts it, 'it was Helen Demidenko rather than *The Hand that Signed the Paper* which was a creation of the post-modern imagination'[11] and 'through this book the fingerprints of a contemporary university education are everywhere to be found'.[12] The youth theme is hammered throughout: according to Manne, it is 'the combination of the moral vision of Australian youth culture *circa* 1990 and the political vision of Ukrainian fascism *circa* 1940 which gives this novel a highly peculiar feel'.[13]

Darville, by the end of Manne's book, ends up thoroughly infantilised, like the Ormond women by the end of Garner's. She is living proof that young people don't know anything about justice, meaning, history or truth, and need 'proper' parental directives, not the sort they have received from 'postmodern' teachers. They are frivolous. They too lightly invoke the Holocaust, or too lightly question a prominent man's right to his job. There is no question of their being able to think for themselves.

Manne doesn't seem to know much about youth or postmodernism. If he did he wouldn't suggest that either has anything to do with an absence of truth. But why use the words 'postmodern' or 'youth' at all? They function not as useful definitions that move his argument forward, but as markers designed to delineate the perceived difference between his world and another, alien, worrying world. Manne puts both young people and postmodernism on the outer, perhaps as a way of avoiding a more difficult question: 'Am I postmodern?' As the US theorist Judith Butler forecast, fears about postmodernism are all too often 'articulated in the form of a fearful conditional, or sometimes in the form of a paternalistic disdain toward that which is youthful and irrational'.[14]

There are strong similarities between Manne's and Garner's books, just as there is an oft-noted similarity between Garner's book and Janet Malcolm's *The Silent Woman*. All are searches, even quests: Malcolm criss-crosses England by hire-car; Manne

An illiberal education

jets about the country interviewing Darville's associates; Garner bicycles around inner Melbourne. All are stories about missed meetings. Malcolm, in *The Silent Woman*, never gets to meet her quarry, Ted Hughes, just as Garner never interviews the Ormond women, and Manne never meets Darville. All three fantasise obsessively about their missing objects, and all three books are structured around the absence of that vital interview.

All three also struggle with the conventions of what constitutes fiction and non-fiction, with varying degrees of success. The rules of biography are Malcolm's subject: she explicitly poses questions about the relationship between ethics and convention, biographer and biographee. In *The First Stone*, Garner clearly doesn't accept my view that, in dealing with the day-to-day lives of real people in a book that is undoubtedly non-fiction (no-one speaks of *The First Stone* as fiction except to defend its lapses), empirical validation is required; speculation and hearsay are not enough. Manne, on the other hand, apparently doesn't understand that there is no requirement for a strict empirical relationship between the narrator of a fictional work and its author. Or that, even where there is a close fit between a work of fiction and historical events, fiction writers don't suffer a historian's obligation to empirical facts, even if this doesn't absolve them from the obligation to act responsibly.

★

The Holocaust and feminism are very big stories. Along with 'literary studies', they are foremost among the things that the aforementioned postmodern literary critics, deconstructionists, destabilisers and cultural studies practitioners have supposedly twisted, hijacked, subverted and lied about. What makes these books by Manne and Garner emblematic is that they epitomise contemporary anxieties about the breakdown of morals, writ large in a postmodern, lit-theory, generational frame. Once again we're in the realm of the big bad wolf.

Gangland

Christopher Koch's acceptance speech for the 1996 Miles Franklin Award made the newspaper front page when he claimed that young writers were in danger of being tainted by 'the plague called deconstructionalism'.[15] Koch's assumption was that 'postmodernism' and 'theory' are the natural enemies of writing and young writers. Again his speech raised the question of whether well-known cultural figures of a certain age know what they're talking about when they discuss postmodernism. Many creative writers inflect their work with recent feminist, postcolonial, poststructuralist or postmodern ideas. One might cite Walter Abish, Julian Barnes, Jorge Luis Borges, Italo Calvino, Marion Campbell, Angela Carter, Brian Castro, Gabriel Garcia Marquez, Hanif Kureishi, Amanda Lohrey, Gerald Murnane, Georges Perec, Thomas Pynchon, Salman Rushdie, D. M. Thomas and Jeanette Winterson. Or the young Australian author Bernard Cohen, who once said 'It was such a liberation for me to read about the death of the author and to think of authorship as a social construct. Authors weren't people who hung around with muses or something.'[16]

Koch's speech constituted a *de facto* defence of the 1950s New Critical aesthetic that dominates local writing, but offered no useful definition of 'deconstructionalism'. But you can hardly blame Koch. Disinformation about 'theory' is rife among the intelligentsia. Public commentary about 'postmodernism' or literary theory is often based on superstition and hearsay rather than any knowledge of the field.

The major charge levelled at theorists is that of cultural relativism. Keith Windschuttle, for example, has said theorists 'believe that truth is also a relative rather than an absolute concept',[17] the idea being that literary theory tends to undermine the idea of intrinsic value and foster nihilism. Yet none of the 'big three' French theorists is a relativist — quite the opposite. Jacques Lacan is dedicated to the idea that language has a biological basis. Most of Michel Foucault's work is devoted to understanding what makes truths seem unassailable.

Jacques Derrida famously argues that there can be no concept that doesn't defer to the idea of a higher truth, and no idea without an inbuilt sense of origin. What most theorists propose isn't relativism so much as a scheme for questioning the assumptions on which taken-for-granted values are predicated, on the basis that such values aren't easily negated. This is a far more sophisticated position than Windschuttle makes out.

But Windschuttle isn't alone. When theory is presented in a journalistic context, popular mythologies take over and subtleties tend to go out the window. In a deservedly controversial article, Luke Slattery wrote that 'for many deconstructionists there is no such thing as truth or falsehood, good writing or bad; or indeed, no reality outside of texts'.[18] No 'theorist' argues anything remotely so ridiculous. To argue that social convention makes truths true and falsehoods false isn't the same as saying there is no such thing as truth or falsehood, or that they are a matter of whim.

Slattery, like many who argue against theory as if this were a war between religions, seemed tangled up in his own binarist *non sequiturs*. The assumption is that what challenges received truth must be relativist, or that what asks questions about the real is therefore idealist. Most theorists aren't interested in taking up a position on one side or the other of such oppositions so much as working out how the oppositions themselves operate. Slattery received a welter of letters of refutation, but they didn't seem to interest him. Two years later he wrote: 'Many intellectuals believe, and teach, that there is no such thing as truth or knowledge.'[19] Again, quite the opposite is true. Even notorious 'theorists' like Derrida and Foucault think truths and knowledges are everywhere. My own postgraduate work, I should add, is partly as a (critical) Derrida scholar. There is a difference, though, between challenging what someone says and misrepresenting their position. Most people who write about Derrida are aware of his well-known assertion that 'the value of truth (and all those values associated with it) is never contested or destroyed in my writings'.[20]

I don't want to labour the point, but it's important to sort out truth from fiction here. If this is a major cultural 'battle' then it's much like other 'wars' when it comes to that old cliché about the first casualty. The issues at stake are central to understanding how the cosy world of the post-Whitlam cultural establishment has reacted to the cultural forces currently being brought to bear on it.

Misconceptions, exaggerations, errors of logic and plain bunk have persisted, more or less unchallenged, throughout discussions of 'theory' in the mainstream media. Among the cultural elite they are holy writ. To cite just a few examples:

- Robert Hughes thinks academics fetishise 'texts' at the expense of 'real life'. He says: 'the idea that you become one kind of person if you read one kind of book seems to me staggeringly naive'.[21] Quite true. It *would* be staggeringly naive. The position Hughes attributes to theorists is a position no-one today holds. Precisely the opposite is the case. 'Theory' is primarily interested in the way different people respond differently to the *same* texts. What theorists don't like about literary canons is that they tend to exist as apparatus for dignifying the elitism of their various promoters, which, I suspect, is precisely what Hughes' statement is designed to disguise.

   The irony is that the position Hughes describes was one held by the famous conservative critic of the 1940s, '50s and '60s, F.R. Leavis, whose style of criticism had much in common with Hughes'.
- Humphrey McQueen thinks that 'those cut off from the canon are left unaware that many of the bright ideas of their gurus had occurred to dead white males. Plato was aware of an arbitrariness in language.'[22] Not only was Plato aware of an arbitrariness in language, as McQueen coyly puts it, he

An illiberal education

argued specifically against it. His targets were poets afflicted by the muse — in other words, creative writers. *Ion*, one of the dialogues in question, is discussed at length in Derrida's *Of Grammatology* and his long essay *Pharmakon*. Contrary to McQueen's charge, critique of the canon (as many a tired postgrad will tell you) tends to involve more intimate contact with it than ever.

- Barry Oakley seems to think deconstructionists think 'one-text-is-as-good-as-another'.[23] Actually, they don't. To want to know, say, what the underlying assumptions of value are is quite different from saying all texts are the same.

- A major misconception is that theorists hate literature — 'Who wants to end up with a Literature major and hate literature?' asks Angela in *Dead White Males*.[24] The logic, I guess, is that if you do one thing, then you automatically can't do the other. Most theorists are voracious readers for pleasure, many are creative writers and many are prominent advocates for books and writing as reviewers, organisers of 'events' and editors of non-mainstream publications.

- Williamson writes that 'the predominant intellectual stance in vogue in much of our humanities and social sciences is a modern version of the behaviourism of Skinner', and is called 'cultural determinism or cultural relativism'.[25] Really? In my own years as a student in such departments I have never heard the word 'determinist' used except as a pejorative. The monkey-see, monkey-do theory of language couldn't be further from what most literary theorists think, which is that language is interactive — a two-way street. Strangely, later in the same essay Williamson argues that we select moral choices because we get certain rewards — now *that's* behaviourism. In his eagerness to oppose the 'essentialist' 'liberal humanist view' of human nature to the 'cultural determinist view', Williamson winds up sounding like a neo-Darwinian *biological* determinist.[26] He seems to suggest that gender is destiny ('nor can it be ignored that in our present society women still do more food preparation than men')[27] and not only is this a scientific fact (that's what they said about behaviourism), but morals are biologically determined too. Now *there's* a bleak view of humanity! The problem with predicating morality on biology is that it cuts both ways — apologists for racism, misogyny and homophobia (which, by the way, I assume Williamson is against as much as I) all argue in terms of biology. For all his faith that 'evidence emerging in neurophysiology and evolutionary biology' supports what he calls the 'liberal humanist view' of essential subject production, Williamson doesn't explain how scientific knowledge might be used in a plane that isn't itself social.

- Another popular anti-'theory' line is articulated by British classicist Peter Jones in an article reprinted in the *Australian Higher Education Supplement*, where he claims that Cultural Studies is presided over by 'twentieth-century French philosophers who argued that language could never reflect or describe external reality, only create it. Reality was therefore personal to the creator; that is, the speaker (and especially, for some reason, the writer). It could not be shared by anyone else.'[28] This sounds more like seventeenth-century Idealism to me. Most twentieth-century French theorists say *precisely the opposite* — that reality is always social and never personal. No major twentieth-century theorist denies the existence of the real.

- Another charge levelled against theorists is that they are involved in a sort of crypto-fascism, along the lines of 'you think everything is text; therefore you must think that the Holocaust is just text'. The assumption rests on an excessively narrow understanding of the word 'text', which many people take to mean 'fiction' or 'book', when it can be better understood as 'language'. The Holocaust was real. No-one seeks to excuse it or deny it. Poststructuralists don't seek to obviate the real, but say that whenever someone

An illiberal education

thinks or talks meaningfully about the Holocaust, or anything else, they do so using language, and that this opens up a range of rather difficult philosophical questions — as both theorists and traditional philosophers agree. This is an entirely different thing from saying the Holocaust doesn't exist.

- Attacks on literary theory often descend to the ludicrous. John Carroll, criticising Simon During's book on Patrick White, has defended the idea of literary canons by drawing comparisons with sport. He poses the question 'Do great works of art, music and literature — "classics" — exist?' then goes on to say:

  > It is difficult to credit that anyone could raise this question. It is equivalent to doubting objective standards which judge that Don Bradman was a greater batsman than anyone else who played cricket. Similarly, no sensible fan would deny that a football ladder records a hierarchy in which the teams at the top are simply better than those at the bottom.[29]

  Of course they wouldn't, but that's not how literary canons work. Sports scores are objective, canonical lists subjective. Sporting teams aren't awarded points for style or other intangibles. Nor do literary canons have commonly agreed rules about how goals are scored or runs tallied, much as their defenders like to pretend otherwise.

  Carroll had no mortgage on illogicality when it came to attacking During's book. According to Peter Craven, 'the mystery by which White . . . sometimes had to write badly in order to write well is one into which During has never been initiated'.[30] Opponents of critical theory would have a field day if its practitioners tried to pass off such drivel as logic.

- A further charge often levelled at theorists is that they tend to use technical language. Quite true. But theory is philosophy (whether traditional philosophers like it or not) and is generally less complex than the Hegel, Heidegger, Husserl or Nietzsche it's variously descended from, just as philosophers writing in a broadly humanist tradition such as Wittgenstein, Sartre, Descartes or Kant are rarely an easy read. Questioning everyday ideas involves defamiliarising them — something that's difficult to do in everyday language. When I first went to university I kept hearing this claim, mainly in the press, about the difficulty of the language. But what was so hard, I wondered, about learning a few new terms? This *was* tertiary education, after all. A more interesting question, given the complexity of the languages in which 'postmodernism' and 'theory' are sometimes discussed, is why so many so-called 'ordinary' people are interested in them now.

In its most extreme forms, the demonisation of theory produces a scenario that Meaghan Morris calls the 'invasion of the body snatchers' argument, in which academic theorists are portrayed as an inhuman, alien species, colonised by foreign knowledge.[31] 'What sort of people could these be?' Helen Garner asks of young feminists in *The First Stone*, raising the possibility that they aren't people at all. One has a hand that is 'narrow and hard', while another's hands are blue. Another is 'cold-faced'. Another barely eats. The photo of one is 'from a different planet'. Beware the 'permafrost of a feminist', Garner sternly warns, as if to suggest they had recently been tucked away in cryogenic capsules for their earthbound journey.[32] Kate Jennings, also not averse to a little hyperbole, talks of recent 'difference' feminisms as 'cults' presided over by long-winded 'guardians of the faith' who 'primp and preen', 'promising esoteric knowledge in exchange for blind obedience'.[33] I'd have to say my own tutors were far more professional. A cult? If only 'theory', from Althusser to Zizek, were so singular.

An illiberal education

★

If, as they say, there is a 'war' going on, then it's terribly one-sided, or else a war fought out in overripe imaginations. It's an irrational 'war', a war of fearful obsessions, phantoms, hidden fronts and imaginary terrors. A 'war', even, of self-inflicted wounds and ritual self-martyrdom. I say this because the other *faux*-rhetoric of this strange non-encounter is to do with death, obsolescence and replacement. If there's a scrapheap out the back somewhere, then the intelligentsia seem to be throwing themselves on it as hard and fast as they can, uttering a stream of apocalyptic hyperbole as they go.

Keith Windschuttle, somewhat poignantly lamenting the rise of Cultural Studies and 'theory', has said:

> In this environment, the prospects of a new, younger generation being attracted to empirical history dwindle all the time ... Unless all this changes dramatically, the retirement dinners given to the current generation of traditional historians, now mostly middle-aged and older, will represent the *funeral* of their discipline.[34]

The italics are mine, as are those that follow. Don Anderson, self-consciously claiming to 'belong to a traditional university English department', when asked the question 'What is Cultural Studies?' replies:

> It is what is *replacing* the study of 'literature' in universities. It is spreading across our sunburnt country like Paterson's Curse ... It is what your sons and daughters, your ex-wife, nay, you yourself are likely to be reading at University whereas, a decade ago, you would have read 'literature'.[35]

Note, once again, the assumption about the age of the readership. Another article by Anderson is full of self-identifying, self-indulgent references to 'dead art', 'dinosaurs', 'old men cast out from the zoo', and 'early voluntary retirement'. Lamenting his supposed membership of a 'class that has had its day', he summarises: 'I . . . have been *passed over*, and what has succeeded me?'[36] Barry Oakley thinks that 'with the advent of Cultural Studies in universities', the quest to 'know thyself... has been abandoned. Poetry has lost its primacy.'[37] Why one should be mutually exclusive of the other, Oakley doesn't say. Mark Allinson laments the loss 'of the symposium of wine, music and poetry'.[38] Helen Garner refers (yet again) to 'our scrapheap generation'.[39] At Sydney University, academic and reviewer Andrew Riemer responded to changes to the core English curriculum by declaring: 'I will continue to teach in the *ruins* of the English department.'[40] Phillip Adams is similarly nostalgic: 'Instead of being able to read a novel, one must now deconstruct a text.'[41] Who are the phantoms that issued such orders? Adams doesn't or can't say.

This is truly a community that fears being forgotten, that thought its particular truths were going to hang around forever, and is shocked that they haven't. These pundits seem to think they should be able to walk into an English department in any reputable university, twenty, thirty or even forty years after they received degrees, and find that their knowledge is still *the* knowledge, their paradigms *the* paradigms. Change is equated with decline: when *we* fade, truth fades; when *we* are gone, truth is gone.

Will we be the last generation that knows of the Holocaust? asks Tom Shapcott, echoing Primo Levi's famous line, to an approving Robert Manne, who quotes him in *The Culture of Forgetting*. Well, actually, no. As an instance of bureaucratically planned and systematically enacted genocide, the Holocaust stands alone. Holocaust studies are alive and well. Anti-antiSemitism remains a powerful discourse, as does anti-Nazism. One effect of a varied immigration intake, in my own experience, is that many non-Jews know someone whose family was directly affected by the Holocaust. To take a slightly sideways step in this line of argument, against Robert Manne's concern

An illiberal education

that younger people are caught up in a 'culture of forgetting', the youth turnout for Anzac Day in 1996 was the largest ever — and there was an outcry in 1997 when the RSL decided that the marches had become too long, and barred veterans from bringing their descendants with them in the procession.

Perhaps what this elite most needs to be saved from is their own logic of generationalism, with its relentless narrative of replacement. Most are still capable of producing great work, and there's nothing stopping them from doing precisely that. If they weren't so busy worrying about what theorists are doing, they'd all probably be at the peak of their careers. I like the fact that Williamson attempts plays of ideas and, perhaps unfashionably, I enjoy his works. But why oppose academic didacticism with a descent into, well, populist didacticism? Koch has interesting things to say about how to structure narrative, and the motivations and background of his writing. So, given the opportunity to talk about his craft, why not do so? Why waste time on an intemperate attack on supposed intemperance? Despite Les Murray's complaints about 'literary totalitarianism', no-one is stopping him writing poetry; on the contrary, he has never been more prominent as a poet.[42] Windschuttle has done some interesting work, notably in his 1979 book on unemployment. The remarkable thing about *The Killing of History* is that he can't find a single good thing to say about critical theory, not one. Why waste energy on what looks like an unproductive fixation? Nobody is stopping Windschuttle from writing traditional history. Despite his hyperbole about the 'funeral' of a discipline, even a casual look at any reputable academic publication list shows that solid empirical histories are still being published. Likewise, although Don Anderson thinks literature is on the way down the chute, a quick check of any bookshop reveals a vast storehouse of newly minted, conventional literary fiction.[43]

Is there more at stake, perhaps? The figures that make up this cultural elite have, after all, had a powerful influence on cultural agendas for a long time. Their hyperbolic language of 'war' often seems to be about little more than border-policing, moulding public perceptions, organising public space. At the centre of every narrativisation of this 'war' is a middle-aged white male figure whose previously taken-for-granted authority has been questioned. But if the intellectual world such figures grew up in, the world in which their cultural authority is grounded, seems set to disappear, this isn't primarily because of pressures from 'theory'.

Academic disciplines such as history and literature are declining in prestige for a number of reasons, including changes in secondary school curricula, a labour-market-led emphasis on vocational training, cuts to funding for non-vocational courses, a general decline in the prestige of Western knowledges and the erosion of the divide between high and low culture. Theory is itself driven by these social changes, and by the need to find languages and models to explain their complexities. Writers such as Manne, Windschuttle and Williamson, however, have made no attempt to address these wider pressures. Instead, they've looked for scapegoats.

The New Establishment's opposition to new academic knowledges has found a willing ally in the press. As Meaghan Morris points out, newspapers have been involved in their own competition with the academy for cultural authority.[44] The background to this is another shift. According to McKenzie Wark, where writers and artists gained cultural ascendancy through the Whitlam years, in the Hawke–Keating years it was the turn of the universities.[45] The broadsheets want to appeal to a middle-class, middle-aged audience who would like to think it's possible to walk into an institution with their arts degrees tucked under their arms and find them still relevant. One response to theory by the broadsheets has been to pander to precisely those things the academy is deemed to have neglected. For instance, the 1996 Boyer lectures by Pierre Ryckmans sparked a renewed burst of activity around the idea

An illiberal education

of the 'public intellectual'. Ryckmans was apparently supposed to deal a killer blow against 'theory' and for the idea of the 'public intellectual' although, as it happened, the lectures turned out to be boring and a non-event. Luke Slattery touted the lectures as a kind of second coming and a return to older-fashioned notions of public space.[46] But, much as the broadsheets like to think of themselves as being at the centre of such a space, is this really possible? As Simon During has pointed out, the media have their own agendas and constraints, including the requirement that they return a profit. In order to do so they can try for wide audiences and provide superficial coverage, or focus on narrower, niche audiences and provide more specialised information. Neither of these approaches is compatible with the traditional idea of the 'public sphere'.[47]

Robert Dessaix has also championed the idea of the 'public intellectual'. Dessaix, like Ryckmans, has blamed the academy for the decline of the idea, claiming that any artist who dared to speak publicly on an issue 'would soon be shouted down for failing to distinguish between the dead parrot of structuralism and the merely stuffed parrot of post-structuralism'.[48] Dessaix's tacit demand is that academics should take the traditional languages of public space seriously, or forfeit the right to occupy it. But, as Meaghan Morris has said:

> We hear much breast-beating these days about the difficulties academics have in the media, and a supposed decline of the 'public' intellectual in an age of specialisation . . . People who bemoan the good old days of the public intellectual (in historical practice, a leisured white gentleman) forget that a 'public' these days is no longer the same thing as a mass market, let alone a homogeneous milieu composed of bearers of a common culture. A 'general' public is a network, potentially infinite, of specialists — some academic, some not, some professional, some not, some forming larger social groups and some, constituencies of one.[49]

Newspapers have also tried to take over the process of canon-building, which is something else the academy is deemed to have neglected. It was almost too much of a coincidence when, at the height of the Darville-Demidenko crisis, Slattery kicked off such a campaign in the *Australian* with a feature entitled 'The Books that Made Us'.[50] A classic piece of canon maintenance, it made specific reference to *The Hand that Signed the Paper*, not disparagingly, but with enough force to hint that the book had raised concerns about national identity and what people were reading. The list of twelve 'books that have influenced us most' contained few surprises. Included were Manning Clark's *A History of Australia*, Garner's *Monkey Grip*, Patrick White's *Voss*, Henry Handel Richardson's *The Fortunes of Richard Mahony*, C. E. W. Bean's *Official History of Australia in the War of 1914–18*, Henry Lawson's *Joe Wilson and His Mates*, Robin Boyd's *The Australian Ugliness*, Miles Franklin's *My Brilliant Career*, Donald Horne's *The Lucky Country*, Germaine Greer's *The Female Eunuch*, Norman Lindsay's *The Magic Pudding* and George Johnston's *My Brother Jack*. A similar predictability was evident in the cast of 24 'keen readers' assembled to 'pass judgment' on the books: the vast majority were from the generation of '68, mainly big names at that. Evidently no-one under forty reads. Women were in the minority, and were asked to pass judgement only on books written by women. The panel was entirely drawn from within the ranks of industry professionals: publishers, authors, journal editors and old-guard academics.

A follow-up piece by Slattery the next day, engagingly entitled 'Canon Fodder', elaborated on these concerns.[51] It worried that children are more interested in films than books, and, worse, are allergic to being told what to read. What followed was a diatribe about teaching the 'right' books in schools to foster an appreciation of the national heritage. Curriculum advisers should make such books compulsory, according to Slattery, because otherwise they won't be read. It didn't seem

An illiberal education

to have occurred to him that this might be because books such as Lawson's short stories and Bean's mythologising war history could no longer be regarded as representative of Australian life — if indeed they ever were.[52] There's something rather puzzling about Australians' obsessive search for national myths. As the novelist Brian Castro has said:

> Maybe Australia's the odd country that expends more time and energy worrying about itself, about its cultural and racial composition, perhaps because it is constantly in the grip of its own fear and loathing . . . a tribalism resolutely mired in myth which iconizes a past which cannot be wholly remembered . . . instead of defining itself, and realising itself as a continually changing society, it has nostalgically yearned for stasis, drawing on a large number of myths which, while uniting segments of its population, retards its overall ability to absorb newness and deal adequately with others.[53]

Slattery's articles were followed two days later by a balancing piece from the historian Stuart Macintyre, 'Teaching books that matter'. While the title underscored the primarily pedagogical function of canons, Macintyre at least made a gesture towards a less didactic model of canon-setting, espousing the idea that what was significant for one was not for another. He reminded readers that 'important as these books are, it would be difficult to argue that any one of them is indispensable to national awareness. That would be inconsistent with the cultural diversity we celebrate.'[54]

But if we needed a reminder that canons and crude nationalism go together, it was there the following day with Barry Oakley's follow-up to the follow-ups, 'Aussie Kids Grab Back Your Roots', placed alongside another feature on Darville, whose bogus ethnic identity had just been revealed.[55] Perhaps the most striking thing about Oakley's column was its assumption that its reading audience was exclusively Anglo-Australian. If you listen, he melodramatically intoned, 'you can hear the soft, sliding sound of an entire culture slipping away'. According to Oakley, with a nod in the direction of literary establishment pin-up boy Robert Hughes, a good dose of *The Fatal Shore* is just the thing to cure the malaise afflicting the national curriculum.

The finale in this blitz was Austin Gough's 'Canon study needs its space'.[56] This time the remedy for educational malaise was to cut out all secondary reading so that students would have time to read the fundamental canonical texts. To this Gough added a familiar refrain about keeping students out of the clutches of all those dreadful 'feminist critics, neo-Marxists and post-modernists'. Gough, a retired academic who has lobbied against the return of Aboriginal human remains held in universities,[57] neglected to mention that academics of his generation pioneered the use of secondary texts, usually in the name of solid humanism. Notably, Gough failed to account for his own piece, itself a secondary text that, like all the other pieces on canon-setting, was designed precisely to tell readers what to read and how to read it.

This lack of self-reflexivity is the nub of the matter. If there's an underpinning story to this 'war', it's about the accusers' inability to come to terms with, or admit, their own positionality, especially political positionality. Swain, the academic satirised in *Dead White Males*, repeatedly uses the word 'ideology'; the implication is that to a normal, liberal person, the idea that everything involves positionality, and hence politics, is irrelevant. Similarly, Manne has said 'ideology is a great way of avoiding serious thought',[58] the presumption being that 'serious thought' is ideology-free, according to the classic liberal paradigm. The pretence is that 'liberal humanism' is a universal doctrine, and therefore requires no explanation or justification. In fact, the post-enlightenment idea of universality is the height of ideology, grounded as it is in a taken-for-granted acceptance of European supremacy. It came in handy when Europe colonised the world, and it's no less self-serving now.

An illiberal education

The idea of the public too, as in public space or public intellectual, pretends to be without ideology. Yet the English word 'public' descends partly from the Latin *pubes*, the word for adult male. Roman public space was exclusively occupied by senior males, who nevertheless considered their voice the expression of the greater good.

Liberalism, humanism and literary studies have never been without theory, often set down in highly technical and programmatic language. F.R. Leavis and Matthew Arnold are two of the big-name literary 'theorists' from the past. Literature has always had political uses. The rise of English as a discipline, and Shakespeare as a canonical figure, had a basis in inter-European rivalry. The conflation of Shakespeare and English nationalism was still doing explicitly political work as recently as 1994, when John Major's Conservative government wanted to introduce a 'Shakespeare test' for all 14-year-olds to counter the social decline allegedly brought about by immigration and Europeanisation. *Dead White Males* writ large.

The main change that has taken place in English as a discipline is that it has started to take the question of its own ontology seriously. Liberalism, however, hasn't really started to do the same. Prominent advocates of liberalism such as Manne, Ryckmans and Dessaix are hanging on to the doctrine of liberalism's universality and its dispensation from 'ideology' for all they're worth. These twin blindnesses are at the centre of many current debates. The 'PC' panic, as David Bennett argues, is 'primarily a panic about the inscription of politics in the traditionally "non-political"'.[59] The conceit in each case is that everyone else is being ideological, but you aren't.

But this is where the 'battle' gets fraught with problems. The logic of postmodernism, like the logic of ideology, has a certain inexorability. When it comes to postmodernism, popular culture is way ahead of the academy. The TV series *Frontline*, for example, often includes critiques of nationalism and ethnicity, played out in precisely the way that poststructuralist theory anticipates: that is, by revealing how 'truths' operate according to the framework they are in.[60] *Absolutely Fabulous* does a similar thing, unravelling the white middle class's assumptions of privilege and portraying them as grotesque, while critiquing the way Western culture thrives by appropriating the East. As the writer Delia Falconer pointed out in a review of E. Annie Proulx's *Accordion Crimes*:

> Like *The Shipping News*, *Accordion Crimes* demonstrates Proulx's uncanny ability to write for a 'postmodern' audience . . . In the light of Christopher Koch's recent demonisation of English teaching in the universities, and his claims that general readers and academics are at odds, it is interesting to ponder how incredibly popular such novels are, which share many academics' interests in fragmented histories, subcultures and everyday life. And, for that matter, how the forum (academic or literary) in which such ideas are put, affects their reception. I can almost hear the howls of derision — a history of the *accordion*. Its meaning to different cultural groups — if Proulx's ideas were taken up by a cultural studies academic.[61]

Even critics of postmodernity are tied up in its logic. Pierre Ryckmans, writing as Simon Leys, is the author of *The Death of Napoleon*, a postmodern 'alternative history' of Napoleon's demise. *Dead White Males* too is constructed around postmodern ideas of pastiche. *The First Stone* tries to blend fiction and non-fiction in a postmodern way, though most postmodern 'faction' works to different effect. As it happens, most of the speaking positions occupied by journalistic critiques of postmodernity are highly mediated by postmodernity. Such speaking positions are made available on the basis that certain sorts of public figures are needed to 'take up space' on certain issues. Their 'opinions', as we've seen already (and will see more of in the next chapter), are often pastiched from an array of ready-to-wear discourses.

An illiberal education

I'm going to risk a massive generalisation here and suggest that, while it is fashionable for certain elites to deny the inscription of politics and ideology in the everyday, many younger people of a different cultural generation take that sort of politics for granted. The certainties of 1970s liberalism aren't so important for them. As a young artist told me, at college students are constantly told that explicitly political art doesn't sell. In government arts funding too, conservative 'truth and beauty' aesthetics are the yardsticks. But political art, she says, is what everyone is doing. And why not? She and many of her generation suspect they aren't going to get to be middle-class, and politics-free comfort zones are something only a middle class can afford.

This generalisation about politics, I think, is supported in a wider sense by the current explosion of cultural energy. People are starting new 'little magazines' that turn their backs on tired rules about what poetry is, or what fiction is, or even what an academic essay should and shouldn't do. They're writing and recording songs in their bedrooms, using sampling technology that wasn't even thought of twenty years ago. They're revelling in ironic decor, designing clothes and even cooking in restaurants according to principles of hybridity and pastiche. They're inventing multimedia companies, designing typefaces with questionable legibility and writing software hypertext. They're writing books that do exactly what Koch warns against doing, with a vengeance. They're running businesses, farming, and being activists in ways that cut across the traditional modernist paradigms of how culture is made. I'm not trying to say that younger people are somehow 'postmodern' (for various reasons that I'll get to in the last chapter, I don't like the word either), but simply that older paradigms about cultural forms can no longer describe what is going on.

One of the things that I think is happening here, that isn't happening in the public utterances of the cultural elites (but is sometimes happening in their art), is an acknowledgement of pluralism and a commensurate self-consciousness about positionality. And, to risk another generalisation, this is exhibited primarily by younger people. As I write, a friend of mine is putting together her first exhibition, a collection of pastiched photos that traces the histories of the representation of some famous women. She wouldn't call her work 'postmodern', and hated 'theory' at university. But part of what she wants the exhibition to do is undermine her received assumptions about her own speaking position. Her *modus operandi* displays a casual scepticism about positionality, and a self-consciousness about form and production, that happen to be similar to what 'theory' does.

But if there is currently a 'war' going on about 'postmodernism', I don't think the intelligentsia are entirely to blame. The 'theory wars' have been a public-relations disaster for the academy. Academics, with some notable exceptions, have been slow to argue their case. There are reasons for that. Since the Dawkins reforms in the late 1980s, most are massively overworked. The points system by which academics work towards promotion favours publication in peer-reviewed, specialised journals. They worry that the press tends to misreport them and trivialise 'theory' in precisely the sort of normative terms they want to critique. As even Beatrice Faust, who is anti-'theory', has said: 'I used to regard journalists as necessary and useful. Now I see many of them as obstacles to the spread of *critique* to the public.'[62]

But there are other problems. Theorists often like to have the last word, and are sometimes slow to grant other knowledges their contexts. Few theorists have attempted to build alliances with the media. Some theorists also tend to dismiss the power of the press too easily. It is both valuable and necessary to talk about how power can cut both ways in the media, and how readers are powerful textual producers who don't necessarily read passively. The press, over the past few years, has nevertheless managed to make theory-academics' working lives more difficult. Terms originally coined to deride academics, such as 'political correctness', have had powerful political effects.

Theorists, according to Meaghan Morris, need to learn where their shared languages stop and others begin: 'what we should do, as academics,' she says, 'is learn to translate — and that means learning to use other languages with grace, complexity and skill'.[63] As sites for such translation, traditional public spaces do matter, not because they are where 'real' debates happen, but because of the sorts of power that their imagined audiences are deemed to possess. The popular produces powerful effects.

The possibility of creative coalitions across a range of media and a range of professional differences is particularly important for students. The entire *faux* 'battle' between liberals and postmodernity is staged as a crisis of moral authority in education. Its rhetoric is one of undue influence, even brainwashing. The elites evidently prefer to believe students can't think independently — it suits their conspiracy theories better, and gives them a screen on which to project their fears and fantasies about their own supposedly waning influence.

Young women are the persistent stars of these scenarios. The young men are generally portrayed as easy-going buffoons. The women are just that little too bright, too dangerously overconfident. Feminism, perhaps, has made them vulnerable. Angela, the central character in *Dead White Males*, acts out what is evidently Williamson's ideal scenario of contemporary student life when she wakes up, as if from a dream, to think for herself at last, rejects the overtures of her self-deluded feminist mother and the evil theorist Swain, and falls for happy domesticity and Shakespeare instead. Darville, for Robert Manne, is not so much a product of her own unique psychology as of university arts faculties. For her there was no escape, and the evil brainwashers have had their way. The feeling throughout *The First Stone* is that the Ormond women were a borderline case. If only someone else had got there first, they might have been saved. So much error, so little time.

At no time do any of these pundits concede that the rise of theory on campus might be the students' choice. Very few universities now have compulsory core courses in arts subjects beyond first year (though the vast majority still teach Shakespeare, a fact the intelligentsia rarely mention, just as they rarely mention the boom in creative writing courses). The moment the opportunity arises, many students choose theoretically based courses, sometimes migrating *en masse* to new departments, and even faculties, where such courses are available. One reason for this is that older intellectual paradigms tend to delegitimate the cultures that students inhabit, passing them off as frivolous. Windschuttle, for example, displays his own prejudices throughout *The Killing of History*. He is incredulous every time he comes up against the fact that contemporary music history is taught on some campuses.[64] But is contemporary music not a legitimate form of culture, with a history? What about the relationship between black urban protest and music, from blues to rap? A course in 'grunge' at Sunshine Coast University met with a similarly querulous response from Kerry O'Brien on the ABC's *7.30 Report*. For many students, theory-based courses provide ways of avoiding the blind spots of classical humanism.

Universities are important. They are where future cultural agendas are mapped out in embryonic forms. New social movements routinely start there, driven by student politics, much to the anxiety of the cultural establishments of the day. The driving force behind campus radicalism is student activism, rather than generous vice-chancellors or academic staff. It's students who have fuelled the thirty-year-old 'fashion' for critical theory. Rather than being construed as the passive object of these debates, they deserve credit for initiating them.

Universities are powerful symbols of change. And that is why they are so crucial to this debate. Whenever there's a

An illiberal education

social crisis, the role of universities is contested by established cultural elites with agendas to run. The myth of the 'ivory tower' persists without regard to the fact that students and staff are involved in all sorts of ordinary life elsewhere. In this particular debate, the myth functions as an abstract idea that the intelligentsia, with their populist instincts, can use to put the possibility of social change at a remove. Perhaps what makes the notion of the ivory tower so precious to the cultural elite is that it allows them to locate the 'postmodern symptom' elsewhere, according to a logic of place, sparing them from having to think in terms of a logic of time.

There's a further level of denial at work here. Despite the persistence of the ivory tower ghetto metaphor, many of these critics were once academics and some still are. It is *de rigueur* in Australian public life, as Adrian Martin has pointed out, to disavow any previous academic life. Before they began a long slow drift into fashionable neo-conservatism, many of this cultural elite also considered themselves radicals. Like the students and academics they criticise, they too were caught up in ideas and movements. Perhaps they too found it exciting to be in the middle of something, where ideas are still unfolding even as you work.

The most pressing questions in this 'debate' aren't so much to do with postmodernism or critical theory as with the malaise currently afflicting liberalism itself. Why the paranoia? Why stop thinking and accommodating at a certain point? Whatever happened to that most old-fashioned and liberal of ideals, the spirit of properly informed, fully engaged inquiry?

9. Canned goods and culture wars: the Metropolis comes to town

There's not an idea in your head or a word in your mouth that I haven't put there.

Henry Higgins in *My Fair Lady*
(Alan Jay Lerner and Frederick Loewe)

I think one of the qualities of Australian life is the way ideas pass through without resistance . . . I think we lack an immune system to new ideas . . . it is part of the shallowness.

Robert Manne[1]

Triumphant returns are a feature of local cultural life. When any of the famous arts-expats of the 1960s sets foot on local shores, it's as if some process of national validation takes place. Brett Whiteley, Richard Neville, Germaine Greer, Clive James and Robert Hughes, having escaped the claustrophobia of Menzies' Australia, all returned (if only to visit) to spark another episode in the indexing process that is constantly at work measuring the progress of the local against the global. Their impressions about 'how Australia compares' were judged against the yardstick set by the returns of an earlier, prototypical generation of arts-expats, that of Patrick White and Christina Stead.

Perhaps such figures, too, find this faintly embarrassing. I think of the famous photo of Whiteley stepping off the boat from New York, with his wife Wendy and a very young Arkie, all of whom were fêted like rock stars. It was a good career move. The Metropolis comes to town. And the benefits cut both ways. If the painter had instant canonisation bestowed on him, Sydney could register itself as being a good enough place for an artist who had been touched by the Metropolis to settle down. But in the photo the Whiteleys do look a trifle nonplussed.

Robert Hughes often seems similarly nonplussed on local visits. No wonder, if the commentary is anything to go by: 'In my book . . . he's a saint, to whose shrine of good sense I will ever make the pilgrimage', wrote one critic.[2] Another celebrates Hughes as 'an Australian cultural hero'.[3] Another, reviewing one of Hughes' books, wrote 'there are moments when Hughes seems a bit too right for words, as if a massive rhetorical intelligence were being deployed to tell us what we had always known'.[4]

Hughes' books, *The Fatal Shore*, *The Shock of the New* and, most famously, *Culture of Complaint*, are a *cause célèbre* among local cultural elites. The arguments of *Culture of Complaint*, as well as its strident, hectoring tone, fit well with the predominant culture of, well, complaint that has infected a widening circle of journalists, columnists, writers and playwrights who make it their business to be distressed by the various bogeys Hughes likes to complain about.

The embarrassing idolisation of those touched by the metropolis is part of what the critic Sylvia Lawson calls the logic of the 'great Elsewhere'. The 'Archibald paradox', as Lawson calls it, after J. F. Archibald, the famous early editor of the *Bulletin*,

> is simply the paradox of being colonial. Metropolis, the centre of language, of the dominant culture and its judgements, lies away in the great Elsewhere; but the tasks of

living, communicating, teaching, acting-out and changing
the culture must be carried on not Elsewhere but Here.[5]

'Elsewhere', according to Lawson, is only two places: Europe
and America. Other places such as, say, Asia don't rate as possible sites of cultural validation. Neville, Greer and James owe
their sanctification to their having been touched by Europe.
The quasi-religious reverence with which Hughes is treated in
Australia owes much to his having made a reputation in
America. Whiteley had an each-way bet — he made a name
in both. Even now cultural contact with places other than
Europe or the USA carries little weight among the cultural
establishment. When the Australia Council launched an arts
mission to India, the TV host and journalist Caroline Baum
expressed her disapproval:

> I am willing to bet this venture will not increase our arts
> export market one iota. If it really wanted to do that, it
> would be sending these performers, or others . . . to the
> major arts festivals and cultural shopping centres where we
> have already built up links and a reputation. Those places are
> called Europe and America.[6]

Almost half a century after A. A. Phillips wrote his famous
essay on the cultural cringe, signposts to the great Elsewheres
of Europe and America remain everywhere in Australian culture. The Metropolis comes to town in the form of ideas too.
Shakespeare, in *Dead White Males*, functions as a pointer to
where we should be heading. The old cities of Europe in
Robert Dessaix's *Night Letters* don't only speak of a lost past,
but lament a lost possible future, bereft of European-style
sophistications. Dessaix's Europe emphatically isn't that of
Jean-Marie Le Pen or the embattled former Yugoslavia, just
a few kilometres across the Adriatic from his 'enchanted'
Venice, but is *the* place of high art and high culture, offering

sanctuary from a necessarily impoverished and too recently formed Australia. Robert Manne's and Andrew Riemer's differing books on the Darville-Demidenko affair are similarly full of cringing comparisons between the local and the supposed sophistications of the 'global', as represented by Europe. The irony is that, as Leigh Dale points out, when the 1995 Miles Franklin judges awarded *The Hand that Signed the Paper* its prize, they too looked to Europe as the home of history's great events.[7]

In the great Elsewhere stakes, though, Europe can hardly hold a candle to America. *Culture of Complaint* is but one of many books to make a local impact hot off the presses of the US 'culture wars'. As I've already said, these are a series of 'scandals' showcased by the US right to demonstrate the decline of civilisation that has supposedly taken place as a result of the liberalisation of censorship and the rise of popular culture, feminism, queerness, multiculturalism and contemporary literary theory. Like *Culture of Complaint*, the founding texts of the US 'culture wars' — D'Souza's *Illiberal Education*, Roger Kimball's *Tenured Radicals* and Allan Bloom's *The Closing of the American Mind* — have been granted an easy passage through local cultural waters and have become the stock in trade of local conservative columnists, often used though seldom cited, but their influence on debate hasn't been fully acknowledged. Nor have the books been properly discussed.

Rather than admit their own debt to overseas thinkers, the local elite constantly rebukes protagonists of contemporary critical theory for *their* supposedly uncritical importation of ideas. Even the model for these accusations is itself imported, based on similar US attacks. According to Keith Windschuttle, who dismisses the 'Parisian labels'[8] that have permeated local academic circles, 'one of the most striking things about the output of late twentieth century literary and social theory is . . . its slavish devotion to seminal texts'.[9] The problem is that *The Killing of History* begins and ends with missives from the great Elsewhere. It opens with cringing genuflections to Bloom, Kimball and D'Souza, which set the tone and form the basis for Windschuttle's argument, and closes with a paean to their works, from which it draws its conclusions. The book's finale comprises an endorsement of 'Allan Bloom's call for a return to teaching from the canon of the great works of western learning as an answer to the relativism and incoherence cultivated by late twentieth century intellectual fashion', with no further discussion of whether or not Bloom's charge of relativism is sustainable, nor any serious critique of the objectionable intellectual baggage it carries.[10] Windschuttle apparently takes his missives from the great Elsewhere as read.

There's a further irony here. With a couple of notable exceptions, few members of Australia's present cultural elite have much of an overseas profile. By and large the intellectual traffic only goes one way. Amid their own slavish veneration of that which comes from Europe and the US, and for all their criticism of the supposed importers of French critical theory, they overlook the fact that local critical theorists write back. For them the traffic goes both ways. One of the things that surprised me when I first went to university in the early 1990s, amid the hype and panic about the supposed dominance of French relativism, was the extent to which Australia produces its own distinctive, pragmatic, anti-determinist versions of critical theory. Writers such as Ien Ang, Tony Bennett, Paul Carter, Dipesh Chakrabarty, Greg Dening, Simon During, John Frow, Elizabeth Grosz, Sneja Gunew, John Hartley, Ian Hunter, Annamarie Jagose, Sylvia Lawson, Stephen Muecke, Meaghan Morris, Paul Patton, Suvendrini Perera, Graeme Turner and McKenzie Wark might have little media profile locally, but all have their work widely published and discussed, not just in the great Elsewheres of Europe and America, but from India to Taiwan as well.

Against this, for local importers of the 'culture wars' the chief *modus operandi* has been plug and play. Rather than accurately detail distinctive local events, they write as if drawing on a giant smorgasbord of goodies, most of which, when reproduced for a local audience, have offered up a rich complement of headlines, created controversy (primarily due to the lack of local fit, but advertised as the outcome of our blindness to our own cultural malaise), and provided an opportunity to play the most favoured of all roles available to the local elites: that of heretic-cum-martyr. It's a lucrative business, for both local and US writers. As one US critic said, if Allan Bloom proved nothing else, he showed that 'it is possible to write an alarmist book about the state of higher education with a long-winded title and make a great deal of money'.[11]

Given that most of the above controversies have pointed towards tradition (such as literary canons and the 'great books') and away from popular culture, postmodernism and so-called cultural relativism, the irony is that, in their US form, these attacks on postmodernism are themselves so intertextual and lacking referents. As the journalist-on-the-spot Lewis Lapham has reported, most of the US 'culture wars' texts have no basis in direct experience, but take their cue from shared mythologies, many of which emanate from the press offices of the US far right (such as the John M. Olin Foundation, funders of D'Souza's *Illiberal Education*, Christina Hoff Sommers' *Who Stole Feminism* and Bloom's *The Closing of the American Mind* — Bloom was director of the Olin Center at the University of Chicago until his death).[12] Whether it's Bloom or Newt Gingrich talking — and, as Lapham points out, they share many themes and sponsors — 'the facts of the matter have been suborned by the preferred image'.[13] Lapham also notes the similarities between the conservative revolution of the 1990s and the theoretical abstractions of 1960s counterculture: 'Just as the mock insurgents of the 1960s staged their masques and dances against a backdrop of cardboard scenery, the rebels of the 1990s shape their morality play from images they have seen on television and abstractions they have discovered in books written by their friends and former economics professors.'[14]

For local detritivores of the 'culture wars', any direct experience is at least twice removed. They are working from texts based on other texts that are themselves calculated to conjure up spectres, not invoke anything remotely resembling a referent. The spiral is as vertiginous as the panics are unreal. This lack of a basis in direct experience is perhaps one of the reasons why the audience in the performance I went to laughed so uneasily in those parts of *Dead White Males* that attacked multiculturalism. Williamson's use of the word as a term of abuse echoed that of the US 'culture wars'; Bloom, for example, attacks multiculturalism every step of the way, laying most of the blame for the malaise supposedly affecting American culture at the feet of those who would democratise elitist traditions in order to accommodate minority groups. Even Robert Hughes, a critic of US multiculturalism, has carefully pointed out that Australian multiculturalism (of which he heartily approves) is quite different from the US version, and requires different responses. (The rest of Williamson's play takes its cue from the 'Shakespeare debate' that filled the pages of the *London Review of Books* for a month or two in the early 1990s, and attempts to map this onto 1990s Australian academic culture.)

Helen Garner's *The First Stone*, as I have already suggested, is similarly mediated through US orthodoxies about 'victim feminism'. Such fashionable mythologies and potent images of rampant feminists on the loose all too easily replace the real story. I don't want to mix Garner up in some equally vacuous logic of conspiracy, but anti-victim campaigners Camille Paglia and Katie Roiphe also have the seal of approval of the US far right. The impression of ideological compatibility was cemented when the US rights to *The First Stone* were sold to the Free Press, publishers of D'Souza's *Illiberal Education* and a range of other US 'anti-victim' texts. In the blurb to the US edition, Garner is given the full neo-conservative treatment as the heroic intellectual who rails against fashionable minority politics, in this case feminism. Billed as a feminist who has recanted, Garner is constructed as a hero for sacrificing her previous ideology in the name of a higher truth and is thereby granted licence to tell other feminists to get real. The book is unproblematically billed as non-fiction, and Garner's Australian opponents are summarily dismissed as self-interested hard-line feminists. To bolster the idea that Garner faced an uphill battle against cant, and that her entry into the case constituted a *cause célèbre*, a transcript of Garner's speech, 'The Fate of *The First Stone*', is included as an afterword. The back cover features an approving endorsement from Katie Roiphe. It's a nice bit of circularity.

In this import-export business, sentences and sentiments from US 'authorities' are endlessly recycled. Allan Bloom's opening sentences in *The Closing of the American Mind* have been echoed by every second columnist wanting to talk about the supposed relativism of the contemporary arts academy. Such columnists seem to have been equally misled, in the sense that their information all came from the one place. Bloom's and Kimball's central claim that the West is 'under siege' looms large in the thinking of local commentators, as does Kimball's idea that contemporary university educations portend 'nothing less than a new form of thought control based on a variety of pious new-Left slogans and attitudes'.[15]

Other similarities are equally arresting. Kimball claims in *Tenured Radicals* that the academy is now being run by 1960s radicals, whereas Windschuttle, in *The Killing of History*, proclaims that the 'movers and shakers' of 'the new humanities' aren't the younger generation, but 'the Old New left crowd of the 1960s'.[16] In fact many academics pore over postgrad research tables in an effort to keep pace. Bloom's claim that 'the glory days of social science from the point of view of liberal education are over'[17] dovetails nicely with Don Anderson's claim that he is being 'passed over' or Windschuttle's claim that he is witnessing the 'funeral' of his discipline.[18] And Dinesh D'Souza's idea that deconstructionists can't say one text is superior to another fits neatly enough with Barry Oakley's statement that deconstructionists think 'one-text-is-as-good-as-another'.[19] Actually, none is right, but the normal practice of local columnists has been to swallow whole the erroneous hyperbole produced by D'Souza, Kimball and Bloom.

There are also echoes of Bloom's vituperative rantings about rock-and-roll in Windschuttle's similar rantings in *The Killing of History*.[20] Strangely, before the incipient neo-conservatism of the late 1980s and early 1990s began its flow along the global trade routes, Windschuttle took rock-and-roll quite seriously, and gave an engaging and still pertinent account of punk, disco and the politics of youth joblessness in his broadly Marxist 1979 book on unemployment.[21]

According to Lapham, the tracts of US neo-conservatism, from the books of D'Souza and Bloom to the pages of the *New Criterion* (first publishers of Kimball's essays, and also funded with a US$100 000 start-up grant and office space from the Olin Foundation) to the utterances of Newt Gingrich, William Bennett or Rush Limbaugh, follow more or less the same pattern of complaint:

> Once upon a time, before the awful misfortunes of the 1960s, America was a theme park constructed by nonunion labor along the lines of the Garden of Eden. But then something terrible happened, and a plague of guitarists descended upon the land. Spawned by the sexual confusions of the amoral news media, spores of Marxist ideology blew around in the wind, multiplied the powers of government and impregnated the English departments at the Ivy League universities, which then gave birth to the monster of deconstruction that devoured the arts of learning. Pretty soon the trout began to die in Wyoming, and the next thing that

anybody knew the nation's elementary schools ha[...]
debased, too many favors were being granted to w[...]
and blacks, federal bureaucrats were smothering cap[...]st
entrepreneurs with the pillows of government regulation,
prime-time television was broadcasting continuous footage
from Sodom and Gomorrah and the noble edifice of
Western civilization had collapsed into the rubble of feminist prose.[22]

He could have been describing the favoured themes of any number of Australian commentators and columnists.

★

But it's not only the cultural elites who have trouble working in direct response to local issues. The problem occurs across the board. The newspaper hysteria following the death of Anna Wood followed hot on the heels of similar coverage in the UK following a similar death, also supposedly due to Ecstasy. Both were given precisely the same treatment. The press demonisation of black youths in Australia as a synonym for crime follows precisely the pattern set in the USA, where black youths were targeted by influential right-wing writers such as D'Souza and lately Charles Murray and Richard Hernstein in their book *The Bell Curve*. Police forces in Australia, to the dismay of youth workers, have begun to talk of adopting 'zero-tolerance policing', copying a recent New York model, where specific communities are targeted on the basis that making arrests for trivial crimes now will prevent more serious crimes later.[23]

Local political pundits and politicians suffer a similar lack of imagination. The political scientist James Walter cites as an example the reception of Francis Fukuyama's famous essay 'The End of History', the influence of which can be seen in everything from Paul Kelly's book *The End of Certainty* to foreign policy under Gareth Evans.[24] Walter points out that

Fukuyama's essay, which proposed that political and economic liberalism had triumphed and all ideological alternatives had exhausted themselves, was fallacious in its historical premise and in its assumption that liberalism was homogeneous and uncontradictory, yet it was uncritically taken up as wisdom from on high.

What makes the cultural elites important is the role cultural debate now plays. The displacement of social debate from religious and political issues into the cultural domain has had a range of effects. On the one hand, the shift has signalled the possibility of questioning canonical certainties across the broader spectrum of issues, opening the door for new kinds of social movements. On the other hand, for conservatives 'culture' has played a more limited role, as a heading under which to speak about the nebulous symptoms of moral decline. Critique is in short supply in the newspapers, or on radio or current-affairs television. Discussion of social, political or economic issues is everywhere, but rarely goes deep. It's simpler to talk of 'political correctness', 'victim feminism' and youth crime, where the moral outcomes are decided *a priori* as a condition of the plot and both the bogeys and the good guys are obvious. This sort of cultural debate has filled the vacuum left by the end of the Cold War, which is when the US 'culture wars' really got going. As Lapham puts it, after the fall of the Berlin Wall, 'in the absence of enemies abroad, the protectors of the American dream began looking for inward signs of moral weakness' — and what better place to look than in higher education?[25] Lapham cites *The Closing of the American Mind* as an instance of such a diagnosis. It is almost in the same breath that Robert Manne starts talking about a 'culture of forgetting', the affliction he sees as inhabiting Australian culture.

In some ways, the speaking position Manne occupies is one made possible by Bloom, and certainly by the 'culture wars'. The titles of Bloom's and Manne's respective books have a similar resonance: one talks of closing, the other of forgetting. Both place themselves at the end of something, and embark on a grand tour across national memory to diagnose the reasons for the supposed decline of their respective civilisations. Both take up an overdetermined, postmodern speaking position from which certain things can only appear credible, and certain institutions only be cited, in the light of certain debates. Both Bloom's and Manne's moral worlds centre on a Europe-based transcendental, which functions as an unquestionable absolute. For Manne it is the Holocaust, for Bloom the canon of great books. Manne laments that Darville would never have got *The Hand that Signed the Paper* published in Europe, whereas Bloom frets that the 'longing for Europe has been all but extinguished in the young'.[26]

The brilliant trick of *The Culture of Forgetting* is that Manne feeds post-'culture wars' anxieties about the failure of literary transcendentals into his own concerns about the failure of moral transcendentals, so that Darville's supposed postmodern tertiary education becomes a way of talking about a national cultural forgetting. Manne, like Bloom, argues that young people, beset by such educations, lack cultural memory. Bloom, like Manne, sets himself up as the authorised rememberer, figuring his flawed students as congenital forgetters, just as Manne figures Darville. Everyone forgets, and everything is eventually in some way forgotten, but in the process of memorialising everything to suit the particular life-span of the present cultural elite, the *faux* scandals of the 'culture wars' have made forgetting into a pathology that is specific to the young.

★

The 'culture wars', as I've already suggested, owe their very existence to the realignment of conservative thinking that took place after the Cold War. Many of its protagonists are former Cold Warriors out of a job. I'm not one for 'dark hand' versions of history, but many of the writers of its central tracts have received lavish grants from far-right US think-tanks and editorial largesse from the far-right press. Certainly there is a confluence of interests. *The Closing of the American Mind* was apparently a big hit with George Bush's 1988 campaign speech-writers. *Illiberal Education* is credited with putting 'political correctness' on the US think-tank agenda. And a more recent entry to this pantheon, *The Bell Curve*, which claims that non-whites are genetically inferior to whites and have taken up the low rungs of the social ladder accordingly, was reportedly a huge hit with elements in the US administration dedicated to cutting welfare spending and obsessed with finding ways for 'small government' to avoid the hard questions about social inequity.

Designed to emit a superficial, common-sense liberal appeal, none of these books stands close scrutiny. They rely on their readers' accepting cardboard cut-out stereotypes about their targets, on the assumption that they lack access to other information. D'Souza's readers, for example, aren't to know that when he talks about traditional courses in Western culture being cut at Stanford University, in fact the course in question didn't constitute the entire curriculum, but was only one of eight streams. He certainly doesn't tell them. Other salient facts also go missing. When he rails against the deconstructionists' supposed attack on Western knowledge, D'Souza fails to mention that none of the major pioneering figures of US poststructuralism (Paul de Man, J. Hillis Miller, Geoffrey Hartmann and Harold Bloom) ever strayed from the standard male Western canon in their writings. Or that the traditional canon itself, which D'Souza, Bloom and Kimball all like to pretend is a stable, fixed entity, has in fact only been in place since the 1940s. *Illiberal Education* originally received favourable reviews from commentators such as C. Vann Woodward, a leading US moderate liberal; as the writer John K. Wilson points out, these reviews 'were important in promoting it as a supposedly moderate and truthful account of what was happening in college campuses . . . cementing the image of D'Souza as a responsible journalist reporting on a national crisis'.[27] Woodward later retracted his praise of the book, criticising its errors of fact and its stretching of evidence to score points. This too suggests local parallels.

The local cousins of these publications operate on a similar presumption of reader ignorance. *Dead White Males* relies on the fact that most of Williamson's audience haven't set foot in a university for many years, but have children who do. Manne's thesis about a culture of forgetting relies on a similar willingness to suppose that the 'fingerprints of a contemporary university miseducation are everywhere' in *The Hand that Signed the Paper*.[28] *The First Stone* is similarly dependent on Garner's readers having too little familiarity with contemporary feminisms to realise how inaccurate her account of them is.

When so many templates have lately been imposed on events they don't really fit, I can't help but wonder how the local importers of this rhetoric would feel if *they* saw *their* sources up close. They too seem to have been insulated by ignorance. Camille Paglia is unpopular in the US with precisely the middle-aged liberal set who admire her here. Over there she's too close and the flaws are all too obvious. Dinesh D'Souza is very good at positioning himself as a liberal, but what the various author blurbs on his book don't state is that he made his name as editor of the non-white-bashing *Dartmouth Review* (also funded by the Olin Foundation), where he used a staged photo of a lynched black student hanging from a tree to illustrate an interview with an ex-official of the Ku Klux Klan. He also proudly published private correspondence stolen from gay and lesbian Dartmouth students.

Bloom's nostalgia for traditional liberal virtues also tends to function as a mask. Much as he claims to be conducting a campaign in the name of classical humanism, his own stance has little of humanism's inclusiveness, but instead makes clever use of the liberal arts to supply a veneer of sophistication, reasonableness and credibility to an extended series of blatantly racist, misogynist and anti-democratic remarks. Just as Newt Gingrich regards minority groups as an unsustainable burden that can be accommodated only at fatal cost to the traditions that sustain the polity, so Bloom regards the minority interest as a burden on a proper literary tradition and, as a corollary, on the American soul. According to Bloom, feminism is 'the latest enemy of the vitality of classic texts . . . the Muses never sang to the poets about liberated women'.[29] So far as non-whites go:

> Affirmative action now institutionalises the worst aspects of separatism. The fact is that the average black student's achievements do not equal those of the average white student's in the good universities, and everybody knows it . . . a disposition composed of equal parts of shame and resentment has settled on many black students who are beneficiaries of preferential treatment.[30]

The achievement of Kimball, Bloom and D'Souza is to disguise their own partisan treatment of social justice issues as a paean to reasonableness, fairness and justice, neatly packaged by way of allusions to classical values.

These rhetorical strategies dovetail neatly with Republican-style 'attack politics', which, as Lapham puts it, aims to 'convert the emotions rooted in economic anxiety into the politics of cultural anxiety' on the basis that 'the comfort of the rich rests upon an abundant supply of the poor'.[31] This sort of divide-and-rule strategy has been effective in other respects as well, and on both sides of the Pacific. The spectacle of old-fashioned liberals scrapping with new-fashioned post-liberals for the right to call each other philistines has undoubtedly been arresting, and has taken up plenty of media space. Meanwhile, a far more dangerous set of philistines has been hanging around the various treasury offices of this land, their activities largely uncommented on by those who claim their works deal specifically with the politics of disciplinary and cultural decline.

★

The US 'culture wars' functioned both directly and indirectly as an attack on younger people and their interests. Much of the attention was directed at higher education, the rest going to the corrupting effects of popular culture, specifically of the *Beavis and Butthead* kind, and attacks on photographers of the Robert Mapplethorpe kind, the latter ushering in a new wave of indirect censorship in US art, through Bible-belt-driven government manipulation of appointments and funding.[32] Australian cultural elites have proved particularly adept at imitating this thrust of the 'culture wars'. Mickey Mouse and Madonna have emerged as standard figures to be invoked every time there is talk of the rise of 'cultural studies' as a discipline and the supposed decline in the teaching of Shakespeare. Recent local pro-censorship debates have followed the US pattern to the letter, and have had much the same targets, such as Quentin Tarantino's *Pulp Fiction*, Bret Easton Ellis's *American Psycho* and the World Wide Web.

Young people, in the 'culture wars', get to side with the popular, the postmodern, the untruthful and the self-deceived, while the writers of the seminal 'culture wars' texts, looking down from the high-culture road, get to side with tradition, content and cultural memory. *The Closing of the American Mind*, subtitled *How Higher Education has Failed Democracy and Impoverished the Souls of Today's Youth*, opens with a long whinge about just what is wrong with the youth of today, the main charge being that they are degraded by popular culture. Students, Bloom claims, 'as long as they have the Walkman on . . . cannot hear what the great tradition has to say. And, after its prolonged use, when they take it off, they find they are deaf.'[33] Bloom, here, like many local commissars of the canon, assumes that a proper high-culture/low-culture divide is central to meaning in a civilised culture, and would like nothing more than to reinstate such a divide. He knows, as do most cultural conservatives, that the real danger to the pre-eminence of writers such as Shakespeare isn't academics, but the sheer volume and variety of popular culture, even if academics make a handy populist target.

The Closing of the American Mind is full of such disparaging remarks about youth culture, with plenty of suggestions for ways to get them back on track, most often via a remedial dose of high culture. 'Just say no' is the Bloom prescription for youth tempted by either popular culture or contemporary literary theory — a similar message to that implied in *Dead White Males*. 'One of the strange aspects of my relations with good students', Bloom says, 'is that I frequently introduce them to Mozart.'[34] Bloom's young people turn out to be quite similar to the young people in *The First Stone* or *Brilliant Lies*. According to Bloom, 'young people, and not only young people, have studied and practised a crippled *eros* that can no longer take wing'.[35] Where Robert Manne has approvingly quoted the historian Eric Hobsbawm as saying 'most young men and women at century's end grow up in a sort of permanent present', adding that 'he might have had Helen Demidenko in mind',[36] Bloom has said 'the only common project engaging the youthful imagination is the exploration of space, which everyone knows to be empty'.[37]

Bloom's book, like the writings of many local commentators, is also full of references to things 'lost': 'students arriving at the university today hardly walk on the enchanted ground they once did. They pass by the ruins without imagining what was once there.'[38] It's all part of the long great sigh, the long great ending, which is finally self-pitying and self-imposed.

★

No account of the 'culture wars' in their local guises would be complete without canvassing the work of Robert Hughes. In a way, and I say this with all due respect, the 'culture wars' made Hughes, or at least remade him. Without them his masculinist hyperbole would look more like a relic from a bygone age than a manly antidote to the feminised, feminist, multiculti perspectives he thinks are taking over art. *Sans* the 'culture wars', I suspect he'd look like someone recently teleported onto the flight deck of the *Starship Enterprise*, beamed up from a debating class *circa* 1955.

In *Culture of Complaint*, Hughes sets himself up as the man-on-the-spot in the 'culture wars', the one prepared to do a little plain speaking when all else is humbug. His arguments *sound* good. They have a sort of diesel-powered robustness that suggests that they are sweeping humbug aside and replacing it with obvious, commonsense solutions. It's easy to get carried away by such robustness. Many local commentators do. Luke Slattery is much taken by Hughes' argument that, while academics spent the 1980s theorising that 'language and the thinking subject were dead, the longing for freedom and humanistic culture was demolishing the very pillars of European tyranny':

> But did Vaclav Havel and his fellow intellectuals, playwrights and poets free Czechoslovakia by quoting Derrida and Lyotard on the inscrutability of texts? Assuredly not. They did it by placing their faith in the transforming power of thoughts — by putting their shoulders to the immense wheel of the world.[39]

It's a wonderful image, but there's a catch. Derrida was himself one of those 'putting their shoulders to the immense wheel of the world'; he was arrested in 1981 in Prague, where he had gone to take part in a symposium organised by dissidents. Derrida is also well known for his activism against apartheid in South Africa. That's the trap for old-style rhetoricians like Hughes (or Slattery). Before you start appropriating other peoples' struggles and posturing on their behalf, accusing others of being mere rhetoricians, it's wise to remember that you might be open to the same charge.

Culture of Complaint is as much an attack on the far right of US politics as on the 'multi-culti' left. On the one hand, Hughes is critical of what he sees as the closed circuits of reasoning, the reliance on manufactured terms such as 'political correctness', and the in-house think-tank funding that dominate US neo-conservative thinking. As he says, 'the choir of conservatives denouncing "well-subsidized left academics" as bludgers, whilst taking their own subsidies from various right-wing foundations, is truly one of the wonders of American intellectual life'.[40] On the other hand, Hughes also targets the left, and here he encounters a problem: in attacking the left for its supposed adoption of 'pettifogging PC virtue'[41] and 'victim cults', he buys into the logic of the right.

Culture of Complaint is largely populated by the standard fictions and bogeys of the 'culture wars', presented in the cut-down, simplified silhouettes that most such tracts prefer. There are plenty of feminist 'academic thought police' who form a 'large repressive fringe'.[42] Attacks on the complexities of academic language include the standard tacit demand that if left-leaning (read theoretical) academics wish to enter public spaces and become relevant, they need to recognise that only a certain traditional type of language is acceptable: 'If the American left is to revitalize itself, it will have to re-learn plain English . . . and it will never do that with the present encumbrance of theory'.[43] The book also rehearses the standard misconceptions about and misrepresentations of literary theory. Hughes thinks that 'those who complain about the Canon think it creates readers who will never read anything else'[44] — a view that no-one holds. It is 'the belief of French poststructuralism', according to Hughes, 'that the "subject" . . . of every sentence was an illusion'.[45] No French poststructuralist, so far as I am aware, has ever said this, although you might come close if you substituted 'construction' for 'illusion'. It is a telling slippage, though, from a word that can denote a variety of things to one that can denote only falsehood.

Hughes is keen to portray literary theorists as tied up in a kind of linguistic determinism. The stranger thing is that, were he a little more up-to-date, he might discover more compatibility between his ideas and theirs than he admits. Much as Hughes wants to tar theorists with the same brush as puritans or racial supremacists, essentialism and separatism are largely out of fashion in the academy. Tabloid caricatures aside, a lot of recent academic work isn't so much about the political incorrectness of speaking for each other as the inevitability of speaking for each other.[46] Hughes' championing of the hybrid and the impure is quite compatible with the poststructuralism he otherwise decries, as is his idea that 'culture and history are full of borders but they are all to some degree permeable'.[47] Poststructuralists too are happy to say that people read for pleasure, even if Hughes wants to claim the high ground of reading for pleasure for himself. The main thrust of *Culture of Complaint*, though, isn't to seek out this sort of compatibility. Rather, it's to set up a strict Manichean divide between 'excellence' and a crude caricature of alternative cultural forms supposedly sponsored by theorists with a 'PC'-driven commitment to democratisation as a system in which no-one can fail.

In many respects Hughes is a straightforward, old-fashioned liberal. He wants to make a clear distinction between the merely linguistic and the sovereign real (language, Hughes knows, equates with the social, and that means politics), but in so doing he is forced to rely on more and more layers of language. Like most of those who claim that language provides — or should provide — transparent access to the real, he can't finally produce the goods, but lets the rhetoric pile up anyway. This isn't to say that there is no such thing as the real, but finding referents unmediated by language is a little more difficult than is often imagined.

Hughes has reasons for wanting to talk about the real as transparently self-evident. He wants to make the same claim for self-evident excellence in art (and for art itself), in order to be able to claim that certain 'intrinsic aesthetic merits' are not just subjective, but objective.[48] The job of the critic, as far as he is concerned, is to pick out the things that will stand for all time, not to indulge politics: 'Politics ought not to be all-pervasive. Indeed, one of the first conditions of freedom is to discover the line beyond which politics may not go, and literature is one of the means by which the young (and the old) find this out.'[49]

But, again, despite all his assertions about the disadvantages of politics and the advantages of eternity, Hughes is unable to define just what 'intrinsic aesthetic merits' are, or what the job of those setting out to find them might actually entail (other than making even more lists). Faced with this difficulty, he defers, filling in time by bashing academics and multiculturalists. The problem with knowing what excellence is, the argument apparently goes, is that these people are standing in the way. Both this argument and its underlying strategy have found much favour with local cultural elites, who endlessly talk about 'excellence' without defining what it is.

As it happens, Hughes' own concerns turn out to be politicised. *Culture of Complaint* is full of citations from poems, nearly all from the stereotypical dead white males. The same is true of his generally enjoyable TV series *American Visions* (and the book). Women artists just don't cut it in the Hughes world; at best he is quietly disparaging. Although he accuses women artists of retreating into feminist ghettos, Hughes himself tends to recycle the ghetto logic in order to dismiss them from the art mainstream. Feminists will be familiar with these sort of loaded dice. Artists such as Georgia O'Keeffe are damned if they do, damned if they don't. If *Culture of Complaint* defends cultural elitism by arguing that the 'composition of . . . elites is not necessarily static',[50] then Hughes' own judgements nevertheless follow a well-worn pattern.

Canned goods and culture wars

Time and time again, in *Culture of Complaint*, Hughes returns to the fantasy of the politically empty space that, paradoxically, goes by the name of 'elitism'. 'Elitism' here refers to a hierarchy of skill and imagination rather than a hierarchy of race, money or social position. Unfortunately, saddled with a doctrine that says language is transparent and that there is unmediated access to the real (self-evident 'excellence'/'intrinsic aesthetic merit'), Hughes is left without a theory of reception. He cannot explain how artists of arguably similar talent, or whose works might give similar pleasure (to use his yardstick), are nevertheless differently received, often as a result of the very social factors he derides.

Instead of talking about reception, he leaves the job up to the museums. It is finally their business, in his account, to actualise the possibility of a politically empty space and to arbitrate on excellence. But which museums might these be? And who staffs them? Are they politically neutral in their choices? Do they make no assumptions in assessing the value of the work? Or are they trained not to? In which case, is the training also value-neutral? What about the museums themselves? Do such institutions build themselves on conveniently vacant patches of land without state intervention or private patronage? Are their budgets magically assigned without lobbying or notice of proposed acquisition programmes? Who sits on the boards and committees where choices are often finally made? Are they too entirely disinterested? Do they not make choices, thereby invoking differences, and with them politics? Museums, in Hughes' argument, are made to count for a lot. They are given the last word. But ultimately they can't adequately stand in for a lack of a more thoroughgoing engagement with problems of aesthetics.

★

To discuss *Culture of Complaint* in this way, though, only tells half the story. Hughes' attacks on the right are at least as vituperative as those he makes on the left, and he regards the right as more vindictive and more influential. As Hughes declares, 'the American right has had a ball with Political Correctness. Yet its glee is hollow, and there is something distasteful about its caperings, its pretence to represent "real" language.'[51] *Culture of Complaint* includes dismissive attacks on most of the central 'culture wars' figures, including Bloom, D'Souza, Kimball and William Bennett, with swipes at D'Souza's grasp of the Western tradition and Kimball's romanticisation of a non-existent 'less ideological' past.[52] As Hughes points out, 'when one hears the often-repeated conservative charge that the modern American campus is "politicized", it is worth remembering that it always was'.[53] He points out that most of the neo-conservative conceits about radicalised campuses are little more than a scare campaign, citing a survey of 35 000 US professors in which less than 5 per cent considered themselves 'far left' and 17.8 per cent considered themselves conservative.[54]

Culture of Complaint is also full of asides about the mechanics of Republican attack politics. There is a rundown on the overall strategy, complete with a neat summary from arch-conservative Pat Buchanan to the effect that 'if we tear the country in half, we can pick up the bigger half', and 1950s red-baiter Joe McCarthy, who said 'to divide a polity you must have scapegoats and hate objects — human caricatures that dramatize the difference between Them and Us'.[55] As an example of the hyperbole that has been allowed to circulate around minority politics, Hughes cites Buchanan's assessment that the proposed Equal Rights Amendment was produced by 'a socialist, anti-family political movement that encourages women to leave their husbands, kill their children, practise witchcraft, destroy capitalism and become lesbians'.[56]

From these descendants Hughes sketches lines through to the funding of recent neo-conservative thinkers by organisations such as the Olin Foundation and the Heritage

Foundation. He draws connections between the privatisation of previously state-owned media and the censorship-by-stealth that follows, and explains how this is commensurate with both 'competitive-market dogma' and conservative attacks on public broadcasting.[57]

But these aspects of *Culture of Complaint* don't generally get much of a mention in Australia. Mostly what you get is the academic-bashing. The circle of reviewers and interviewers who make it their business to watch over Hughes' local reception is as small as his reputation is large. While certain sectors of the cultural establishment have a special investment in Hughes (some of the coverage has been spectacularly sycophantic), they rarely detail his scathing attacks on the conceits of the culture wars.[58] *Culture of Complaint* has also been accepted wholesale by a range of other local commentators as the authoritative tract about just what's wrong with the US, and therefore us (the only difference, apparently, being the capital letters), in spite of the fact that Hughes is careful to place his remarks in the context of US puritanism. An example was an interview with Mary Delahunty that could only be described as a 'flirt piece', in which she kept wanting to ask Hughes about the evils of victimism, much to his obvious unease, and in spite of his attempts to talk about other aspects of his work.

Maybe this skewing of Hughes' reception in favour of his attacks on minority politics and academics, and away from his critique of the US right's deeper role, is final evidence of how uncritically local cultural elites have consumed the US 'culture wars' rhetoric. Once again they swallowed whole, preferring myth to a more balanced reading, especially those myths whose origin could be traced to the great Elsewhere.

10 All hands on deck in the 'Year of the Helens'

I fake it so real I am beyond fake.

Courtney Love

You come into the world naked and all the rest is drag.

RuPaul

Collective rites of passage aren't so highly publicised as they once were. There don't seem to be so many of those single, binding incidents that make us think: this is us. 'Ties that bind' seem not so much universal as optional. There's no contemporary equivalent to the question: 'Where were you the day JFK was shot?' Potentially galvanising events like the collapse of the Berlin Wall have passed easily into memory. Even the debates over *The First Stone* or the Demidenko affair didn't galvanise 'us' into a single community, or provide a 'snapshot of the *Zeitgeist*', as writer and publisher Michael Heyward claimed, but instead resulted in rancorous debate.[1]

But the idea of *Zeitgeist*, as Heyward's remark suggests, isn't dead. It thrives among certain communities as a way of speaking about the objects of their collective knowledge, endowing such knowledges with the slick gloss of universality. The period Heyward referred to, from early 1995 to early 1996 — the 'Year of the Helens' as the columnist Helen Daniel dubbed it

All hands on deck

— was by any reckoning a gala year among the intelligentsia. It was the year books, writing and 'ideas' hit the front pages: first with the publication of Helen Garner's *The First Stone*, then with the scandal that erupted after the awarding of three major literary prizes to Helen Darville-Demidenko's controversial novel, *The Hand that Signed the Paper*. More controversy followed with Garner's address on the 'fate' of her book to the Sydney Institute. At around the same time there was a ruckus over the reviewing of David Williamson's play *Dead White Males*. Then came Hilary McPhee's headline-making speech to the arts community, and Les Murray's persistent badgering of the Australia Council through the press. Then, almost precisely a year after the publication of *The First Stone*, there was another controversy when the 1980 winner of the Vogel award, Paul Radley, revealed he hadn't written the winning book.

As it happened, the controversies lingered on well after that year had elapsed. 'Culture', as a talking point, had arrived. A minor kerfuffle broke out over Simon During's quietly iconoclastic book on Patrick White. Then 1996 Miles Franklin Award-winner Christopher Koch made the papers with his inflammatory acceptance speech. There was a scandal when the Brisbane *Courier-Mail* accused the late historian Manning Clark of having been an agent of influence for the Soviet Union and a recipient of the Order of Lenin. The claim filled front pages and radio airwaves for weeks. There was another squall when it was alleged that the writer Mudrooroo, who had written for many years as an Aboriginal, was of Creole background. And another when Leon Carmen, a 47-year-old white male, revealed he was the author of *My Own Sweet Time*, a hoax Aboriginal biography written under the name Wanda Koolmatrie and published by the Aboriginal press, Magabala Books.

Perhaps what Heyward said is true. In these events there did appear to be a snapshot of a culture at work. Even the expression 'Year of the Helens' seemed to signal how important the arts had become. Certainly it was a year of high debate, which, according to the prevailing mythology, was 'good for us'.

Often the spectacle seemed to be one of reputations rising and falling. The debate over *The First Stone* damaged reputations on all sides. Opinion is still divided, sometimes angrily so. I was at a party among relative strangers where a lively discussion was taking place about Sydney–Melbourne rivalries, and famous migrations from one to the other, when a journalist who knew Garner mentioned her opinion on the matter. The room went quiet. 'Why is Helen Garner being cited as an authority?' someone coolly asked. On the other hand, most of the early reviewers of *The First Stone* followed it through as ongoing defenders. The reorganisation of public space that took place in the wake of the controversy was striking.

The fierce protectionism that prevailed was symptomatic of a new turn in cultural debate. If Garner's book had caused sharp disagreement, the book's defenders spoke as if she had been demonised and persecuted. Egos were on the march, at the expense of issues. Luke Slattery wrote a piece in the *Australian* that sought to portray key figures in the Ormond case as dangerous, radical ideologues because they attempted to protect themselves and their careers by telling their side of the story in their own way.[2] Slattery also suggested that Jenna Mead had tried to white-ant Garner's account by publishing her own in the journal *RePublica*. This seemed a bit rich, considering that Mead was writing as someone with first-hand involvement in the affair. These stratagems, like those of so many recent debates, relied on demonising key figures as ideologues and conspirators.

This new populism found its way into Garner's address to the Sydney Institute. Fitting neatly into the genre of angry and intemperate speeches by established literary figures against the various scourges of the 'culture wars', 'The Fate of *The First Stone*' was short on argument and long on character assassination.

All hands on deck

Most of its fire was aimed at the usual bogeys: doctrinaire feminists and 'tenure-hungry' academics. Garner attacked one of the opponents of her book for being full of 'dangling earring-hubris'.[3] But the really notable thing about the speech was the coverage it attracted. It's not often that a speech by a local writer makes a front-page story, complete with colour photo. The *Sydney Morning Herald* ran the story on page 1, plus an edited transcript of the address over a full page inside the paper.[4] The *Australian* too gave it front-page coverage, plus an editorial and a full-page feature inside headlined 'A Story that Needed to be Told'.[5] The *Age*, more sanguine, gave it a page 4 news story and transcript. All ran follow-up stories over subsequent days. The voices of young women were absent here too. The *Sydney Morning Herald* interviewed a range of people who approved of the book — all over fifty — under the heading 'Feminists, Public Figures Back Garner Book Defence'.[6] The *Australian* ran a full-page feature the following Saturday, with a range of views, all from prominent forty-something women, entitled 'Helen Garner's Telling Truths'.[7]

The furious contestation of public space from within the literary community, and the concerted effort to protect the reputation of the canonical author, were equally striking. I've already mentioned Rosemary Neill's gratuitous response to the young-feminist-writes-back books by Virginia Trioli and Kathy Bail.[8] Morag Fraser, who originally reviewed *The First Stone* for the *Age*, claimed Garner had raised the ire of ideologues because she was a 'gadfly' whose position was hard to pin down (Fraser compared Garner's feminism to that of Simone de Beauvoir and Germaine Greer).[9] In Fraser's *Age* review of Trioli's *Generation F*, Garner's name is mentioned almost as often as Trioli's, and it is Garner who is quoted at length.[10] The journal Fraser edits, *Eureka Street*, later published a speech of Garner's, defending the right of artists as visionaries who peer into people's lives (and invoking Virginia Woolf, Guy de Maupassant, Nadine Gordimer and Raymond Carver).[11]

Peter Craven made sure that every single utterance by Garner's so-called antagonists, Jenna Mead and Cassandra Pybus, met with a rebuttal in his fortnightly column for the *Australian*, right down to disputing the latter's claims about the type of coffee Garner drinks.[12] Kerryn Goldsworthy wrote a critical monograph on Garner, which turned out to be mainly an analysis of the reception of *The First Stone*. Many of Goldsworthy's criticisms of critics of the book relied on taking them out of context in order to be able to say they had taken Garner out of context. Goldsworthy claimed, for example, that critics of *The First Stone* unreasonably found the book wanting because it didn't offer a solution to sexual harassment.[13] But most prominent critics of the book expressed disappointment that Garner didn't seem to understand what sexual harassment is, which is quite a different thing.

Most strikingly and brilliantly, Michael Heyward had the idea of signing up Garner at Text, and released a collection of her non-fiction, *True Stories*. The cover of *True Stories* features a wonderful shot of Garner, photographed as philosophers were once photographed in the first half of the twentieth century: looking upwards in three-quarter profile with the light coming from below. Garner looks quizzical, sage-like, yet authoritative. She touches her fingers lightly together, as if undoing some philosopher's puzzle (the fingers are repeated, enlarged, on the back cover). The title of the book is written across her chest in an informal script, suggesting her as a kind of philosopher of the people. Above it is her name, in a similar script. Both her name and the words 'true stories' are emblazoned on her, each as much a part of her as the other. It is a shot that makes you feel you have been present at a canonisation.

★

The efforts to keep the writer of *The First Stone* on a pedestal were in complete contradiction to the efforts made to knock Helen Darville-Demidenko off hers. By the end of 1995,

Darville's portrait was being used to sell satirical Christmas editions of news magazines.[14] I have no intention of defending *The Hand that Signed the Paper* or its author here; I find both the book and the claims Darville later made in interviews offensive and, in particular, anti-Semitic. But the questions that were asked of *The Hand that Signed the Paper* weren't asked of *The First Stone*, even if, as it turned out, many of the protagonists in both debates were the same.

On the contrary, most commentators made a dogged effort to keep discussion of the two books apart. The central fear seemed to be that just as one book by a canonical writer might leave the canon (which could upset the whole show), so another might enter. Most defenders of *The First Stone* relied on more or less the same argument: that the book had been written by a reputable artist and was therefore art, and possessed the requisite writerly virtues. Therefore they didn't consider that they even had to answer charges that the book could have been written artlessly, say, out of malice, or was a biased account. Critics of *The Hand that Signed the Paper*, on the other hand, were equally determined to read it as artless, against any claims it might have accrued on the basis of having won three major literary prizes. 'It's not very well written' became the stock-in-trade comment, which, true or not, nevertheless tended to undermine the possibility that inclusion in the category 'art' might obviate the charges made against the book.

Here, at the centre of the Year of the Helens, was a spectacle of two very different literary receptions, each with its own affect and dispensations. Though *The Hand that Signed the Paper* was widely regarded as fiction, it was held up for critique in quite a different way from *The First Stone* — a book commonly asserted to be a work of non-fiction. Garner's credentials as a leading feminist were never examined in the same way as Darville's ethnicity. Nor were her research methods, her treatment of evidence, or her frequent and dismayed defence that critics of the book seemed to be reading something quite different from what she thought she'd written. Indeed, her prevarication was held up as a shining example of what it means to be 'human'.

The controversy over *The Hand that Signed the Paper* has faded very quickly, considering the intensity of the storm that broke out. Thus far, the sky remains in place. Briefly, for those who haven't caught up, or who have forgotten, Helen Darville wrote the book under an assumed name and assumed Ukrainian identity. As Helen Demidenko, she presented an account of the administration of Nazi death camps, written from the Ukrainian side, as a piece of family history. The first controversy over the book concerned its argument that the Bolsheviks who had persecuted Ukrainians before the war included a large number of Jews, and that this in some way explained, or even justified, why Darville-Demidenko's Ukrainian ancestors had been willing to administer Nazi death camps. The book didn't mention that this supposed association of Bolsheviks and Jews is a historical fiction with a basis in Nazi propaganda. The second controversy broke out when it was revealed that Darville's identity was fake. She wasn't Ukrainian but English, and the book therefore wasn't a family history. A third controversy concerned allegations that parts of the book were plagiarised. Darville defended herself through lawyers who, among other things, submitted that this was typical postmodern fictional practice.

Striking as the controversies over Darville's book were, they haven't had the effects forecast. The affair was spectacular but not lasting. It was, as a senior writer on a major broadsheet has said, 'a media feeding frenzy . . . an embarrassment'.[15] But the affair remains compelling, not only as a reminder of the insidiousness of anti-Semitism, but also because of a few things that went largely unnoticed at the time, being less to do with the controversies themselves than the way they were played out. Most fascinating is the way the book enabled a certain community of critics, columnists and journalists to go over some agendas that were firmly in place long before *The Hand that Signed the Paper* stumbled onstage.

Typical was a piece that appeared in the *Sydney Morning Herald* at the height of the affair under the headline 'The Art of Being PC'.[16] It used the controversy over Darville's assumed Ukrainian identity to pontificate that arts funding was more likely to go to a 'basket weaver' than a 'proper artist', or to an ethnic writer on the basis of their ethnicity. But on the list of previous Miles Franklin Award winners, Demidenko stands out as the only conspicuously non-Anglo name apart from Malouf in the forty-year history of the award. Affirmative action and multiculturalism were in the firing line here. Cited on this ethnic-funding controversy were the usual suspects, including Les Murray, Bob Ellis and David Williamson. They were joined by the sculptor Ron Robertson-Swann, the poet Mark O'Connor, the pianist Roger Woodward, the president of the Fellowship of Australian Composers, John Colborne-Veel, the Sydney composer Ian Shanahan, Canberra economist Stephen Rimmer, and *Adelaide Review* editor Christopher Pearson. A club, apparently, for the white, male, and over-40. Countervailing quotes from three women — Marion Halligan, head of the Literature Board, Hannie Rayson, who sat on that board, and Hilary McPhee, chair of the Australia Council, all of whom spoke in their official roles — occupied about one-fifth of the article's length, at the end. Otherwise the voices of younger, non-white, or female artists were completely absent. This, I would have thought, confirmed the need for exactly the kind of affirmative action that the article argued against. What the article did instead was set up and police a set of polar opposites: white art *vs* migrant art, legitimate art *vs* illegitimate art (craft, as in 'basket weaving'), and high culture *vs* low.

Many other commentators succumbed to a similar reflex. 'She's ethnic, she's young, a woman and a victim to boot. Wow! Have I got a politically correct award winner for you,' wrote Barry Cohen in the *Australian*.[17] 'Demidenko's false identity has clearly been designed to exploit our culture's overweening need to be seen to be promoting its obscure or exotic minorities,' wrote Rosemary Neill.[18] Explaining how the book won the prizes, Terry Lane wrote: 'It is written by a young (score one point) woman (move close to the top of the queue) of "non-English speaking background" (home and hosed).'[19] 'Agenda Setters Brought to Book' was the title of another piece, which took Darville's side but used the affair to question the credibility of the 'spurious government-patronised arts establishment'.[20]

The debate was less than representative in other respects too. Of the four books on the affair, three were instigated by middle-aged men with strong press connections. Andrew Riemer wrote *The Demidenko Debate*, John Jost compiled *The Demidenko File* with Gianna Totaro and Christine Tyshing, and Robert Manne wrote *The Culture of Forgetting*. The fourth book, *The Demidenko Diary*, was written by Darville's friend Natalie Jane Prior as an exposé of Darville's personal life. It seemed that the figure of Darville was being battled over by the sort of middle-aged patriarchs who routinely set themselves up as arbiters of public morals. Both Manne's and Riemer's books, despite their disagreements, are notable for the number of times they use the word 'youth'. Both doubt the suitability of younger people as cultural heirs. Like Manne, Riemer draws a straight line between cultural theory, postmodernism and youth:

> In her university years Helen Darville would have been thoroughly exposed to such notions, which are almost universally advocated, with lesser or greater conviction and lesser or greater clarity, by contemporary literary academics . . . It is by no means unlikely that she would have been attracted to the pervasive scepticism and potential nihilism that inform such intellectual inclinations . . . Helen

All hands on deck

Darville, her novel and the deceptions she practised may well represent the malaise of contemporary youth, the lack of moral sensitivity her critics detected in her, and even perhaps a morbid fascination with violence unrelieved by pity or compassion.[21]

As if to further demonstrate what was at stake in the Demidenko affair, towards its end the major protagonists started fighting among themselves. The debate degenerated into a four-cornered contest between Riemer, Manne, P. P. McGuinness and Gerard Henderson, each baiting the others and working over old agendas and enmities. It was a fascinating exchange, played out almost entirely within the self-contained logics of the cultural establishment. This is a pattern in Australian public life. When Robert Manne faces off with Humphrey McQueen over Manning Clark, or Phillip Adams does battle with Stuart Littlemore or Ray Martin, or any combination of the above, I suspect that they see themselves as occupying great and opposing positions. They'd be surprised, I think, by how alike they all look to outsiders.

In the Darville-Demidenko affair, the catalyst for open hostilities was the appearance of Riemer's book, which accused attackers of *The Hand that Signed the Paper* of being 'politically correct' and totalitarian. Manne, a long-time campaigner against 'PC', clearly stung by Riemer's accusation, devoted a whole chapter of his book to Riemer's argument, and was goaded into stating, apparently in contradiction to his earlier utterances on 'PC', that 'criticism, however harsh, is not censorship'.[22] The nerve Riemer exposed was Manne's tendency to exempt his own 'ism' — anti-anti-Semitism — from the scepticism with which he treated other 'isms'. Manne seems to have applied the cultural establishment's golden rule: other people's ideals are instances of 'political correctness'; mine are 'ethics'. Once Henderson and McGuinness had weighed in, the net effect was of listening to a closed conversation in which each participant was keen to hand down his own version of the final judgement, not just on the book, but on its other judges.

Other circles of commentary on the affair were similarly limited. Although Henderson and others have claimed that the Darville-Demidenko debate was an example of the literary establishment closing ranks to defend its members, the opposite was the case. Much of the debate took place among a remarkably small but influential literary circle. Henderson's claim, in a sense, came with a caveat; 'literary establishment' was in part code for 'Miles Franklin Award judges'. Far from being an organised front, most of Darville's defenders looked isolated and friendless. The bulk of the literary community closed ranks not to defend Darville, but to attack her.

Many of Darville's most prominent critics were journal editors, who shared out a fair slab of public space on the affair among themselves. The rule here seemed to be 'you publish in my journal and I'll publish in yours'. Manne, who is the editor of *Quadrant*, published in *Australian Book Review* and *Quadrant*. Ivor Indyk, then involved with *Southerly* and subsequently founding editor of *Heat*, also published in *ABR*. Morag Fraser, editor of *Eureka Street*, wrote on the book's reception for *Meanjin*. Peter Craven, former editor of *Scripsi*, was published in *ABR*. Helen Daniel, editor of *ABR*, was a prominent critic of the judges, and called regularly for their resignation from her editorial chair, as well as from the floor of the 1996 Sydney Writers' Festival. The forum *ABR* published on the affair gives a vignette of how it all worked. Despite claims that the forum comprised 'a number of people', tending to suggest that participants comprised a representative cross-section of the community, all turned out to be editors, writers and critics.[23] Contributors included Manne, George Papaellinas, then editor of the journal *RePublica*, Louise Adler, then arts editor of the *Age*, Riemer, then literary editor of the *Independent Monthly*, Margaret Jones, former literary editor of the *Sydney Morning*

All hands on deck

Herald, and David Bernstein, editor of *Australian Jewish News*. Of the eleven participants, all but two denounced the book or expressed reservations about the judging of the Miles Franklin Award.

The charmed circle set up by the journal editors spread through to the newspapers. Manne was prominent in the *Age*, and along with Henderson was Darville's most prolific critic. Ivor Indyk wrote for the *Australian*.[24] Ian Syson, then assistant editor of *Meanjin*, now editor of *Overland*, wrote for the *Age*.[25] Guy Rundle, an editor of *Arena Magazine*, also wrote for the *Age*, as did Peter Christoff, a contributor to *Arena Magazine*, *ABR* and the *Australian*.[26] Daniel also attacked the judges in her regular *Age* column.

Those writing for the *Age* constituted a powerful front. Henderson's regular anti-Darville columns and pieces by writers such as Pamela Bone and Jacques Adler joined the paper's anti-Darville editorials. At one point the *Age* ran three virulently anti-Darville pieces on a single day. At the height of the affair a solitary piece by David Marr provided a dissenting voice. If Riemer raised the ire of some of these commentators by suggesting they behaved in a totalitarian manner, then perhaps there was something in what seemed at first a hyperbolic charge. Embarrassing moments included a hysterical column by Guy Rundle calling for the book to be withdrawn from sale — at least he didn't suggest it be burnt — which appeared near an anti-Darville editorial that followed Robert Manne's theme on the affair, commenting on 'a poverty of intellect and feeling at the core of the Australian literary culture which is truly shocking'.[27] Louise Adler, Rundle's editor, later commented that if Rundle's column appeared it therefore meant she agreed with its content.[28]

Peter Craven, who commented frequently on the affair from his column in the *Australian*, was an interesting case. He started off as a defender of the book, writing 'I do not think the book is a fictionalised fascist tract. It is a talented novel, by a young writer, full of vividly conceived action.'[29] Later he wrote 'there is no reason why a work that is actually and unambiguously imbued with fascism cannot win a literary prize',[30] citing George Orwell's famous defence of the awarding of the Bollingen prize to Ezra Pound just after World War II, when he was on trial for making pro-fascist broadcasts. To be fair, this was before the problems of Darville's falsified ethnic identity arose, and before parts of the book were alleged to be plagiarised. Yet Craven's change of heart couldn't have been more complete. A year later he was to announce 'The next Miles Franklin Award shortlist is upon us. Still from the team that brought you Helen Demidenko.'[31] In the interim he wrote a column quoting a three-paragraph slab of Manne's damning review of the novel for *ABR*.[32]

Craven's quoting Manne was part of a trend. Suddenly everyone was writing on the issue, and no-one seemed to notice it was a tag-team event. Rosemary Neill, writing in the *Australian*, also quoted Manne.[33] Craven later praised Manne, Heyward (Manne's publisher) and Daniel for their contribution to the debate.[34] Daniel, in her *Age* column, praised Heyward for his commentary on the affair.[35] Gideon Haigh, another of Heyward's authors, writing in the *Australian*, quoted Syson, Indyk and the poet John Forbes, as well as Daniel, and announced that *ABR* was about to publish four pages of letters on the affair.[36] Syson, writing for the *Age*, approvingly quoted Forbes.[37] Rundle, in his *Age* piece, commended Daniel as an 'honourable dissenter' from the bulk of the 'literati'.[38] In his *Age* column, Henderson approvingly cited Christoff, and mentioned his *Age* colleagues Daniel and Adler as evidence that 'some leading figures in the literary world did speak out about the book'.[39] Ex-politician Barry Cohen, meanwhile, approvingly quoted Henderson.[40]

The reviewing of the books on the affair followed a similar pattern. Craven reviewed Riemer's *The Demidenko Debate* and Jost et al's *The Demidenko File* for the *Australian*.[41] In his review of Manne's *The Culture of Forgetting*, also for the *Australian*, he claimed that, despite his misgivings about Manne's understanding of fiction, Manne had produced the 'last and best word' on the affair.[42] Christoff, who is quoted in *The Culture of Forgetting* as claiming 'that a book like this would not have been published in Europe let alone honoured',[43] wrote the review for the *Age*.[44] Andrew Rutherford wrote a slightly sceptical but ultimately approving review of *The Culture of Forgetting* for the *Sunday Age*,[45] as well as a blanket review of the three other Demidenko books.[46] In an extraordinary feature-length profile of Manne and his book for the *Age*, Michael Gawenda was struck by Manne's sincerity and the courage with which he took a stand on a controversial issue. *The Culture of Forgetting*, Gawenda wrote, is a 'superb book . . . this is a book written out of pain'.[47] For a moment it seemed that Manne might achieve sainthood. Soon afterwards he did the next best thing, accepting a post at the *Australian*.

Given that plagiarism was one of the charges levelled at Darville, it's ironic that many non-'literati' journalists writing on the affair also repeated each other's copy. The Darville-Demidenko debate was conducted mainly in the 'quality press' and the ABC. Commercial television and radio hardly touched it. There was no footage to speak of, and for once the broadsheets had an issue all to themselves. This provided them with a unique opportunity to differentiate themselves from other forms of media. Only talkback radio can match the broadsheet press's penchant for 'opinion' journalism, but the broadsheets have an edge because of their greater news-gathering ability. The repetition of more and more 'opinion' is important for the broadsheets, given that they cater for a narrow demographic, and seek to create a certain moral tone. The affair served as a reminder that journalists too are involved in a postmodern art that, like some postmodern fiction, places more emphasis on 'the story' than on the real — though postmodern novelists signal their 'borrowings' as part of the effect.

Most of the interesting commentary on the Darville-Demidenko controversy took place outside the circuits set up by such columnists, with their hard-wired mythologies about 'PC', multiculturalism and postmodernism. The cycle of hagiographic reviewing of the books on the affair was broken by Philip Cassell's review of *The Culture of Forgetting* in the Melbourne *Herald-Sun*. He pointed out that Manne's book, apart from documenting the anti-Semitism of *The Hand that Signed the Paper*, mostly functioned as systematic character assassination designed to discredit Darville:

> If we read Helen Darville as someone whose fantasies and political views result from her need to find a way of expressing her acute personal problems, and if she is an entirely idiosyncratic self-creation, then clearly she is not an agent in a 'culture of forgetting', and it is pointless to blame the education system or youth culture for her sorry condition.[48]

Some of the best commentary on the affair appeared in the letters pages. 'To Bring Off a Demidenko You Still Have to be a Darville' was the title of one letter debunking the anti-multicultural argument. Its writer claims that any first-generation immigrant knows 'only an Anglo-Saxon can effectively work the system that exists in the elite circles of this culture, even when it comes to affirmation of the ethnic experience'.[49] In Darville's case it would seem that only an author with a certain Anglo background and education would be likely to pull off a scam like winning the Miles Franklin Award on false pretences if, in fact, that was what Darville did.

Literary hoaxes are often to do with race, or bring anxieties about race to the surface. This was later evident in the Carmen–Bayley hoax, where the writer Leon Carmen, with the blessing of his agent John Bayley, set out to prove that non-white writers are advantaged in Australia by writing a mock-Aboriginal biography. Most hoaxes play out as a form of phobic narrative about the influx and representation of the

All hands on deck

'other'. In both the Darville-Demidenko hoax and the Carmen–Bayley affair, it was whites who set out to show the error of non-white ways by formulating an exposé of identity credentials and multiculturalism. Much as hoaxes pass commentary on the fragility of *all* cultural identity (as RuPaul says, we're all in some sort of cultural drag), no local hoax has ever reflected adversely on the primacy of white identity. It is non-whites who are inevitably asked to defend a position in terms of white concepts of cultural identity, and who, as 'newcomers', whether they be Eastern European migrants or post-Mabo Aboriginal writers, tend to end up bearing the brunt. No doubt Carmen and Bayley thought their hoax a clever commentary, but against the background of white male whingeing, Aboriginal-bashing and multiculturalism-bashing that had taken place in the previous few years, it seemed all too predictable.

Despite Craven's claim for Manne's book, perhaps the last word on the Darville-Demidenko affair went to the marchers in the Demidenko marching group in the 1996 Gay and Lesbian Mardi Gras. 'Is it a critique or a homage,' I asked one of them before the event. It was definitely a homage, came the reply; 'she is a cross-dresser and so are we'. With its blonde drag splendour, complete with little woven Ukrainian baskets, the marching group was pure pastiche. Like much pastiche, it implicitly asked whether there is any such thing as an original, raising the possibility that everyone, in some way, is in drag, and is somehow a performer of their gender. What comes first: performance or gender, fake or original? Queer culture has a big stake in questions like this, because they anticipate another that is equally ingrained in Western culture, with an inbuilt answer: what comes first, heterosexual or homosexual? Pastiche, by destabilising the possibility of originals, points to the idea that there is no naturalised, original sexuality, and that heterosexuality, like homosexuality, is as much a construct as everything else — not a primary, natural state.

Gangland

If the Darville-Demidenko debate had a stature larger than it otherwise might have deserved, that was at least in part because anxieties about cultural primacy were a feature of many of the issues against which it was projected: anti-multiculturalism, anti-postmodernism, anti-academicism and the unsuitability of youth as cultural heirs (Henderson is an exception here — he was one of the few commentators to stick to his basic objections to the book's anti-Semitism). Much of the argument turned out to be based on anxieties about centre and periphery. In *The Culture of Forgetting*, running alongside Manne's disquiet that the lessons of the Holocaust may be forgotten (an anxiety that, incidentally, I share) is a parallel worry that Europe might be forgotten.

One of the problems with this sort of cultural nostalgia is that it sets up a further set of polar opposites. To the playing-off of migrant art against white art, illegitimate art against real art and low culture against high can be added local versus European. Such oppositions though are almost always conservative. And they have their traps. The *Australian* got so carried away with the white-centre-*vs*-multicultural-margins orthodoxy of the debate over *The Hand that Signed the Paper* that it tricked itself into some racism of its own. 'Nothing Ukrainian, Please' ran the headline on an article about the following year's Vogel award.[50]

When critics of *The Hand that Signed the Paper* sought to present themselves as representatives of a European-style 'sophistication' and depth of 'cultural memory', they implicitly suggested that other cultures couldn't provide the same. The hidden subtext was a narrative about cultural primacy, not only to do with whiteness, national identity and cultural origin, but also to do with their own role as social commentators. These sorts of assumptions, which seek to validate the critic's role as moral arbiter, are a recurrent, if subterranean, feature of local cultural life. At the centre of *The First Stone*, for example, is a set of questions about 'what sort of public figure am I?' —

All hands on deck

one of the mainsprings of the book's narrative drive being the failure of the Ormond complainants to recognise Garner's book as the public space for a debate about feminism. But if Darville's detractors seemed less anxious, and even a little smug, in their eagerness to judge they seemed guilty of a little provincialism of their own.

Few of those who pontificated most loudly on the Darville-Demidenko affair seemed able to cope with the fact that, according to the generally accepted conventions of fiction, authors' names don't have an agency function, only a copyright function. *The Culture of Forgetting*, in part, reads as an extended failure to comprehend that fiction as a genre makes no necessary link between fact and written word. The irony of Manne's striving to make that connection is that, while he chides the judges of various awards for their provincialism in not spotting the text's anti-Semitism, in seeking a precise match between Demidenko (as he insists on calling her) and the narrator of the book, he makes the same crude mistake as the judges did when they honoured the book as a first-person account. Henderson too seemed determined to blame the 'literati' for what is in fact an essential fictional convention. I'm not a fan of arguments about art for art's sake — when Frank Moorhouse starts talking about the free rein of the 'feral imagination', I switch right off. But fiction is by definition granted a certain licence from fact (though not from responsibility). Henderson failed to make the distinction. His main strategy, in radio interview after radio interview, was to buttress his arguments against Darville with the fact that she had described the book as 'faction'. But this seemed a weak excuse for failing to investigate what fiction actually is. The first thing any critic learns is never to take writers' claims for their work at face value or premise arguments on them.

If we're going to talk 'provincialism' and indulge in hyperbole about 'a culture that has drifted from its moorings',[51] then debating the stuff of fiction should be different from questioning the right of fiction, its writers and its critics to function in accordance with the wider social conventions that govern their work. Other critics too claimed that Darville had misrepresented herself and thereby betrayed our trust in her as an author. It was all a bit like someone who went to the big city complaining that they'd got their pockets picked. A defining characteristic of the novel as a genre is that empirical validation is not required — and writers and critics didn't just make that rule up yesterday.

Again, I should stress that I'm not trying to defend *The Hand that Signed the Paper* as a responsible work — I don't think it is — but there is a difference between censuring Darville's exploitation of the conventions of fiction and blaming the affair on those conventions and those who defend them, whether they be other writers or 'literary critics who are infatuated with the free play of texts'.[52]

This more or less systematic misunderstanding of some basic conventions set up a further set of binary oppositions. As in the debate about Garner's book, there was a logic of 'same' and 'other' at work. Opponents of Darville's book and supporters of Garner's united to demonise the rest. In each case, roughly the same group — academics, feminists, multiculturalists and the 'literati' — were cast as congenital non-truth-tellers about themselves and their professions. Despite Manne's bland assertion that 'during the Demidenko controversy the principle of free speech in its essential and noble meaning was, quite simply, not under question',[53] bully-boy tactics were common throughout the debate.

The orthodoxy was that *The Hand that Signed the Paper* was universally anti-Semitic and universally bad, not just for its critics, but for everyone.[54] So strong was this orthodoxy that the scandal almost took on a new life as the basis for a 'theory of everything'. If the book won the Miles Franklin Award, so the logic went, then the award itself evidently needed rethinking. If the literati supported it, then they too needed rethinking. If

All hands on deck

multicultural bias was one of the reasons for the award being made, then that policy should be questioned. At one point it seemed as if anyone who defended any aspect of the book risked condemnation as anti-Semitic by association. People were labelled revisionists, postmodernists and even Nazi sympathisers because they differed from the orthodoxy, or because their view was more complex. Reviewers were accused of moral emptiness just because they found something to like about the book. A reluctance to judge was confused with a lack of interest in morality. Character assassination, vilification and *ad hominem* attacks became the norm. As David Marr said, 'the core humanity of those who have admired the book is being casually questioned'.[55]

Populist strategies of demonisation that single out 'feminists', 'critical theorists' and now the 'literati' are the pattern of recent cultural debates. Again, the logic is polar. All of these groups are figured in opposition to 'common sense', 'ethics', 'social responsibility', the common interest of the 'mainstream', or a grip on the real. The Holocaust, in this case, figures as the ultimate version of the real. But is it possible to defend alternative ways of thinking about the Holocaust without being anti-Semitic? Contrary to the textual fundamentalism put about by some of the critics, it is. In fact, asking such questions has a bearing on the controversy, and on the role often played by members of cultural elites.

Unique in its horrors though the Holocaust is, it would be a mistake to think of it as an 'originary' or sacrosanct moral moment, as some critics of Darville-Demidenko seemed to want to do. Most authoritarian movements have their basis in a similar absolutism. Holocaust absolutism brings the danger of closing off ways of thinking about similar horrors, such as the slaughter of millions on the Russian front, or by Pol Pot, or in Rwanda. The risk of putting the Holocaust at the centre of one's moral universe and declaring that 'it should never happen again' is that it may blind one to the fact that it *does* keep happening, if in slightly less systematic forms. In the case of *The Hand that Signed the Paper*, much of the debate took place against a background of 'ethnic cleansing' in the former Yugoslavia, but few commentators mentioned this. A notable exception was Craven, who commented that, if not for the likes of Henderson or Manne, some 'might have imagined on the basis of Darville that the Holocaust was *simply* another Bosnia or Somalia'.[56] (The italics are mine.) Tempting as it is to think of events like the Holocaust as instances of pure evil, essentialising evil tends to render it a problem without solution. Thinking in less transcendental terms allows us not only to condemn the Holocaust, but also to question those who exploit the Holocaust as a token of moral righteousness to set themselves up as prophets. It was at this level that Darville too deserved to be criticised, not demonised at the level of absolutes.

★

Scandals, as someone once said, are satisfying. They seem to provide the clear demarcation between good and evil so often missing in everyday life, bringing events into a kind of clear relief. The Year of the Helens was a good solid year of scandals, yet none was as simple as it seemed. In fact, in both of the leading events the prevailing wisdom could easily be turned on its head. The real scandal of *The First Stone* isn't about 'feral feminists' but about the power of literary reputation. The scandal of the Darville-Demidenko affair isn't just to do with anti-Semitism, but is to do with the power of the press, and the ability of prominent individuals with powerful connections to lobby and skew debate. Like Stalinist art, the reputations of prominent figures in Australian culture are accorded a certain monumentality. A famous comedian once said to me that Australian culture's greatest single talent is elevating the middlebrow to the highbrow, accompanied by an unwillingness to ask the really hard questions, all the time muttering darkly about the 'tall poppy syndrome'. But a strong cultural climate should have critics as able as its artists, and artists who can withstand critical commentary.

If the above debates were mainly run by a middle-aged partisan sect of much the same age and background in such a way that coverage tended to reflect what editors assumed were the received ideas, prejudices and interests of a certain generation, other branches of popular culture were covered in much the same way. The so-called 'Year of the Helens' wasn't just the Year of the Helens. It was also the year of the Beatles, the Rolling Stones, Hendrix, the Eagles, David Bowie and Queen.

'Purple Haze of Time Fails to Dim the Legacy of Hendrix's Genius' went the headline in the *Weekend Australian*.[57] The Eagles and the Rolling Stones toured and generated heaps of press coverage. But the biggest act of the year was the Beatles. One paper devoted a full page and a half to an article celebrating some new Beatles recordings that 'will make The Beatles the world's biggest act — again'.[58] 'Strawberry Fields for Ever and Ever' was its title. Another devoted two full pages to the story, under the headline 'Still Fab Forever'.[59] The *Sunday Age* devoted three pages to what they called 'The Second Coming'.[60] As the Beatles hype machine rolled on, news filtered through of a new album from 1970s glam rockers Queen, featuring the vocals of Freddie Mercury, who had been dead for four years. It only reinforced the impression that baby-boomers would rather raise the dead than listen to new music. Queen also got the full-page feature treatment. One article was headlined 'The Immortal Freddie'.[61] The tide of 'legislated nostalgia' was already in full swing in the lead-up to the Year of the Helens, with Woodstock '94, where nearly all the media attention was on Bob Dylan and Crosby, Nash and Young, as opposed to Nine Inch Nails and Green Day, who reportedly got the best crowd reactions. When younger bands were mentioned, it seemingly came with a caveat. One article on silverchair appeared alongside a feature on Hendrix, twice the size, as if to say, hey kids, don't forget who the masters are.[62]

The Year of the Helens, at least as far as music coverage in the 'quality press' went, was a year of diminished public space for younger people. It was also the year when Anna Wood died, the year of the Paxton beat-up, and the year in which importation of the book *E is for Ecstasy* was banned. It was the year first news came through of the invention of a pill to stop ageing, and the year of *Smoky Joe's Cafe*, featuring the songs of Leiber and Stoller. 'Who could forget the Delltones?' Charles Wooley intoned in the *60 Minutes* tribute to the stage show.[63]

It was a year in which women were pilloried, more than usual, as producers of unreliable narratives. Running alongside Helen Garner's interrogation of the Ormond complainants as 'disingenuous' and the protracted judgement of Helen Darville were the media trials of the Hindmarsh Island women and the trial of Carmen Lawrence, all of whom were deemed to have failed the test as 'truth tellers', while their accusers, who were often male, set themselves up as 'truth measurers'. In some ways all these controversies seemed a throwback to an earlier age.

I'm not a huge believer in the idea of public space, or that the broadsheet press should be some kind of prime mover, dominating a culture with its moral authority. Nor do I think the media always 'get it wrong' and are so monolithic that no-one can intervene. In fact the Year of the Helens seemed to show precisely the opposite — that the broadsheet media feel under siege from other forms of media (tabloids, the Internet and on-line services, the mass electronic media, niche publications and so on) and are looking to enhance their declining prestige by sponsoring certain kinds of debates (and the figures to run them). Over the past fifty years, per capita newspaper circulation has fallen 75 per cent.[64] What keeps the broadsheets important and makes the idea of public spaces useful is that representative government relies on them. As these recent

All hands on deck

debates have shown, younger people don't have much of a space in these imagined zones. Almost all the commentary is played out by the same elites. Perhaps that, after all, is what it means to be part of the *Zeitgeist*.

Dark underbelly: youth, culture, policy

The idealization of youth, which formed so central a part of the culture of the twentieth century, is losing its material basis as youth unemployment remains high and as the former virtues of youth turn into disadvantages.

Keith Windschuttle (1979)[1]

Society is based on complicity in the common crime.

Sigmund Freud

A snapshot of the *Zeitgeist*? If the shenanigans of the Year of the Helens suggested that younger people struggle to find a voice within 'mainstream' culture, there were parallels in some of the government policy-making surrounding it. Without wanting to suggest that poor social policy-making is somehow the 'fault' of a cultural elite, or that any of those mentioned so far are consciously 'anti-youth', the way questions about youth and generationalism have circulated in recent cultural controversies is at least symptomatic. It points to a more general culture of demonisation and neglect.

Lately, for example, there has been a flurry of activity on the issue of youth 'gangs'. In a single month the vast majority of State governments presented measures to deal with the 'problem'. In New South Wales, premier Bob Carr announced he was considering legislation to give police the right to break up 'gangs' of more than three. The South Australian Minister for Youth Affairs, Dorothy Kotz, suggested a youth curfew as a 'crime prevention tool', to deprive young people of the 'opportunity to commit crimes that you see in your own street now, that you didn't see five years ago'.[2] In Western Australia such a curfew was introduced in the town of Geraldton, and Richard Court, the Western Australian premier, defended his military-style boot camps, designed to put errant youth 'back on track' by involving them in community projects and local businesses, and expressed surprise at the young people's ability to work.[3] In Tasmania, the Groom government proposed banning repeat offenders from certain areas of Hobart, targeting 'gangs' and homeless young people.[4]

That all this took place within a few weeks in August and September 1996 doesn't so much suggest the arrival of a new social problem as a wave of hysteria. Governments seemed to be latching on to a perceived vote-winner — the old law-and-order argument with a new twist, and a new and defenceless target. A target that could be pilloried without offending the mainstream media audience or alienating swinging voters.

Don't think they're being original: the strategy is imported. Bill Clinton's 1996 re-election platform proposed the reintroduction of school uniforms and a curfew for teenagers, promises that campaign adviser Dick Morris said would appeal to swinging voters.[5] The US Congress has passed a Youth Predators Act that puts juveniles on the same legal footing as adults. The UK Conservative Party under John Major, in its unsuccessful 1997 re-election campaign, proposed that offenders over ten years of age be required to wear electronic tracking tags. The Tories also proposed the introduction of curfews and the electronic tagging of parents to make sure they stayed at home with their children.[6]

This hysteria reflects a change that has taken place since the late 1980s in the way youth crime has been reported, and even demarcated as 'youth crime'. The 'gang' has emerged as a reporting phenomenon and as an occasion for moral panic. It's no coincidence that this has happened alongside other moral panics involving youth, such as the 'victim feminism' debate, the debates about 'political correctness', rave culture and campus speech codes, and even debates about the emergence of 'grunge' fiction and the 'decline' of literature. What the 'gangs' phenomenon has in common with all the above moral panics is sustained and prejudicial misreporting, and the construction of younger people as 'outsiders' who threaten the proper business of a wider community, whether it be an urban community supposedly threatened by crime, an imagined feminist community that sees its achievements 'betrayed', or a conservative literary community fearing that 'standards' are under threat.

'Youth Gangs Problem Blights Our Big Cities' ran one headline in the *Australian*.[7] The article opened with tales of the bizarre behaviour of graffiti gangs who travel over 80 kilometres by rail to deface Gold Coast tourist sites. Promisingly for its thesis, Asians and drugs emerge as issues in the very first sentence. In the tradition of the spotters' guides mentioned in chapter 1, there is material about heroin gangs, race gangs, bikie gangs and the amphetamine trade. Alongside is a map showing how the problem has spread through every State, illustrated with a picture of a surly stereotypical homeboy youth, his arms folded, in what newspaper editors evidently imagine to be the youth uniform of jacket and baggy trousers, complete with the ubiquitous baseball cap. But read the whole article and you discover that, according to the director of the New South Wales Bureau of Crime Statistics, 'crime statistics did not show any increase in gang-related crimes'. The article depends on conflating a range of criminal activities carried out by various groups under the heading 'youth crime'. (It's a long time since most bikie gangs were 'youth'.) Another strategem is to label any youth group a 'gang'. Evidence of gang activity in Perth, for example, is labelled on the map as 'some groups of Aboriginal youth'. Under what circumstances, I wonder, is a group a gang?

'Gangland Victoria: Youth Crime Booms' ran a full-width screamer on the front page of the *Age*.[8] In this case the evidence for a rising 'tide of crime' consisted of statistics noting an increase in the number of children appearing before the courts, 'partly because of an increase in gang violence'. The argument was buttressed by quotes from welfare, judicial and police figures, arranged so as to foreground their expressions of 'concern'. In the context of the article such 'concern' registers as alarm, but might otherwise read simply as an expression of proper professional interest. Read further, and it is revealed that, in spite of an increase in 'offences against the person' by young offenders, juvenile offences remain a small proportion of crimes — hardly enough to warrant the front-page treatment. Read further again and it turns out that most of the so-called 'boom' had nothing to do with gangs at all, but was the result of a tripling of arrests for petty matters such as public transport offences and failing to wear a bicycle helmet. This article was illustrated with a photo of a group of homeboy youths.

'Children Who Kill' was the headline above a full-page feature in the *Sunday Age*.[9] This one kicked off with a couple of lurid and emotive anecdotes, speculating that 'new figures show a dramatic rise in the number of young teenagers charged with homicide. Are we following the American trend?' As it happened, the increase in homicides cited was from 2 in 1989–90 to 8 in 1994–95, down from 9 in 1993–94. Hardly evidence for the scaremongering that preceded. A barrister, John Smallwood, noted that most killings seemed to be accidental, and, in the case of stabbings, resulted from a single wound. Frank Vincent, a Supreme Court judge and chairman of the Parole Board, was quoted as saying he was unaware of any substantial variation in youth homicides.

The murder of a taxi driver by a 13-year-old was nevertheless reported in such a way as to suggest that youth were on the rampage. 'Young and Out of Control' was the headline for a full-page article that played on the 'cold-bloodedness' of the murder, suggesting that 'the case reveals the growing Australian and worldwide problem of juvenile crime, depression and alienation, often stemming from family breakdown'. Several experts were cited to similar effect, one saying the boy was typical of 'hundreds' of similarly 'out of control' young people, and another claiming that the case was typical of 'a growing number of disillusioned young kids with very negative life experiences, no hope and no sense of vision', the implication being that there is any number of similarly dysfunctional, potentially dangerous young people lurking on the city streets at night.[10]

'Kids 14, Dealing Heroin on Streets' ran another page-1 headline in the *Sunday Age*.[11] Again, the way such headlines are constructed is interesting. The article itself is about children who are at risk and vulnerable to exploitation by older criminals. So, for the headline, why not 'Drugs Exploitation, Kids at Risk'? 'What do Your Kids do After School?' was another headline, with a lurid half-page colour photo of a kid snorting a powder track.[12]

'The New Untouchables' screamed a *Bulletin* headline.[13] An introductory line in bold type below read: 'Mob rule: They are being called the plague — gangs of lawless children who terrorise the residents of outback towns . . . there is little the local police can do to stop them.' Again the strategy was to deal with any problem as a 'law-and-order' issue. The article quoted local business people and homeowners who claimed to have had their premises or homes vandalised by Aboriginal children. There was only one countervailing quote from a member of the Aboriginal community, and scant discussion of those towns' desperate economic and social problems, their specific racial problems, or the dearth of attempts to tackle such problems by non-law-and-order means.

Dark underbelly

These and a host of similar headlines and articles have tended to treat young people as pariahs — and, in an increasingly populist legislative climate, governments are listening. As mentioned in chapter 1, an early instance was the Western Australian government's *Crime (Serious and Repeat Offenders) Sentencing Act (1992)*. This followed a wave of hysteria whipped up by radio talkback host Howard Sattler and Perth's daily newspaper, the *West Australian*. The writer Paul Sheiner has detailed how the *West Australian* structured a narrative about juvenile crime and constructed a picture of the typical juvenile offender, placing him in a sort of stagnant US-style undercity, using a series of emotive headlines similar to those above ('Aboriginal Gangs Terrorise Suburbs').[14] These stories functioned as a background for a further set of stories about high-speed police chases involving young people — many of them Aboriginal — in stolen cars. Sheiner points out how a series of earlier stories on youth crime, while generally not dwelling on questions of race, were placed alongside stories to do with Aboriginal gangs, glue-sniffing, and the drain on taxpayers' money resulting from Aboriginal claims to the Swan Brewery site, so as to forge a connection between crime and Aboriginals. Howard Sattler's radio broadcasts on 6PR, according to Sheiner, regularly attacked young offenders and their families, and incited racial hatred. The upshot of the stories was a series of public meetings, organised and publicised by Sattler, that had the effect of panicking the government into drastic action.

One feature of the resultant Act was that it watered down the category 'juveniles', blurring the distinction between juvenile and adult sentencing. It also provided that repeat offenders would be subject to mandatory imprisonment with indeterminate sentences. The Act has been criticised as unworkable, racist, in violation of human rights conventions, and open to manipulation by the police. Its main effect, however, was to raise the stakes on 'law and order' issues. Other

State governments, keen to be seen to 'do something', have followed suit:

- According to Robert Ludbrook, executive director of the National Children's and Youth Law Centre, the Victorian *Crimes Amendment Act (1993)* granted police powers that are in breach of the UN Convention on the Rights of the Child.
- Meanwhile, Human Rights Commissioner Chris Sidoti has pointed out that a New South Wales government proposal that police be granted powers to 'move on' groups of younger people means that 'any group of young people playing a doubles tennis match will henceforth be able to be moved on by the NSW police'.[15] The New South Wales government is also moving to remove the long-standing ban on the publication of the names of young people who appear before the courts, and wants to incarcerate them in special areas of adult jails. When these proposals were criticised, Bob Carr replied: 'If a 13 or a 16 year-old is bobbing up on the streets of Cabramatta time after time dealing in drugs, they are going to be treated as an adult. If they are dealing in death on the streets of Cabramatta they will lose their juvenile status.'[16]
- Several State governments have given police the power to apprehend young people simply for being in the wrong place at the wrong time, whether or not they have committed an offence. The New South Wales government piloted a scheme of this kind in two country towns in 1994. A review of the pilot programme found that it had done nothing to reduce juvenile crime, had gone against the grain of the recommendations of the Royal Commission into Aboriginal Deaths in Custody, and had been abused in ways that breached the International Convention on the Rights of the Child. The State government then announced that the programme would be made available to communities

throughout the State, by application from local councils to the minister. A few years earlier, when he was leader of the opposition, Carr produced an 'anti-gang strategy' that included descriptions of 'roaming gangs of youths . . . their baseball caps turned back to front'.[17]

In Queensland spray-painting graffiti now carries a maximum sentence of seven years. Police have been given powers to stop and search youths suspected of carrying graffiti apparatus, including marking pens; those who refuse to comply are liable to a sentence of up to two years. As the columnist Elizabeth Wynhausen points out, the maximum sentence for spraying graffiti in Queensland is now four years longer than the maximum sentence for common assault.[18] Commenting on this wave of repressive legislation by various State governments, Chris Sidoti has said:

> Juvenile justice laws and Cabinet submissions were driven by opinion polls and media reports that sensationalised crime. Such laws would not cut crime and only further deteriorated relationships between police and young people . . . Why are we looking at doubling the number of children in detention in Queensland at the cost of $100,000 a year when we are cutting the funds to youth services that stop crime occurring in the first place?[19]

The irony is that a 1995 Criminal Justice Commission report found that in Queensland the number of cases processed by the courts for crimes such as break and enter had declined. Less than 2 per cent of the Queensland juvenile population is likely to appear before a court for any reason.[20]

Mandatory sentencing is the latest idea to be floated in many States as part of a 'get tough' response to youth crime. But the problem with mandatory sentencing, as the criminologist Rob White suggests, is that it effectively shifts discretion from the judiciary to the police, who decide whether or not a young person picked up for a minor offence will be charged, or let off with a caution. Police forces have a well-documented history of discriminatory practices in this area; one Victorian study showed that in 1994–95 only 11.3 per cent of Aboriginal juvenile offenders were cautioned, while for non-Aboriginals the figure was 35.7 per cent.[21] Furthermore, police are especially likely to charge young people when there is public pressure to 'do something' about crime.[22] Once a young person is charged, often things get worse. Under pressure of a courtroom situation 90 per cent of young people plead guilty, and judges are then obliged to apply whatever the mandatory sentence might be.

The trend towards longer sentences on the grounds that they have a deterrent effect is similarly misconceived; in fact, they can be counterproductive. According to a Victorian Parole Board survey, young people who committed crimes in the 1960s and 1970s, when short sentences were the rule, had a much lower reoffending rate than those subject to the generally longer sentences of the 1980s, because the latter had lost their twenties and become imbued with crime culture.[23] In August 1995 the federal Labor Attorney-General, Michael Lavarch, initiated an inquiry into children and the legal process. The preliminary findings of the inquiry, released in May 1997, were highly critical of mandatory sentencing legislation in Western Australia and the Northern Territory.[24] In the present climate of moral panic, however, the chances of reform seem remote.

As it happens, those targeted in legislation against juvenile crime are often non-white. Successive federal and State governments have failed to act on the recommendations of the Royal Commission into Aboriginal Deaths in Custody: as of June 1996, the rate of detention of indigenous children nationally was 21 times that of white children.[25] Young people of Indo-Chinese, Pacific islands and Lebanese origin were also overrepresented in the juvenile justice system. According to Amnesty International, there are reports that police have threatened Aboriginal children by referring to the death of 18-year-old Daniel Yock, who died in custody in 1993 shortly after an altercation with police.[26] A 12-year-old Aboriginal girl was reportedly arrested in January 1996 after she slapped a police officer who threatened to 'do a Daniel Yock' on her younger brothers and sisters. According to Amnesty, 'Aboriginal communities across Australia have repeatedly complained about continuing instances of juveniles being harassed, intimidated and ill-treated by police patrols for no apparent reason.'[27]

As the criminologist Chris Cunneen has pointed out, Aboriginal youths are subject to higher rates of police harassment than whites, are less likely to receive a discretionary caution, and are much more likely to be arrested. Young Aboriginal people also tend to be subjected to extreme bail conditions (including banishment) that seem almost calculated to increase the possibility of reoffending.[28] The differences between the sentencing regimes applied to Aboriginal and non-Aboriginal youth could be seen when two Aboriginal children in Queensland were remanded in custody for a proposed period of six weeks for allegedly spitting at Pauline Hanson. When it was suggested that their detention might have been in breach of the UN Convention on the Rights of the Child, Hanson said: 'what we are doing with it, having the convention, is we are allowing children to abuse the law'.[29] At around the same time, a non-Aboriginal Sydney boy with 23 charges outstanding against him was released on bail to spend a week with his social worker on the Gold Coast.[30]

★

Rarely mentioned in the sensationalist reporting of youth crime is the background of youth policy neglect for Aboriginal and non-Aboriginal alike. Youth support programmes were among the first casualties of the Howard government's 1996 cuts to the Aboriginal affairs budget.[31] More generally, younger people have borne the brunt of the economic policy shifts of the late 1980s and the readjustments that followed the recession of the early 1990s. Long-term unemployment is highest among younger people; unemployment among 20 to 24-year-olds is three times that of people aged 40 to 44;[32] those who are employed are more likely to be employed in unskilled service-industry jobs. The minimum youth wage has been reduced, youth employment programmes have been slashed and unemployment benefits abolished for under-eighteens. One of the first acts of the Howard government was to clear the way for wage cuts for apprentices and trainees, and remove allowances for paid TAFE and off-the-job training.[33] The government has also proposed that unemployment benefits to people under twenty-one be means-tested on their parents' income.[34] All the Coalition's pre-election promises to 'do something' about youth unemployment materialised in the form of a self-surveillance diary system for the unemployed, a work-for-the-dole scheme and a 'dob in a dole cheat' hotline that had to be abandoned because it was being used almost entirely for vengeance calls.

It nevertheless remains the fashion to argue that the reason for youth unemployment is high youth wages. Columnists such as P. P. McGuinness, who is an advocate of economic rationalism, have argued that the only things keeping young people unemployed are 'controls, regulations and union rules' and high youth wages. According to McGuinness, this suits the interests of the 'compassion industry' of 'priests and moralists who wring their hands over the immense social and moral problem of unemployment, dwelling with an almost gloating joy on the misery involved'. 'The reason why we have high rates of unemployment and scandalous rates of youth unemployment', he claims, 'is simply that the vested interests of our community want it that way.'[35] The evidence is otherwise. According to a 1996 OECD report:

Dark underbelly

> The employment or unemployment rates of youth, women and unskilled workers do not appear to be significantly correlated across countries with the incidence of low-paid employment . . . factors other than wages such as the overall level of aggregate demand, or the amount of training received, may be more important for determining labour market outcomes of these groups.[36]

Other policy settings militate against young people's interests as well. That's a major difference between this and earlier outbreaks of generationalism: young people are facing institutional discrimination and legislative neglect as never before. Often young people who have spent years in tertiary education, dodging unemployment, end up being better educated than those they serve. As one magazine editorial put it, 'We've got the best educated generation in history waiting on tables for the luckiest generation in history.'[37] But even this looks set to change, with the upping of higher education fees and the tightening of means tests for student allowances. In the 1996 federal budget the age threshold for independent Austudy allowances was raised to 25. Money spent on education in the short term is often money saved later on social problems such as unemployment and crime, yet retention rates are falling. In some States retention rates have dropped 10 per cent in five years. Rather than address this problem with targeted funding (students at risk were allocated a paltry $10 per head in 1996), the tendency has been for education ministers to fall back on the economic rationalist mantras of 'competition', 'opportunity' and 'choice'. The federal Schools Minister, David Kemp, has suggested the problem could be solved if schools advertised their literacy rates so parents could choose where to send their children. The Victorian minister for education, Phil Gude, recommended that schools advertise their students' VCE results for the same reason.[38] A twenty-year study of literacy has found that almost one-third of 14-year-olds lack basic literacy skills.[39]

Gangland

According to Chris Sidoti, youth homelessness has risen since the National Homeless Children Inquiry report was released in 1989.[40] One national study found that the risk of homelessness among high-school students is about one in ten.[41]

A similar picture emerges in health. Suicide accounted for 26.5 per cent of deaths among males aged 15 to 24 in 1990, compared with 14.8 per cent in 1975.[42] For males aged 25 to 34, the figure went from 18.3 to 29.5 per cent. Figures for women were much lower, though they showed a small increase over the same period. Jerry Moller of the National Injury Surveillance Unit has suggested that one reason for the lower suicide rates among young women is that they tend to use drugs, especially analgesics and tranquillisers, rather than more violent methods. Girls aged 10 to 14 are treated in hospital for overdoses of painkillers 14 times more often than boys.[43] Younger people comprise the highest risk group for HIV/AIDS, and have the highest infection rate. According to the Anti-Cancer Council, more young people smoked in 1993 than in 1990.[44] Younger people lead in hard drug use, at an escalating rate, but rehabilitation units are being closed down. In one State as of May 1996 there wasn't a single bed dedicated to teenage detox or rehabilitation.[45] At the same time, the State government was accused of covering up the deaths of 36 children from a variety of causes, all traceable to welfare system failures that remained uninvestigated by the relevant departments.[46]

There is little crossover between the regular newspaper articles about youth crime and those about youth unemployment or homelessness. The editorial concern comes from two completely different places. Younger people lack control over the way they appear in the media; they are represented, but aren't allowed to represent themselves. Similarly, at the level of policy-making, they are isolated from the machinery, acted on, but not allowed to act or set priorities. Reports on youth drug abuse, truancy and crime tend to obscure the fact of

Dark underbelly

policy neglect, representing the problem as something to do with the internal machinations of youth culture.

Younger people, including those born at the tail end of the baby boom, face another daunting problem. By the year 2025, 27.1 per cent of the population will be aged over 65, and the median age will reach 40.[47] Baby-boomers, who comprise the largest single group in the population, will start retiring in the year 2010. Most of them have been notoriously poor savers, who had notoriously thrifty parents. Baby-boomers stand to inherit around $200 billion from their parents over the next twenty years.[48] Having been the recipients of free tertiary education, an adequate health system, job security and generous superannuation schemes throughout most of their working lives, they'll benefit again from their inheritances. Chances are they won't be passing much on to their children. Due to the steep decline in the post-baby-boom birth rate, there will be a shortage of taxpayers to support this influx of retirees. Having been the first generation in recent history to inherit a standard of living lower than their parents', post-baby-boomers will be paying for the baby-boomers' pensions as well as their own (compulsory) 'user-pays' superannuation. According to ABS projections, currently for every person over 65 there are six working people paying taxes. This number will halve over the next 35 years.[49] It's also likely that younger people will still be paying off the huge overseas debts run up during the 1980s boom.

One reason for many of the above problems is the widespread reluctance to pay higher taxes, which has been exploited by the political parties with endless variations on the 'fistful of dollars' election promise. Again this looks like evidence of a 'looking-glass culture', where people would rather perpetuate their own relative social privilege than look at the wider perspective. Australia is one of the lowest-taxed nations by international standards. When recent governments have shifted infrastructure from the public to the private sector, they have overlooked the significance of public institutions' ability to provide services on the basis of needs rather than wealth. Voters have been happy to play along because taxes are kept low, but there are hidden costs. Currently governments are trying to balance their budgets, not by judiciously increasing taxes on the employed, but by penalising the unemployed through the abolition of job-creation programmes, support programmes, youth housing subsidies and other benefits, as well as by cuts to public employment generally. The social costs of such cuts might not show up in budget estimates, which are mainly designed to keep the markets and the ratings agencies happy, but sooner or later they show up as tangible costs in other ways.

★

Some day someone will write an intelligent popular appraisal of the relationship between moral panics and economic rationalism. I suspect they'll say that moral panics often function as a smokescreen, put forward by leading figures of the day as a way of not talking about the underlying causes of social problems. Take, for example, a column by P. P. McGuinness, attacking Pauline Hanson's detractors, not because McGuinness agrees with her racism or her populism — to his credit, he is appalled by both — but because he believes that, instead of attacking Hanson, commentators should investigate why she feels so insecure, and why her remarks proved so popular. So far, so good. But all the reasons McGuinness comes up with are equally populist. It's the fault of 'political correctness', he fumes, which makes ordinary people feel they can't say what they want to, preventing them from expressing their anxieties about immigration from day to day, resulting in outbursts like Hanson's. It's because of feminists and cultural studies experts, who misdiagnose everything and impose a climate of rigid intellectual orthodoxy.[50]

Dark underbelly

What McGuinness fails to mention, and what makes people most uneasy, has very little to do with any of these things, which are furphies from the self-contained world of columnists, politicians and other elites, whose own orthodoxies aren't so far removed from some of Hanson's. What makes people anxious is high unemployment, deteriorating working conditions and insecurity about education and health services. It's the effects of two decades of ruthless economic restructuring, to what long-term advantage? It's the problems brought about by mounting pressures on income and time. It's the fear of crime. It's the promised recovery that never comes, except for the already rich, and the increasing gap between rich and poor that haunts the promise.

Australia currently has almost the highest level of inequity between rich and poor of the 24 OECD countries.[51] According to one report it also has the second-worst level of child poverty in the industrialised world.[52] There are very few people who have passed through this wave of economic restructuring unscathed. All too often the benefits of economic rationalism have been sold as a lowering of expectations, or with a caveat that names one of the recent social movements as the cause of the problem. A reliance on markets can sometimes be useful, but lately governments have been completely blind to the disadvantages of 'letting the market decide'. The free-market ideologues of today are more interested in developing models based on questionable assumptions about human behaviour — encapsulated in the sexist term 'economic man' — than in studying the real world, where market outcomes have not always been so tidy.

McGuinness isn't alone. A similar logic pervades an article from the *Economist*, extracted in the *Australian*, about the decline of the blue-collar worker. Blue-collar workers, the argument goes, have been pushed out of work by feminism. Economic restructuring and the decline of manufacturing industry barely get a mention.[53]

Another article in what is an increasingly popular genre was Jane Freeman's 'The Nervous Nineties'. As well as being overtly baby-boomer focused, it helped to promote the idea that what makes us 'nervous' about the 1990s is splinter groups:

> In the '90s, we are too nervous to use words like fat or short or disabled or old; the ogre of political correctness is having its dying spasm of strength. Childcare centres are told what toys boys and girls should play with; a city in England bans Christmas decorations for fear of offending non-Christians; even sign language for the deaf is revised to make it ideologically approved.

Asked to comment is Michael Fitzpatrick, a director of CS First Boston:

> There are forces which continue to act as thought police ... People's ability to do what they want is restricted by elements in the community who get legislators to agree with them. We have an increasingly complex set of restrictions on industry and lifestyle which make us uncompetitive.[54]

Uncompetitive with whom? And whose 'lifestyle' is being restricted? When terms like 'ideologically approved' and 'political correctness' are dragged out in what should be a debate about economic disparity, the likelihood is that readers are being told where to look for scapegoats. Some will recognise CS First Boston as the organisation that oversaw the privatisation of the Victorian electricity industry and the 1996 rationalisation of Telstra, when thousands of jobs were shed.

Most of the draconian anti-youth legislation has been introduced in a climate of moral panic that obscures the social effects of economic restructuring and the increasing stratification of wealth and opportunity. If baby-boomers stereotypically defined themselves as a generation who had choices, then post-baby-boomers have been encouraged to think of themselves as

Dark underbelly

having few choices, and to 'face the facts' about 'market forces' when it comes to health, education, career and lifestyle. While baby-boomers have lately ruled the marketplace, it's apparently OK for those that follow if market forces rule them.

Moral panics and climates of fear tend to suit mainstream economic orthodoxy. As Moira Rayner has said, the basic principles of democracy, equity and free speech are difficult to sustain in user-pays, economic rationalist societies based on competition, insecurity and fear; communities that exhibit healthy democratic values tend to be based on mutual respect, co-operation and trust.[55] In recent years, though, the measure of successful government has become its ability to urge citizens to ruthlessness. Rhetorical attacks on 'minority politics' have translated into policy attacks on legal aid funds and the independence of the judiciary. As James Walter points out, political parties that develop rhetorics of competition, centred on the rhetorics of individual choice, have 'a daunting task to develop a convincing language of social unity'.[56] Often, as with campaigns against 'youth gangs' and unemployed youth, the gap is filled by finding some common enemy, who is portrayed according to the few collectivist rhetorics left, either as a threat to public order or as a 'drain on the taxpayer's dollar'. The irony being that, as Walter points out, during the Thatcher years in England crime increased in proportion to the growing gap between rich and poor. The more individuals who committed crimes felt marginalised, the less they felt duty bound to see themselves as being in any moral contract with the state or general community.

★

There are other links between economic rationalism and the policing of 'youth crime'. It all boils down to the same argument about young people's exclusion from public spaces that I've been using throughout this book. According to the criminologist Rob White, one of the factors in the present hysteria about juvenile sentencing is the transformation of what was once public space into private space. Young people tend to meet in privatised spaces such as shopping malls, convenience store forecourts and fast-food takeaways. Such places are important to young people because they can associate with little or no parental control, and can see others and be seen while remaining relatively anonymous and secure among like-minded peers. Yet these aren't so much public spaces as private spaces of consumption, designed to keep people moving. When occupying such spaces, young people find themselves subject to new forms of surveillance from security guards and cameras, which represent a more narrowly focused set of priorities than the traditional police balancing of public responsibility and personal liberty.

Shopping malls and the like are also relatively bereft of places to socialise that don't involve spending money. For many young people who congregate in malls such consumption isn't possible. According to White, they therefore tend to be constructed as 'outsiders' according to a logic that figures them as virtually 'worthless' as members of consumer society. Like other 'outsiders', such as criminals, they are targeted accordingly — whereas young people who present as potential consumers are rarely seen as a problem by business owners, security guards or police. As White summarises it: 'commodification of public space (via the extension of private ownership and control), and the commercialisation of public activity (by privileging monetary exchange relations over casual social interaction), set the immediate context for police–youth relationships'.[57]

Public spaces are evaporating in other ways too. For example, the Tasmanian government has proposed banning 'street kids' from open city spaces and installing surveillance cameras. These moves were supported by newspaper editorials on the grounds that similar bans exist in hotels.[58] Hotels, of course, are private spaces, but the distinction wasn't made. These bans will expose young people — especially young women — to greater risk, because they'll be dislodged from the parks to back lanes and other places where they are less visible. Contrary to the hyperbole, young people are much more likely to be victims of crime than the middle-aged and elderly, and are much less likely to report it.

Increased surveillance is the pattern when it comes to younger people. In May 1997, for example, drug-taking by students in a high-school toilet was secretly taped and broadcast on national television, with little media discussion of young people's right to privacy. Surveillance was also the order of the day in many of the recent debates surrounding other youth cultures, from the debate over 'victim feminism' to the Paxton affair, to the Darville-Demidenko debate. One of the things that characterises what I've called the new generationalism, in fact, is the way that sections of the media have figured youth as a particular category of surveillance: they've got to be watched.

One of the ironies of the situation is that the economic logic behind the widespread social disfranchisement of youth is the same as that behind the reduced availability of physical 'public' space. In the name of 'downsizing' the public sector, public spaces are being sold off, as when schools, hospitals and other institutions are closed and their sites sold to developers. One Melbourne municipal administration proposed to meet rate cuts by selling off some of its parks, which it referred to as 'non performing' assets.[59] At the same time, services are being contracted out, and formerly subsidised services are being put on to a 'user-pays' regime. This tends to shut out less affluent potential users and cater for niche markets at the expense of young people who want to use the facilities in less structured ways.

The nexus between business and the media provided the background to the *West Australian*'s original story about teenage gangs. As the media critic John Hartley points out, on the day that the *West Australian* ran its 'Aboriginal Gangs Terrorise Suburbs' front page, the front-page story in the *Age*, the *Australian* and the *Sydney Morning Herald* concerned the unenviable record notched up by Bell Resources, with half-year losses of $862.5 million, the biggest in Australian corporate history. Bell was at the time part of the troubled Bond group, an organisation close to the *West Australian* and important for Western Australian prestige. The Bell story ran in a couple of small paragraphs on page 4 of that day's edition, with a pro-Bond story appearing on the front page next day. To check the 'Aboriginal gangs' story, Steve Mickler, a researcher for the Royal Commission into Aboriginal Deaths in Custody, approached the local police in the suburbs named. All reported no change in arrest rates, nor any incidents involving Aboriginal youths in the period before the article appeared. One asserted that crime in those suburbs wasn't as serious as people think and that most offenders were white.[60]

Such reports, as Hartley suggests, tend to create one group who can be thought of as 'us' and a set of other, shadowy, alien groups who can be thought of as 'them'. 'Moral panics' and the recent political climate both tend to militate against the very groups who have never enjoyed mainstream political and economic patronage, and embolden conservative sectors of the community and right-wing policy-makers. Women, non-whites and migrants, as well as young people, are consistently the targets of recent moral panics to do with land rights, feminism, youth crime, youth culture and immigration.

★

On the face of it, it is surprising how far the cultural elites who have been the focus of this book, given their broad left background, have learnt to mimic the ideals and language of the new right. But that is what has happened as the failures of 1970s liberalism have transmogrified into an anti-collectivist, anti-'victim' rhetoric that mimics the language of economic competitiveness used by politicians. Both the political and cultural elites have constructed a two-tier culture where younger people are on the outer, denied full participation, consistently set up as ciphers for 'what is wrong' and represented as an alien race. At the level of government the situation is patently worse. The culture of abuse against younger people has led to a diminution of their human rights. When the Howard government announced its work-for-the-dole scheme in 1997, for example, there was little discussion of whether it compromised the human rights of the younger people it targeted (such as a right of refusal, and a right to equality of access to community welfare funds). By then it seemed to be taken for granted that younger people somehow deserved to have such a scheme imposed on them. The construction of younger people as certain types of subjects with less than full moral agency had already had its effects.

In other aspects of government policy, the erosion of younger people's basic social rights was justified in an ever more naked language of economic rationalism. The Australian government refused to support an international study of child labour and opposed the inclusion of 'social clauses' in a World Trade Organisation trade agreement, a move that was defended by Tim Fischer on the implied grounds that child labour, including forced labour, helps make countries where it takes place economically 'competitive'.[61] The Howard government also obstructed US and European Union moves to reduce child exploitation on the grounds that they might be used as a form of protectionism, hindering free trade.[62] This was part of a trend, as could be seen when the prime minister personally intervened against the inclusion of human rights clauses in a trade agreement with the European Union, arguing that human rights had nothing to do with trade.

But perhaps to some extent we are all guilty here — guilty of 'complicity in the common crime', as Freud put it.

Gangland

Compassion is currently out of fashion. To some degree we've all learnt to think like free-market individuals, and to behave in a self-interested way when we're convinced that others, be they the bogeys of 'minority politics', 'welfare cheats' or youthful criminals, seek to threaten our 'freedoms'.

Theory, death and me: a Realpolitik of generationalism

It's the end of the world as we know it — and I feel fine.

REM

*I am ashamed of my century
For being so entertaining
But I have to smile.*

Frank O'Hara

Sometimes I feel a bit sorry for Douglas Coupland, the author of *Generation X*. These days he never mentions the book in interviews; it became a millstone around his neck. Generationalism is partly a form of marketing, a way of ushering in the new, and a whole lot of new products with it; and his book became just that — a new product. As Coupland has said, looking back on the phenomenon generated by his book, 'X got hypermarketed right from the start'.[1] It became a term beloved of marketeers and baby-boomer journalists wanting to put a bit of self-justifying spin on stories about themselves and sell a few newspapers or magazines at the same time. If the moniker 'Generation X' first appeared as the name given Billy Idol's original punk band, it's now a demographic. Advertising industry conferences seek ways to target this ad-wise 'elusive new market'. Books such as Karen Ritchie's *Marketing to Generation*

Gangland

X have appeared in business bookshops. And ads for everything from jeans to tampons use lines that their creators apparently imagine are straight out of the current lexicon of media-wise Gen-X hip. An ad for Pepe jeans features the slogan, 'I used to be a target market'. Reebok goes further, announcing 'no slogans' as their slogan. Coca-Cola, having decided that the 'Gen-X' market was fragmented, launched a television campaign featuring literally dozens of different ads, aimed at no less than thirty different subcultural groups their market researchers had identified within 'Generation X'.

It's easy to see why they're interested. Australian teens and twenty-somethings have an estimated annual spending power of $8.5 billion dollars.[2]

Coupland's book spawned a wave of imitators. Books like *The GenX Reader*, *The Official Slacker Handbook* and *Revolution X* all had the magic 'X' in the title, in the foreword and/or in the blurb. Publishing had found itself a new niche market. Hollywood got in on the act too. The black comedy *Heathers* was the first, incidentally launching the career of the actor who would be billed as Gen X's first starlet, Winona Ryder. A swag followed, such as *Reality Bites*, *Threesome* and *Before Sunrise* (directed by Richard Linklater, whose low-fi movie *Slacker* popularised that early Gen-X buzz-word). These were marketed at the twenty-something demographic as ferociously as *Mighty Morphin Power Rangers* was marketed to sub-teens. All failed. By far the best was *Clueless*. By then the slacker figure (Cher's brother, parked by the pool with Nietzsche) was a figure of fun. In the course of *Clueless* he is progressively rehabilitated, and by its end has rediscovered desire.

Television fared better. *Melrose Place* and to a lesser extent *Beverly Hills 90210* continue to be successful. The great thing about *Melrose* is that it doesn't pretend to be anything other than what it is: good, honest trash, flaunting its own kitsch with a self-awareness that lets everyone in on the joke. Fox, the network that owns the show, loves it too. Its creator, Darren

Star, attributes the support he gained at Fox to the fact that *Melrose* provides the network and its advertisers with one of the few reliable opportunities to reach the otherwise very difficult to get 'youth demographic' of 18 to 34-year-olds.[3]

This wouldn't be the first time a group had its cultures shrink-wrapped and sold back to it in simplified guise. The invention of the 'teenager' in the late 1950s had a lot to do with marketing and the new affluence of 15 to 20-year-olds. With that the whole postwar idea of generationalism came of age. Then, as now, the techniques are more or less the same. Marketeers feed off mainly black, working-class culture to remanufacture a product suitable for mainly white, middle-class mass consumption. You can see how it works in the music industry. Young rock and roll artists such as Elvis, Chuck Berry and Little Richard had their gestures and attitudes stolen and their culture mimicked by sanitised musicians who were more manageable and marketable. In the 1950s there was Fabian, in the 1980s Vanilla Ice.

I'm not in the business of suggesting that marketeers, or the media for that matter, have people hypnotised. The ways people interact with the media are various and impossible to anticipate. But marketing can nevertheless affect the way people define themselves, especially when the self-definition takes place under a rubric that is so closely linked to the globalisation of markets and information. Baby-boomers came of age as consumers just as modern advertising and marketing techniques developed a new, sophisticated edge. The boomers' sheer numbers ensured that they were pandered to. Marketeers learned to identify discrete markets, matching them to given brand names and product ranges. Major product releases were designed to match their tastes, oriented around the key ideas of freedom and individualism. During the 1960s and early 1970s, everything from Levis to Volkswagens was marketed this way (these days it's insurance and superannuation products). Such products themselves became emblematic. Baby-boomers felt entitled to think of themselves as people who mattered, and who were defined by the choices they made.

No group was ever so closely tied to the ideology of the future, progress and the promise of social change as the (supposedly) banner-waving baby-boomers. All the catch-cries of the 1960s were to do with new freedoms: freedom from outdated sexual mores, establishment thinking, stifling gender roles and nuclear family norms, freedom from limited forms of consciousness. With them the idea of generationalism gathered a cachet of progressivism and change. The popular ethic surrounding drug-taking was about enlightenment, self-development and self-knowledge, befitting an era of unrivalled prosperity. The quest for newness was also reflected in the availability of new products that made life easier. The 1960s were the golden age of the labour-saving device. Domestic appliances were designed to save women from the drudgery of the kitchen and laundry, as the pill had apparently saved them from the tyranny of unwanted conception. The 1950s and 1960s were also the golden era of new entertainment technology — cinemascope, stereo, long-playing records and TV. Even the moon landings seemed to underline the promise that progress, scientific and economic, could bring unlimited social change.

At the risk of making another broad generalisation, many younger people seem to have a more sophisticated understanding than their forebears of the links between themselves, the media, marketing and generationalism. When someone asks a younger person about generationalism, a typical response is 'What's your marketing stereotype?' No-one wants to know about generationalism. It's a non-question, and everyone seems to understand that it's largely a construction. Not that this implies the idea comes from above. The way people work with the media, and the way they understand the media as working with them, is more sophisticated than that. One of my favourite current generational tropes is the goatee.

Theory, death and me

Incidental as it might seem, the adoption of this appearance detail by many young men in the early 1990s said a lot about under-30s culture. Youth culture had skipped a generation, and was looking to the Beat generation of the late 1940s and 1950s for its influences. But rather than prizing the Beats for their pioneering individualism, their love of travelling and the search for a new high, as the hippies of the 1960s did, younger people read them for their rootlessness, dissipation and buddy-nihilism. Moreover, they were being read as mythology. If the goatee was a purposely inauthentic pastiche on Beat culture — a form of intertextual cultural reference — slacker culture was like 'the road' trip on the couch. For Chevvy window, substitute TV.

But slacker culture, like the Beat culture it emulates, is notoriously male-centred. Interesting female role models are thin on the ground, unless you count Joan Burroughs' hopeless amphetamine addiction, or enjoy the prospect of getting your head shot off in a party stunt, or love the idea of playing second fiddle and surrogate mother, *à la* Caroline Cassady, to an endless passing parade of more famous 'poetic souls'. Perhaps that's why, in the original comic strip (*not* the movie), Tank Girl farts in Jack Kerouac's car.

One thing that seems clearly understood is how the baby-boomers' continuing tenure puts a spin on our contemporary definition of generationalism. Postwar notions of generationalism, like the baby-boomer culture they exemplify, tend to be chock-full of overwhelmingly white, male and middle-class presumptions, centred on the patrilineage of the nuclear family. 'Generation-X' is itself an overwhelmingly white category, an idea out of a soup-can that doesn't reflect contemporary diversity. Check out the range of non-white characters or the attitudes towards women across the range of youth-marketed films from *Wayne's World* to *Threesome*, or the race and gender politics of any of the 'Gen-X' books, and you'll see what I mean. When did any gangsta rap outfit ever talk about

Gangland

Gen X? Or any serious contemporary feminist? Or an immigrant? Or anyone poor?

One of the problems with generationalism as an idea is that in many respects it simply doesn't work. What about all the people who don't fit? Who are just that little bit too old, or that little bit too young, or who just don't identify with the sort of ideas and beliefs that 'their' generation is supposed to have? Looking at the nostalgic *1968* exhibition at the National Gallery, you might suppose that all people did then was turn on, tune in and drop out. But what about those who volunteered for Vietnam, or raised families in the suburbs rather than frequenting outdoor rock concerts? To read the features pages of the newspapers, with their endless Hendrix anniversary tributes and Jim Morrison valedictions, you'd think that no-one ever listened to the Monkees. So if we were to speak of 'Generation X', which 'Generation X' would it be? The 'Gen X' of 'slackers' who have disengaged in a sort of post-beatnik tradition, forming small groups and setting up their own communes-on-a-couch? The 'Gen X' of gangsta rap, with its tough-guy gun obsession and hard-edged racial politics? The 'Gen X' of third-wave feminism, with its commitment to multiplicity and critical theory? The 'Gen X' of pseudo-careerism, with its fancy business card titles ('executive sales officer') disguising low-paid, dead-end jobs? The 'Gen X' of skate culture? The 'Gen X' of second and third-generation immigrant kids who don't feel Greek/Italian/Vietnamese, but are alienated by the 'skips' and their racism? The 'Gen X' of rampant born-again Christianity? The 'Gen X' of compulsive *Melrose Place* addiction? The 'Gen X' of youth homelessness? The idealism of rave culture?

The thing about rhetorics of generationalism is that they frame themselves in terms of a narrative progression. They have a beginning, a middle and an end. The beginning in the currently dominant rhetoric of generationalism is the pre-baby-boomer generation. Baby-boomers are in the middle, which is the high point of this narrative. Younger people are at the end. Currently there is almost no popularly imagined future in which youth play a positive role.

★

This book got started as an essay about possible futures. In particular, I was interested in academic debates about postmodernism. It seemed to me that if the cultural elites I've spoken about in earlier chapters are allergic to new knowledges and figure them as retrograde and 'postmodern', something similar was also happening within the academy. Much as the Whitlam-era liberal cultural establishment generally blames academics for postmodernism, it seemed to me that many academics were similarly conservative. Postmodernism in the academy has circulated predominantly as a discourse about the decline of Marxism, primarily among a group of male critics of similar age and professional standing (sound familiar?). While feminism had a lot to do with the destabilisation of centralised notions of truth and meaning that many see as being part and parcel of postmodernism, feminists got short shrift within what came to be called the 'postmodern debate'. When the participants in that debate spoke about 'postcolonialism', which they often did, it also seemed that they spoke about ethnicity and the postcolonial subject with a certain lingering essentialism. Like the liberal cultural elites, they seemed to be suffering from a nostalgia for the old days, but were hiding it better.

But what interested me most about the 'postmodern debate' was that it divided itself into two 'sides' who were implicitly making similar claims. Marxists, on the one hand, lamented the fragmentation of the great 'master discourses', including their own, in the name of market capitalism. Their narrative was one of decline. Poststructuralists, on the other hand, spoke of liberation from the tyranny of these master discourses, and from the tyranny of essentialism. Poststructuralist feminists, for example, continue to question the idea of biological determinism.

Knowing a little about the history of poststructuralism is useful here. Its noisiest but most naive stage was in the 1970s, when a bunch of very 1970s mid-career males at Yale University in the USA colonised the discourse with their idea that everything could simply be thought of as 'textual play'. (This is the position that David Williamson sends up with the Swain character in *Dead White Males*.) Since then poststructuralism has come a long way. Many critics find it offers useful, practical tools for critique. But the version of poststructuralism that featured in the 'postmodern debate' was as dated as the version offered up in *Dead White Males*. It too operated on a narrative curve that featured, at one end, a grand vanguardist-cum-apocalyptic statement about 'the end of the West'.

Postmodernism, as I've mentioned throughout this book, is a term that figures heavily in current cultural debates. Whether one is 'for' or 'against' postmodernism, it operates as a powerful sign of the 'future'. It's also a term I'd like to disown. Not as an argument against critical theory; on the contrary, for me, without critical theory it would be almost impossible to discuss the way many cultural phenomena operate — be they the intertextuality of the mainstream media, magazines like *The Face*, or movies such as *Total Recall*. On a personal level, the ideas implicit in contemporary critical theory tend to take cultural diversity for granted in a way that fits with the world I've grown up in.

Old liberal models of diversity don't do this. They're too patronising. But I don't think this is only my personal response. 'Theory', of a kind, is intrinsic to the way many people live now. You don't need to have done some kind of undergraduate course, or wander around with a copy of the latest tome under your arm, to have noticed that the central terms and concepts of theory have entered the popular, as was the case with movements like romanticism, impressionism, surrealism

Theory, death and me

and modernism. The theorist Jean Baudrillard has written that 'the age of simulation thus begins with a liquidation of all referentials — worse: by their artificial resurrection in systems of signs . . . It is no longer a question of imitation, nor of reduplication, nor even of parody. It is rather a question of substituting signs of the real for the real itself.'[4] This isn't so far from Courtney Love's saying 'I fake it so real I am beyond fake.' Similarly, Roland Barthes, in his famous essay 'The Death of the Author', has said that 'we know now that a text is not a line of words releasing a single "theological" meaning . . . but a multi-dimensional space in which a variety of writings, none of them original, blend and crash'.[5] This is echoed when Malcolm McLaren says 'Originality is the art of concealing your sources.' Theorists' recent obsession with 'the body' crosses over to wider contemporary obsessions with piercing, tattooing, sado-masochism and cybernetics.

But I remain sceptical of the word 'postmodernism'. As it happens, I don't think it's possible to be 'for' or 'against' postmodernism. I don't regard postmodernism as any one thing, or as having any intrinsic qualities, whether it be a style or a set of ideas. But I do think that, as a way of describing what is happening now, it has become a disabling term. In particular, the notion of the future that it proffers, no matter who is doing the talking, is a kind of endism. It speaks of a world where everything is 'post'; where all the best things are already done. This is an idea that theorists of postmodernism keep repeating — that everything has been done, which helps explain the dominance of pastiche and 'borrowings' in contemporary arts. I don't think, though, that such theorists have come to grips with contemporary life. The terms offered up by the postmodern debate don't adequately describe the new cultural forms and trends (in art, fashion, music, media) being produced everywhere you look, with a sheer energy that is daunting. In some ways the postmodern debate tends to look like nothing so much as another way of saying 'lights out, we're done now'. 'Post', after all, is everything that the generations following the baby-boomers are supposed to be. A testimony to the centrality of all that came before. This cult of endism, it seems to me, remains a way of keeping everything else in its place. Ironically, it tallies neatly enough with the endism of neo-conservatives worried about their loss of white, male privilege, and predicting a cultural implosion in the wake of *that* loss.

Postmodernism may or may not be a handy way of speaking about contemporary cultural conditions, but it doesn't provide much in the way of useful narratives for a hopeful future. One thing that 'post' addicts of all colours have not been able to anticipate is the remarkable degree of political engagement on the part of the young. Younger people have never been more serious about issues, despite their cynicism about mainstream politics and the fodder served up on mainstream news and current-affairs programmes and in the newspapers. That we live in postmodern times has not resulted in the atomisation of all political reflexes or disabled the will to organise, as some critics and theorists of postmodernity have predicted. Nor has it resulted in the empty, 'relativistic' nihilism that many conservatives take as an article of faith. This complex, multi-layered world might be confusing and disquieting for some, but younger people, it seems to me, are by and large making sense of it. They are familiar, even comfortable, with contingency.

One of the persistent strands of argument in this book has been about public spaces, and the relationship of younger people to the media. So far, I've tended to talk in terms of patterns of representation, suggesting that they are biased against younger people; a cultural elite has sponsored a certain idea of public space, and a certain notion about what the media do, and what being a media spokesperson entails in terms of cultural authority, so as to perpetuate the media's hegemony. In addition to the sorts of politics many young people are

Theory, death and me

already involved in, one of the places for an emergence of a Realpolitik of generationalism that tries to undo this hegemony, I think, is, perhaps paradoxically, through their relationships with the media.

I've taken the attitude throughout this book that the media aren't any one thing. There are all sorts of media, from talkback radio to 'zines, all of which are context-sensitive at the point of reception. I also believe that people aren't dupes to the media, or high culture for that matter, and aren't mindlessly 'swept along' by them. Sections of the media might want to put certain discursive strategies in place, but these are only strategies. The media aren't programmatic. Most people are too good at being critical readers of the media for that.

Nor are the media a constant. They change, just as people's relationships with them change. Currently the authority of the quality press is under threat. An underlying argument of this book has been that this is one of the reasons for the struggles for cultural authority that have been taking place between the press and the academy. A similar struggle is currently going on between 'quality' and 'tabloid' media, as a battle between highbrow and lowbrow. The quality press is also struggling for readership, especially among the under-35s. As I've suggested, their focus on the dominant over-35 readerships is one of the reasons they've become involved in the complex web of interrelationships between neo-conservatism, global economics and the cultural establishment (also trying to hold on to its authority) that produces phenomena such as the unprecedented coverage given the *First Stone* 'victim feminism' scare, or the youth gang scare, or three-page features on the Beatles. The media might look monolithic, but in fact, they are vulnerable. They always have been. And I think that younger people's familiarity with how the media work puts them in a strong position from which to intervene in a rapidly changing situation.

Audiences are also changing in what they expect of various media. One of the reasons for the focus on the quality press here is that it is still important to governments, having an influence on 'public opinion' disproportionate to its numbers of readers. At the moment, a liberal, humanist model dominates perceptions of how the quality press should work. Critics of the media often take the high moral ground, arguing that the only way for the media to 'improve' themselves is to redouble their moral efforts and their commitment to fundamental, universal, often 'high-cultural' values. The liberalism of the media themselves, in turn, can be seen in the way they continue to treat, say, ethnic interviewees primarily in terms of their ethnicity. They pretend to be inclusive, but still use whiteness as a base paradigm.

As it happens, I don't think liberalism is all bad. There is a lot to be said for the classic liberal virtues of factual accuracy, freedom of speech, freedom of association and, indeed, democracy. Nor do I think eras, or groups of people, replace each other according to some logic of generationalism. Rather, they overlay each other and interact with each other. Currently there is a complex intermelding going on between the quality press and values that have been introduced by other forms of media. The traditional idea of the unified public sphere is being broken down, mainly by niche media forms that have been made possible by new technologies.

It's fascinating to watch how the quality media are coping. Some papers have produced cheesy lifestyle sections, or new computer sections with their own embedded 'hypertext', consisting of underlined words, just like a web browser. The emphasis has gone off hard news and on to catering to 'special interests', some of which meld the voice of the paper and its sponsors in 'advertising features'. One positive impact of this has been a proliferation of outside 'guest' columnists and editorial writers who specialise in various issues. It's been fascinating too, and slightly horrifying, to watch governments trying to cope. They have introduced powerful nation-building rhetorics of togetherness, and keep harking back to the idea of a 'mainstream'. I don't think these strategies can work for long, though. To cope with the new diversity, new social technologies will be needed.

Many are already available. I'm not a believer in the Utopian claims made for the Internet, but I do think the way people use it gives insight into the new forms of imagined community that are currently becoming possible. I also take heart from the fact that many recent forms of activism do without the vacuous ideas of Utopias or apocalypses, yet sustain narratives of social change (I'm thinking especially of queer activism in its recent forms). Even something so seemingly irrelevant as governments' increased willingness to sponsor harm minimisation campaigns rather than 'just say no' campaigns when dealing with drugs issues, it seems to me, is evidence of new social technologies at work. Such absences of (moral) absolutism are commensurate with a Realpolitik where social work (rather than gesturing to transcendentals) actually gets done.

A Realpolitik of generationalism might begin in much the same way. The idea of generationalism, in the first instance, is useful in some ways. It provides a way of speaking back to what looks like monolithic power. It might, say, provide access to media on the grounds that a generational imbalance needs redress. In the longer run, though, it isn't very enabling. The big strength of younger people is their ability to step into the breach with, dare I say, an innate understanding of how the media work, formed on the basis of a lifelong relationship with them, at the very moment when they are most under threat. Already newspapers are starting to employ, and show interest in, a wide range of media and intellectual skills. Several prominent young journalists work across a range of topics, with a brief that draws on their interdisciplinary background. This is because the media cannot afford not to be interested in new ideas. The quality press might pretend to be highbrow, and might want to sponsor old versions of the literary canon with certain conservative agendas in mind, but at heart it is a beast of cultural studies — as most younger people are.

Lately, in line with the sorts of crises that have swept many Western democracies, to do with the crisis of authority afflicting the Western male subject, sections of the media have tended to sponsor the idea that privilege needs protection *especially* from youth. These crises, whether to do with gangs or victim feminism, have had at their centre the idea that younger people are radically unknowable. Even the label, Generation X, says the same thing. Given, in part, the long-standing invisibility of younger people in the media, except in certain default subject positions ('young feminist', 'Internet expert', 'gang member', 'depressed unemployed youth'), it's been something of a self-fulfilling prophecy. Younger people, though, are prominent in the very sections of the media that threaten the cultural authority of the quality media. They own desktop publishing systems. They run home pages. They publish 'zines. They run alternative subscriber radio. They write the very sort of lowbrow novel that the literati see as challenging the highbrow (the rest of us realise it's not a one-on-one arm-wrestle). Sooner or later the quality media, if they're to survive, will have to listen more closely. Not only because they're currently pinning their hopes on an audience that can't live for ever, but because younger people, in the main, have the conceptual understanding and the skills the media, from lowbrow to highbrow, will need, in audience and journalist alike.

New knowledges, as I've said, don't necessarily replace the old. But they do affect the way old knowledges are used.

Before this can happen, something else is required. I want to talk, for a moment, in terms of policy-making. Clearly recent State government legislation about youth crime is prejudicial and ill-informed. In most cases it is made possible by racism. The rhetoric underpinning scares about high-speed car chases, and 'youth crime' generally, once again involves a logic of apocalypse. In most cases politicians are responding to

Theory, death and me

footage that depicts a kind of Mad Max scenario, with out-of-control cars whizzing across the landscape at high speeds functioning as a metaphor for the end of the world as we know it. The background tune to the political rhetoric always consists of a populist 'law and order' refrain, derived from a nostalgia for an explicitly 'non-apocalyptic' past — the past that talkback radio strives so hard to generate.

As it happens, there is no apocalypse. Younger people are also less inclined to think in terms of racial absolutes. It is impossible to imagine a band such as Yothu Yindi having a nationwide hit twenty years ago. It seems to me that countering this kind of legislation, in part, involves producing rhetorics that involve a viable notion of 'future'; one that has younger people in it. Doing this requires an awareness of just what is at stake when people talk about generationalism.

Ringing in the changes: life after liberalism

Dislike and resentment of younger writers is something fairly universal among writers . . . My father said to me that when a writer of twenty-five puts pen to paper he's saying to the writer of fifty that it's no longer like that, it's like this. The older writer, at some point, is going to lose touch with what the contemporary moment feels like.

Martin Amis[1]

For anyone my age and younger the cold war is a piece of history. Gorbachev is the first Soviet leader that we can remember. The ALP is the party of Hawke and Keating — Gough Whitlam is mainly remembered as the man they named the band after.

Marcus Westbury[2]

It can't be easy being a cultural icon of the 1970s and finding yourself washed ashore in the 1990s. Even harder when it seems as if you've got a whole generation snapping at your heels, demanding space, making claims about the validity of *their* culture. According to the writer Frank Moorhouse, these are desperately 'unexciting times'.[3] All the good fights have been fought and won — mainly, as it happens, by Moorhouse and friends. That's why today's young people lash out at their elders, says Moorhouse:

not because things need to be done and an older generation is standing in the way, but because nothing needs doing any more.

Tragically, the good old days of Frisbee-throwing and nipple-painting are all over for counter-culture icon Richard Neville. 'We were as good as it gets', he claims, so 'up yours, Xers!' Neville then offers today's young 'a few home truths' in his distinctive house style — disarming wit with an undercurrent of chip-on-the-shoulder bile. And what might these home truths be? Well, back in the old days of Frisbee-throwing and nipple-painting they did it all, you see. Setting himself up as a spokesperson for his generation (and perpetuating the myth that the sixties were owned by the counter-culture), he writes:

> We gave you the gay Mardi Gras. You made it an arm of the tourist industry . . . Work was just another four-letter word, not the meaning of life. You've managed to turn the world of business into the whole world . . . Our universities were hotbeds of revolution, not composts for careers. We kicked the arse of the establishment, not licked it.[4]

Well, ain't that just the problem? Far from being the everlasting counter-culture he so fondly imagines, these days Neville and his cohorts *are* the establishment, in more ways than one. For those born into a time of full employment with depression-era parents who saved, it can't have been too hard to become feckless arbiters of style in 1960s Paris and London. Not so easy for those who follow. So misted are Neville's hexagon-framed rose-tinted glasses that he not only forgets that his cohort were the ones who subsequently ushered in managerialism, economic rationalism and massive levels of youth unemployment, but also manages to suggest that all this is the fault of young people. Perhaps someone should point out to him that young people are among the major victims of these things. According to one academic, those who currently fail to complete secondary schooling stand a fifty–fifty chance of *never* having a full-time job.[5]

But Moorhouse and Neville were both provoked. They were responding to the first edition and the first twelve chapters of this book (though not explicitly in Neville's case). The pity is that they did it in such a way as to exemplify one of the book's main points: that members of the cultural establishment find it difficult to write about young people without resorting to clichés.

Moorhouse and Neville weren't alone. Today's young people, according to the journalist George Negus, comprise 'a generation that is largely apolitical and discouraged from questioning . . . the society in which they live'. Apparently that's why Negus doesn't feel the 'hot breath' of up-and-coming talent on the 'back of his neck', and why he and his journalist peers 'don't feel . . . surrounded by talented, intelligent, questioning young people'.[6] According to another journalist, Mike Carlton, also responding to *Gangland*, 'our successors dwell in broad, sunlit uplands' compared to the trials of previous generations, including his own.[7] So much so that 'There is not enough of life left to waste even an hour on the upstart whingeing of Generation X . . . Generation X can wait its turn. We babyboomers are not going to f-f-f-fade away just yet.'

The real problem, says Moorhouse, is that young people didn't grow up in the 1960s and '70s. Today's young, he says, are a 'generation without a coherent world view — not because they are not smart or that they have been marginalised — but because history has not given them that sort of stage. It looks as if history has not given them a grand dramatic role.'[8] As Negus said: if his generation 'failed to change society's values to the extent that we would have liked to, that's no reason for handing over to a generation that's got no values'.[9] So the cultural establishment *still* hasn't got any further than the same old stereotypes: that compared to the one true generation of the 1960s and '70s, young people today have no authentic ideas or commitment; that it's all been said and done; that today's youth are harbingers of ethical and aesthetic decline;

that young people don't have some sort of claim to share in speaking the contemporary moment, even if only because, so far as Moorhouse is concerned, it's hardly worth speaking about. At least *he* doesn't slander young people. There's nothing of Paul Keating's contempt for the young unemployed when he was prime minister ('get a job'), Amanda Vanstone's vitriol for university students when she was education minister ('get a reality check'), or Helen Garner's condescension to young feminists in *The First Stone* ('get a life').[10]

The strange thing is that, despite the assertions of the likes of Moorhouse, Neville, Negus and Carlton that the sum of human endeavour peaked just as they reached adulthood, and that they are some kind of bulwark against inevitable decline, elsewhere there's an overwhelming sense that this isn't an era of decline so much as one of massive and dynamic change, even renewal. Just as once seemingly impregnable institutions — church, state, family and science — have seen their authority dwindle, so new forms of media have grown up alongside existing forms of media. New arts have grown up alongside the old, opening up innovative forms of creative expression. Computer technology has transformed the very idea of what knowledge is and how it is circulated. Genetic science has challenged the very definition of life itself. The end of colonialism has brought forward voices that challenge Western culture's claims to universality, while the new colonialism of economic globalisation has shaken accepted ideas of where the borders are, so that nations are having difficulty maintaining their territorial integrity and governing themselves — and so on. And with these shifts have come new ways of thinking, new ideologies, new institutions, new forms of association, new forms of public and new forms of social and cultural space.

As I've already argued, the consequences of such changes are all the more remarkable for the fact that they go largely unreported in the mainstream media, which tend to report change primarily in so far as it operates as a showcase for new technology. The present shifts in artistic and political practice are taking place in what the writer Marcus Westbury has called the 'undergrowth' of Australian culture.[11] They're taking place in multimedia studios, in design studios, within activist groups, research groups, web-based discussion groups and editorial collectives, and are being reported on in 'zines, community radio, universities and web-sites. These conversations are taking place where people are using sampling to make music, or using technology to manipulate images, or where people are discussing what happens when Western media conventions are used to represent non-Western subjects. They're taking place among film-makers, among festival and event organisers, at rave parties, and among independent media producers.

Probably the hardest thing about being a member of the seventies cultural establishment and finding yourself washed ashore in the 1990s is that the cultural maps have radically changed. If the members of the contemporary cultural establishment seem to have little eye for the present, and aren't its ideal readers, then it's not because they are of the wrong age or the wrong generation or the wrong class or the wrong gender, but simply because they have turned away — often quite pointedly. Moorhouse has said, 'I may be proved wrong: these may be times of massive social transformation. But I doubt it.'[12] So what counts as 'massive social transformation'? If the tumult and turmoil of the 1960s 'sexual revolution', or the rise of the New Left, or 1960s-style mass anti-war protest are what register on your cultural Geiger counter as social transformation, then these aren't times of massive change. The social transformations presently taking place are all the more profound for the fact that they are happening in the substructures of life, heralded by comparatively little in the way of sixties-style hot air. As Westbury says:

> We have grown up in the shadow of two revolutions. One that occupies the imagination that never quite made it in the late sixties and the real revolution in the eighties: globalisa-

tion, telecommunications, the collapse of communism, the rise of multinational corporations and the decade that marked the most tumultuous and revolutionary upheaval of any since World War Two.[13]

The magnitude of recent shifts can also be seen in the decades-long debate about multiculturalism. In the words of the writer Ghassan Hage:

> The move from assimilation to multiculturalism did not happen because some white Australian sat there, with their index on the lips, asking: 'Let's see now, what shall I choose? Assimilation or multiculturalism?' It happened because Australia's demographic and socio-cultural reality changed such that assimilation could no longer work.[14]

Similar forces can be seen at work right across the social and cultural spectrum. They are the reason the highbrow media are battling for cultural authority. They are the reason for the anxiety that underlies so much public debate across a range of issues, and perhaps for the sorts of nostalgia that Moorhouse, Neville, Negus and Carlton exhibit. They are the reason, too, for the white cultural backlash that inflects the cultural output of a range of figures across the cultural establishment, whether it be an essay by Robert Dessaix, a book by Paul Sheehan, or the dedication in a novel by David Foster — all of which have insinuated the virtues of assimilation.[15] Indeed, the depth of recent cultural shifts is such that the present cultural establishment can no longer take their own ascendancy for granted. They've had to articulate their position. This isn't something they enjoy being forced to do. Having to articulate a position tends to show that you and your views aren't such a natural, invisible part of the landscape of 'common-sense' ideas and beliefs as it might have once been possible to pretend.

But what position? What's at stake here? Moorhouse, near the end of the article I quoted from above, comments that 'we are in a time of reanalysis and realignment . . . a time for cool and subtle analysis and new negotiations with reality'.[16] The problem is that he so radically underestimates just what reanalysis and realignment might involve. At stake is the fate of the dominant ideologies that have structured mainstream Australian cultural life since World War II. This doesn't simply mean that new issues need to be debated; the changes are more profound than that. Also at issue is the present cultural establishment's failure to engage with the shifts in thinking that are fast becoming necessary to accommodate change in a just, equitable way — in fact, many of them have resisted the forces of change in terms designed to place beyond criticism those cultural institutions that have lately been most open to question. The negativity of their cultural gatekeeping, designed to ensure that certain status quos stay firmly in place, has been far from 'cool and subtle'. Manifestly lacking a better idea, and having failed to anticipate — let alone forestall — the social calamities of the past decade (at first they fanned the flames), they've instead howled, Neville, Negus and Carlton-style, Garner and Mannestyle, across a *faux* generational divide. Even as the committees who invite them to festivals, the boards that award them grants, the reporters who routinely call them first, the publishers who call on them to head up and contribute to anthologies, continue to covet the idea that these people and their ilk are somehow the personification of 'debate'.

But it's not enough, simply, to have a debate about generationalism. The argument here, as I've suggested in previous chapters, isn't about what age you are. Quite the contrary: age shouldn't matter. The only viable debate about generationalism is one that centres on the question of why generationalism, especially against young people, is such a feature of contemporary cultural life. And if quite a vicious generational war is already going on, then what other ideas is the 'new generationalism' at the expense of? What other discussions might be had instead? What cultural institutions seemingly remain beyond criticism? What emerging ideas remain sidelined? What does the 'everyday ideology' of generationalism obscure?

★

Perhaps it's bad taste to talk about the reception of your own book, but I'm going to anyway. Moorhouse, Neville, Negus and Carlton weren't the only ones to lapse into something approaching self-parody when they responded to the first edition of *Gangland*, but at least their language wasn't abusive. Elsewhere I was accused of suffering sibling rivalry, of youth-envy, of undertaking a 'prolonged exercise in go-getting infantilism', of a 'pantingly implied desire to be a journalistic opinion maker', of being 'in your face, on the make and hard to take', of being 'a kind of Ubu', of having no values or implicit understanding of literature or art, and of suffering 'all the anxieties of ageing'. And that's just from Peter Craven's review of the book in *Australian Book Review*.[17]

Craven later described the review as 'impersonal'.[18] His work is examined on pages 30, 40, 119–27, 132–3, 167–8, 212, 218–19, 220, 223 and 228.

The journalist Luke Slattery, reviewing the book, bellowed that 'the generationalism that [*Gangland*] purports to explore is actually an obsession of the author's'.[19] He later added, 'the things Davis mentions . . . moral panics, youth crime scares; they relate mostly to Davis's subjective and highly coloured interpretation of social facts'.[20] A quick chat to a cross-section of teenagers, a talk to a youth worker, or a quiet look at Rob White and Christine Alder's *The Police and Young People in Australia* might have disabused Slattery of his fantasy.[21] As the books editor of the *Age* kindly noted shortly after the review appeared, Slattery's work is criticised on pages 30, 47, 49, 53, 120–2, 126, 156–7, 163, 173–4, 201 and 210.

Other responses were not so much abusive as bemusing. *Gangland* was immortalised in the Paul Kelly song, *Nothing on my Mind*, where Kelly tells us about someone (him?) who never did anything worthwhile before he was thirty. The book has had poems published about it in highbrow literary magazines.[22] It provoked one columnist to write at length that I was a 'dalek' who wanted to exterminate everything.[23] It has provoked threats of physical violence and a bit of actual push and shove. After an alleged stand-over man was shot dead in Melbourne's Lygon Street I received a number of calls from reporters wanting to know if I was the guy who'd written a book about ganglands, and could I give them the lowdown on the insularity of Melbourne's Carlton Mafia and their system of paybacks. Well, yes, but not that kind of Mafia.

But most of all I was surprised to discover that what I thought of as a book about the decline of certain kinds of 1970s liberalism, and their mutation into something more dangerous and defensive, was received by many mainstream commentators as a book attacking baby-boomers. There's comparatively little material on baby-boomers in the book. In a bit over 90 000 words in the first edition, baby-boomers get a scant 48 mentions. Nearly half the book's chapters don't mention them at all. Aborigines, academics, feminism, political correctness, economic rationalism and David Williamson are among the many topics that take up more space. Of those 48 references to baby-boomers, most are in the reported speech of self-identifying commentators, in the style of Richard Neville or Mike Carlton, to illustrate *their* obsession with age, obsolescence and generationalism. Of the rest, more than half are statistical matters of fact, and of the remaining half-dozen or so references, most appear in the introduction, where I claim that 'this is not a book that sets out to attack baby-boomers' (xiv). True, there's a mention in the all-important blurb, and among the remaining references to baby-boomers there are several cheap shots. Classic hits radio does that to you. But none of this adds up to a book about baby-boomers.

Some commentators went further. The journalist Virginia Trioli implied that the book simplistically equated age with

Ringing in the changes

'use-by date'.[24] She seemed not to notice the book's assertion that 'age should be no barrier' (127), nor its championing of older figures 'outside the loop' as positive examples. She also apparently missed the book's repeated insistence that no-one should be put on any sort of notional cultural 'scrapheap' (xv, 21–2, 155–71), and didn't notice that throughout *Gangland* not a single person's work is criticised on the basis of that person's age. She also seemed to have neglected the chapter that argues for a plural, heterogeneous 'as-well-as' model of culture, rather than a generational-replacement model.

If newspapers are full of one kind of story, then they tend to be short on space for other kinds of stories, leaving serious debate up to others. Few of the 60 or so commentators and journalists working in the independent media who interviewed me about this book even mentioned baby-boomers. The same was true of many of its non-mainstream reviewers. They read *Gangland* as a book about the cultural investments and ideas that dominate certain sections of the media, a book about what has happened to 1970s liberalism and those sectors of the cultural establishment that profess it. A book about economic rationalism, moral panics and youth crime scares; about the present longing for the 1950s that besets so many established commentators; about the way contemporary culture isn't taken seriously in the mainstream media; about having your work and way of thinking chronically dismissed; about the difficulties of breaking into a career when you don't agree with its dominant, dated methodological or aesthetic paradigms; about the 'culture wars', neo-conservatism and the fate of 1970s radicalism; about why so many self-professed 1970s radicals have ended up as supporters of censorship and attackers of multiculturalism, feminism, and so-called 'political correctness'. What they've been interested in, in other words, is the dominant paradigms that shape public cultures. What they tended to do, I suspect, was start at the first page of the book, and not with the index.

The writer Sue Luckman summed up:

> Much of the debate, especially in the major press, centred on [the book's] generationalism thesis at the expense of more considered debate on the real central premise of the book: the role of this generational discourse in the construction and maintenance of an Australian intellectual, artistic and media elite (hardly surprising given the ensuing discussion was conducted almost exclusively within the elites identified by Davis) . . . little discussion has ensued regarding the way in which this elite has occluded the creative and/or political contributions of an increasingly educated cohort of younger people to Australian intellectual and artistic life. Not to mention the role played by younger people — since the sixties — in the maintenance and growth of organised political dissent.[25]

If the mainstream media tend to reconfigure unfamiliar debates into discussion about familiar topics (baby-boomers?), then some commentators failed to see the organising logic of *Gangland*, in particular why disparate commentators were discussed together. As Trioli wrote in her review of the book for the *Age*, 'You can no more say Manne's intellectual and economic outlook is like Henderson's than you can suggest Adams's broadcasting shares anything with Laws's.'[26] I suspect Trioli, like many media insiders, underestimates the degree to which these people *do* look the same to many people outside the professional media network. They look the same because they are the familiar faces of routine, banal commentary — the rent-an-opinions who, in the process of delivering 'reliable product', are always going over the same things, rarely raising any new or real issues; who are always pushing the same barrows and who, even when they disagree publicly, are nevertheless always fighting the same old battles, most often with each other. The world these commentators occupy may be agonistic but it's no less a charmed circle for that. What insiders often underestimate is the degree to which people feel alienated from the mainstream media.

But there's a deeper organising logic that shapes the cultural establishment and the public cultures they preside over. For all their differences, what Adams, Manne, Henderson and even to some small degree Laws share (besides the fact that the last three lined up together on the Demidenko affair), indeed, what establishment figures such as Don Anderson, Peter Craven, Robert Dessaix, Morag Fraser, Helen Garner, Drusilla Modjeska, Richard Neville, Pierre Ryckmans, Anne Summers, David Williamson and so on all share is some kind of specific debt (but not necessarily the same debt) to particular kinds of postwar liberalism. The kind of debts that accrue from having been formed by the particular ideas that dominated university arts faculties in the 1950s, 1960s or 1970s. The kind of debt expressed in certain attitudes to the sanctity of art and literature. The kind of debts that tend to a veneration of Western high culture as *the* source of legitimate knowledge, history and truth, and a suspicion of popular culture as corrupting and relatively knowledge-free. The kind of debts that often lead to a suspicion of the usefulness of the new kinds of knowledges that have circulated during the past two decades in universities and elsewhere — in popular culture, in multimedia studios, in 'zine culture, cyberculture or contemporary feminism.

True, within this broad grouping there are important differences. Some are anti-libertarian and tend to moral conservatism; others are (or once were) libertarians. Robert Manne's careful transition from cold-war shock trooper to mainstream conservative–liberal defender of 'core values' has little in common with Richard Neville's path from 1960s libertarian to 1990s savant who worries about *South Park* and increasingly seeks to defend, well, 'core values'.[27] Yet both have lately lionised the past as a place where 'lost' values might be rediscovered. Both have written about the redemptive force of high culture and the corrupting tendencies of popular culture, when to many people such values are by no means self-evident.[28] Both have expressed anxiety about young people's values, or supposed lack thereof.[29] Most of the figures whose work is criticised in this book have implicitly taken a similar stance to Manne and Neville on high and popular culture, and most have also attacked youth culture, just as many share particular assumptions about the natures of freedom, equity, and what truth-telling involves. Again, these assumptions are by no means self-evident to many others, and besides, they haven't been backed up by the work of their exponents themselves.[30]

Perhaps Manne put it best when he wrote that he 'was educated in a world where voices like those of F. R. Leavis and Lionel Trilling — who thought that the task of criticism was vital to culture — still mattered'.[31] The type of criticism Manne means is broadly referred to as Leavisite liberalism. Many of the people whose work is criticised in *Gangland* habitually write and speak from inside this or related formations. As the publisher and film-maker Tony Moore has said:

> Many of our broadsheet critics belong to a tradition that stretches from Matthew Arnold in the nineteenth century, through FR and QD Leavis and onto the Marxists of the Frankfurt School, a tradition that presents mass entertainment as antipathetic to art and a false ideology.[32]

These ideas are the products of a particular kind of university education (the academic 'theory' of the past); a shared experience of sorts, which, while not without its own ruptures and internal controversies, in a very general sense continues to shape public culture, in so far as it pervades the lives, morals and aesthetics of many who went through university arts faculties in the fifties, sixties and early seventies, many of whom are now Australia's cultural establishment.

As such the cultural establishment tends to share the idea that cultural value equates with print culture and the so-called 'quality media'. Social decline is invariably measured in terms of a perceived decline of print culture (literature, essays, academic history) and highbrow electronic media ('quality' documentaries and current affairs) and a corresponding proliferation of low-end electronic media (popular television, video games, recorded music, the internet) which, so the story goes, is meaningless and corrupting. It's a class-bound stance that rests on the reflexive assumption that elite culture is inherently superior to popular culture. Yet these clichés seem to have an uncanny power: they are used to explain everything from the so-called decline of the public sphere to the 'death of childhood', adolescent violence, drug abuse and sexual promiscuity.[33] They overlook the fact that popular culture is full of ethical and critical content, and that most of us quite satisfactorily draw meaning from it and are more capable of filtering out what we don't want than media critics often give us credit for. Popular forums such as the internet and talkback radio offer many people a 'public' voice that they mightn't otherwise have. Besides, the so-called 'quality media' are by no means a level playing field.

If what I'm moving towards here is an argument about cultural renewal, then it seems necessary to question this establishment. The truism that the cultural sphere is presently structured by irreconcilable differences ('Adams versus Laws') tends to mask other underlying patterns of similarity. Where, for example, after 25 years of immigration, are all the Vietnamese columnists?

The argument about the fate of liberalism is an important one in contemporary Australian cultural life, not least because of the claims various types of liberalism made for inclusive and plural social reform. One ethic of this version of liberalism is that its key exponents comprise an elite clerisy who almost literally embody a certain set of values, as is often expressed through notions such as the idea of 'felt art' and 'felt morality', so prevalent in the work of writers like Manne and Garner. A clerisy who attribute finer values to themselves and nominate themselves to speak these values to the rest of society as 'moral good'.[34] All this hardly seems a viable notion in the late 1990s. Besides, the social programme of this kind of liberalism has shown itself to be almost bankrupt. For all the claims postwar liberalism has made about its ability to deliver freedom, equity and moral good, those at the notional centre of this society see it as their due to live in first-world conditions, whereas those at the margins increasingly live in third-world conditions. The most the latter seem to be able to expect is to become the object of professional concern from coterie commentators, who, in any case, seem as interested in generating cachet among an audience of their peers as in anything else, to the extent that an industry has developed around monumentalising such figures and praising their superior sensibilities.[35] Otherwise little has been developed in the way of mechanisms for analysing, speaking across, or redistributing power across the difference between centre and margins.

★

What does cultural renewal mean? What does it look like? Where is the present energy for cultural change coming from? Not only has mainstream liberalism failed to redistribute privilege from centre to margins, it's also in internal crisis. Other voices and ideas have risen to challenge it, to the point where classical liberal notions of universal truth and value raise more questions than they answer and are starting to look ethnic-specific. But there's nothing new here. In a sense liberalism has always been in crisis; the very precariousness of its position, perched between the right (which scorns liberalism as wishy-washy and sentimental) and the left (which traditionally derides liberal notions of freedom as bourgeois and individualist), has helped liberalism to naturalise itself as the safe middle of the road. But society's newly emerging voices owe no more to the organised left or traditional conservatism than they do to liberalism. And they're where the energy for change is coming from.

High liberalism increasingly persists as a kind of geek culture whose tokens are conferred back and forth among a cultural elite. In Australia this can be seen in the claims recently made for The Essay, and the way recent collections of essays produced from within the cultural establishment were reviewed. Helen Garner puts together a collection of essays. It is reviewed by Morag Fraser, Peter Steele and Peter Craven.[36] Les Murray produces a book of essays. It is reviewed by Peter Craven.[37] Drusilla Modjeska, Amanda Lohrey and Robert Dessaix put together a collection of stories and essays. It is reviewed by Morag Fraser and Peter Craven.[38] Imre Salusinszky puts together a collection of essays. It contains essays by Robert Dessaix, Helen Garner, Les Murray, Barry Oakley and Pierre Ryckmans, and is reviewed by Morag Fraser and Luke Slattery.[39] Morag Fraser puts together a collection of essays. It contains essays by Robert Dessaix, Helen Garner, Kerryn Goldsworthy, Les Murray, Barry Oakley and Peter Steele. It is reviewed by Peter Craven and Luke Slattery.[40] Robert Manne puts together a collection of essays. Peter Craven defends it against a querulous review.[41] Peter Craven puts together a collection of essays. It comprises many essays previously published in *Quadrant* during Manne's editorship and in *Eureka Street*, edited by Fraser, and includes essays by Helen Garner, Robert Manne, Drusilla Modjeska, Pierre Ryckmans — in fact, it showcases almost the entire Craven canon. It is reviewed by Kerryn Goldsworthy, Barry Oakley and Peter Steele.[42] Robert Dessaix puts together a collection of essays. It is reviewed by Peter Craven and Morag Fraser.[43] Pierre Ryckmans puts together a collection of essays under the pen-name of Simon Leys. It is reviewed by Morag Fraser and Peter Steele.[44] It's as if the world no longer validates them: they're reduced to validating each other — even if they're still granted acres of newspaper reviewing space to do so.

Gangland

A striking characteristic of the anthologies among the above books is that they contain so few new voices. When it comes to practising inclusion (as opposed to preaching it) the same old criteria get in the way. Liberalism centres on the doctrine that things have immanent aesthetic and moral qualities: objects are inevitably described in terms of their intrinsic properties (beauty, authenticity, originality) or those of their genius–creator (all the adjectives generally applied to Robert Hughes). Coterie liberalism as practised by the above elite tends to avoid analysing the material or historical conditions under which objects, tastes, desires and artistic and social practices are produced. It's OK to *muse* on politics, but don't offer up anything much more than evidence of a finer sensibility. The influence of postwar liberalism has been such that this divorce of art and politics has until recently been taken for granted. But it's still there, hanging on, for example, in the definition of the essay adopted by Imre Salusinszky for his collection:

> The essay may include narrative or analysis: however its rhythm comes not from these but from thought . . . that is why the familiar essay is intensely personal . . . It is also why political, or republican, or monarchist, or religious polemics belong to another genre.[45]

It's a far cry from the definition offered by Germaine Greer at the 1997 Melbourne Writers' Festival. The essay can be anything, she said, so long as it's non-fiction. Yet Luke Slattery, reviewing Salusinszky's book, found the essays not personal enough. Perhaps the Australian essay, Slattery mused, 'has been too much a vehicle for the working through of the postcolonial conundrum'.[46] For all the extravagant claims made for some of these books, and for all their pretensions to address contemporary social issues, none opened up room for the new voices that they speak about. Morag Fraser's introduction to her collection, too, canvassed the terms of admission using a definition of the essay at its most deeply Eurocentric, circling around the idea of literary excellence. Yet such criteria, as even a self-professed conservative like Tom Wolfe has lately acknowledged, are increasingly looking like a form of cultural chauvinism by which the few protect themselves from the many — 'See? We include everybody — but notice how few are up to our standards!'[47]

More importantly, in the context of recent Australian cultural history, liberalism's tendency to think primarily in terms of the intrinsic, immutable qualities of individuals or objects is precisely the strategy the New Right has used with such success over the past decade to demonise marginal social groups. It's hardly surprising, then, that the most striking failure of the liberal establishment throughout the 1980s and 1990s has been their inability to counter the increasingly influential strategies of a strident new conservatism.

But perhaps it's fitting that liberalism be reduced to the status of a sub-culture. That's certainly the status of the sovereign art forms at its centre. As the summary for a session at the 1998 National Young Writers' Festival put it: 'Literature . . . how do you tell if your parents are reading it?'[48] Literature was discussed at the festival, naturally, but alongside a number of other forms of writing, all of which were given equal validity.

Emerging cultures of political and artistic thought have lately developed in places outside liberalism, and outside mainstream commentary and party politics. The first move of such cultures, it seems, is to abandon the sovereign oppositions that liberalism uses to get itself going. For example, the Adelaide-based Virtual Artists produce collective works on the assumption that art and design are inherently political. They are involved both in making commercial art and in organising corporate boycotts and various other actions.[49] The Newcastle-based Octapod collective, as well as staging exhibitions and workshops, functions as a hub for local activism.[50] The Brisbane-based Soapbox gallery, formed to disturb these same oppositions, has held shows centring on refugees, masculinity and indigenous issues.

Gangland

In a sense there's nothing new here. The compatibility of art, analysis and activism can be seen in working-class and social realist traditions of painting and writing running from the 1930s through to writers such as Dorothy Hewett, or in novels such as Christos Tsiolkas's *Loaded* or journals such as the now-defunct *RePublica*, as well as in a long tradition of what was once called 'migrant art'. All of which have been barely acknowledged by the present liberal establishment.

All these contemporary projects in some way talk of life after liberalism. At the same time they talk about cultural renewal, often quite explicitly. All are notable, too, for opening up space for voices that aren't the 'usual suspects'. In fact, such projects assume that giving space to voices that don't fit standard paradigms is necessary in order to challenge and stretch the very definition of art, and with it the wider definition of culture.

A similar collusion of art and politics, famously, has lately taken place in the arts faculties of universities. It's no accident that *all* the above collections of essays and many of the reviews, too, explicitly position themselves against contemporary academic culture, often with a vengeance. The essay, it seems, is the one last thing that might be *preserved*, the last bastion of literary boutique culture — the irony being that the essay is the very form that the contemporary humanities have turned into a multi-million-dollar global industry. But with their sometimes vehemently anti-intellectual editorials, reviews and essays, these recent collections seem like a last shot in the culture wars, following on from the salvo of books and plays such as *The First Stone, Dead White Males, The Culture of Forgetting*; all obsessed with universities and the things that take place in them (from contemporary feminism to the way literature and history are taught). What they are manifestly unable to discuss is how the culture wars have functioned as a smokescreen behind which important recent social shifts — including a shift of power to capital from labour, to name but one — have taken place.

Ringing in the changes

★

The best commentary on *Gangland* came without the standard agendas of the culture wars. As many noticed, *Gangland*'s coverage of regional issues is weak in the extreme.[51] Reading it, you could be forgiven for believing Melbourne and Sydney are the only major cities in Australia. It tends to concentrate on print media at the expense of electronic media, and on the literary scene at the expense of the other arts. As Helen Elliott pointed out in the *Herald-Sun*, it also concentrates too heavily on the broadsheets.[52] Its brief might be to take aim primarily at the liberal intelligentsia, but it's nevertheless too weak on the Talkback Kings and the politicians who listen so carefully to them. As critics such as Michelle Sabto and Ken Gelder pointed out, the book is also very short on the voices of young people themselves.[53] This, I admit, is the result of an editorial decision I took very early on. As a late thirty-something, I didn't feel qualified to write about youth culture from within, so I decided to concentrate on the cultural establishment. Nor did I want to set myself up in the business of anthropologising or 're-representing' young people, which are among the very tendencies I was arguing against. But it's still a damn good criticism.

It's nevertheless impossible to talk about cultural renewal without talking about young people, and especially the relationship between young people and the media. Again, the initial reception of this book threw up some curious responses. Luke Slattery, in his review, claimed young people are well represented in the media. His standout evidence? That Lachlan Murdoch (his boss) has a job at the *Australian*. It was a silly thing to say and Slattery evidently knew it. Later he tried to qualify his remark, saying that what he actually said about Murdoch was 'not that he had a media job but that he, at age twenty-six, was a most powerful print media baron. Quite a different thing'.[54] Nice try, but I think that everyone knows that the bottom line here is that Lachlan Murdoch is Rupert's son.

Gangland

The commentator Guy Rundle, similarly keen to land punches against the book (both Slattery and Rundle are associates of Peter Craven's, and all their reviews of the book shared similar arguments, including a scepticism about cultural gangs) also claimed that young people are well represented in the media, citing the number of young producers working for the *7.30 Report*.[55] Perhaps this was a joke. Lately young journalists have almost entirely disappeared from on-camera roles on the *7.30 Report*. Despite there being a large number of young behind-the-scenes staff, the young radio and television producers I've spoken to all have a similar story to tell, of being a high-turnover, revolving shift of young support staff serving a pantheon of stars who stay more or less in place, though this has lately started to change (more on that in chapter 15). As Ted Emery, a veteran executive producer for Channel 7, has said about his peers' attitude to new talent:

> What staggers me about the complete lack of generosity in this industry is that surely in your bones . . . you get to a certain age where you say . . . 'it's time to be a mentor', and hand over what you know, or what's relevant, to people who have other ideas — as opposed to just putting the lid on them and still doing the same stuffy load of old crap you've been doing for years.[56]

But the issue, in any case, isn't so much to do with numbers as with power.

Both Rundle and Slattery, by pretending *Gangland* is primarily a book about the number of young people working in the media, overlooked important questions about the dominant cultures of local commentary. Do these young journalists participate in organised networks of common opinion? Are they on the rosters of shared information and old contacts? Can they start debates? Is what they say reported by others? Do they participate in the groupthink of a particular kind of coterie liberal culture? Could they get on the phone and put together a bloc of opinion, then have it published, as happened during the debates over *The First Stone* and *The Hand that Signed the Paper*? Most of the commentators criticised in *Gangland* have one of two things in common: either they get stuck into young people on the basis of prevailing mythologies about them, or they participate in other fashionable journalistic mythologies about the imposts of 'political correctness', multiculturalism or victim feminism — both agendas dating from the culture wars, and both of which have taken up a disproportionate amount of mainstream media space. It may well be, as Rundle says, that the editor of *Time* is young, that section editors of many of the dailies are young, but this says nothing about whether such journalistic cultures are shifting or whether new ideas and approaches are being allowed to percolate through. That's the real issue here.

The will to shift paradigms in the mainstream media is coming from young journalists, film-makers and producers themselves. Since the book came out I've spoken to literally scores more young media professionals, and none of them have contradicted its basic arguments about media power. One spoke of the closed cultures of the Canberra press gallery — and her disappointment with the limitations of the Canberra genre, coupled with her fear of stepping outside it. A number of TV producers talked about how, when they wanted to do something different — to do an interview without the 'noddies' or the hokey reverse-shot; to cut something a slightly different way, that reflected, say, developing trends in other media; to try a new kind of story idea or cover a subject that they regarded as political and contemporary (several mentioned rave parties) — they were howled down by 'seventies blokes', who seemed to think they had a mortgage on good ideas. They felt, in other words, as if they were working behind enemy lines, to a set of outdated aesthetic and political paradigms. Independents in particular speak of their frustration with the 'fucking baby-boomers' — their words, not mine —

and the tired ideas–cultures that dominate funding body grants committees.

But what else might this mean?

Slattery inadvertently let the cat out of the bag with his admission that, among media professionals, 'if the balance is held in favour of age, this merely follows readership demographics and, to an extent, the value of experience'.[57] Quite so, though the line about experience tends to be a self-fulfilling prophesy, as any young job-seeker knows. Having conceded the existence of media demographic targeting, what Slattery fails to canvass is the fact that every politically influential form of mainstream media in this country, from talkback radio to current affairs television to the broadsheet press, is aimed at a 35-plus demographic, and that powerful populist sections of the media catering to this demographic increasingly tend to construct Australia as an ideally homogeneous place under threat from cultural difference of the sort represented by immigrants, Aborigines, feminists or young people. What might it mean for youth policy if the dominant forms of media are demographically skewed in this way? What effect might this demographic biasing have had on public culture, as reflected in law-making, reporting of youth affairs, youth stereotyping in the media, and the sorts of stories that are told in the public sphere about youth-oriented arts and media? The problem, then, isn't simply to do with whether or not young people make media, but how young people and their cultures are depicted *in* the media.

Slattery claims it's 'patently wrongheaded' to suggest that 'the young are being "discredited, even demonised" by the media'.[58] A recent survey confirms otherwise. Alcoholics and drug abusers, criminals, bludgers, lazy, complaining and aggressive — these were the main stereotypes used to portray young people in the media, according to research commissioned by the federal government in 1998.[59] The two-pronged study included a Roy Morgan survey of 600 people, which found that only 18 per cent could remember positive stories about young people in the media over the previous twelve months. A parallel analysis of 3052 media items from television, print and the radio between April and June 1998 showed only 23 per cent were positive, that 'most articles seemed to appeal at a disturbingly emotive level using sensationalism as an effective tool', and that the voice of youth was notably absent. So bad has the situation become that in early 1999 the federal government launched the National Youth Media Awards to help counter the negative media stereotyping of young people.

Shane Paxton, who was the object of an extended media beat-up about unemployed young people and who has since worked in TV current affairs, says of his experiences:

> When working on *Today Tonight* I discussed doing a report on some terrible things that were happening to homeless people in Melbourne . . . I was stopped mid-sentence with the reply 'homeless people don't rate'. Ideas for current affairs reports involving young Australians were met with: 'Little old ladies (the show's demographic) don't want to hear that young people are doing positive things.'[60]

A Rockhampton high-school student commenting from the audience at a 1998 conference on regional youth sums up: 'the thing is, young people are always represented by other people . . . we're sick of seeing and hearing ourselves misrepresented on the media, but we're never allowed to represent ourselves.'[61]

In the months that followed the publication of *Gangland* I spoke privately to a range of senior print-media figures, all of whom were in general agreement that young people were underrepresented both among their decision-making staff and in their audiences — but especially that contemporary culture and ideas were underrepresented in their coverage. None had any trouble with the proposition that the serious end of Australian opinion-making was largely served by a greying fleet of commentators and that, while there were more and more 'young' journalists about, by and large they weren't being given the same opportunities as today's senior commentators had been given at the same age.

But age isn't really the point, is it? As the independent radio commentator Drew Williamson has said, even when young people are present in the mainstream media 'you get the feeling they're there just to look young and cute and to give the publications a bit of cred. Not because they are going to really be listened to or allowed to change things. They're just made to fit in with existing journalistic paradigms.'[62] This is a crucial point for Williamson. As he sees it, if the media are to come to terms with the fact that this is a truly diverse society, then the way the media are presented and the production paradigms that underpin them are going to have to adjust in such a way as to acknowledge the Eurocentric assumptions about conversation and opinion, and about question and response, that underpin even something so apparently simple as a radio interview. The required changes, in other words, are fundamental, and the will for such change, as Williamson's comment indicates, is coming from younger media workers.

The writer Bernard Cohen tells a similar story:

> There's space in the media for liberal humanists and conservative humanists, but only for humanists . . . When I've had stories accepted by the mainstream media, I've often had to rework them towards the standard 'strong opinion' format. Sub-editors' introductory paragraphs have sometimes recast the pieces to fit humanist outcomes. Most editors don't understand the value of uncertainty or of equivocation to reflect contemporary experience of culture.[63]

As Cohen also points out, in some respects this is presently changing. What isn't changing is that the media no longer broker new ideas — not even the broadsheets, which among all mainstream media outlets are arguably in the best position to do so. Yet it's vital that this situation should change. While many commentators have spent the past decade worrying about various 'faux' cultural crises — from the 'political correctness' scare to the supposed activities of young feminists and young novelists — they've been failing to provide powerful, erudite accounts of the present, which is crucial given the policy influence of the mainstream media, and given the current need for wider social renewal and change.

Here's an example: *Among the Barbarians*, Paul Sheehan's jeremiad against the 'multicultural industry', elicited a strong response across the board of Australian opinion. The word that was settled on in a string of conversations I had with journalists, and which Peter Craven used in his commentary on the book, was the euphemistic 'brave'.[64] Craven is a master of the sting-in-the-tail back-hander, but in this case I think he got it half-right. Whenever the word was used, it seemed to signal a sense of misgiving; a sense that perhaps the book was ill-judged and in some respect foolish; that it somehow overshot its mark. But that word, 'brave', also signalled that there seemed to be no real way of talking about the book. 'You simply must read it', was what Craven and others said, often in lieu of providing any sort of proper analysis. It was as if there were otherwise no words, no language, to describe precisely what was wrong. Robert Manne appeared on television to debate it, and wrote a column that pointed out some of its failings. Gerard Henderson made a few sideswipes. Anne Henderson wrote a searching review.[65] But no-one seemed to get to the heart of the assumptions about cultural primacy that underpinned the book.

But is there really no such language? In my own experience the required language isn't hard to come across. It's used in the kind of everyday conversations about Australian whiteness that regularly take place in working and middle-class migrant and Aboriginal households across the country. I heard it, for example, in a recent conversation I had with a 19-year-old Jackie Chan fan who, having read Chan's autobiography, was commenting on the whiteness of America, Chan's decades-long difficulty in establishing a career there in anything but an Asian-villain role, and her experiences as an Asian in Australia. Like many people, she was taken with the out-take at the end of the recent Chan–Chris Tucker film, *Rush Hour*, where Chan commented that he had to learn the whole English language to act in the film, whereas his American co-star couldn't even memorise three words of Cantonese.

Such languages also exist in more formal contexts. In *White Nation*, Ghassan Hage points out that recurring calls for a race debate in Australia have been based on the fiction that no debate is already happening. Such calls usually come from more or less the same place and, Hage says, represent attempts to reinstate white mastery over multiculturalism. Multiculturalism itself, he argues, always gives whites the final say; the power flows one way, and there is a backlash the moment this hidden contract is challenged.[66] Here and in the above conversation are at least two concepts that begin to provide a thoroughgoing language with which to critique Sheehan's book. Why aren't they part of everyday media conversation?

In a forum on *Gangland,* Morag Fraser argued that we should put arguments about cultural succession to one side in order to concentrate on important issues such as Wik and Pauline Hanson.[67] No offence to Fraser, but I see these issues as being intrinsically linked. Not because the present intelligentsia has nothing to offer or should be made obsolete — a ridiculous and unfair proposition — but because so many people feel profound disappointment with the present liberal establishment, because of the silence that has reigned on youth issues, the lingering patrician assumptions that permeate mainstream discussions about race, and the establishment's failure to anticipate what New Right political strategies would do to democracy.

Listening to Fraser's call I heard again the echo of a claim for the omnipotence of the present cultural establishment. A call that suggested that *they* would be the ones best to preside over debates about Hanson. What skills might they bring to these debates, I wonder, given what we've seen in the past few years? What knowledges? While they provided us with the popular critical consciousness of Leavisite and other breeds of liberalism, ethics that have dominated mainstream commentary for decades, it seems these very doctrines, with their aversion to identity politics and their tendency to regard criticism as a moral rather than a political duty, as a universal and enlightening aesthetic rather than a specific social function, have failed to forestall disaster, and have in some respects fomented it.

Young people have a claim here, not because they are necessarily politically progressive by nature (something I have never argued) but because in my experience, both in the research I did for *Gangland* and in the trips I've subsequently made up and down the east coast of Australia, from Hobart to Mackay, listening to young Aborigines, high-school students, youth workers, youth group members, media workers, 'zine editors, student newspaper editors, independent film-makers and so on, I frequently heard the language I'm speaking of.

While some (guess who?) have scoffed at *Gangland*'s claim that younger people are 'less inclined to think in terms of racial absolutes',[68] recent research indicates that many young people show a range of positive attitudinal effects from having grown up in a more plural, heterogeneous culture than their elders. As Noel Pearson has said, speaking of those older Australians attracted by Pauline Hanson's One Nation Party:

> It is the hardest thing for older white Australians. The challenge of coming to terms with our history is the hardest for your generation . . . It is the hardest because you people have gone through the history of assimilation policies, of *terra nullius*, of the denial of the humanity of Aboriginal people. The goodwill and the paternalism and the desire for greater good for indigenous peoples — these are all part

of the troubling emotions which your people must come to account.[69]

As Pearson concluded, many younger indigenous people in jail wanted race 'war', while older indigenous people wanted to work for peace. Among white Australians the opposite seems to be the case, with younger white Australians wanting to work towards peace while, sadly, many older white Australians do not.

Recent figures support Pearson's observations. According to a poll conducted in 1998 by the Australian Democrats with a sample of more than 1000 people aged between fifteen and twenty, 65 per cent believe Australians are racist, and 54 per cent think that the Prime Minister should apologise to the stolen generation of Aboriginal children. On other issues, too, younger people tend to be more progressive than the rest of the population, even if, as Democrat senator Natasha Stott Despoja has said, 'Young people are under-represented in the political process and their voices are often ignored.'[70] Ninety per cent believe that the government is weak on environmental issues, 73 per cent oppose laws designed to 'move on' young people from public spaces, 75 per cent believe condom vending machines should be installed in schools and 67 per cent think Australia should be a republic.[71] According to Green senator Bob Brown, speaking of the protests against the Jabiluka uranium mine, 68 per cent of young people put the environment first as a political priority, whereas the overall population puts it fifth.[72]

I admit it was gratifying, too, that shortly after *Gangland* came out I got an exasperated call from the head pollster of a national research company brusquely wanting to know where I got my information from. He told me he'd just spent tens of thousands of dollars on a nation-wide attitudinal focus-group survey of young people and discovered absolutely nothing that wasn't already in this book.

Ringing in the changes

In his book *Generations*, the social researcher Hugh Mackay, backed up by one of the nation's most formidable attitudinal research teams, paints a useful picture of young people's changing outlooks:

> This is the generation born into one of the most dramatic periods of social, cultural, economic and technological change in Australia's history: the age of discontinuity, the age of redefinition, the age of uncertainty — call it what you will. They don't share their parents' or grandparents' conscious anxiety about the rapid rate of change and its destabilising effect on society . . . This is the generation for whom the women's movement was already 'history' by the time they hit thirty . . . who have always known that the global environment is a precious resource . . . our most highly educated and media-stimulated generation.[73]

Unfortunately Mackay's discussion points rarely range beyond the traditional middle-class concerns of family, job and love-life, but they nevertheless give a picture of the sorts of social changes that have shaped young people's attitudes.

But this is to say nothing of the 2000 or so people, most aged between eighteen and thirty, who passed through the blockade camp at Jabiluka — itself a historic instance of black and white protest coming together — in its first few months alone.[74] Or of the nationwide anti-Hanson classroom walkouts organised by the student activist group Resistance, which led to the arrest of five students at one school, and the formation of Students Against Racism.[75] Wendy Robertson of Resistance has said: 'The Hanson stuff runs against the grain of their reality . . . The less the mainstream parties are representing young people, the more we will be on the streets.'[76] If the spontaneous formation of political organisations is itself an indicator of the level of activism and will to social change, then the formation of the group STARS, Students Who Action Reconciliation Seriously, in the wake of the National

Youth Reconciliation Convention in Darwin in 1998 (itself organised on the initiative of students at Darwin's Kormilda College) is another demonstration of how seriously young people take politics.[77] As the activist Annie Beck has said:

> We have been sold as Generation X, alienated and uncaring, but the truth is that we are very political, deeply concerned and prepared to be active. We have been abandoned by the mainstream parties and it is harder for young people to survive. Now we are financially dependent on our parents until we are 25 [*per* recent Howard government legislation] and that is very patronising.[78]

The various forms of contemporary cultural activism share a disdain for mainstream media commentary and mainstream party politics (according to the Australian Democrats' Youth Poll 98, less than 2 per cent of young people have faith in politicians).[79] It's perhaps fitting, then, that mainstream commentary doesn't acknowledge contemporary activism. 'Where is the underground press? Where are the festivals of dissent?', Richard Neville has asked.[80] The Internet Resources for Australian Activists web-site includes links to over 100 activist organisations.[81] It's a pity that the forms of activism Neville and his contemporaries recognise — festivals, demonstrations and high-profile court appearances — are those that facilitate self-congratulation. But it's no coincidence that you don't read much about contemporary activism in the morning news, or hear much about it on anything apart from youth, community and subscriber radio.

So what *do* people listen to on the radio?

Before that question can begin to be answered in the next chapter, there's a final claim to be made here, and that's for the role of criticism. For me the responses to *Gangland* illustrate the need for a stronger form of criticism than currently exists. I'm not suggesting this is a perfect book — far from it. But it seems to me there needs be a way of articulating ideas that goes beyond the kind of personal sniping and sectarian defensiveness that pass for legitimate comment. Criticism should discomfort, but it should also discuss ideas in good faith. When commentary is simply another excuse to work over old agendas, then I note that with regret. Not because I have any personal regrets from my experience writing *Gangland*, but because it seems to me that the idea of criticism itself holds so much promise.

14 Who is at the centre?

The politicians have been playing real, hard politics and the analysts have given us gammon analysis.

Noel Pearson[1]

Young people today feel locked out.

Tan Le[2]

Shortly after the 1998 federal election the media monitoring company Rehame found that Alan Jones, who has more than 20 per cent of Sydney's breakfast radio audience, made not one positive comment about the Labor Party during the election campaign, and was extremely supportive of the Liberals. According to Rehame, Jones mentioned the ALP tax package 22 times, without once saying anything positive. The Liberal tax package was mentioned 32 times, without a single negative comment being made.[3] During the campaign Jones interviewed Liberal chief John Howard four times and his opposition counterpart, Kim Beazley, just once, during which Beazley was accused of being a liar.

But Jones's broadcasting apparently had an effect. According to Liberal powerbroker Michael Kroger, the part played by Jones was important to the coalition victory.[4] So there it was at last in black and white: a tribute to the power of talkback radio. A tribute, too, to the power of divisiveness.

Who is at the centre?

The background to all this was a series of Liberal Party attacks on another media outlet for its alleged bias. The ABC, according to the government, had taken a consistent stance against the government throughout the campaign, and was a hot-bed of 'political correctness', though the government could produce no figures to back up its allegations. So paranoid had it become that when Tim Freedman, lead singer of the Whitlams, announced his own political leanings on ABC Radio JJJ, the network was forced to apologise to the government. All this despite the fact that the chairman of the ABC, Donald McDonald, endorsed Howard's platform at a Liberal Party function during the election campaign, and despite the appointment of Kroger himself to the board of the ABC.

There's a pattern to such attacks. They might be irrational, but they fit contemporary neo-conservative political strategy. This strategy dates to the mid-1980s, to Ronald Reagan's second-term election campaign, when the Republicans identified 'wedge' issues, designed to split the Democrat vote in two by wresting away blue-collar voters who had seen their standards of living drop throughout the 1970s, and who could be made to think that this was a result of minorities rorting the system, egged on by 'politically correct', white-collar, soft left democrats. In Australia the strategy was a centrepiece of the 1996 Liberal campaign, and again in 1998. As Noel Pearson has said:

> For those doubtful of the wedge theory, read *The Victory*, Pamela Williams's candid account of the 1996 election. The 'us' versus 'them' strategy was key to the Robb–Howard campaign. Us versus the bludging Paxtons, us versus the immigrants on the dole queues. Us versus the Aboriginal industry. And so on.[5]

It's good advice. Aborigines, young people, feminism, multiculturalism, welfare, human rights — all have been used as wedge issues, all branded as playthings of the 'politically correct'. Yet local political commentators, as Pearson says, with one honourable exception (he names Malcolm McGregor) have failed to give any sort of analysis of 'wedge' politics. For Pearson the question is why, during the growth of Hansonism, 'serious commentators consistently refused to focus on the political calculations made, not by David Oldfield and Hanson, but by Andrew Robb (during 1996) and Howard . . . The politicians have been playing real, hard politics and the analysts have given us gammon analysis.'[6]

Such attacks have other generic characteristics too. 'Political correctness' is always located in public institutions — universities, the public service and public broadcasters — in conformity with the New Right's attack on the public sphere. A vote against 'political correctness' also becomes a vote against the maintenance of the public sphere, and a vote that aids and abets privatisation. In turn, right-wing political parties have tended to align themselves with private broadcasters, many of whom aren't open to the same sorts of public scrutiny for political bias as publicly owned broadcasters. Enter Rush Limbaugh, doyen broadcaster of the Republican Party. Enter Alan Jones. Just as Limbaugh has close ties to the Republican Party, so Jones does to the Liberals. He has twice run unsuccessfully for Liberal preselection, and he was a speech-writer to Prime Minister Malcolm Fraser. He is close to the present Liberal hierarchy and to broadcasting magnate Kerry Packer, who also endorsed Howard in the 1998 Federal election.

Campaigners against 'political correctness' also like to portray themselves as beleaguered. The parties of the right have been in power for quite some time now, but it seems they find it hard to believe. They and their supporters often slip back into the same old paranoid rhetoric: that they are a 'brave besieged minority', silenced by the forces of political correctness; that the 'real' debates (on multiculturalism, on immigration, on Aboriginal land rights) haven't yet taken place because of ideological censorship; that they are courageously speaking out when everything is against them, and that the good common sense of ordinary people is likewise repressed. Not only are these ideas staples of New Right strategy, they are staples of radio talkback, where Aboriginal activists, environmentalists, single mothers, welfare recipients, all still get a regular going over. They remain staples, too, for the local cultural establishment, for commentators such as P. P. McGuinness, Michael Duffy and Paul Sheehan. Wedge politics strategists seem to have effectively exploited the fact that free speech is the last liberal fantasy for middlebrow commentators with populist leanings, to the point where such commentators hardly seem capable of talking about anything else. So pervasive has the anti-democratic cancer of this rhetoric become that it can be heard across the political spectrum, effacing the division between 'left' and 'right'. So former Labor minister Barry Cohen, decrying complaints about a sports commentator who called Matt Shirvington the fastest white man alive, says that those who complain about such comments risk returning us to the era of 'political correctness' and censored speech.[7] But always there's a question. Whose right to speak as they like is being defended here? The remarks about Shirvington would hardly have been made by a non-white person, would they? The talismans of free speech being handed out here are hardly being passed freely around the entire community; they come with a built-in assumption about just who is a member of the speaking community.

In practice, the 'refreshing . . . freedom of speech' that Prime Minister John Howard observed overtaking the nation in the wake of Pauline Hanson's notorious maiden speech to Parliament has turned out to be selectively applied, and there's nothing new in the pattern being used.[8] Describing negotiations to conclude the ratification of the Howard government's 10-Point Plan on native title, Noel Pearson has said:

The fact is we are returning to a dialogue about indigenous rights that takes us back to the period before the 1960s.

> That's where the blacks stayed out on the woodheap, while the whitefellas worked out the details inside the station house.[9]

Nor did Howard's support for free speech seem to extend as far as Pat Dodson, when the Prime Minister's Department unsuccessfully requested Dodson to remove 'inappropriate' political comments from his eulogy for H. C. (Nugget) Coombs.[10] Nor did it extend to the Australian Law Reform Commission. According to the federal opposition, the attorney general, Daryl Williams, improperly tried to stop the commission making its criticism of the government's Wik legislation public.[11] Nor did it extend to the Biological Diversity Advisory Council, whose draft press release on the negative environmental impact of the Wik legislation never saw the light of day, according to then opposition spokesman on the environment, Duncan Kerr.[12] Nor did it seem to extend as far as student unions, given 1999 federal government attempts to curtail their funding and compromise their independence, and the independence of student newspapers with it, with voluntary student unionism legislation.

The voice. That's what counts here: the voice. And Alan Jones has *the* voice. The voice of the highly successful ex-football coach, the voice of the ex-drama teacher, the Queen's English of the ex-private boys' school English master. The voice that reaches up to 600 000 listeners per day, 80 per cent of them over the age of forty, 58 per cent over the age of fifty-five.[13] Along with, it seems, every politician, senior bureaucrat and policy adviser in the country. But what else is distinctive about the voice? The most perennial of all contemporary voices, it seems, is the voice of the middle-aged man complaining about recent social changes. Think Stan Zemanek, think John Elliott, think Paul Sheehan. Zemanek's book *The Thoughts of Chairman Stan* sold out in a fortnight. Elliott has described Aboriginal land claims as 'ludicrous'.[14] Sheehan's best-selling anti-multiculturalism tract, *Among the Barbarians*, was launched by Jones.

And what's at stake here? Clearly the use of 'wedge' issues to win government involves power politics at its most ruthless. But something else is going on too.

★

'Who is at the centre?' This simple question currently haunts Australian life. It's being asked in the platform of Pauline Hanson's One Nation Party, which aims to reorient the definition of the national interest to reflect the perceived interests of its white population. It's there in recent changes to childcare funding that advantage working men and traditional families compared to working women, who will be further discouraged from working by changes to taxation that will accompany a GST.

The questions of who is at the centre and who gets to speak for whom are writ large in debates about so-called 'political correctness'. Who has the last word in such debates if not those already privileged enough to speak from the centre? The same questions haunt the Wik debate. What sorts of 'payments' are being made when the Howard government, acting on behalf of white pastoralists, takes it on themselves to deny Aborigines the right to negotiate on native title? Who pays the price for what has been, in effect, a land-grab? Whose opinions are holding sway? Who finds themselves back on the margins, not just in terms of the right to speak, but lately also in terms of media coverage? Since the Howard government pushed its Wik legislation through the Senate in 1998, land-rights issues seem to have slipped almost entirely off the public agenda. The government, again, has been able to set the priorities, and for the mainstream media Wik has become a 'dead issue'. 'Dead', that is, for those already at the notional centre.

Similar assumptions were at work in the 1999 judgment on the land claim made by the Yorta Yorta people of southern

New South Wales. According to Justice Olney, who ruled against the Yorta Yorta, their claim to their ancestral homelands had been swept aside by the 'tide of history'. Whose history? Whose tide?

If one group is to occupy the centre, then what is the cost of keeping them there? And who pays that cost?

Who pays too when one group nominates itself as the dominant arbiter of the general interest? What happens if the people doing the talking set themselves up as the voice of progressive opinion without canvassing the assumptions that underpin their own place at the centre? The rules here aren't so different from the rules of talkback radio: public opinion is massaged, but issues are rarely discussed transparently.

★

In 1998 I again attended the Melbourne Writers' Festival. It's become a kind of compulsive habit, I suppose. A masochistic one too, as it turned out. There, as I sat in 'the gods' — the upper row of seats of the main theatre — as a paying customer, I had the pleasure of listening to an entire panel of speakers talk at length about this book. The topic was the 'culture wars', and the speakers were the critics Robert Manne, Adrian Martin and Meaghan Morris, with Morag Fraser in the chair. Manne was given a rousing introduction by Fraser, who expatiated on the number of times they had appeared on radio together and how eminently sensible he was. Manne's speech was also by far the longest, taking up almost precisely the same amount of time as Martin and Morris put together. It included one of the most interesting descriptions of this book yet: Manne suggested to the audience that *Gangland* was interested only in mere cultural matters, whereas he, of course, was interested in important matters like race, economic rationalism and countering the forces that produced Pauline Hanson's One Nation Party. This struck me as odd given that, as you'll have seen, these matters are covered in some depth in chapters 3, 5, 9 and 11 here, including a detailed account of the complicity of the present cultural establishment, throughout the late 1980s and early 1990s, in fostering the rhetorics of crude anti-multiculturalism, anti-political-correctness and anti-identity-politics that have been so cleverly used by Hanson — and Howard — ever since. These people, as the above chapters show, include Manne himself.

But what struck me most about Manne's speech was that, for all his concern about race matters, throughout the speech he didn't refer to a single Aboriginal person or peoples or traditional lands by name. Instead he spoke of 'the Aborigines', which is an expression I haven't heard for a long time.[15]

This isn't simply a cheap shot. Manne has lately made useful observations about race issues in Australia, especially on *Bringing Them Home: The Stolen Generations Report*.[16] But if self-appointed saints of the public sphere are nevertheless mired in ways of thinking that objectify those they are concerned with and misrepresent the work of others, then my question again is, who is at the centre? What is the price of keeping them there? What kind of community of ideas is this? What kind of public culture is this? What kinds of public thinking are possible?

It's impossible to ask 'who is at the centre?' without asking further questions about media commentary. The writer, activist and thinker Marcia Langton has spoken of the 'unbelievably low standards of the newspapers in this country . . . the low standards of journalism and the low standards of public debate'.[17] She's right. The prognosis for commentary is poor. The past decade or so has seen the rise of doctrinaire economic rationalism, disastrous youth unemployment and suicide rates, the rise of racism and the fraying of the idea that democracy is meant to serve those at the margins in favour of the idea that democracy goes too far when it doesn't primarily serve those in the mainstream. While all these developments were occurring more or less under the noses of our present media establishment, many of them did little but whinge, Robert Hughes-style, about the imposts of multiculturalism and minority politics.

And if, since Hansonism, many regular commentators have started to change their approach, issuing a series of motherhood statements about the virtues of cultural tolerance and the perils of Pauline, one effect of their abrupt and often unacknowledged back-tracking has been to maintain their own incumbency. Their audiences — and, indeed, their producers and publishers — seem to hope that in their traditional role as articulators and arbitrators of the 'common good', they'll be able to solve some current dilemmas.

I don't think it's going to happen.

The trouble with putting yourself at the centre is that this, increasingly, is a decentred world. To speak as if it is possible to serve some moral absolute is to speak as if this is still a monoculture, when it's clearly not. In particular, it seems to me that those who speak, however unconsciously, from a position of patrician white privilege — which is the very definition of what it means to be at the centre — will never be able to say anything new about the issue of race in Australia.

In 1997 Robert Dessaix interviewed Marcia Langton for his series of radio interviews with Australian public intellectuals. The interview never made it to air, but did make it into the book of the radio series, edited by Dessaix, entitled *Speaking Their Minds: Intellectuals and the Public Culture in Australia*. In that interview Langton talks about what it's like to be Aboriginal and a social commentator in Australia. She says:

> I'm never invited to contribute to white Australian public life, except to comment on Aboriginal matters. I'm not invited, say, to write a film or theatre review or to comment on any piece of work that is not produced by an Aboriginal person, unless it touches on Aboriginal life. But to say something about *Priscilla, Queen of the Desert* . . . no. For me it's

another aspect of the way the Australian version of apartheid works. It wouldn't occur to the ordinary white person that I might have a contribution to make to Australian culture in general.[18]

Throughout the interview Dessaix was sympathetic with this. He seems almost shocked, in fact. Yet, as the writer Foong Ling Kong has pointed out, his interview with Langton is entirely circumscribed by the question of her Aboriginality.[19] At no point does *he* give her the opportunity to present herself under any sign but the sign of her race, or to speak on any other issue. The only art she is asked to comment on is Aboriginal art. The only culture she is asked to comment on is Aboriginal culture. Throughout the interview Dessaix seems unaware of the irony of this, given what Langton is saying. Instead, the interview traces a long, slow arc: even as Dessaix expresses sympathy for Langton's position, she is pushed again to the margins whereas he, as the interviewer, as the editor, as the commentator, never once questions his position of authority at the centre. He never once imagines what it might be like if she were where he is, and he were 'elsewhere'. His framing of her words in the name of his whiteness, and the privilege he assumes as he organises his own speaking position in relation to Langton's throughout the interview, couldn't be more complete.

In 1998 Jana Wendt did almost precisely the same thing in a television interview, when she asked the writer Toni Morrison if Morrison planned ever to write about white people. As Morrison said, Wendt couldn't even begin to understand how racist that question was — no black person could ever ask the same question of a white writer.[20] It was an uncomfortable moment for Wendt. I was interested that, attempting to explain herself later, she claimed the question 'was not race-based at all', implying that it was meant, instead, as a literary question. According to Wendt, 'Morrison's aggressive response was a powerful illustration of her acute sensitivity, some say over-sensitivity on this issue'.[21]

But if it wasn't a race-based question, what was it? To suggest that it was a literary question and therefore devoid of racial content is to draw on one of the commonplaces of Australian literary and public life — the thirty-years-out-of-date idea that literature and politics don't automatically intersect. It's a distinction that anyone who has closely read Morrison's writing should find impossible to sustain. As Wendt ultimately conceded, the point Morrison made 'was well worth making: that is, that we, those of us with white skin, are so used to being at the heart of life, at the centre of everything, that we find it very peculiar when all of a sudden we are shifted to the periphery.'[22]

Then there's the 1998 book, *Two Nations*, about the rise of Pauline Hanson's One Nation Party. It contains many excellent contributions, but what's most striking about the book is the absence of Aboriginal contributors, given that there are so many excellent Aboriginal writers and thinkers in this country. No Noel Pearson, no Jackie Huggins, no Ruby Langford Ginibi, no Marcia Langton, no Lionel Fogarty, no Sam Watson. Nor are there any Asian contributors to this book, which also seems odd given the many excellent writers of Asian background living in Australia. No Ding Xiaoqi, no Sang Ye, no Beth Yahp, no Yang Lian, no Ien Ang, no Brian Castro. Also absent are writers of Southern European origin, despite the fact that Australia has some of the largest populations of people of Greek and Italian origin outside those countries. No Fotini Epanomitis, no George Papaellinas, no Angelo Loukakis, no Mary Kalantzis, no Christos Tsiolkas, no Zita Antonious. Any book called *Two Nations* that suffers these sorts of omissions runs the risk of self-parody.[23]

Two Nations is part of the renaissance in the idea that the essay is a sustaining part of public culture. Some of the other recent collections, such as Morag Fraser's *Seams of Light* and

Who is at the centre?

Peter Craven's *Best Australian Essays, 1998*, were also promoted by their editors as interventions in the race debate.[24] With the exception of an essay by Brian Castro in *Seams of Light*, both suffer from precisely the same sorts of omissions as *Two Nations*.

Perhaps such omissions will continue to be the orthodoxy in a place where it remains possible for a sports commentator during the 1998 Commonwealth Games to speculate without embarrassment that Matt Shirvington may yet turn out to be the first white man to run a certain distance under a certain time. Or where the *Sun-Herald* can run a full page asking whether or not the Ana Kokkinos film, *Head On*, misrepresents Greek culture, presumably because in Australia Greek culture needs be singular.[25] Or where ABC television could run a short piece on emerging Aboriginal musicians in which their white 'mentors' took up the overwhelming proportion of screen time and were referred to by name, while all but one of the Aboriginal musicians were referred to as 'some other Aborigines'.[26]

So what assumptions are being made here about the colour of Australian public space? What does this say about Australian commentary? What kinds of ideas are possible here? What kinds of silences are endemic? For all the cultural establishment's 'well-meaning' thinking on race, is what we are seeing a form of white colonial liberalism, where concern is expressed on race matters but little power or agency is granted to those on the periphery, where the white voice remains sacrosanct, and where white people, having been complicit in injustices, now claim an implicit mortgage on the moral high ground, to emerge, again, as the heroes of the piece?

★

In 1998 I also attended another writer's festival, the Brisbane Writers' Festival. This festival was notable for its relative lack of patrician white voices advertising their wares. Instead, a wide range of sessions simply had Aboriginal participants. Ernie Dingo, John Graham, Mary Graham, Jackie Huggins, Sam

Watson and Archie Weller all spoke. As did Asian writers such as Kee Thuan Chye, Lau Siew Mei and Alfred Yuson. The audience too was notable for its representative diversity. It was also notable for its numbers of young people.

★

It's impossible to ask questions about who is at the centre and the price of keeping them there without considering young people. On top of a youth unemployment rate of around 25 per cent and one of the highest youth suicide rates in the world, both of which are higher in regional areas, and a massive increase in youth homelessness, we have a worsening prognosis for youth wages, youth rights, and youth welfare. For example, the recently introduced Common Youth Allowance, which is designed to eliminate the financial incentive for people to stay on unemployment benefits, thereby pushing the young into work, is structured so that about 25 000 16- and 17-year-olds are no longer eligible for benefits. Many more have lost benefits because of the introduction of parental means-testing for people aged between eighteen and twenty-one.[27] As a result many young people from regional areas have been forced to stay in — or return to — places of low employment opportunity because they cannot live independently elsewhere. Yet the income threshold for the means test is set so low that in many cases their families are unable to support them.

Meanwhile, the nation's peak body for young people, the Australian Youth Policy and Action Coalition (AYPAC), lost $330 000 in federal government funding, effective on the day before the Common Youth Allowance was introduced. The cut was announced shortly after AYPAC criticised the government's youth policy, especially the Common Youth Allowance, the work-for-the-dole scheme, and the introduction of the privatised Jobs Network.[28] At the same time as AYPAC funding was cut, the government announced the establishment of a hand-picked Roundtable to function as the government's sole youth policy advisory body. The 50 members of the body have been told not to broadcast their thoughts on education and employment matters, to stay away from 'serious' policy areas and to make only 'broad vision statements'. When members working on education conducted a questionnaire on voluntary student unionism and the findings were circulated on the Net, officials from the Department of Education, Training and Youth Affairs removed the information from the Net because it conflicted with the government's position. These same officials have been given power to dismiss members who behave in a way perceived to be 'against the Roundtable's interests'. As one member has said, 'we're basically a tokenistic organisation'. According to another member, Ryan Heath, 'It's been made clear that we are to find a range of opinions and give them to the Government but not come up with policy suggestions of our own.'[29]

In 1998 funding was also withdrawn from Beat, the Bridging Education and Training Service set up by the Salvation Army and the federal government as a joint programme to help troubled teenagers expelled from school to find jobs, and to deal with problems of homelessness, crime and drug use. Apparently this was because Beat might compete with the interests of contractors in the private employment service.[30] Breaking the Cycle, a specialised programme for long-term unemployed youth, was forced to close in late 1998 after government funding cuts. A non-profit organisation, since 1992 it had found jobs for 1200 young people referred to it by the now-defunct Commonwealth Employment Service as most difficult to find work for. According to a spokesperson for then Federal Employment Minister, David Kemp, while Breaking the Cycle was a 'very worthwhile centre which does a great deal for young people', it was not part of the then-new Jobs Network.[31] Both this decision and the winding-up of Beat are good examples of how privatisation cuts across welfare provision.

A report prepared by the National Drug and Alcohol Research Centre has found that more than 10 per cent of Australians aged eighteen to thirty-four have a drinking problem, more than twice the rate among people aged fifty five and over.[32] A survey undertaken by Melbourne's Centre for Adolescent Health found more than 40 per cent of 17-year-old men and 33 per cent of 17-year-old women had engaged in a bout of heavy drinking in the previous week.[33] The problem is worse when it comes to hard drugs. In Victoria, by mid-February 1999 the State death toll for heroin overdoses was running ahead of the annual road toll, with 60 deaths versus 45.[34] According to Andrew McGregor, who has worked in youth legal aid for nine years, youth unemployment is an important factor contributing to an increase in hard drug trafficking amongst teenagers.[35] Twenty years ago the average age of heroin addicts was in the late twenties. Now it is seventeen.

A 1998 report, 'Australia's Youth: Reality and Risk', compiled by the Dusseldorp Skills Forum, has found that for every young person officially listed as unemployed, another is scraping by on the margins, neither in full-time employment nor full-time study. According to the report, 190 000 people aged fifteen to nineteen are unemployed, in part-time work, or not in the labour force. This represents about 46 per cent of the non-student population in this age group.[36]

Another report prepared by the Australian Centre for Equity through Education, and based on an eight-year academic study, says almost one in three of the 100 000 young people who experience homelessness at some time each year are still at school. The authors of *Youth Homelessness, Early Intervention and Prevention*, David MacKenzie and Dr Chris Chamberlain, point out that 'young people who leave home because of family conflict are unlikely to get full-time employment if they drop out of school', whereas 'in the 1950s and 1960s most of them avoided homelessness because they got jobs. Now they cannot.'[37] MacKenzie and Chamberlain suggest that there is a danger that a new underclass will emerge if large numbers of young people become chronically homeless.

In the 1998 federal budget, the government allocated almost $300 million for an incentive programme to provide 120 000 new apprenticeships, provided an extra $2.2 million to assist the homeless, financed an extra 10 000 university places, allocated $70 million over four years for the running of the new Common Youth Allowance, and budgeted $259.5 million as running costs for its Work for the Dole programme.[38]

But the clever rhetoric claiming that this last initiative embraced a principle of 'mutual obligation' disguised the fact that welfare payments have always involved a principle of mutual obligation as a condition of citizenship. What the Work for the Dole programme in fact involves is a notion of citizenship where some citizens are less equal than others. The unfairness of the social contract for youth can be seen in the ever-present drive to reduce youth wages for those who do have work. As Tan Le, 1998 Young Australian of the Year, has commented, in an economy increasingly geared to global efficiency, the pressure for wage competitiveness is being borne disproportionately by the nation's youth.[39] In effect, young people have led the way in the new era of globalised political hard-ball. They are the guinea pigs in the push to demonstrate how high levels of unemployment can be used to justify and create wage 'efficiencies'; they are disproportionately disfranchised by the effects of privatisation, welfare shrinkage, the erosion of rights and a biased social contract; and they are the demons in the 'divide and rule' politics of victim-blaming.

For so long as governments continue to play political hard-ball with young people it's difficult to see any of their initiatives actually achieving structural solutions to the problems young people face, or to see headline-making funding initiatives as anything more than sophisticated window-dressing. According to 'Australia's Youth: Reality and Risk', during the

1990s Australian young people have gone backwards on almost every major indicator, from employment to education to training, especially compared to adults.[40] The report said that the young have 'gained few substantial benefits' despite the rhetoric and money spent on them. It named dead-end, insecure and low-paying part-time jobs as a particular trap — precisely the area where there has been the largest jobs growth. These are the jobs young people are forced into when they are forced off benefits. At a conference held before it lost its funding AYPAC concluded that the first Howard government had made no positive initiatives on youth apart from spending $18 million on youth suicide prevention. As AYPAC's head, David Matthews, said, 'We feel that young people are still blamed rather than included in society . . . Instead of being encouraged, they're being penalised.'[41]

Successive federal governments have failed to act on the 1989 National Homeless Children's Report, in spite of claims from Chris Sidoti, the Human Rights Commissioner, that youth homelessness has actually risen since the report was released.[42] According to the Centre for Youth Affairs, Research and Development at RMIT, in 1998 there were 21 000 homeless Australians aged under eighteen.[43] The 1997 joint report by the Human Rights and Equal Opportunity and Australian Law Reform Commissions overwhelmingly found that Australia isn't fulfilling its commitments under the United Nations Convention on the Rights of the Child. According to the report, 66 per cent of young respondents to one survey felt that they were 'never' or 'only sometimes' treated fairly by the police, and many young people complained of feeling harassed by police, security guards and shopkeepers. The report called for realistic bail conditions, especially for Aborigines who live in remote areas and are often remanded in detention centres hundreds of kilometres from their homes; it also stressed the importance of providing a legal advice line and police training in youth affairs, and recommended a national summit on chil-

Who is at the centre?

dren, to be attended by heads of government, focusing on youth homelessness and suicide.[44]

A National Children's Summit held in late 1998 was virtually ignored by political leaders.[45] In 1997 the Northern Territory government, surfing a wave of media-driven populist sentiment about youth crime waves, considered introducing curfews for children and night 'tags', in the form of a sensor strapped to the ankle,[46] and has proposed removal of the right to remain silent. The Northern Territory also became the latest government to join the fashion for mandatory sentencing. In 1998, under its one-strike-and-you're-in programme, Margaret Nalyirri Wynbyne, a young woman with no previous convictions, was separated from her four-week-old baby and jailed for fourteen days, then left on the side of the road without a bus fare home — all for receiving stolen goods in the form of a $2.50 can of beer.[47] In Western Australia mandatory sentencing has meant that young people are often imprisoned for trivial offences and held hundreds of kilometres away from their families. Following recent legislation, in New South Wales young people can be forcibly evicted from public places by police, without police having to show any evidence of illegal activity.

According to a recent New South Wales study, measures against anti-youth crime are acting disproportionately on Aboriginal and migrant youths, who are more likely to end up in detention despite being no more likely that white youths to commit crime. Recent outcries about migrant youth gangs, according to Don Weatherburn, the director of the NSW Bureau of Crime Statistics and Research, tend to overlook a deeper malaise. According to Weatherburn, the real problem isn't 'ethnic youth gangs', but the poor economic and social conditions among migrant communities.[48] According to the sociologist Paul Tabar, there has been an 'ethnicisation of crime', with racist outcries against ethnic gangs by the police, politicians, the media and talkback callers constructing an overwhelming community consensus that disguises the real problems, which are to do with class and endemic underprivilege rather than race.[49]

A decade on from the Royal Commission into Aboriginal Deaths in Custody, few of its recommendations have been implemented. A key objective of the Commission was that incarceration rates among Aborigines be reduced, yet Aboriginal incarceration rates have skyrocketed. In New South Wales jails alone, the proportion of Aboriginal prisoners has risen markedly from 8.5 to 14 per cent; over the same period, the overall national prison population has increased 29 per cent. According to Human Rights Commissioner Chris Sidoti, the rate of Aboriginal incarceration is rising because 'unfortunately we still have this great auction on who will be tougher on crime'.[50] Four Aborigines died per year between 1992 and 1997 in New South Wales jails, with three losing their lives in 1998. According to the journalists Wendy Bacon and Bonita Mason, writing in 1995, one reason for the failure of governments to implement the recommendations of the Commission is that the media have by and large failed to comment on their inaction.[51] As Ruby Langford Ginibi, whose own son attempted suicide in jail, said in 1998, 'the killing times are not over'.[52]

Yet evidence is mounting that the populist 'get tough on crime' approach favoured by the New South Wales, Northern Territory, Queensland and West Australian governments is not only ineffective but expensive. According to US research published in 1996 by the Rand Corporation, economic analysis shows that the most cost-effective way of preventing youth crime is to re-include youth in the wider social contract by redressing economic, social and educational inequities. The research found that programmes supporting young people to stay in school were more effective in preventing juvenile crime, and were five times more cost-effective, than punitive measures such as the 'three strikes and you're in' schemes favoured by southern US States, and fashionable among Australian State governments. Income support to prevent eco-

Who is at the centre?

nomically disadvantaged families from breaking up was similarly effective.[53]

In Australia, a national study has found that one in ten high-school students is at risk of becoming homeless.[54] Higher education budgets have been cut, and participation and equity compromised, via changes to successful programmes such as Abstudy, which made it possible for disadvantaged young Aborigines to get tertiary education. A 1998 federal government initiative means that the 9000 young Australians presently receiving homeless support payments will have their eligibility for benefits determined by their parents, with parents of children who have left home because of domestic violence and other abuse being encouraged to use a 'hotline' to voice their views on whether their children should receive benefits. According to a spokesmen for Senator Jocelyn Newman, then Minister for Social Security, some parents felt it was 'too easy for their kids to claim they're homeless'.[55] In the 1998 federal election campaign the Work for the Dole programme received broad bipartisan support, with the major parties even bidding to outdo each other, despite the questions such programmes raise about human rights.

At the heart of the Work for the Dole scheme are questions, again, about how democracy and the media work. Is welfare to be distributed according to a ledger-based model, which is what 'work for the dole' suggests, or a rights-based model? Amid the thousands of newspaper column inches and hours of electronic media time devoted to the scheme, this fundamental question was glossed over.

In January 1999, John Howard upped the ante further with an announcement that dole recipients would be subject to a literacy test and that those who couldn't read and write would have their benefits reduced. In other words, young people were going to be directly penalised for the failures of the education system, a system that has itself been subject to ruthless cutbacks. It's called getting them coming and going.[56]

Gangland

★

It's difficult to imagine that the government could canvass this sort of 'double-dipping' if the TV current affairs shows hadn't already done part of the job for them. Indeed, little of the above would have been possible without the demonisation of young people in the media. The teenage drug-dealer, the youthful dole bludger, the single mother, the juvenile delinquent with a baseball cap on backwards, looking for a pensioner's open window to climb through — all have become both media and policy staples, marching hand-in-hand with the currently fashionable idea that young people deserve lesser access to full human rights, to welfare, to equity before the law, than the rest of the community.

So let me ask again, who is at the centre? Who presided over the moral and cultural milieu in which all this became possible? What is the price of keeping them there?

Beat-ups about young dole bludgers and youth crime are themselves evidence of how the interests of the centre override those of the margins. They are examples of how the media trades in 'folk devils' and false perceptions to drive circulation and ratings. Governments have been complicit in the demonisation of young people in order to create a false sense of shared community among a predominantly middle-aged constituency, by appealing to a shared enemy. In the case of young people these are remarkably similar 'folk-devils' to those lately peddled by the cultural establishment to drive book sales — that is, young people are irresponsible, prone to criminality, and devoid of moral sense or social memory.

Young people have nothing to say. Those who do are the exception, not the rule. That's the message from the soft-news end of the media. 'Believe it or not, students revolt', was the patronising headline that accompanied an article on a sit-in by university students protesting against up-front higher education fees.[57] It's a fashion among established commentators to complain that youth rules the world. 'Sorry teenagers, the power game is up . . . Teenagers think the world revolves around them', went the leader in a soft-news story in one newspaper, remarking on the rise of Leonardo DiCaprio as evidence that teenagers are all-powerful.[58] There is a tragic irony here in the use of the word 'power'. The marketing of youthfulness, in the form of attractive young bodies and faces, whether it be young newsreaders, young novelists, or movie stars, needs to be distinguished from the asking of real questions to do with the diminishing rights and social power of young people. It was, needless to say, a distinction the article failed to make.

The US social commentator Henry A. Giroux places this problem in a broader context:

> As the state is hollowed out and only the most brutal state apparatuses remain intact, children have fewer opportunities to protect themselves from an adult world that offers them dwindling resources, dead-end jobs, and diminishing hopes for the future. At the same time, children are increasingly subjected to social and economic forces that exploit them through the dynamics of sexualization, commodification, and commercialization throughout vast segments of the culture.[59]

There are many parallels between the US and Australian situations. Giroux points to the drying up of public funding and support services, and the elimination of extracurricular activities from schools, along with the fact that 'corporations increasingly provide the public spheres for children to experience themselves as consuming subjects and commodities' (shopping malls, for instance).[60] All these are examples of the hollowing out of the state that has occurred with the rise of neo-conservative-inspired, free-market-oriented policy-making. The result, he says, is that 'young people find themselves in a society where there are very few decommodified public spheres for them to identify with and experience'.[61]

Alternative media creators and thinkers have demonstrated that the media aren't monolithic or omnipotent, yet mainstream media representations of young people remain extremely powerful. So powerful that, for example, in early 1999 free needle services for young intravenous drug-users in New South Wales were precipitately dropped after a newspaper published a picture of a supposed 12-year-old shooting up in a lane. This despite the possibility that the new ruling would expose young intravenous drug-users to the risk of HIV and hepatitis, and despite the fact that the drug-user in the picture turned out to be aged over 16. As the mainstream media colonise the idea of what public space is, so they become more and more important to the political process. Governments listen to newspaper editorials, TV current affairs and talkback radio before they start formulating policy.

When someone puts their hand up to speak about youth issues, established commentators sigh ''Twas ever thus'. Yet those born after 1975 are the first generation for many decades to look forward to a lower standard of living than their parents enjoyed. Never have young people been the object of such vehemence in the media and government policy as they are now. Never have they been so subject to welfare and rights shrinkage, or such iniquities as the drying up of free education, the removal of community services such as legal aid, or the diminution of free or subsidised municipal facilities, especially in regional areas.

Today's young are the first generation to bear the brunt of the shift in government thinking in welfare and economics that has taken place since the early 1980s, and the subtle shifts in media story-telling style that have gone with it. This new style of story-telling, based as it is on a standard set of mythologies and demons, seems almost tailor-made to the weakening of traditional notions of community that occurs in highly

Who is at the centre?

competition-oriented societies, where notions of community have to be galvanised by fear-mongering and scapegoating.

The term 'youth' no longer simply describes a life stage. Instead it is increasingly defined by its place in a complex geopolitics in which New Right political strategies are linked with changes in the global distribution of wealth and power, changing patterns of media ownership, fashions in journalism and opinion-making, battles over university curricula and the canon of core Western values, and the wider range of mechanisms currently being put in place to protect an increasingly inegalitarian economic and social status quo.[62]

So the question remains: who is at the centre?

15
Damning the torpedoes: politics after punk

Tentacular networks of chummy patronage, mutual puffery and cultural power . . . this new elite is the most intellectually thin in Australian cultural history.

John Docker[1]

Another problem with the libertarian generation is that, because of their confrontational politics, they refuse to recognise the power they have acquired themselves. Caught up in their fantasy of 're-presenting' the oppressed, they have become blind to their own position. They refuse to see, for instance, that for younger women feminism can be perceived as the mainstream. Post-punk politics shaped these younger women's political sensibility.

Rosi Braidotti[2]

Australian cultural life is like Ancient Greek theatre. In it you'll find the full gamut of emotions to do with life and death, envy, jealousy, betrayal. And as in Ancient Greek theatre, the same characters keep appearing time and time again.

The cultural establishment who were the main target of *Gangland* are still in business. The same old people are still talking about the same old thing, and reviewing each other's books about it. It's all based on a set of generic mythologies — op-ed meets Epic Theatre. Four years after the publication of *The First Stone*, Anne Manne is still talking about Helen Garner as a victim of 'intolerance and venom', without ever asking if perhaps *The First Stone* wasn't itself intolerant and venomous.[3] The columnist Anne Neumann too is still peddling the myth about 'highly politicised feminists who refuse to temper the revolution with mercy' — and we all know who *they* are.[4] Bettina Arndt, having run full circle from libertarian to defender of 'family values', still seems determined to drag the clock back to darker days, arguing that homosexual teachers should remain closeted because homosexuality is supposedly a difficult topic to broach with children. It's a bit like saying children don't know anything about heterosexual sex. Meanwhile, homophobia and a lack of role models for homosexual youth are figured by many as leading causes of youth suicide.[5]

The broadsheet art critics are still at it too. Giles Auty in particular writes as if everything after modernism is a nightmare from which we'll soon wake. His work is full of paeans to 'truth' and truisms such as 'significant art of all kinds has an original message embedded in it'.[6] And who decides what's a suitably original message? Well, Auty, of course. Like so many journalists, Auty likes to set himself up as the 'besieged dissenter'. The perceived enemies are always more or less the same. For Paul Sheehan — who, as McKenzie Wark pointed out, has built his career on being besieged — it's the multicultural industry.[7] For Auty it's 'militant gender groups'.[8] It's a professional tic. The *Age*'s Peter Timms too likes to whinge about artists who are 'more downright socially engaged than the rest'.[9] Both Auty and Timms compulsively gesture to Europe for *real* cultural values; you know, truth and beauty — not that nasty socially inflected stuff. But newspaper art criticism is like newspaper feminism. Just how did mainstream commentary get so far from what people are saying on the street, and from what actual practitioners are doing in both these areas? Why is what is going on not being so much reported, as actively filtered by the most conservative of possible voices?

In mid-1999 members of the visual arts community petitioned against the appointment of conservative *Sydney Morning Herald* art columnist John McDonald as head of Australian art at the National Gallery of Australia. Auty and Timms cheered the appointment from the sidelines, and there was wide press comment in support of McDonald, whom some labelled an iconoclast.[10] It's hard to see how someone so proudly hostile to experimentation might be called an iconoclast, especially given that McDonald was appointed at a time when the gallery had radically curtailed its acquisition of contemporary paintings. It's a measure of how timid and backward-looking public culture has become that the voice of the sinecured and well-paid conservative status quo can get away with presenting itself as the voice of wild and free dissent.

Four years after the year of the Helens — Darville-Demidenko and Garner — the Big Boys came to town, each to take his own turn at controversy. Robert Hughes, Bryce Courtenay, John Laws, Alan Jones, Paddy McGuinness, Bob Ellis: all got walk-ons in the parade of familiar faces that tends to stand in for national events and national debate. John Laws got stuck into fellow 2UE radio talkback host Alan Jones for his political views. Hughes found himself the object of a charge of plagiarism. Courtenay found himself the target of newspaper bias. Ellis found himself the victim of a libel suit involving the federal treasurer, Peter Costello, and Tony Abbott, another Liberal minister. McGuinness found himself the editor of *Quadrant*. And Helen Garner found herself back in the news too, in a brief but intense reprise of the year of the Helens.

As well as its crisis, each event had its chorus. Some wrote in disbelief, such as David Marr in his querulous yet withering reports on the Abbott and Costello libel case. Others wrote in, well, disbelief. Only this time it was *their* idols being cast down. The effect was often comical. It's doubtful that the discovery that Robert Hughes's review of a show in *Time* had plagiarised passages from a review of the same show written by Patricia Macdonald for *Australian Art Collector* would have received more than a column or two of newspaper attention, if not for the zeal with which Peter Craven and Luke Slattery sprang to his defence. Hughes, Craven wrote, was a victim of his own genius: his absolutely photographic memory had got the better of him without his realising. Where was Craven when all those other recent perpetrators of literary hoaxes needed him? 'Repressed total verbal recall'. That was what Craven put it down to, writing in the *Age*.[11] His friend and colleague Luke Slattery wrote two articles on the affair for the *Australian*. He too laid it on thick about Hughes's genius. Hughes, after all, 'can still "regurgitate" classical works learnt by rote at school'.[12] It was all a case of '"Unconscious" appropriation', argued Slattery. After all, 'Human beings are imitative creatures — it's how we learn to speak'.[13] And besides, Slattery opined, 'before the Romantic era placed a high premium on individual genius, creativity was regarded as a matter of reworking older, traditional material'. Hughes, according to Slattery, was simply following in the footsteps of that pre-Romantic 'genius' Shakespeare, because like Shakespeare he was reusing other people's material to his own ends, adding a little bit of his own charismatic magic along the way.

Or is the whole idea to take up space like this? If not for their assiduous efforts, perhaps other people might have done something different with the news. Evil people, unlike Craven, who devoted an entire issue of a journal he once edited to Hughes, and unlike Slattery, who once travelled to New York to interview him. People who hadn't reviewed so many of his latest books and paid homage to him so frequently in their articles and columns.[14] For the record, Hughes promptly and instinctively offered an apology to Macdonald, which was accepted.

The cult of celebrity is still alive and well in Australian cultural life. In one newspaper a review of Allan Gurganus's novel, *Plays Well with Others*, was illustrated not by a picture of Gurganus, but by a photograph of his reviewer, Robert Dessaix.[15] The same newspaper — the *Age* — published a review of Germaine Greer's *The Whole Woman*, accompanied by a photograph of its reviewer, Helen Garner.[16]

Have the over-inflated reputations of public sages really become more important than straightforward veracity? That seemed to be the case when the *Sydney Morning Herald* pulled a debunking review of *Sandstone Gothic*, an autobiographical account of academic goings-on at Sydney University written by Andrew Riemer, a regular book reviewer for the *Herald*. The reviewer, Stephen Knight, an old colleague of Riemer's, called the book 'the longest complaint I've read since *Piers Plowman*, and not as well written'.[17] 'Riveting reading' was the conclusion reached by *Herald* regular and another old colleague of Riemer's, Don Anderson, in the review that finally appeared.[18] Anderson is entitled to like the book more than Knight did, but the *Herald*'s concern for Riemer's reputation ensures we hear only the reinforcement, not the criticism.

All hands were on deck, again, in mid-1997 with news that Janet Malcolm, that doyen of 'new journalism', had published an excoriating review of Garner's *The First Stone* in the *New Yorker*.[19] Craven dashed into print to protect Garner, accusing Malcolm of being a 'snake'.[20] Given the characteristically restrained, highly coded language of New York journalism, the review wasn't so much damning as homicidal. 'These are not the reactions of a seasoned journalist, but the ravings of a rejected lover', wrote Malcolm. 'What makes *The First Stone* such an extraordinary book, a book unlike any other study of sexual harassment, is Garner's enactment — in her obsessive pursuit of Nicole Stewart and Elizabeth Rosen — of the very misdemeanor she has set out to investigate'.[21] But this, according to Craven, was merely a sign of Malcolm's 'repressed admiration'.

'How to stymie a debate in order to protect a reputation': that must be the name of the manual that circulates among the cultural establishment. I was fortunate, or unfortunate, to see the system in action recently, though that wasn't what I was expecting when I sat down in the upper row of seats, almost directly above the stage, at a panel session on writers and reviewers at the 1998 Melbourne Writers' Festival. The chair, Peter Pierce, a critic and academic, got up and opened the session with the request that *Gangland* not be discussed. 'That was last year, this is this', he told the audience. It was good to think, just for a moment, that the issues in this book were all so fleeting as that. Then he handed over to his panellists: Helen Daniel, editor of *Australian Book Review*, Peter Craven, the writer and critic Dean Kiley, and Bryce Courtenay.

The first three papers proceeded straightforwardly enough, but it was Courtenay's that got the attention of the audience, when he read out a section from an offensively patronising review of one of his books, then attributed it to Pierce. Why is it, Courtenay asked, that overseas reviews of his books are so different from local reviews? Why do Australian reviewers so despise his work, when overseas reviewers at least give him a fair go? His Australian reviews, he said, 'hurt like buggery', whereas American critics, not having preconceived notions of his work, had compared books of his such as *The Potato Factory* with Peter Carey's *Jack Maggs*, had reviewed them alongside each other, and had even ranked his book ahead of Carey's. The crowd, from my vantage point up above both the audience and the stage, were firmly on Courtenay's side. During his paper there were cheers and murmurs of approval. When Pierce rose to say Courtenay should have referred to Tolstoy as 'Count Tolstoy', not 'Mr Tolstoy', he was roundly booed, having unfortunately confirmed the audience's impression of him as a literary snob. Why is it, Courtenay asked, that Australian reviewers of his work seem so out of kilter with the millions of readers who have bought his books? He then went into a long recitation of his local sales figures. Craven rose to defend Australian reviewers as not being anti-popular fiction, but there was popular fiction and popular fiction, he said. During this the audience again booed, and some began rhythmically stamping their feet. Everything Craven and Pierce said seemed to confirm the gulf between popular opinion and literary elites. Clearly unused to being openly jeered at (who isn't?), they looked less and less comfortable as the session went on, and were clearly relieved when it closed. It must have been a humiliating experience.

During the session various personages came and went. The books editor of the *Age*, Andrew Clark, arrived late, and left before the session ended. Bob Sessions, Courtenay's publisher, sat among the audience off to one side of the stage. Robert Manne and his friend Raimond Gaita sat quietly among the audience just a little further along. Michael Heyward, their publisher, took a seat in the body of the audience. At the very end of the session Gaita asked Courtenay whether his sales figures solved the question of literary merit. It was a *non sequitur*, because Courtenay had already acknowledged his work wasn't intended as high literature, and the issue was the difference between local and overseas reviews. But the question nevertheless provided a sense of closure. Gaita and Manne then moved onto the stage to comfort Craven. In a genuinely tender display, Manne even put a comforting hand on Craven's shoulder.

But the way the session was reported put paid to any remaining doubt that Australian literature involves a complex system of patronage and paybacks. A report by Andrew Clark in the *Age* the following day opened with a quote from Michael Heyward, who claimed that Courtenay had said during the session that he was responsible for the success of other Australian writers. 'I don't think I've seen anything as shameless and vulgar at a writer's festival', Heyward ranted. 'It suggests a lack of contact with reality.'[22] I have enormous respect for Heyward as a publisher, and can only suggest that perhaps he was in a darker spot than I was and hadn't taken notes. Courtenay in fact said that if his work, by proving popular, led readers to other

Australian writers they might not have otherwise read, then this was a wonderful thing. But the piece was a stitch-up. After a full column of Heyward's comments about how 'offended' he was by the session, which he wasn't directly part of — comments that amounted to little more than value judgements on his part — Courtenay was finally given space to rebut the concrete allegations made against his character. According to Heyward, Courtenay's remarks about *Jack Maggs* besmirched Carey's book to the advantage of his own. According to my notebook, Courtenay's remarks about Carey's book were all in the context of his mentioning a US review that compared *The Potato Factory* favourably with *Jack Maggs* — it was not a comparison Courtenay himself made. In fact, he qualified the US appraisal by praising Carey's work. In a nod to the power of properly literary reputation, Clark then gave Gaita's *non sequitur* the last word. None of the issues raised by Courtenay, nor indeed by any of the other panellists, were mentioned.

Finer sensibilities than Courtenay's had been offended, it seemed. Indeed, as if to confirm or parody Courtenay's claim about the snobby divide between the way critics review popular and literary fiction, the language used to disparage him was almost entirely the language of class: the language the old rich use to describe the new rich. Gideon Haigh, writing in the *Australian*, ignored the basic questions at the heart of the session too, reducing them to a question of how his delicate sensibilities had been assailed by 'one of the most graceless and unedifying performances by an author it has been my misfortune to sit through'.[23] His head was in his hands, he tells us, which is why he couldn't tell if at one point Courtenay 'was claiming to be largely responsible for the fact that more Australians are reading Australian authors'. But there you go; he's raised the allegation anyway. What was most striking about Haigh's report, given that it was written as a first-person account of the event, was that the audience was entirely absent. There were none of the hoots, none of the foot-stamping, none of the clapping, and none of the boos, of the session I saw and heard — predominantly in support of Courtenay. Even with your head in your hands, I would have thought you would have at least heard a dull roar.

If it might seem that the way the event was reported in these two newspapers canvassed a wide range of opinion, then it's worth remembering that Haigh, like Gaita and Manne, is published by Heyward at Text Publishing. Heyward and Craven are ex-colleagues and old friends, and Craven has described Haigh as 'the finest Australian journalist of his generation in any field'.[24]

I'm not entirely comfortable with defending Courtenay. I've never read one of his books, and I find his brand of haranguing populism tedious. Nor should writers be naïve about what critics actually do — they *criticise,* and have every right to do so, as long as it's done in good faith. It gives me no pleasure, either, to be criticising Heyward or Haigh, whose work I've admired. But doesn't everyone have a right to be represented fairly and honestly in the media, no matter whose finer sensibilities might be offended?

★

How does all this look to an outsider? The Irish writer Nuala O'faolain was a guest at the 1998 Melbourne Writers' Festival. Commenting on Courtenay's presence at the festival and having attended a reading he gave, she remarked:

> Bryce Courtenay tells me he has sold 20 million books and that this is the first time he's been invited to the festival . . . Why, then, are there only 30 people here to hear him, not to mention me? Perhaps intellectual snobbery survives where class snobbery is absent.[25]

Describing a session involving Robert Manne and Raimond Gaita, she said:

Damning the torpedoes

The occasion is fairly ponderous, since the interviewer is reverent to an unfortunate degree. The chances of the men qualifying their warm approval of themselves or each other is zero.

Of a discussion about race at the festival, she remarked:

How do Australians start off an indigenous moral sense? Is it, as Manne implies, by reference to the Aboriginal people? If so, shouldn't there be a few Aboriginal people at the festival? Ireland has its own shame, in its treatment of the travellers. But you don't get any kudos for saying in public how sensitive you are about them.

★

The gangs came out to play, too, with the publication of Jenna Mead's book *Bodyjamming: Sexual Harassment, Feminism and Public Life*, about some of the issues surrounding contemporary feminism, published in the wake of *The First Stone*, in which Mead emerges as a principal villain. I have an interest in this book, both as a friend of Mead and as a contributor; but what was interesting was how the reception panned out. The usual suspects got on board: after all there was a reputation to protect. The class-bound nature of the mainstream media public sphere was again at issue — the language used here, again, was of finer sensibilities having been offended. All homed in on the same thing: Rosi Braidotti's contribution debunking the urban legend that surrounds Garner's time as a teacher at Fitzroy High School, before she was sacked for using explicit sexual language in class. Braidotti had been a student at the school at the time, and as a high achiever at a school with a very low success rate, had seen her academic career, and those of several other students of non-English-speaking background, nearly scuttled by a Garner publicity juggernaut at a crucial moment when the school had been trying to improve its academic reputation. As Braidotti says, 'The whole circus was played out on our backs'.[26] The essay, I agree, contains several short passages that are regrettable for the vehemence of their personal feeling against Garner. But the rest is important, and besides, what was this if not Braidotti's story to tell; one of an injustice she had bottled up for twenty years while having to listen to the slavish perpetuation of quite a different mythology?

But it's a cardinal rule of gatekeeping (of the negative kind so often practised by the local cultural elite) to go for the soft target — might I say the non-WASP target — ignoring everything else. Not only is the public sphere here middle-class (finer sensibilities, again, having been offended), but also Anglo-white. The irony being that it's a non-Anglo voice again being denied, as was originally the case in the Garner-at-Fitzroy-High affair according to Braidotti's account. But there's another problem here, and a kind of lesson. What many found objectionable about the several short passages in Braidotti's piece was her strategy of mobilising strong personal reactions. In fact, this is hardly different from Garner's own narrative strategy in *The First Stone*, but the cultural establishment, with its blinkered view of its own icons, isn't good at noticing such uncomfortable symmetries. Reacting to *Bodyjamming* the journalist Kate Legge wrote, 'I felt the public space under scrutiny shrinking to within a square centimetre'.[27] Funnily enough, Legge described precisely how many people felt about *The First Stone*.

Robert Manne, too, spoke of the many 'strange' essays in *Bodyjamming*. Is it a coincidence that the two he nominates are by writers with non-Anglo names? Is this, in its own quiet way, a measure of how public space is meted out? According to Manne, *Bodyjamming* was an attempt to 'destroy the reputation of Helen Garner once and for all'.[28] Yet despite its even and moderate prose, his column could itself be read as an obvious attempt to do damage to the book (an all-too-common mission among the self-professedly 'tolerant' liberal establishment), by the tried-and-true method of damaging its author.

Damning the torpedoes

Manne painted Mead as an unreliable and unreasonable witness because of her account of a meeting of the Politics Society at La Trobe University in which they both participated. Manne mentions a tape made of the event, which, so far as he is concerned, gives a different picture to Mead's account. It would, of course, be surprising if Mead hadn't been apprehensive at the meeting, given that she was at the time the centre of a national media furore — though the possible reasons for her apprehension (people's facial expressions, gestures, the way they sat) are unlikely to be disclosed by a tape recording. But the interesting thing about Manne's piece was its tendency to reduce the whole question of Mead's veracity in the case of *The First Stone* to a tape that happened to be in his possession and over which he claimed rights of interpretation, and which he is given a newspaper column to discuss. What does this add up to? Given his exclusive access to the tape, Manne is the sole custodian of important information. He claims some kind of right of ownership, in fact, over the memory of an event, and consequently labels a woman as an unreliable narrator. He then uses his media opportunities, and indeed, what turns out to be his exclusive media voice on the event, to make his view public. The irony is that it appears to have escaped Manne's notice that all this is a handy working definition of patriarchy.

But what passes for debate, here, still has little to do with engagement. It's still little more than an attempt to discredit motives and reputations. And to our class- and ethnic-bound account of the sorts of public space broadsheet newspapers offer, we might add gender-bound. Only certain sorts of women, especially certain sorts of feminist, it seems, get space — unless they're Germaine Greer. The affair had a sequel when the newspaper where Manne's piece appeared (the *Age*) declined to grant Mead right of reply. That's a little story, perhaps, about the things you *don't* see in the paper.

It's perhaps appropriate here to talk briefly again about the reception of this book, given that the gangs who were criticised

· **Gangland**

in *Gangland* were for the most part the gangs that lined up to attack it, and in doing so they gave a demonstration of what cultural power means. All three reviews of *Gangland* in the major broadsheets — the *Age*, the *Sydney Morning Herald*, and the *Australian* — and a number of other reviews, were by people whose work is explicitly criticised in the book. Possible conflicts of interest hardly seemed an issue for their editors.[29] In fact, they seemed to go out of their way to publish reviews by writers with scores to settle. Unlike its supporters, most of the book's critics took the opportunity to publish on it a number of times, arranged to publish each other, and commented on each other's reviews. Virginia Trioli wrote on the book three times.[30] Peter Craven wrote about the book five times, and republished his friend Guy Rundle's critical review of the book in his *Best Australian Essays, 1998*.[31] Robert Manne's piece on the book appeared four times, first as a column in the *Age* and *Sydney Morning Herald*, then as an editorial in *Quadrant*, then in his book *The Way We Live Now*.[32] What transpired, in other words, was something of an inadvertent parody of this book's arguments about cultural gangs and gatekeepers.

The exercise of this sort of media power has other effects. Craven's republishing his friend Guy Rundle's critique of the book had the effect anthologisation often has, neatly detaching the review from the conversation that took place around it. Rundle's review was the only one I replied to, given the extremity of his misrepresentations of the book. Someone always gets suckered. In this case the critic Kerryn Goldsworthy swallowed whole, going out of her way to praise the review effusively in her review of Craven's book.[33] Her work is criticised on page 212, Rundle's seven pages later.

★

It's startling how, in the name of fighting the conformities of 'political correctness', a rump of commentators (most, as it happens, middle-aged white males), have all started sounding like each other. Frank Devine, Peter Coleman, Les Carlyon, Michael Duffy, Paul Sheehan: who can tell the difference? Especially when they're on about their favourite subjects: multiculturalism, feminism and, well, themselves. Especially their heroic deeds as 'dissenters' against the imposts of fashionable 'elite' opinion. Contrast the literary reception of Mead's book with the welcome given Paul Sheehan's *Among the Barbarians*. While liberal commentators dithered about *Among the Barbarians* (see chapter 13), the anti-'PC' crew uttered a collective roar of approval.

Among the Barbarians is a book arguing against the 'multicultural industry', replete with hysteria about Asian crime syndicates, clichés about Chinese sojourners, and its own brand of patriotic jingoism. The commentators chosen to anoint the book could hardly have been more appropriate. Having launched the book, Alan Jones gave sales a good start when he interviewed Sheehan on his radio show. Les Carlyon, a veteran campaigner against so-called 'political correctness', who, like Sheehan, was then a Fairfax employee, reviewed the book for the *Sydney Morning Herald* and the *Age*.[34] Michael Duffy reviewed the book for the *Australian*.[35] Duffy has elsewhere argued that, although multiculturalism has some good points (when it helps migrants assimilate) it's also notable for 'the ideological function it has served in helping the 60s generation, and those who think like it, to undermine a version of Australia with which they disagree . . . a new sort of official religion'.[36] The only major counter-review was Anne Henderson's in the *Australian's Review of Books*, with a carefully worded editorial/apologia from Kate Legge on the facing page.[37] Given that *Among the Barbarians* opens with a chapter in which Sheehan paints himself as a martyr to 'received opinion', it's perhaps appropriate that Duffy has gone on record as saying he is simply against all prevailing political fashion.[38] Perhaps someone should remind such figures just how fashionable and influential their own brand of right-wing correctness really has been over the past decade. Surely it's time for nationally syndicated columnists to put the martyr badge away and stop pretending that they lack freedom of speech, and that the views they air regularly in the media have no forum?

The publication of *Among the Barbarians* signalled a number of trends in Australian debate. Rather than be seen to support Hanson, key conservative commentators instead tried to identify with her supporters, to explain their anger and sense of economic dispossession, and to claim it was justified because, all over again, these people had been censored and lied to by the politically correct multiculturalism industry. In other words, it was a case of being able to have your anti-'PC', anti-multiculturalism debate and be anti-Hanson too. The problem is, though, that the space such commentators occupy is rapidly becoming less credible, in part because of the very success of popular movements like Hansonism. Such commentators depend on setting themselves up as the voice of the 'dispossessed', re-reporting their discontents to the average punter, who is always positioned as more intelligent and literate than the so-called 'dispossessed', just as the commentators are always themselves members of an educated media elite (these are the little hypocrisies of such commentary). Yet one of the things Hansonism and other popular movements show is that the 'dispossessed' can speak for themselves. And, in the case of Hansonism, the anti-'PC' campaigners have yet to grapple with the central problem: it's their language that's being used by One Nation.

Others among the usual suspects got on board with the publication of *Among the Barbarians*. Not just Carlyon and Duffy, but Miranda Devine and Christopher Pearson too. A veritable anti-industry industry, running on all cylinders, foot to the floor, flush with enthusiasm about the new conservatism.[39] A dissenter was P. P. McGuinness, usually keen to jump on the anti-'PC' bandwagon, who rued the possibility that Sheehan had written the 'manual for the next five elections'.[40] As it happened, Sheehan hadn't even written the manual for one election. But McGuinness had his own problems.

Almost two months earlier he had taken over the editorship of the conservative journal, *Quadrant*, following the resignation of Robert Manne. The new editorial advisory board appointed in the wake of Manne's resignation read like a roll-call of the conservative cultural establishment: David Armstrong; Peter Coleman; Miranda Devine; Bill Hayden; Christopher Pearson; Imre Salusinszky. All sometime dissenters against prevailing orthodoxies; all successful public figures; all accepting a place on a magazine board. As the prize-winning novelist Christopher Koch, a member of the magazine's board of management, complained:

> It's reached a stage where you can't hold an opposing opinion on a whole range of topics — education, feminism, post-modernism — without being shouted out of the ring and abused.[41]

Manne resigned his editorship following a dispute with the much-lauded poet Les Murray, who is the literary editor of *Quadrant*, and who believes debate is dominated by a prevailing orthodoxy, just as the journal had been subsumed by 'dog obedience trials'.[42] Dog obedience trials? Who among these established literary figures are the truly obedient? And who are the dogs? Manne had lately fallen off the anti-'PC' bandwagon to express sympathy for the stolen generations in the pages of the journal, supporting the idea that the government owed Aborigines an apology.

★

My desire, here, in this list of events, as in the rest of this book, has been to put things on the record. To narrate an alternative history comprised of things that happened in the background; the connections everyday consumers of the media often suspect, but don't have the opportunity to follow up. But if the above were some of the dominant local 'cultural controversies' of late 1997, 1998 and early 1999, then notice something? Apart from the welcome intervention of Tim Freedman in the fracas over supposed political bias in the ABC (well, perhaps not so welcome for him), who has agency? The usual suspects. Middle-aged blokes, mainly, who share out so much among themselves, all the time whingeing about how hard done by they are.

Indeed, the other signal event of this period, the taping by John Safran and Shane Paxton of an 'exposé' on Ray Martin using the same kind of invasive techniques employed by the show he then hosted, *A Current Affair*, became famous precisely because it *wasn't* shown at the time, as a result of an exchange of letters-between-people-in-high-places designed to ensure it would *never* appear. Richard Ackland eventually broke the silence, showing an edited version of the tape on ABC television's *Media Watch*. But the tape was famous well before that; pirated copies circulated widely and were widely discussed. It showed how much hunger there was for *something else* in the otherwise highly choreographed flow of information, ideas and reputation-mongering that passes for a pluralist public sphere.

★

Bob Ellis, in his memoir *Goodbye Jerusalem*, pictures a Labor Party in its glory days. The old days when politics was driven by policy and personality, not by opinion polls. Ellis got into a lot of trouble for his memoirs. A court found that in them he had libelled two women, Tanya Costello and Margaret Abbott, and their husbands — Peter Costello (the federal treasurer) and Tony Abbott (the employment services minister). It's hard not to feel sympathy for Ellis, both the Ellis of the libel case and the Ellis of the book. Party politics, it's worth recalling, was once a passionate thing. It involved vision, even a dream of what a

Damning the torpedoes

better future might look like (as opposed to endless excuses for the regressions of the present). Which is why young people today take their political passion, vision and need for a better future elsewhere. But in other respects, the Jerusalem Ellis talks of is a myth. The Labor Party never truly had a Golden Age: just a century of bickering, faction-fighting and ongoing contestation, most of which has been spent in opposition. These days even the would-be Jerusalem of the Whitlam years peers out from under the shadow of Timor Gap.

And then there's that other Ellis to consider; the one whose own media politics seem all too symptomatic of the way media power is often handed out. Ellis is a long-time anti-'PC' campaigner and freedom of speech advocate, but when Penelope Nelson, who had been his lover at the age of nineteen, wrote an account of the relationship in her 1995 book *Penny Dreadful*, the publisher, Random House, reportedly showed Ellis the proofs and gave him the right to delete unfavourable references to himself from the book, bowdlerising Nelson's account.[43]

But other Jerusalems are changing too. Especially the Jerusalem Ellis is himself part of — the Australian media and cultural establishment. Recently we have seen the demise of *In Melbourne Tonight*, the resignations of veteran newsreader Brian Naylor and TV current affairs host Ray Martin. *Midday* with Kerri-Anne Kennerley was taken off air. Mushroom Records was sold, and at the same time celebrated its twenty-fifth anniversary with a gala gig and television event. And all this amid talk of a 'youth-quake' (even if Viagra did hit the streets at around the same time). Television shows like *The Panel* and *Good News Week* seemed to be taking over.

But what did this 'youth-quake' really mean? Is it a triumph of youth culture, or simply of demographics? *The Panel* and *Good News Week* aside, much of the recent 'youth-oriented' programming, like the broadsheet press's drive to lighten up their formats, seems designed to appeal to a caricature of what young people want. Such programming, I think, is doomed to fail. The trend towards the 'bright and bouncy' turns the widely perceived vacuousness of youth culture into a self-fulfilling prophecy. It never seems to occur to media executives that young people might want *content*. Instead the media serve up their version of what they think youth culture is: a spectacle. One that, to some extent, provides titillation.

Television shows like *The Panel* have to some extent changed things by putting on screen what everyone already knew: that current affairs need not be presided over by godheads, but can be discussed by ordinary people. But Roy and HG are also innovative, as was John Clarke's *The Games*. And, with due respect to the panellists and despite the industry hype, *The Panel* is hardly the voice of youth ('I don't watch these granny shows', one 19-year-old said to me about the programme). It's a marker of how backward television is that other 'fresh faces' such as Andrew Denton and Paul McDermott are hardly new to the industry either. Having been a television and radio regular for over a decade, Denton is amused to hear himself still described as the 'new boy'.[44] But is the increasing emphasis on marketing the idea of youthfulness (as opposed to really examining the social plight of many young people) going to result in a situation where commentators in their fifties will find themselves facing premature obsolescence, while at the journalistic coal-face it remains as hard as ever to challenge the macho assumptions at the heart of newspaper publishing and the electronic media? Are young journalists, young presenters, just new faces for a conceptually tired machine, a demographic fillip?

Demographics is hardly a useful or even a plausible basis for a society. Demographics-driven revolutions that rely on putting young faces in front of a camera are ultimately empty. What a wide range of viewers, listeners, readers, *participants* in the media want, I suspect, is to see a deeper shift, one that can deliver debates on contemporary issues that have some real content and are more properly democratic and inclusive across the range of possible voices; that don't rely on the same old arbiters of the 'common good', speaking from a position of self-appointed moral superiority.

★

The literati, as I've mentioned throughout this book, are superbly symptomatic of how 'culture' runs, but they aren't where the real power lies. The real power is at the top end of town, in boardrooms, on dealing screens, and wielded by industry lobby groups. In other respects too, the particular type of power once enjoyed by the literati is decreasing. 'Culture' is increasingly the heading under which social debates take place — which is partly why the 'culture wars' are so hotly contested — but the very diversity of the field 'culture' has diminished the authority of high culture. If the cultural establishment has thrown its lot in with high culture, and has based its cultural authority on holding the high ground, and has fought the 'culture wars' and many of the battles of the New Right accordingly, then high culture has been one of the first things to go. Among all the things that the real instigators of the culture wars — the populist far right — were fighting for, high culture was the most expendable. The Australian cultural establishment — the 'new establishment', as I've called them here — has been sold a pup.

At the beginning of this book, I mentioned how I came of age in the era of punk, which saved me from the 'summer of love'. Despite a million T-shirts proclaiming the contrary, punk is dead, at least in the form it took then, and a generation or more out of date. It too is something that happened in the seventies, even if late in the day, as a specific reaction against what had gone before. When I say 'punk', I don't speak widely — I mean the punk I knew: the Australian punk of the Saints, early INXS, the Crystal Ballroom, the News and the Birthday Party (in our arrogance, we thought the Sex Pistols were poseurs) and the culture that went with them. A culture that, to my surprise, has turned out to have an enduring political legacy. Following in the wake of the oil shocks of 1973–74 and that moment in the mid-seventies when real incomes started to decline for the first time since World War II, punk arguably marked the moment when the great elitist project of modernity came unhinged.

For me it was a profoundly democratising moment. I and dozens of others would never have dared pick up a guitar and started bands if not for punk. Two decades later, I would never have dared think I could write a book. Nor, having originally left school at 16, would I have dared go to university or start work on a PhD. For me, punk marks the end of the top-down model of cultural production and the beginning of a do-it-yourself model. Punk also marks the moment when left and right started to fold together, creating a space for something else.

There's a crisis at the heart of contemporary cultural struggles; a crisis that's reflected in the weakness of local mainstream criticism (because this crisis is yet to be acknowledged by local mainstream critics); and one that, for me, was first articulated in the politics of punk. That is, people who were thought oppressed and therefore had to have someone (often a well-meaning member of the 'left') to represent them, to speak on their behalf, now speak for themselves. How this 'crisis' is negotiated — whether it even remains a 'crisis' — and the question of how existing cultures stretch, change in structure, dissolve, meld, hybridise, or vehemently resist, those voices now daring to speak for themselves, remains *the* question of the moment.

It's a 'crisis' that animates almost all the controversies spoken of in this book — from the political correctness debate, to the victim-feminism scare, to the literature wars, to moral panics about youth culture and popular culture, the culture wars and controversies about university curricula. Old centres of cultural authority are being destabilised. And not just the white patrician liberalism I mentioned in the previous chapter. Who these days wants the old left, or the old 'new left', to represent them with monolithic programmes? What use conservatism, what use the left, when new forms of media and new knowledges have undermined the remarkably similar Archimedian speaking position that the seventies left and contemporary conservatives try to occupy? The terms 'left' and 'right' continue to be useful, especially in an era where the New Right has been resurgent, where there has been a shift of power from labour to capital, and at a time when it's increasingly important to articulate the difference between social justice and corporate capitalism, but they no longer demarcate ready-made positions or programmes. Newly emerging cultural voices use knowledges in ways that have little respect for the traditional assumptions of the left or the right. Contemporary feminism, for example, is highly critical of the assumption of white cultural supremacy at the heart of seventies left-libertarian feminism, partly because contemporary feminisms cover a wider ethnic and cultural base than left-libertarian feminism. Rather than seeking to identify with a pre-set position on a political spectrum, people want knowledge they can use themselves, just as they increasingly have the power to represent themselves — in part because of the blurring of the line between tabloid and highbrow media that the old cultural establishment tends to deride.

My argument, then, is for reform. A revolution, I think, has already taken place with all the shifts that the cultural establishment has tried so hard to resist and often refused to recognise. Even if these shifts — postwar immigration; the increasing prominence of Aboriginal peoples; the blurring of divisions between highbrow and lowbrow media; the destabilising of top-down, elitist models of culture; the commensurate changes in university arts curricula — are yet to gain lasting and secure institutional recognition and power. Even if the dominating discourses of the public sphere, in the past decade and more, have been supplied to the media almost directly by the think-tanks of the right with a view to eroding whatever institutional power has been gained (I'm thinking of the attacks on affirmative action, political correctness and so on that the New Right has orchestrated via its peddling of 'wedge politics' to both middlebrow commentators and conservative political parties). The New Right might have supplied the sound-bites, the language and dominant journalistic mythologies of the recent past — the soundtrack — but none of these things has curbed the growing propensity of people, especially once 'marginalised' people, to represent themselves. The question remains one of how such voices are accommodated. And it's not simply a matter of incorporating new voices into the existing system. If egalitarianism, fairness and democracy are to be priorities, then not only do the necessary debates need to avoid the rhetorical clichés and habitual tics of the culture wars of the 1980s and 1990s, and the even older truisms of patrician white liberalism, they need to acknowledge that the increasing diversity and heterogeneity of culture means the system itself needs to change.

How might such change take place, given the rules of debate that are in place at the moment? 'Justice', 'public', 'equality', 'nation': all these historically important ideas are presently in the process of being redefined. If this is an increasingly post-Fordist world — an increasingly non-top-down, horizontally stratified world (as opposed to a rigidly hierarchical, vertically stratified world), where people, famously, have choices, and where the old centres have lost some of their moral authority, then what might a post-Fordist democracy look like? How does democracy work once you acknowledge there is a wide array of publics and forms of media? How do ethics work? Given that multiple public spaces exist alongside each other, and that society is increasingly decentred, then how centralised does government need to be, or should it be, and what might a decentralised administration look like?[45] What do the diverse groups that make up postmodern society have in common that can enable them to articulate a shared sense of purpose? At the same time, what forms of hierarchy continue to structure

Damning the torpedoes

and underwrite the freedoms of choice that Western subjects allow themselves? The continuing orientalisation and exploitation of the 'third world'?

It's no coincidence that, as society becomes more and more plural, more radically heterogeneous, globalised, ideologically diverse, and so uncontainable as to stretch conceptual boundaries, the old, seemingly straightforward journalistic umbrella ideas like 'national identity', 'political correctness' and even 'multiculturalism' are being asked to do more and more work. And are looking less and less up to the task. On the other hand, you will find almost no discussion in the press of the patrician white liberalism that continues to structure so much public debate. The question, then, is how to instigate a wide-ranging discussion about identity and the ways an increasingly diverse and diffuse society might be structured so as to be able to articulate common purpose and a shared system of ethics in terms that don't simply resuscitate old white paradigms of 'national identity'.

Obviously these are complex issues, all the more so when the very media forums where they might be widely canvassed seem so inadequate to the task. Yet they are urgent questions. They are just a few of the many questions that might be raised in the context of the social, cultural and economic changes that have recently taken place. In the context of this book, with its focus on youth issues, I would add that it's time, too, to mount a critique of the age delineations that increasingly structure society. The actions of the global economy have afflicted older people almost as much as the young, and both at a vulnerable time in their lives. The current tendency in the media is to play the interests of one group off against the other. The irony is that the increasing delineation of generations is itself a facet of global capitalism. If there's a tendency, for example, to think that young people 'have it all', then this is to focus on the way youthfulness is commodified in the media and marketplace, at the expense of thinking about the

Gangland

actual conditions most young people live under. It might be better for a range of people of all ages to mount a collaborative critique of the way governments increasingly disburse opportunity and rights according to age in an economic and philosophical climate where we are constantly told universal welfare is no longer possible. At the same time, there's an urgent need to critique and destabilise the way cultural identities, party political strategies, the media and global markets interact with each other.

As a possible first step, it needs to be recalled that ordinary people still have power in the face of global markets. We're paying for them. Nor are 'we' without agency. Little that has happened in the development of postwar global capitalism has taken place without widespread consent or at least acquiescence, including withdrawal from formal political processes and collective thinking and action.

I remain interested in the mainstream media, and in the idea that there is such a thing as a media 'mainstream'. Much as I'm impressed by the actuality of alternative public spheres, much as the 'mainstream' and its 'margins' are undoubtedly dissolving into each other, and much as independent media are thriving (and, incidentally, supplying my own media ideal), I'm also yet to see a 'zine, a web-page or a pay-TV channel that reaches 600 000 people per day — the number that listen to Alan Jones's show on 2UE. I don't suspect for a moment that this audience isn't critical. I'm always amused by media 'experts' who seem to assume that they alone are capable of critical readings of the media. Contrary to what such pundits seem to believe about the way people less educated than themselves 'mindlessly consume' the media, I'm yet to be in the company of anyone listening to Jones's show — from taxi drivers to the target audience of conservative over-55ers — who hasn't had some erudite criticism to make. But the insidious power of the media isn't in audience readings. It's in the perceptions politicians have about those audiences.

Damning the torpedoes

There are many public spheres, but the mainstream media increasingly manage to pass themselves off as the sovereign public sphere. It's they who continue to set agendas. Their priorities, then, need be open to critique. There will always be cultural gangs. The question, finally, is one of ethics. What patterns of influence are at work? Who is benefiting whom? What kinds of voices are given prominence? What ideas are being taken for granted so as to facilitate the perpetuation of those voices? What space is being taken up by huffing and puffing, by rants and bigotry, by personal agendas and petty vindictiveness, by pissing in pockets and reputation-mongering, by barely re-digested New Right rhetoric, that might otherwise be used as a space for productive, interesting, ambitious, even optimistic debate?

The above questions won't be addressed by pitting one generation against another. Nor will social renewal be achieved by the longing for the past that afflicts government and the cultural establishment. Nor will problems be solved by lamenting the passing of the old monoculture, or by the way commentators reach for clichés when they should reach for new ideas. Nor will they be solved by nostalgia for old speaking positions and the notional certainties of the old, centralised public sphere.

If many pundits habitually tend to speak in terms of decline rather than renewal, then perhaps it's time to do something other than lament the passing of the old monoculture. What's replacing it — the thing many commentators, the rump of 'usual suspects', don't yet have the language for — is rich, multi-dimensional and heterogeneous. Much more has been gained, I think, than has been lost. It's time, finally, to stop fearing the present.

Notes

Preface to the second edition

1 The critic Peter Craven, for example, complained three times in print that *Gangland* had accused him of 'log-rolling' for David Malouf, when in fact he'd reviewed Malouf's last three books negatively. One of these reviews turned out to be a radio broadcast made five years before this book was conceived. The other two were by no means as negative as Craven made out — they damned the books, but praised the author in such a way as to reinforce his reputation in spite of the book. Craven's recent review of Elizabeth Jolley's *Lovesong* uses the same strategy. See Peter Craven, 'Gang Warfare', *Australian Book Review*, October 1997, p. 8; 'Inspirational Speech puts PM to Shame', *Australian, Higher Education Supplement*, 24 September 1997, p. 44. See also comments made by Craven in Larry Schwartz, 'The Hands That Write the Crits', *Age, Saturday Extra*, 22 August 1998, p. 7. Craven reviewed Malouf's *Remembering Babylon* in Peter Craven, 'Singing in a Strange Land', *Eureka Street*, June–July 1993, p. 44; and *The Conversations at Curlow Creek* in Peter Craven, 'Tall Tales, but True?', *Eureka Street*, October 1996, p. 38. He reviewed Elizabeth Jolley's *Lovesong* in Peter Craven, 'The Plot Thins', *Weekend Australian, Review*, 5–6.7.97.

Introduction

1 Kate Jennings, *Bad Manners*, Minerva, Melbourne, 1993, p. 93.
2 Ibid., p. xi.

Chapter 1

1 Mike Safe and Mark Whittaker, 'The Baby Boomers of 1994', *Australian Magazine*, 26–27.2.94, p. 18.
2 Bill Wyndham, 'Last Blast for a Rebel Without A Pause', *Sunday Age*, 10.4.94.
3 Francis Leach, letter to editor, *Sunday Age*, 17.4.94, p. 16.

Notes

4 Ruth Gamble, letter to editor, *Sunday Age*, 17.4.94, p. 16.
5 David Martin, 'My Turn', *Newsweek*, 1.11.93, US edition.
6 Deirdre Macken, 'The Grunge Plunge', *Good Weekend*, 6.1.96, p. 38.
7 Quoted in Innes Wilcox, 'Student Protesters are Little Brutes, says Vanstone', *Age*, 3.9.96, p. A3.
8 Helen Garner, *The First Stone*, Picador, Sydney, 1995, p. 16.
9 Deborah Hope, *Weekend Australian, Review*, 17–18.2.96, p. 1.
10 Jane Freeman, *Sunday Age, Agenda*, 6.2.94, p. 1.
11 *Age, Saturday Extra*, 16.3.96, p. 1.
12 Andrew Masterton, *Age*, 3.1.96, p. 11.
13 *Australian Magazine*, 2–3.11.96, p. 3.
14 Mark Whittaker, 'Just Don't Call us Ferals', *Australian Magazine*, 17–18.2.1996, p. 45.
15 Suzanne Brown, *Sunday Age*, 12.5.96.
16 Susan Kurosawa, 'What Tribe is Your Teen?', *Australian Magazine*, 2–3.11.96, p. 85.
17 *Sydney Morning Herald* (henceforward *SMH*), 28.1.96.
18 Robert Friedman, 'Editor's Note', 'The Baby Boom Turns 50', *Life*, Summer 1996 Special, p. 6.
19 Quoted in Tracie Winch, 'Fox on a Roll with Martin and Molloy', *Age, Green Guide*, 6.6.96, p. 8.
20 'Youth Radio Stations do Battle for Spot on Dial', *Sunday Age*, 5.5.96.
21 Ibid.
22 'Code for CD Lyrics Agreed', *SMH*, 26.10.96, p. 3.
23 'Anna's Deadly Party', *Daily Telegraph Mirror*, 25.10.95, p. 1.
24 Quoted in Stuart Hitchings, 'Jagged Little Pill', *Juice*, January 1996, p. 52.
25 Anne Crawford, 'The Reluctant Crusaders', *Sunday Age, Agenda*, 13.10.96, p. 3.
26 David Elias, 'The Hand that Wrote the Paper', *Age*, 14.6.97, p. A19.
27 Virginia Trioli, *Generation F: Sex, Power and the Young Feminist*, Minerva, Port Melbourne, 1996, p. 7.
28 'Be Realistic, Minister Advises Job Seekers', *Courier-Mail*, 29.8.96, p. 2.
29 Kate Halfpenny, 'Hair Trigger', *Who Weekly*, 22.4.96, p. 25.
30 ABS figures cited in Mark Longmuir, 'Myth of Youth Wages Clouds Jobless Issue', *Age*, 18.10.95, p. 15.
31 David McKenzie, 'Study Finds Two Million in Poverty', *Age*, 28.9.95, p. 7.
32 Quoted in Murray Waldren, 'Lit Grit Invades Ozlit', *Australian Magazine*, 24–25.6.1995, p. 17.
33 Quoted in Kurt Brereton, 'Design Crimes: From Graffiti to Grunge and Back Again', *Desktop*, July 1995, p. 40.

Chapter 2

1 Barrie Kosky, 'I See What's Wrong: Kosky's View', *Age, Metro Arts*, 11.11.96, p. B7.

Gangland

2 Garner, *The First Stone*, p. 46.
3 Helen Garner, interview in Candida Baker, *Yacker*, Pan Books, Sydney, 1986, p. 149.
4 Don Anderson, 'Teachers, Intellectuals, Politics', *24 Hours*, ABC Radio, May 1995, p. 59.
5 Barry Oakley, 'That's That', *Australian Magazine*, 20–21.4.96, p. 62.
6 Robert Manne, *The Culture of Forgetting*, Text, Melbourne, 1996, p. 173.
7 'Mixed Feelings on the PM's Tactics', *SMH*, 2.11.96, p. 9.
8 Michael Gawenda, 'Shakespeare by Baz is Just as Sweet', *Age*, 13.1.97.
9 *Media Watch*, 29.10.96.
10 'The Best Young Australian Novelists 1997', *SMH, Spectrum*, 11.1.97, pp. 8–9.
11 Paul Kelly, *The End of Certainty: Power, Politics and Business in Australia*, Allen & Unwin, Sydney, 1994, p. x.
12 Personal communication with Meaghan Morris, 21.5.97.
13 Terry Lane, *Hobbyhorses: Views on Contemporary Australian Society*, ABC Books, Sydney, 1990, p. 62.
14 John Laws, 'John Laws' Book of Irreverent Logic', in *A John Laws Limited Edition*, Pan Macmillan, Sydney, 1996, p. 157.
15 Richard Neville, 'The Kill Culture', *Independent Monthly*, April 1993, pp. 25–7.
16 Peter Coleman, *Obscenity, Blasphemy and Sedition: 100 Years of Censorship in Australia*, Angus & Robertson, Sydney, 1974, p. 1.
17 Interview with Mary Delahunty, *Arts Today*, April 1995.
18 Quoted in Nikki Gemmell, 'You've Come a Long Way Mate', *Good Weekend*, 28.8.95, p. 57.
19 Michelle Grattan, 'Hayden Fearful of Agenda Setters', *Age*, 16.2.96, p. A2.
20 Barry Cohen, 'No Place for Victim Culture Down Under', *Australian*, 11.10.95, p. 25.
21 'Feminist Writer Attacks Girlcott', *Age*, 9.8.95, p. 4.
22 Peter Coleman (ed.), *Doubletake: Six Incorrect Essays*, Mandarin, Melbourne, 1996, introduction, p. 6.
23 Barrie Kosky, 'I See What's Wrong: Kosky's View'.
24 'Beware Bullies who Sap the Beauty from Young Writing', *Age*, 14.6.96.
25 Quoted in Linda Jaivin, 'Feral Animals', *Weekend Australian, Review*, 14–15.9.96, p. 8.
26 McKenzie Wark, posting to 'Auslit' mailing list, 22.8.96. Used by permission.
27 Manne, *Culture of Forgetting*, p. 173.
28 Robert Dessaix, 'Some Enchanted Evening', *24 Hours*, ABC Radio, December 1995, p. 55.

Notes

29 This isn't the first time young people have been demonised. For an account of youth-centred moral panics in the 1950s, see Stanley Cohen, *Folk Devils and Moral Panics*, MacGibbon & Kee, London, 1972.
30 Garner, *The First Stone*, p. 222.
31 Beatrice Faust, 'Time You Grew Up Little Sister', *Weekend Australian*, 12–13.10.96, p. 23.
32 Beatrice Faust, 'Daughters in the Dark', *Weekend Australian*, 15–16.3.97, p. 23.
33 Robert Hughes, *Culture of Complaint: The Fraying of America*, Harvill, London, 1993, p. 5.
34 Dessaix, 'Some Enchanted Evening', p. 56.
35 John McLaren, 'Truths in Fiction', *Overland*, no. 141, 1995, p. 30.
36 Peter Craven, 'A Kind of Boswell', *Australian Book Review* (henceforward *ABR*), 178, February–March 1996, p. 16.
37 Susan Mitchell, 'Vicious Writing on the Wall', *Weekend Australian*, 15–16.4.95, p. 15.
38 Ibid., p. 15.
39 Ibid., p. 12.
40 Rosemary Neill, 'Disunited We Stand', *The Australian's Review of Books*, October 1996, p. 24.

Chapter 3

1 Daniella Petkovic, Maria Kokokiris, Monica Kalinowska, *Livin' Large*, Pan Macmillan, Sydney, 1994, p. 10.
2 Douglas Coupland, *Generation X: Tales for an Accelerated Culture*, Abacus, London, 1992, p. 5.
3 Quoted in Duncan Graham, 'Campbell Says He is a Message to Parties', *Age*, 4.3.96, p. A7.
4 Daryl Melham, quoted in Michael Gordon 'The Risk to Reconciliation', *Weekend Australian*, Focus, 20–21.4.1996, p. 19.
5 'Racism: Big Leap in Asian Complaints', *Sunday Age*, 3.11.96, p. 1.
6 Mary Kalantzis interviewed by Charles Wooley, *60 Minutes*, 26.5.96.
7 Henry Reynolds, 'Unrestrained and Dangerous', *Australian*, 25.9.96, p. 13.
8 Quoted in Tim Stevens and Maria Ceresa, 'Fischer Makes Fatherhood a Poll Issue', *Weekend Australian*, 23–24.9.95, p. 3.
9 Michael Barnard, 'Will "Political Correctness" Kill Free Speech Here Too?', *Age*, 18.6.91.
10 Luke Slattery, 'English Under Analysis', *Age*, 13.8.91, p. 11. Peter Ellingsen, 'The Question of Validity', *Age*, 13.8.91, p. 11.
11 Jane Kenrick, 'How the Fags' Demise has Become a Fad', *Melbourne Times*, 24.5.95, p. 7.
12 Fran Cusworth, 'Girls Just Want to Have a Ball', *Age*, 9.10.95, p. 17.

Gangland

13 See Adrian Martin, *Phantasms*, McPhee Gribble, Ringwood, 1994, pp. 139–48.
14 John Hyde, 'Multiculturalism a Good Idea Gone Wrong', *Australian*, 1.9.95.
15 Leonie Kramer, 'Ideologies are Limiting our Language', *SMH*, 9.8.95, p. 7.
16 Barry Cohen, 'No Place for Victim Culture Down Under', *Australian*, 11.10.95, p. 25.
17 Les Carlyon, column, *Age*, 21.3.96, p. A17.
18 P. P. McGuinness, 'PC Movement Suppresses Serious Discussion', *Age*, 13.4.96, p. A27.
19 Adrian Martin, *Phantasms*, pp. 27–8.
20 *Weekend Australian*, 15–16.5.1993, p. 20.
21 Robert Manne, 'On Political Correctness', *Quadrant*, January–February 1993, p. 3.
22 'Race Card Trumps the Gender Card', *Age*, 11.10.95, p. 14.
23 Quoted in David Bennett '"PC" Panic, the Press and the Academy', *Meanjin* 3/1993, Spring, p. 441.
24 Quoted in Tim Stevens and Maria Ceresa, 'Fischer Makes Fatherhood a Poll Issue'.
25 Cited in 'American Whites in Decline', *Weekend Australian*, 17–18.3.96, p. 16.
26 Hanif Kureishi, *The Buddha of Suburbia*, Faber & Faber, London, 1993, p. 141.
27 ABS figures May 1994, *Age*, 11.5.95.
28 Cited in 'The Sum of Us', *Sunday Age*, 15.10.95, p. 23.
29 Christos Tsiolkas, speech at 1995 Melbourne Writers' Festival.
30 Hugh Mackay, 'The Thought Police are the Real Dissenters', *Weekend Australian*, 12–13.8.95, p. 16.
31 Australian Bureau of Statistics, *Australian Social Trends 1994*, p. 10.
32 Quoted in Barry Dickins, 'Playing on the Water', *Age*, Saturday Extra, 13.5.95, p. 5.
33 'Ugly Republicans with Plastic Bags over Their Heads', *Australian*, 3.10.95, p. 13.
34 'Nation Without a Past', *Weekend Australian*, 8–9.7.95, p. 27.
35 See, for example, *ABC News*, 18.11.96.
36 Garner, *The First Stone*, p. 45.
37 Robert Manne, 'On Political Correctness', in David Bennett (ed.), *Cultural Studies: Pluralism and Theory*, Department of English, University of Melbourne, 1993, p. 186.
38 Beatrice Faust, 'Language Barriers', *Weekend Australian*, 30–31.3.96, p. 26.
39 'A Guilt-Edged History', *Sunday Age*, 1.6.97, p. 14.

Notes

40 John K. Wilson, *The Myth of Political Correctness: The Conservative Attack on Higher Education*, Duke University Press, Durham and London, 1995, p. 64.
41 *60 Minutes*, 20.10.96, report by Tracy Curro.
42 On 12.10.96, at Melbourne University.
43 'Activists Ride Again on US Campuses', *Times Higher Education Supplement*, 22.1.93, p. 9.
44 'Stand Up and Be Counted', *Weekend Australian, Review*, 13–14.4.96, p. 2.
45 Interview with Robert Dessaix, *Rethinking Australia: Intellectuals and the Public Culture*, Radio National, 13.4.97.
46 See John Docker, *Australian Cultural Elites. Intellectual Traditions in Sydney and Melbourne*, Angus & Robertson, Sydney, 1974, p. 144–50.
47 Ibid., p. x.
48 Kate Jennings, *Bad Manners*, p. 54.
49 Anne Coombs, *Sex and Anarchy: The Life and Death of the Sydney Push*, Penguin, Ringwood, 1996, p. 57.
50 Quoted in Lisa McLean, 'PM's Words "Prejudiced, Unforgivable"', *Weekend Australian*, 29–30.6.96, p. 7.
51 Michael Duffy, 'Revisions', *Adelaide Review*, 149, 1996, p. 18.
52 Andrew Riemer, 'Incorrect, but True: Challenging the Pieties', *SMH, Spectrum*, 24.2.96, p. 11.
53 Kenneth Minogue, 'Idols with Clay Feet', *Weekend Australian*, 16–17.3.96.
54 Kenneth Minogue, 'Sisters are Ruining it for Themselves', *Australian*, 11.12.95, p. 11.
55 Kenneth Minogue, 'Notes on Australian Intellectual Decadence', *Adelaide Review*, December 1995, p. 22.
56 See Richard Guilliatt, 'The Art of Being PC', *SMH*, 30.9.95, p. 15.
57 Roy Eccleston, 'Careful, Someone Might Hear You', *Australian Magazine*, 29–30.7.1995, pp. 12–19.
58 Ibid., p. 12.
59 Editorial, *Australian*, 29–30.7.1995, p. 18.
60 Coleman, *Doubletake*, p. 4.
61 John Laws, *John Laws' Book of Irreverent Logic*, p. 217.
62 Quoted in Gerard Henderson, 'Intolerance Makes a Comeback', *Age*, 5.3.96, p. A15.
63 Stan Zemanek in panel discussion with Tony Abbott, Mary Kalantzis and Pat O'Shane, *7.30 Report*, 8.4.96.
64 Richard Goldstein, 'The Politics of Political Correctness' quoted in Bennett, '"PC Panic"', p. 435.
65 Phillip Adams, 'A Case of Right and Wrong', *Weekend Australian, Review*, 6–7.4.96, p. 2.
66 'Unlike Hunted Wu, Our "Disbelievers" Have Nothing to Fear', *Age*, 1.8.95, p. 11.

67 Quoted in Theodore Draper, 'A Dragon to Slay', *Australian, Higher Education Supplement* (henceforward *HES*), 17.1.96, p. 24.
68 Michael Pusey on *A Current Affair*, 30.5.96.
69 Bennett, '"PC Panic"', p. 441.
70 Jim Neilson, 'The Great PC Scare: Tyrannies of the Left, Rhetoric of the Right', in Jeffrey Williams (ed.), *PC Wars: Politics and Theory in the Academy*, Routledge, New York and London, 1995, p. 72.
71 Mike Nahan, 'Re-think Tank', *Australian*, 3.5.96, p.13.
72 *Weekend Australian*, 29–30.6.96.
73 Christopher Pearson, 'Stolen Children: Beyond the Outrage', *Australian*, 8.10.96, p. 13.
74 Robert Manne, Editorial, 'Pauline Hanson and the Three Prime Ministers', *Quadrant*, January–February 1997, p. 2.
75 Henry Reynolds, 'Unrestrained and Dangerous', *Australian*, 25.9.96, p. 13.
76 'Howard Steps up Attack on ABC', *Age*, 8.6.96, p. 1.
77 Adams, 'A Case of Right and Wrong'.
78 See Humphrey McQueen, *Suspect History. Manning Clark and the Future of Australia's Past*, Wakefield Press, Adelaide, 1997, p. 199.
79 Cited in Eccleston, p. 19.
80 Robert Manne, 'On Political Correctness', *Quadrant*, January–February 1993, p. 2.
81 'Race Card Trumps the Gender Card', *Age*, 11.10.95, p. 14.
82 Quoted in Gerard Henderson, 'Nats Just Can't Shake Racist Smell', *Age*, 20.2.96, p. A15.
83 Quoted in Dennis Passa, 'Bullet Proof', *Who Weekly*, 10.6.96, p. 26.
84 *7.30 Report*, 8.4.96.
85 Robert Manne, 'Extreme Views the Right Must Reject', *Weekend Australian, Focus*, 26–27.4.97, p. 22.

Chapter 4

1 Toni Morrison, 'Introduction: Friday on the Potomac', in Toni Morrison (ed.), *Race-ing, Justice, En-gendering Power: Essays on Anita Hill, Clarence Thomas, and the Construction of Social Reality*, Chatto & Windus, London, 1993, p. xi.
2 Garner in Candida Baker, *Yacker*, p. 148.
3 Beatrice Faust, *Backlash, Balderdash: Where Feminism is Going Right*, University of New South Wales Press, Sydney, 1994, pp. 7–15.
4 Susan Mitchell, 'Vicious Writing on the Wall', p. 15.
5 Bettina Arndt, 'Bruising Break-ups', *Age*, 14.12.95, p. 11.
6 Helen Garner, 'The Fate of *The First Stone*', *SMH*, 9.8.95, p. 8.
7 Camille Paglia, 'No Law in the Arena', in *Vamps and Tramps*, Viking Books, New York, 1994, p. 64.

Notes

8. Naomi Wolf, *Fire with Fire: The New Female Power and How it Will Change the 21st Century*, Vintage, London, 1994, p. 147.
9. Rene Denfeld, *The New Victorians: A Young Woman's Challenge to the Old Feminist Order*, Allen & Unwin, Sydney, 1995, p. 61.
10. Katie Roiphe, *The Morning After: Sex, Fear and Feminism on Campus*, Little Brown, New York, 1993, p. 93.
11. Robert Hughes, *Culture of Complaint*, p. 12.
12. Jenna Mead, 'Sexual Harassment and Feminism: Jenna Mead talks to Amanda Lohrey', *RePublica*, no. 2, 'The New Land Lies Before Us', p. 166.
13. See Kerryn Goldsworthy, *Helen Garner*, Oxford University Press, Melbourne, 1996, and Morag Fraser, 'Garner's Stories in Search of Truth', *ABR*, April 1996, p. 5.
14. Garner, *The First Stone*, p. 71.
15. bell hooks, 'Katie Roiphe: A Little Feminist Excess Goes a Long Way', in *Outlaw Culture: Resisting Representations*, Routledge, New York and London, 1994, p. 103.
16. 'Garner Denounces Academic's Attack as a Disgraceful Slur', *Weekend Australian*, 23–24.9.95.
17. Garner, *The First Stone*, pp. 222, 38, 39, 42, 43, 89, 100, 122, 177, 178 respectively.
18. Ibid., p. 218.
19. Ibid., p. 71.
20. Ibid., p. 77.
21. Ibid., p. 54.
22. Ibid., p. 79.
23. Ibid., p. 48.
24. Ibid., p. 48.
25. P. P. McGuinness, 'Feminism Debate Has to Go Far Beyond the Dogmatism of the Wimminists', *Age*, 10.8.95, p. 12.
26. Morag Fraser, 'It's Time for Feminism's Egos to Call a Truce', *SMH*, 10.8.95, p. 13.
27. Terry Lane, 'Burnt at the Ideological Stake', *Sunday Age*, 27.9.95, p. 19.
28. Editorial, *SMH*, 10.8.95, p. 12.
29. Denfeld, *The New Victorians*, p. 86.
30. See, for example, Bettina Arndt, 'Beyond Glass Ceilings', *Age*, 9.4.96, p. A11.
31. John O'Neill, 'After *The First Stone*', *Independent Monthly*, October 1995, p. 51.
32. Anne Summers, 'Shockwaves at the Revolution', *Good Weekend*, 18.3.95, p. 29.
33. Faust, *Backlash, Balderdash*, p. 15.
34. Mitchell, 'Vicious Writing on the Wall', p. 15.
35. Garner, *The First Stone*, p. 88.

36 Ibid., p. 97.
37 Ibid., p. 202.
38 Wolf, *Fire with Fire*, p. 110.
39 bell hooks, 'Camille Paglia: "Black" Pagan or White Colonizer?', in *Outlaw Culture*, p. 86.
40 Paglia, 'No Law in the Arena', pp. 31–2.
41 Ibid., p. 32.
42 Garner, *The First Stone*, p. 89.
43 Paglia, 'No Law in the Arena', pp. 36–7.
44 Camille Paglia, 'The Rape Debate, Continued', in *Sex, Art and American Culture*, Viking Books, Harmondsworth, 1992, p. 57.
45 Garner, 'The Fate of *The First Stone*', p. 8.
46 Garner, *The First Stone*, p. 38.
47 Camille Paglia, 'Rape and Modern Sex War', in *Sex, Art and American Culture*, p. 53.
48 Ibid., p. 53.
49 Camille Paglia, 'The M.I.T. Lecture: Crisis in the American Universities', in *Sex, Art and American Culture*, p. 268.
50 Garner, *The First Stone*, p. 202.
51 Paglia 'No Law in the Arena', pp. 43–6.
52 Garner, *The First Stone*, p. 150.
53 Ibid., p. 99.
54 Drusilla Modjeska, *The Orchard*, Picador, Sydney, 1994, p. 67.
55 Wolf, *Fire with Fire*, p. 132.
56 Camille Paglia 'The Return of Carry Nation: Catharine MacKinnon and Andrea Dworkin', in *Vamps and Tramps*, p. 112.
57 Garner, *The First Stone*, p. 222.
58 Summers, 'Shockwaves at the Revolution', p. 29.
59 David Williamson, *Brilliant Lies*, Currency Press, Sydney, 1993, p. 28.
60 Garner, *The First Stone*, p. 112.
61 Ibid., p. 99.
62 Arndt, 'Bruising Break-ups', p. 11.
63 Garner, *The First Stone*, pp. 91, 108, 153, 184, 187, 196 respectively.
64 Ibid., p. 50.
65 Ibid., p. 39.
66 Ibid., p. 146.
67 Ibid., pp. 5, 4, 133, 18 respectively.
68 Ibid., pp. 59, 134.
69 Ibid., pp. 93, 45, 134, 39, 40, 151, 193 respectively.
70 Roiphe, pp. 108–9.
71 Helen Garner, Interview, *Farrago*, vol. 74, ed. 3, p. 7.
72 Morrison, 'Introduction: Friday on the Potomac', p. xviii.
73 Garner, *The First Stone*, p. 93.
74 Editorial, 'Sex Law is Way Out' *Age*, 22.1.96.
75 Michael Pusey, 'Reclaiming the Middle Ground . . . From New Right "Economic Rationalism"', in Stephen King and Peter Lloyd (eds),

Economic Rationalism: Dead End or Way Forward, Allen & Unwin, Sydney, 1993, p. 23.
76 Summers, 'Shockwaves at the Revolution', p. 29.

Chapter 5

1. Michael Gawenda, *Age*, 7.10.96, p. A11.
2. P. P. McGuinness, 'Constituting the Will of Ordinary People', *Age*, 30.11.96, p. A29.
3. *Publishers Weekly*, 5.6.95, p. 19.
4. Robert James Waller, *The Bridges of Madison County*, Mandarin, London, 1993, p. 107.
5. Coupland, *Generation X*, p. 41.
6. '30 Years Since Yesterday', *Age*, 29.8.96, p. C16.
7. 'Les Back from the Dead, Lighter in Body and Soul', *Weekend Australian*, 21–22.9.96, p. 3.
8. Paul Fussell, 'Thank God for the Atom Bomb', *Independent*, July 1995, pp. 35–9.
9. Greg Sheridan, *Australian*, 19.4.95, p. 11.
10. McGuinness, 'Feminism Debate Has to Go Far Beyond the Dogmatism of the Wimminists'.
11. Terry Lane, 'On Multiculturalism', in *Hobbyhorses*, pp. 87–9.
12. Ibid., p. 89.
13. David Williamson, *Brilliant Lies*, pp. 18–19.
14. John Laws, *John Laws' Book of Uncommon Sense*, p. 287.
15. Steve Price (3AW) quoted in Kate Nancarrow, 'Ernie Makes Unlikely Ruler of the Waves', *Sunday Age*, 3.11.96, p. 4.
16. Kathy Laster and Kirsten Deane, 'Why Gump Sums Up US Self-image', *Australian*, 30.3.95, p. 11.
17. Henry Reynolds, 'Lost in Australia's Great Divide', *Age*, 16.5.97, p. A13.
18. *Forrest Gump*, Paramount Pictures, 1994. Dir. Robert Zemeckis. Story by Winston Groom.
19. Tony Squires, '"Nitwit" the Taunt as Egos Set the Airwaves Hissing Over Hanson', *SMH*, 9.11.96, p. 13.
20. Shaun Carney, 'More Comfort and Relaxation', *Age*, 17.1.97, p. A13.
21. 'Martin/Molloy', Fox FM, 19.11.96.
22. *ABC TV News*, 19.4.97.
23. Hughes, *Culture of Complaint*, p. 39.
24. John Laws, *John Laws' Book of Uncommon Sense*, p. 379.

Chapter 6

1. Helen Garner in Candida Baker, *Yacker*, p. 141.
2. Kate Jennings, *Bad Manners*, p. 92.

3 Joan Didion, 'Preface', in *Slouching Towards Bethlehem*, Flamingo, London, 1993, p. xiv.
4 Gerard Henderson, 'Literary Elite Ripe for Inquiry by Trade Practices Watchdog', *Age*, 18.7.95, p. 13.
5 Hilary McPhee, 'The "Two-horse Town" of Australia's Arts World', *Age*, 31.8.95, p. 16.
6 Docker, *Australian Cultural Elites*, pp. ix–x.
7 Luke Slattery, 'Defying Gravity', *Australian Magazine*, 8–9.2.97, p. 14.
8 Peter Craven, 'Clive's Postcard from the Festival', *Australian*, HES, 16.10.96, p. 45.
9 Peter Craven, 'The Last and Best Word', *Weekend Australian*, Review, 25–26.5.96, p. 8.
10 Andrew Rutherford, 'History in the Faking: the Demidenko Affair Unravelled', *Sunday Age*, Agenda, 2.6.96, p. 6.
11 Quoted in Peter Craven, 'Leopard's Imprint on Quality', *Australian*, HES, 13.11.96, p. 52.
12 Ibid.
13 Luke Slattery, 'Romancing the Poet', *Australian Magazine*, 24–25.8.96, pp. 27–32.
14 Luke Slattery, 'High and Mighty', *Weekend Australian*, Review, 7–8.9.96.
15 Owen Richardson, 'Curtain Up on the Adventures of Young Brennan', *Sunday Age*, Agenda, 8.9.96, p. 7.
16 Peter Craven, reply to letter to editor, *ABR*, May 1996, p. 4.
17 Peter Craven, 'Of War and Needlework: The Fiction of Helen Garner', *Meanjin*, 2/1985, pp. 210–3.
18 Peter Craven, 'Garner has an Encounter with Religion', *Weekend Australian*, Review, 7–8.3.92, p. 7; 'Fighting the Furies', *Weekend Australian*, Review, 25–26.3.95, p. 7; 'This Helen's for Real', *Weekend Australian*, Review, 6–7.4.96, p. 9.
19 Peter Craven, 'The Successful Transition of Helen Garner', *Age*, Tempo, 14.10.92, p. 4.
20 Peter Craven, 'Garner's Controversial Fame', *ABR*, December 1996–January 1997, p. 8.
21 Craven, 'Garner has an Encounter with Religion'.
22 Craven, 'Fighting the Furies'.
23 Craven, 'This Helen's for Real'.
24 Craven, 'The Successful Transition of Helen Garner'.
25 Craven, 'Garner Has an Encounter with Religion'.
26 Quoted in Craven, 'Garner's Controversial Fame'.
27 Peter Craven, *Australian* HES, 10.12.93, p. 17.
28 Peter Craven, 'Crooked Versions of Art: The Novels of David Malouf', *Scripsi*, vol. 3, no. 1, p. 99.
29 Peter Craven, 'Shaped and Transfigured in the Telling', *Weekend Australian*, 2–3.10.93, p. 6.

Notes

30 Peter Craven, 'A Conjuror of Luminous Memories', *Age*, *Saturday Extra*, 8.9.90, p. 8.
31 Morag Fraser, 'Quiet Horrors Among the Polished Spoons', *SMH*, *Spectrum*, 30.9.95, p. 12A.
32 Elizabeth Jolley, 'Helen Garner, Rescuing Fragments', *Scripsi*, vol. 3, no. 2/3.
33 Helen Garner, 'Elizabeth Jolley: The Love of Nurses', *Scripsi*, vol. 6, no. 1, pp. 81–6.
34 'Booked for Christmas', *Weekend Australian, Review*, 16–17.12.95, p. 1.
35 'The Year in Books: Nothing But the Best', *Age*, *Saturday Extra*, 16.12.95, pp. 8–9.
36 Peter Craven, 'A Woman of Theatre', *ABR*, April 1995, p. 14.
37 Drusilla Modjeska, 'Extra to Real Life', *ABR*, April 1995, p. 15. (My brackets.)
38 Elizabeth Jolley, *Mr Scobie's Riddle*, Penguin, Ringwood, 1983; Helen Daniel, 'Riddles of Mortality', *Age*; 5.2.83, p. 10; Jolley, *Foxybaby*, University of Queensland Press, St Lucia, 1985; Helen Daniel, 'A Jolley Comic Horror', *Age*, *Saturday Extra*, 7.10.85, p. 10; Jolley, *The Well*, Viking, Ringwood, 1986; Drusilla Modjeska, 'Many Levels in the Fantasy World of Hester Harper', *SMH*, 13.10.86, p. 44; Helen Daniel, 'Trafficking Between Fantasy and Horror', *Age*, *Saturday Extra*, 27.10.86, p. 12; Jolley, *The Sugar Mother*, Fremantle Arts Centre Press, Fremantle, 1988; Peter Craven, 'Dark Shadows in a Teacup', *Age*, *Saturday Extra*, 23.4.88, p. 11; Jolley, *My Father's Moon*, Penguin, Ringwood, 1989; Peter Craven, 'Life's Grim Heart Transcended', *Weekend Australian*, 22–23.4.89, p. 10; Helen Daniel, 'Painful Passage Into Memory', *Age*; 15.4.89, p. 11; Jolley, *Cabin Fever*, Viking, Ringwood, 1990; Peter Craven, 'A Conjuror of Luminous Memories'; Drusilla Modjeska, 'A Drawn Pause Out of Intention', *Scripsi*, vol. 6, no. 3, 1990, pp. 129–34; Helen Daniel, 'Challenging Echoes in a Continuum of Excellence', *Weekend Australian, Review*, 8–9.10.90, p. 5; Jolley, *The Georges' Wife*, Penguin, Ringwood, 1993; Peter Craven, 'Shaped and Transfigured in the Telling'; Helen Daniel, 'The Self in Three Movements', *ABR*, 155, October 1993, pp. 8–9; Jolley, *Off the Air: Nine Plays for Radio*, Penguin, Ringwood, 1995; Peter Craven, 'A Woman of Theatre', *ABR*, 169, April 1995, pp. 14–15; Jolley, *The Orchard Thieves*, Viking, Ringwood, 1995; Morag Fraser, 'Quiet Horrors Among the Polished Spoons'; Peter Craven, 'Season Adjustments', *Age*, *Saturday Extra*, 7.10.95, p. 9; Helen Daniel, 'Family Fables', *Courier-Mail*, *Weekend*, 7.10.95, p. 6; Peter Craven, 'The Year of Publishing Dangerously', *Independent Monthly*, vol. 7, no. 6, December 1995–January 1996, pp. 87–90. General essays on Jolley include Helen Daniel, 'Elizabeth Jolley: Variations on a Theme', *Westerly*, vol. 31, no. 2, June 1986, pp. 50–63; Helen Daniel, 'Who Killed Madge?', *Age*, *Saturday Extra*, 10.4.93, p. 8; Peter Craven, 'Writing with Gentle Dignity', *Age*, *Saturday Extra*, 2.10.93, p. 7; Morag

Fraser, 'Infinite Variety', *Voices*, vol. 4, no. 4, Summer 1994–95, pp. 91–8; Drusilla Modjeska, 'Extra to Real Life'. Anthologies including Jolley: Elizabeth Jolley, 'A Sort of Gift: Images of Perth' in Drusilla Modjeska (ed.), *Inner Cities: Australian Women's Memory of Place*, Penguin, Ringwood, 1989, pp. 201–7; Elizabeth Jolley, 'The Widow's House', in Helen Daniel (ed.), *Expressway*, Penguin, Ringwood, 1989, p. 6–14; Helen Daniel (ed.), *The Good Reading Guide*, Angus & Robertson, Sydney, 1989.

39 Helen Garner, 'Christina Stead's Magical Stories', *Scripsi*, vol. 4, no. 1, 1986, p. 191.

40 Peter Craven, 'Lighting Up her Landscape', *Age, Saturday Extra*, 29.5.93, p. 7; Drusilla Modjeska: 'Genius Overlooked', *SMH*, 5.6.93, p. 45; Helen Garner, 'The Real Christina Stead', *Sunday Age*, 20.6.93, p. 9.

41 Peter Craven, 'Masterpiece Does Justice to a Master', *Age, Saturday Extra*, 13.7.91, p. 7; David Malouf, 'Something of a Miracle', *ABR*, 133, August 1991, pp. 4–6; Elizabeth Jolley, 'Marr's Patrick White: Some Impressions', *Scripsi*, vol. 7 no. 3, 1992, pp. 27–31; Drusilla Modjeska, 'A Life Apart from Patrick White', *Australian Society*, vol. 10, no. 8, August 1991, pp. 34–5.

42 Peter Craven, 'Whitewash and Cultural Cringe Return', *Australian, HES*, 6.3.96, p. 27.

43 Peter Craven, 'The Kingdom of Correct Usage is Elsewhere', *ABR*, 179, April 1996, pp. 36–41.

44 Ibid., p. 41.

45 Geoffrey Dutton, letter to editor, *ABR*, May 1996, p. 3.

46 'Garner's Stories in Search of Truth', p. 6.

47 ABC FM, 28.8.95.

48 Kristen Williamson, 'My Favorite Book', *Sunday Age, Agenda*, 9.7.95, p. 9.

49 *Age, Saturday Extra*, 19.8.95, pp. 7–9.

50 *Weekend Australian*, 21–22.10.95, 28–29.10.95, 4–5.11.95, 11–12.11.95.

51 'Best Books of '96', *SMH, Spectrum*, 30.11.96, p. 11s, 7.12.96, p. 13s.

52 'Books with Bite', *Sunday Age, Agenda*, 15.12.96, pp. 6–7.

53 Sian Powell and Belinda Hickman, '*Review of Books* reaches for Literary Stars', *Australian*, 11.9.97, p. 3.

54 Shelley Gare, 'From the Editor', *The Australian's Review of Books*, March 1997, vol. 2, issue 2, p. 2.

55 *Sunday Age, Agenda*, 22.10.95, p. 8.

56 *Who Weekly*, 21.8.95, p. 87.

57 *SMH, Spectrum*, 7.10.95.

58 Mandy Sayer, 'A Blistering Ride Underground', *Weekend Australian, Review*, 15–16.6.96, p. 9.

59 *Sunday Age, Agenda*, 23.7.95, p. 9.

60 Owen Richardson, 'When the Pitch is Just Perfect', *Sunday Age*, 17.3.96, p. 9.

Notes

61 Peter Craven, 'Debut of a Born Writer', *Age, Saturday Extra*, 23.3.96, p. 9.
62 Peter Pierce, 'Conventions of Presence', *Meanjin*, 1/1981, p. 113.
63 Peter Craven, 'Sad Vogel Imbroglio', *Australian, HES*, 20.3.96, p. 21.
64 'Fund Our Young Artists: McPhee', *Australian*, 28.9.96, p. 5.
65 McPhee, 'The "Two-horse Town"'.
66 'Is She Right or is She Wrong?', *Australian*, 1.9.95, pp. 10–11.
67 McPhee, 'The "Two-horse Town"'.
68 Garner, *The First Stone*, p. 20.
69 Kate Jennings, 'Love for Lost Souls', *SMH*, 29.2.92, p. 49.
70 Leo Schofield, 'Travels with My Festival', *Sunday Age, Agenda*, 15.10.95, p. 6.
71 Fiona Capp, 'Borderlines: The Responsibilities of Journalism', *ABR*, December 1995–January 1996, pp. 30–1.
72 Morag Fraser, 'Garner's Stories in Search of Truth', p. 5.
73 Club One Membership leaflet, Melbourne Writers' Festival.

Chapter 7

1 Brian Castro, 'Writing Asia', in *Writing Asia and Auto/biography: Two Lectures*, Australian Defence Force Academy, Canberra, 1995, p. 5.
2 *Weekly Book Newsletter*, 14 May 1997.
3 Susan Chenery, *SMH, Spectrum*, 8.4.85, p. 10.
4 Quoted in Diana Giese, 'The Real Work', *Voices*, vol. 4, no. 1, 1994, p. 90.
5 Virginia Trioli, *Generation F*, pp. 137–52.

Chapter 8

1 McKenzie Wark, 'Artists Join Fashionable Culture of Complaint', *Australian*, 17.7.96, p. 40.
2 Keith Windschuttle, *The Killing of History: How a Discipline is Being Murdered by Literary Critics and Social Theorists*, Macleay Press, Sydney, 1994, p. 2.
3 Mark Allinson, 'Towards a Psychology of Resentment in the Modern Academy', *Quadrant*, May 1996, p. 15.
4 Luke Slattery, 'English Under Analysis', *Age*, 13.8.91, p. 11.
5 David Williamson, 'Men, Women and Human Nature', in Coleman (ed.), *Doubletake*, pp. 10, 12.
6 Barry Oakley, 'In the First Place', *Australian Magazine*, 31.10–1.11.92, p. 6.
7 Don Anderson, 'Behind the Lines', *SMH, Spectrum*, 18.6.94, p. 10A.
8 Garner, *The First Stone*, p. 106 [her italics].
9 Manne, *The Culture of Forgetting*, p. 17.
10 Ibid., pp. 15–17.
11 Ibid., p. 78.

12 Ibid., pp. 143–4.
13 Ibid., p. 118.
14 Judith Butler, 'Contingent Foundations: Feminism and the Question of Postmodernism', in Judith Butler and Joan W. Scott (eds), *Feminists Theorize the Political*, Routledge, New York and London, 1992, p. 3.
15 'Beware Bullies who Sap the Beauty from Young Writing'.
16 McKenzie Wark, 'The Courses of True Fiction', *Australian*, HES, 5.10.94, p 34.
17 Windschuttle, *Killing of History*, p. 12.
18 Slattery, 'English Under Analysis'.
19 Slattery, 'I Think Therefore I Think', p. 20.
20 Jacques Derrida, *Limited Inc*, ed. Gerald Graff, Northwestern University Press, Evanston, 1988, p. 146.
21 Peter Craven 'Stuck in the Middle with Hughes', *Age*, Saturday Extra, 8.5.93, p. 7.
22 Humphrey McQueen, *24 Hours*, ABC Radio, June 1996, p. 59.
23 Barry Oakley, 'In the First Place', *Australian Magazine*, 31.10–1.11.92, p. 6.
24 David Williamson, *Dead White Males*, Currency, Sydney, 1995, p. 98.
25 Williamson, 'Men, Women and Human Nature', p. 12.
26 Ibid., p. 13.
27 Ibid., p. 27.
28 *Australian*, HES, 5.6.96, p. 28.
29 John Carroll, 'Mocking the Classics', *Age*, 22.3.96, p. A13.
30 Craven, 'The Kingdom of Correct Usage is Elsewhere'.
31 Meaghan Morris, 'The Truth is Out There . . .', *ABR*, June 1996, pp. 17–20.
32 Garner, *The First Stone*, pp. 18, 146, 100, 58 and 96 respectively.
33 Kate Jennings, *Bad Manners*, pp. 43–5.
34 Windschuttle, *Killing of History*, p. 119.
35 Anderson, 'Behind the Lines'.
36 Anderson, 'Teachers, Intellectuals, Politics', pp. 56–9.
37 Barry Oakley, 'That's That', *Australian Magazine*, 20–21.4.96, p. 62.
38 Allinson, 'Towards a Psychology of Resentment', p. 15.
39 Garner, *The First Stone*, p. 102.
40 Quoted in Tony Stephens, 'Winds of Change Cause a Literary Kerfuffle at Uni', *SMH*, 17.5.93, p. 3.
41 Phillip Adams, 'Dumbo Theory of Deconstruction', *Australian*, Review, 19–20.11.94, p. 2.
42 Quoted in Peter Ellingsen, 'The Question of Validity'.
43 Anderson, 'Teachers, Intellectuals, Politics', pp. 56–9.
44 Meaghan Morris, 'A Question of Cultural Studies', in Deryck M. Schreuder (ed.), *The Humanities and a Creative Nation: Jubilee Essays*, Australian Academy of the Humanities, Canberra, 1995, pp. 137–59.
45 'Artists Join Fashionable Culture of Complaint'.

Notes

46 Luke Slattery, 'Our Man on China', *Weekend Australian, Focus*, 9–10.11.96, p. 23.
47 Simon During, 'Why Academics Cannot Bridge the Gap to Public Culture' *Australian*, 26.5.93, p. 17.
48 Robert Dessaix, 'Dead and Stuffed Poets', *ABR*, July 1996, p. 19.
49 Meaghan Morris, 'Publish or be Damned', *Postgraduate Review*, University of Melbourne, vol. 2, no. 1, Summer 1996, p. 23.
50 Luke Slattery, 'The Books that Made Us',*Weekend Australian* 19–20.8.95.
51 Luke Slattery, 'Canon Fodder', *Australian*, 21.8.95.
52 Bean's history, for example, was a deliberate propaganda exercise; the impressions of the Gallipoli campaign he confided to his private diary bore little relationship to the hero-story that cemented the Anzac legend.
53 Brian Castro, 'Writing Asia', pp. 3–4.
54 Stuart Macintyre, *Australian*, 23.8.95.
55 Barry Oakley, 'Aussie Kids Grab Back Your Roots', *Australian*, 24.8.95.
56 Austin Gough, 'Canon Study Needs its Space', *Australian*, 30.8.95.
57 Austin Gough, 'Black Activists Fight Science: Academic', *Weekend Australian*, 18–19.11.95, p. 3.
58 Robert Manne interviewed by Caroline Baum, *Between the Lines*, ABC Television, 26.6.96.
59 Bennett, '"PC Panic"', p. 436.
60 See *Frontline*, Series 2, Episode 6, in *Frontline: The Story behind the Story . . . Behind the Stories*, Viking, Ringwood, 1995, pp. 217–28.
61 Delia Falconer, 'Dancing out of History', *Age, Saturday Extra*, 13.7.96, p. 9.
62 Beatrice Faust, 'Reflections of a Sceptical Feminist', in Coleman (ed.), *Doubletake*, p. 126.
63 Meaghan Morris, 'Publish or be Damned', p. 23.
64 Windschuttle, *Killing of History*, pp. 20–1, 28.

Chapter 9

1 *Between the Lines*, 26.6.96.
2 Simon Hughes, 'Unabashed Elitist is "a Saint"', *Age*, 3.11.95, p. 17.
3 Luke Slattery, 'Expatriates on a Pedestal', *Weekend Australian, Focus*, 30.11–1.12.96, p. 24.
4 Peter Craven, 'Hughes Jumps the Net of Cultural Politics', *Weekend Australian*, 29–30.5.93, p. 5.
5 Sylvia Lawson, *The Archibald Paradox: A Strange Case of Authorship*, Penguin, Ringwood, 1987, p. ix.
6 Caroline Baum, 'Is Passage to India Necessary?', *Age, Metro*, 9.10.96, p. 5.
7 Leigh Dale, 'The Importance of Being English', *Australian, HES*, 11.6.97, p. 37.
8 Windschuttle, *Killing of History*, p. 7.

9 Ibid., p. 222.
10 Ibid., pp. 248–9.
11 John Searle quoted in Michael Berube, 'Public Image Limited: Political Correctness and the Media's Big Lie', *Village Voice*, 18.6.1992, p. 32.
12 Lewis Lapham, 'Reactionary Chic', in *Hotel America: Scenes in the Lobby of the Fin-de-Siècle*, Verso, London and New York, 1996, p. 355.
13 Ibid., p. 355.
14 Ibid., p. 357.
15 Roger Kimball, *Tenured Radicals: How Politics has Corrupted our Higher Education*, Harper & Row, New York, 1990, p. xvi.
16 Windschuttle, *Killing of History*, p. 5.
17 Allan Bloom, *The Closing of the American Mind: How Higher Education has Failed Democracy and Impoverished the Souls of Today's Youth*, Simon & Schuster, New York, 1987, p. 367.
18 Don Anderson, 'Teachers, Intellectuals, Politics', p. 59; Windschuttle, *Killing of History*, p. 119.
19 Barry Oakley, 'In the First Place', *Australian Magazine*, 31.10–1.11.92, p. 6.
20 Windschuttle, *Killing of History*, pp. 20–1, 28.
21 Keith Windschuttle, *Unemployment: A Social and Political Analysis of the Economic Crisis in Australia*, Pelican, Ringwood, 1979, pp. 60–3.
22 Lapham, 'Reactionary Chic', p. 346.
23 *Insight*, SBS, 24.4.97.
24 Francis Fukuyama, 'The End of History', *Quadrant*, August 1989, pp. 15–25. First published in *The National Interest*, no. 16, Summer 1989, pp. 3–18. Discussed in James Walter, *Tunnel Vision*, Allen & Unwin, Sydney, 1996, pp. 27–52.
25 Lapham, 'Reactionary Chic', p. 347.
26 Bloom, *Closing of the American Mind*, p. 320.
27 Wilson, *The Myth of Political Correctness*, p. 15.
28 Manne, *Culture of Forgetting*, p. 143.
29 Bloom, *Closing of the American Mind*, p. 65.
30 Ibid., p. 96.
31 Lapham, 'Reactionary Chic', pp. 358–9.
32 See Hughes, *Culture of Complaint*, p. 142.
33 Bloom, *Closing of the American Mind*, p. 81.
34 Ibid., p. 69.
35 Ibid., p. 122.
36 Manne, *Culture of Forgetting*, p. 147.
37 Bloom, *Closing of the American Mind*, p. 86.
38 Ibid., p. 136.
39 Hughes, *Culture of Complaint*, p. 64, quoted in Luke Slattery, 'I Think, Therefore I Think', p. 20.
40 Hughes, ibid., p. 70.
41 Ibid., p. 23.

Notes

42 Ibid., p. 30.
43 Ibid., p. 70.
44 Ibid., p. 89.
45 Ibid., p. 63.
46 See, for example, the work of members of the Subaltern Studies Group such as Gayatri Chakravorty Spivak, *In Other Worlds: Essays in Cultural Politics*, Routledge, London, 1987; see also the journal *Subaltern Studies*, edited by Ranajit Guha.
47 Hughes, *Culture of Complaint*, pp. 82–3.
48 Ibid., p. 160.
49 Ibid., p. 98.
50 Ibid., p. 83.
51 Ibid., p. 26.
52 Ibid., p. 53.
53 Ibid., p. 54.
54 Ibid., pp. 53–4.
55 Pat Buchanan and Joseph McCarthy cited in ibid., p. 42.
56 Tom Wicker, 'The Democrats as Devil's Disciples', *New York Times*, 30.8.92, cited in ibid., p. 30.
57 Hughes, ibid., p. 144.
58 See Craven, 'Stuck in the Middle with Hughes'; Slattery, 'I Think, Therefore I Think'; Craven, 'Hughes Jumps the Net of Cultural Politics'; Slattery, 'Expatriates on a Pedestal'; Luke Slattery, 'The Art of Being Robert Hughes', *Australian Magazine*, 12–13.8.95, pp. 16–23; Peter Craven, 'American Stars and Bars', *Age*, 14.6.97, p. 10.

Chapter 10

1 Michael Heyward, speech at Melbourne Writers' Week, 23.10.95.
2 Luke Slattery, 'Cheap Shots in Feminist Fight', *Australian*, 25.9.95, p.11.
3 Garner, 'The Fate of *The First Stone*'.
4 *SMH*, 9.8.95
5 'A Story that Needed to be Told', *Australian*, 9.8.95, p. 11.
6 'Feminists, Public Figures Back Garner Book Defence', *SMH*, 10.8.95, p. 3.
7 'Helen Garner's Telling Truths', *Weekend Australian, Focus*, 12–13.8.95, p. 23.
8 Rosemary Neill, 'Disunited We Stand', *The Australian's Review of Books*, October 1996, p. 24.
9 Fraser, 'It's Time for Feminism's Egos to Call a Truce'.
10 Morag Fraser, 'Turning Over the First Stone', *Age, Saturday Extra*, 7.9.96, p. 9.
11 Helen Garner, 'A World Apart', *Eureka Street*, vol. 5, no. 10, December 1995, pp. 29–30.

12 Peter Craven, 'One Man's Vision of a World at War', *Australian*, HES, 10.5.95.
13 Goldsworthy, *Helen Garner*, p. 39.
14 'My Ukrainian Christmas', *Independent*, December 1995–January 1996.
15 Name withheld. Details in my possession.
16 Richard Guilliatt, 'The Art of Being PC'.
17 Barry Cohen, 'A Lousy Work by any Name', *Australian*, 30.8.95.
18 Rosemary Neill, 'Demidenko Life Fiction Goes too Far', *Australian*, 24.8.95, p. 13.
19 Terry Lane, 'And the Winner is . . . Dull and Boring', *Sunday Age*, 3.9.95.
20 Frank Devine, *Australian*, 24.7.95.
21 Riemer, *The Demidenko Debate*, Allen & Unwin, Sydney, 1995, pp. 196, 248.
22 Manne, *Culture of Forgetting*, p. 167.
23 'Forum on the Demidenko Controversy', *ABR*, August 1995, pp. 14–19.
24 Ivor Indyk and Barry Oakley, 'Literature, Lies and History', *Weekend Australian*, 26–27.8.95, p. 21.
25 Ian Syson, 'Judging the Judges', *Age*, 26.8.95, p. 20.
26 Peter Christoff in 'Forum on the Demidenko Controversy', pp. 15–16; 'Assassins of Memory', *Arena Magazine*, no. 18, August–September 1995, pp. 44–8; 'Same Difference', *Arena Magazine*, no. 19, October–November 1995, pp. 14–15; 'Demidenko's Success Reflects Panel's Naivete and Ignorance', *Australian*, 14.7.95, p. 19.
27 Guy Rundle, '"Tactical Error" a Vile Tragedy', *Age*, 23.8.95, p. 17. Editorial, 'An Imaginary Life', *Age*, 23.8.95, p. 15.
28 Louise Adler in interview with Caroline Baum and Robert Sessions, *Bookchat*, ABC Television, 27.8.95.
29 Peter Craven, 'Innocent Reaction to the Brutal Facts', *Sunday Age*, 9.7.95, p. 10.
30 Peter Craven, *Australian*, HES, 12.7.95, p. 30.
31 Peter Craven, 'Great Prizes Follow Great Themes', *Australian*, HES, 29.5.96, p. 37.
32 Peter Craven, 'Poets Excelled as Literary Editors', *Australian*, HES, 9.8.95, p. 29.
33 Neill, 'Demidenko Life Fiction Goes too Far'.
34 Peter Craven, *Australian*, HES, 1.12.95, p. 35.
35 Helen Daniel, 'Double Cover', 'The Damage done by the Double D', *Age*, 2.9.95, Extra, p. 7.
36 Gideon Haigh, 'Brought to Book: Chapter and Verse on the Literary Prizes', *Australian*, 28.8.95, p. 10.
37 Ian Syson, 'Judging the Judges', *Age*, 26.8.95, p. 20.
38 Guy Rundle, '"Tactical Error" a Vile Tragedy'.
39 Gerard Henderson, 'The Deconstruction of Demidenko', *Age*, 22.8.95, p. 13.

Notes

40 'A Lousy Work by any Name'.
41 Peter Craven, 'All Alone in No-Man's-Land', *Weekend Australian, Review*, 10–11.2.96, p. 9; and 'Mise en Scene of a Literary Crime', *Australian*, 20.2.96, p. 19.
42 Peter Craven, 'The Last and Best Word', p. 8. See also Manne, *The Culture of Forgetting*, pp. 134, 162.
43 Quoted in Manne, ibid., p. 167.
44 Peter Christoff, 'Against Subtle Assassins of Memory', *Age, Saturday Extra*, 8.6.96, p. 8.
45 Andrew Rutherford, 'History in the Faking: the Demidenko Affair Unravelled', *Sunday Age, Agenda*, 2.6.96, p. 6.
46 Andrew Rutherford, 'The Hand that Stirred Up the Controversy', *Sunday Age, Agenda*, 11.2.96, p. 9.
47 Michael Gawenda, 'Awakening for the Culture of Ignorance', *Age*, 1.6.96, p. A27.
48 'Demidenko Unmasked' *Herald-Sun, Weekend*, 25.5.96, p. 14.
49 Dr Michael Montalto, letter to editor, *Australian*, 16–17.9.95.
50 *Weekend Australian, Review*, 16–17.9.95, p. 6.
51 Robert Manne, 'The Hand that Set Australia Adrift', *Weekend Australian, Review*, 1–2.6.96, p. 5.
52 Peter Christoff, in 'Forum on the Demidenko Controversy', *ABR*, August 1995, p. 15.
53 Manne, *Culture of Forgetting*, p. 167.
54 There were prominent figures who disputed that the book was anti-Semitic. See Tony Coady, 'Judging the Defendant', *Age, Saturday Extra*, 27.1.96, p. 9.
55 David Marr, 'Dabbling with Demons', *Age*, 26.8.95, p. 17.
56 Peter Craven, 'The Last and Best Word'.
57 *Weekend Australian*, 23–4.9.96, p. 9.
58 Martin Wroe, 'Strawberry Fields for Ever and Ever', *Weekend Australian, Review*, 14–15.10.95, p. 1.
59 Adam Sweeting, 'Still Fab Forever', *Age*, 11.11.95.
60 *Sunday Age, Agenda*, 19.11.95.
61 Waldemar Januszczak, 'The Immortal Freddie', *Weekend Australian, Review*, 28–29.12.96, p. 5.
62 Richard Jinman, 'Purple Haze of Time Fails to Dim the Legacy of Hendrix's Genius', and John Ellicott, 'Silverchair Go Home to Put Their Feet Up', *Weekend Australian*, 23–24.9.95, p. 9.
63 *60 Minutes*, 1.9.96.
64 Ben Hills, 'The Golden Age: The Decline of Newspapers', *Quadrant*, January–February 1997, pp. 52–5.

Chapter 11

1 Windschuttle, *Unemployment*, p. 70.
2 Interview with Ray Martin, *A Current Affair*, 1.9.96.

Gangland

3 *7.30 Report*, 26.8.96.
4 Report on TAS TV evening news, 5.9.96.
5 Alison Mitchell, 'Downfall of a Spin Doctor', *Age*, 4.9.96, p. A13.
6 'Tories' Anti-crime Measures Include Curfew for Toddlers', *Age*, 6.3.97, p. A11.
7 Madeleine Coorey, 'Youth Gangs Problem Blights Our Big Cities', *Weekend Australian*, 19–20.8.95, p. 10.
8 Paul Conroy, 'Gangland Victoria: Youth Crime Booms', *Age*, 19.9.95, p. 1.
9 Gary Tippet, 'Children Who Kill', *Sunday Age*, 28.4.96, p. 17.
10 Richard Yallop, 'Young and Out of Control', *Weekend Australian, Focus*, 17–18.8.96, p. 25.
11 'Kids 14, Dealing Heroin on Streets', *Sunday Age*, 5.11.95, p. 1.
12 *Age, Saturday Extra*, 5.8.95, p. 1.
13 Damien Murphy, 'The New Untouchables', *Bulletin*, 12.9.95, p. 18.
14 Paul Sheiner, 'Juveniles and Justice in Western Australia', *Meanjin*, 2/1993, pp. 253–64.
15 Quoted in Trudy Harris, 'Juvenile Laws "Victimise Young"', *Weekend Australian*, 7–8.9.96, p. 11.
16 'Child Drug Sellers to Face Adult Sentences', *Australian*, 18.9.95.
17 Quoted in Elizabeth Wynhausen, 'Too Tuff on Teenage Crime?', *Weekend Australian*, 7–8.12.96, p. 26.
18 Ibid.
19 Quoted in Trudy Harris, 'Juvenile Laws "Victimise Young"'.
20 Richard Hill, Tony McMahon and Judith Bessant, 'Don't Damn Young Law-abiding Majority', *Australian*, 4.9.96, p. 13.
21 Cited in Australian Law Reform Commission and Human Rights and Equal Opportunity Commission, 'A Matter of Priority: Children and the Legal Process', Discussion Paper, May 1997, par. 10.8, at http://uniserve.edu.au/alrc/
22 Rob White, 'Street Life: Police Practices and Youth Behaviour', in Rob White and Christine Alder (eds), *The Police and Young People in Australia*, Cambridge University Press, Melbourne, 1994, pp. 102–27.
23 Cited in 'Children Who Kill'.
24 'A Matter of Priority', recommendations 11.2 and 11.3.
25 Ibid., par 11.12.
26 'Australia, A Champion of Human Rights?', *Amnesty International Australian Newsletter*, vol. 15, no. 1, February–March 1997, p. 7.
27 Ibid., p. 8.
28 Chris Cunneen, 'Enforcing Genocide? Aboriginal Young People and the Police', in White and Alder (eds), *The Police and Young People in Australia*, pp. 128–58.
29 'Crown Under Attack over Bail for Boys', *Age*, 24.12.96, p. A3.
30 'Outcry as Boys Jailed for Spitting', *Age*, 23.12.96, p. 1.
31 'Housing and Youth Hit by ATSIC Budget Cuts', *Age*, 17.8.96, p. A3.

Notes

32 'Myth of Youth Wages Clouds Jobless Issue'.
33 'Howard Targets Youth Wages', *Age*, 23.5.96, p. 1.
34 'Purge to End Dole for 25,000 Under-18s', *Australian*, 18.6.97, p. 1.
35 'A Long Term Problem that can be Solved', *Age*, 14.12.96, p. A23.
36 OECD *Employment Outlook 1996*, cited by Tim Colebatch, *Age*, 20.7.96, p. A23.
37 Safe and Whittaker, 'The Baby Boomers of 1994', p. 12.
38 Tony Townsend, 'Reading Between the Lines', *Age*, 25.11.96, p. A11.
39 'One in Three Struggle to Read', *Age*, 22.10.96, p. 1.
40 'Youth Housing Record Slammed', *Age*, 5.9.96, p. A2.
41 '"Homeless Risk" for Students', *Age*, 6.9.96, p. A3.
42 ABS, *Australian Social Trends 1994*, p. 55.
43 'Women's Drug Abuse Begins in Early Teens', *Australian*, 5.6.96, p. 5.
44 'Teens Smoke More to Promote Image', *Age*, 3.11.95, p. 3.
45 'Call to Ease Plight of Young Addicts', *Sunday Age*, 19.5.96, p. 6.
46 'Cover-up Claim on 36 Deaths', *Age*, 3.6.96, p. A3.
47 *Australian Social Trends 1994*, p. 202.
48 James Button, 'Greying Nation', *Age*, 5.8.95, p. A9.
49 Adrian McGregor, 'Too Poor to Retire: The Middle-Class Nightmare', *Weekend Australian, Review*, 3–4.8.96, p. 4.
50 P. P. McGuinness, 'Intolerance of the Enlightened', *Age*, 18.9.96, p. 7.
51 Peter Harkness, 'Market Hits and Myths', *Age*, 4.9.96, p. A15.
52 'Our Children are the Second Poorest', *Age*, 17.10.96, p. 1.
53 'Men: The New Second Sex', *Weekend Australian*, 5–6.10.96, p. 25.
54 Jane Freeman, 'The Nervous Nineties', *Sunday Age, Agenda*, 6.2.94, p. 1.
55 Moira Rayner, *Rooting Democracy*, Allen & Unwin, Sydney, 1997.
56 James Walter, *Tunnel Vision*, p. 73.
57 Rob White, 'Street Life', p. 124.
58 Editorial, 'Banning the Gang Leaders', *Saturday Mercury*, 7.9.96, p. 18.
59 Commissioner for Knox, quoted in Graeme Bannerman, 'The Invasion of Our Public Space', *Age*, 13.12.96, p. A15.
60 John Hartley, *The Politics of Pictures: The Creation of the Public in the Age of Popular Media*, Routledge, London and New York, 1992, pp. 212–3.
61 Tim Fischer, 'Poor Children Losers in the Race to Wealth', *Age*, 23.12.96, p. A11.
62 Sid Spindler, 'Free Trade in the Lives of Our Children', *Age*, 17.12.96, p. A13.

Chapter 12

1 'X Marks the End of a Short, Slack Generation', *Age*, 24.6.95.
2 Ben Crawford and Zarah Perkins, 'The Xorcist', *Not only Black and White*, no. 8, August 1994, p. 36.
3 Matthew Tyrnauer, 'Star Power', *Vanity Fair*, May 1995, p. 114.

Gangland

4 Jean Baudrillard, *Simulations*, Paul Foss, Paul Patton and Philip Beitchman (trs), Semiotexte, New York, 1983, p. 4.
5 Roland Barthes, 'The Death of the Author', in *Modern Criticism and Theory: A Reader*, David Lodge (ed.), Longman, London and New York, 1988, p. 170.

Chapter 13

1 Martin Amis, interview with Francesca Riviere, *Paris Review*, Spring 1998, quoted in *Harper's Magazine*, November 1998, p. 30.
2 Marcus Westbury, *Undergrowth*, Allen & Unwin, forthcoming.
3 Frank Moorhouse, speech to 'Gangs and Gatekeepers' Session, Melbourne Writers' Festival, 19.10.97.
4 Richard Neville, 'We Were as Good as it Gets', *Australian*, 4.2.98, p. 13.
5 Professor Lauchlan Chipman, Keynote Address, Issues of Regional Youth Conference, Central Queensland University (Mackay), 9.7.98.
6 *The Media Report*, ABC Radio National, panel discussion with David Armstrong, Mark Davis and George Negus, hosted by Robert Bolton, 22.9.97.
7 Mike Carlton, 'Sharp Made a Scapegoat', *SMH*, 27.9.97.
8 Frank Moorhouse, 'Peter Pan and the Lost Boys', *Adelaide Review*, January 1998, p. 15.
9 George Negus, 'George Lets Fly', interview with Thornton McCamish, *The Big Issue*, no. 30, 22.9–5.10.97, p. 21.
10 Kind thanks to Ken Gelder, who pointed out the symmetry of Vanstone's and Garner's remarks in Ken Gelder, 'The First Stone in a New Debate', *Sunday Age*, 14.9.97.
11 Westbury, *Undergrowth*.
12 Frank Moorhouse, 'Peter Pan and the Lost Boys'.
13 Westbury, *Undergrowth*.
14 Ghassan Hage, *White Nation: Fantasies of White Supremacy in a Multicultural Society*, Pluto Press, Annandale, 1998, p. 236.
15 Robert Dessaix, 'Nice Work if You Can Get It', in Imre Salusinszky (ed.), *The Oxford Book of Australian Essays*, Oxford University Press, Melbourne, 1997, pp. 239–40. Paul Sheehan, *Among the Barbarians*, Random House, Milson's Point, 1998. In the dedication to his *In the New Country*, Foster writes:

> To my part-aboriginal grandsons Michael, Caleb and Willem Foster, in the hope that Australians may learn to see them, so that they may be permitted to see themselves, as Australians, rather than as aboriginal Australians.

I'm impressed by Foster's obvious affection for his grandchildren, but the rest seems a little more problematic. There are few things more arresting and yet commonplace in the late twentieth century than the spec-

Notes

tacle of white middle-aged men, in the guise of professing equality and expressing humanistic concern, telling ethnic minorities how to think themselves in relation to the mass. David Foster, *In the New Country*, Fourth Estate, London, 1999.

16 Moorhouse, 'Peter Pan and the Lost Boys'.
17 Peter Craven, 'Gang Warfare', *ABR*, October 1997, pp. 7–8.
18 Peter Craven, 'The Critic Who Avoided Adelaide', *Australian*, HES, 11.3.98.
19 Luke Slattery, 'Far-fetched and Fallacious', *Weekend Australian, Review*, 11–12.10.97. Craven pursued a similar theme, arguing that in *Gangland* 'youth is a fetish' and the book's arguments are an example of 'sibling rivalry', not 'generational deprivation' (Craven, 'Gang Warfare', p. 7).
20 Luke Slattery, letter to editor, *Arena Magazine* no. 33, February–March 1998, p. 13.
21 White and Alder, *The Police and Young People in Australia*.
22 Tim Thorne, 'Erechtheus 33's Apologia', *Heat*, no. 9, 1998, p. 73.
23 Frank Devine, 'No Future in Dalek Discourses', *Australian*, 18.9.97, p. 13. There you go, Frank, you're in!
24 Virginia Trioli in 'Symposium: Are There Gangsters and Gatekeepers Dominating Public Space?', *ABR*, November 1997, p. 25.
25 Sue Luckman, 'Forever Young?', *Overland*, no. 151, 1998, p. 82.
26 Virginia Trioli, 'Curse of the Old Farts', *Age, Saturday Extra*, 13.9.97.
27 Richard Neville, 'The Death of Childhood', *Age*, 24.9.98.
28 Robert Manne, *The Way We Live Now: The Controversies of the Nineties*, Text Publishing, Melbourne, 1998. The arguments on pages 206–10, 227–37 and 267–71 all in some way play to the idea that popular culture and 'the way we live now' have something to do with each other. Richard Neville, 'The Business of Being Human', *Age, Good Weekend*, 23.8.97, p. 50.
29 Manne, *The Culture of Forgetting*. Richard Neville, 'We Were as Good as it Gets', p. 13.
30 For example, in *The First Stone* Helen Garner makes much of Milton's 'great challenge' to 'Let warrantable assertion and falsehood grapple' (p. 178). What resonance might this have had for a generation reared on the Romantic poets and a liberal education, gesturing as it does towards Garner's own reputation as a 'truth-teller'? Yet, for all these resonances, her book is clearly partial in its telling.
31 Manne, *The Way We Live Now*, p. 210.
32 Tony Moore, 'Demonising the X Files', *Arena Magazine*, October–November 1997, p. 20.
33 See Henry A. Giroux, 'Nymphet Fantasies: Child Beauty Pageants and the Politics of Innocence', *Social Text*, 57, vol. 16, no. 4, Winter 1998.
34 Readers of Manne's work on *The Hand that Signed the Paper*, or Garner's *The First Stone*, will be familiar with the way both almost literally embody the issues. In *The Culture of Forgetting*, Robert Manne sets up his

diagnosis of the Darville-Demidenko affair so as to present his physical shock, which he details at length, at Darville's anti-Semitism, as evidence of a general national cultural decline, as if he were its living moral barometer. In *The First Stone* Garner's body rattles away like a Geiger counter, a living index of 'truth'. The story gets going with 'rushes of horror', 'twinges of alarm', and a 'stab' of curiosity, follows with 'a rush of terrible sadness', and a 'gradual chilling of my blood', concluding with 'a bomb of fury and disgust' that Garner felt 'go off inside my head'. Garner, *The First Stone*, pp. 16, 37, 122, 125, 156.

35 See, for example, Kate Legge, 'Diffusing the Mindfield: Removing the Oxymoron from Australian Intellectualism', in *Future Tense: Australia Beyond Election 1998*, Allen & Unwin, St Leonard's, 1999, pp. 77–83. Sneja Gunew has commented on how Robert Dessaix was canonised among the intelligentsia for his attacks on academic multiculturalism. See Sneja Gunew, 'Reinventing Selves', in Mary Zournazi (ed.), *Foreign Dialogues: Memories, Translations, Conversations*, Pluto Press, Annandale, 1998, pp. 99–116.

36 Peter Craven, 'This Helen's for Real', *Weekend Australian, Review*, 6–7.4.96. Morag Fraser, 'Garner's Stories in Search of Truth', *ABR*, no. 179, April 1996, pp. 5–6. Peter Steele, 'Having a Go', *Eureka Street*, vol. 6, no. 3, April 1996, pp. 32–3.

37 Peter Craven, 'Grand Flow of Murrayspeak', *Weekend Australian, Review*, 31.1.98–1.2.98.

38 Morag Fraser, 'Troika of Secrets', *ABR*, no. 196, November 1997, pp. 8–9. Peter Craven, 'Triple Bill That Makes No Secret of Quality', *Sunday Age, Inside Story*, 11.1.98.

39 Morag Fraser, 'Inspired Eavesdropping', *ABR*, no. 195, October 1997, pp. 9–10. Luke Slattery, 'Not Personal Enough', *Weekend Australian, Review*, 6–7.12.97.

40 Peter Craven, 'Words Conspire to Dazzle and Delight' *Sunday Age, Inside Story*, 8.3.98. Luke Slattery, 'Maturing in Fine Style', *Weekend Australian, Review*, 9–10.5.98.

41 Peter Craven, 'Manning the Barricade Again', *Australian, HES*, 8.7.98.

42 Kerryn Goldsworthy, 'Essaying the Essay', *ABR*, no. 208, February–March 1999, pp. 9–10. Barry Oakley, 'The Heart of the Matter', *Weekend Australian, Review*, 12–13.12.98. Peter Steele, 'Rambles in Reason', *Age, Saturday Extra*, 5.12.98.

43 Peter Craven, 'Me and My Spirit', *SMH, Spectrum*, 14.11.98. Morag Fraser, 'Grand Miscellany', *ABR*, November 1998, p. 19.

44 Morag Fraser, 'Untimely Truths', *Age, Saturday Extra*, 6.3.99. Peter Steele, 'Angel, Sphinx', *ABR*, June 1999, p. 5.

45 Imre Salusinszky, 'Revival of the Essay', *Australian, HES*, 8.10.97.

46 Slattery, 'Not Personal Enough'.

47 Tom Wolfe, *A Man in Full*, Jonathan Cape, London, 1998, p. 194. For a fuller discussion of these recent essay collections see Mark Davis,

Notes

'Assaying the Essay: Fear and Loathing in the Literary Coteries', *Overland,* no. 156, September 1999.
48 Programme, *National Young Writers' Festival*, Newcastle, 25–27.9.98.
49 http://www.va.com.au/
50 http://users.hunterlink.net.au/~ddsbh/
51 This criticism was made privately. At the kind invitation of Dr Geoff Danaher I subsequently participated in the 'Issues of Regional Youth Conference' at Central Queensland University (Mackay), in July 1998, to address these issues. See Mark Davis, 'Sick, Wicked Culture: The Global Politics of Regional Youth', *Australian Quarterly*, vol. 70, no. 5 (September–October 1998), pp. 16–23.
52 Helen Elliott, 'Outsider Attacks Old School', *Herald-Sun*, 16.9.97.
53 Michelle Sabto, 'Lo-Fi Tales', *Meanjin*, vol. 57, 4/1998, pp. 809–15. Ken Gelder, 'The First Stone in a New Debate', *Sunday Age*, 14.9.97.
54 Slattery, letter to editor, *Arena Magazine*. See also Slattery, 'Far-fetched and Fallacious'.
55 A 'stylish' and 'serious . . . review essay' by a 'young leftie', his friend Peter Craven called his piece. Craven later republished the essay in his *Best Australian Essays, 1998*. See Peter Craven, 'Room for Radical Departures', *Australian, HES*, 5.11.97. See also Guy Rundle, 'Gang-bashed', in Peter Craven, *Best Australian Essays 1998*, Bookman, Melbourne, 1998, p. 160.
56 Ted Emery and Rick McKenna, Interview with John Mangan, 'Seriously Funny', *Age, Green Guide*, 4.2.99, p. 14.
57 Slattery, 'Far-fetched and Fallacious'.
58 Slattery, 'Far-fetched and Fallacious'.
59 Janine MacDonald, 'Media Slate Youth: Study', *Age*, 17.11.98.
60 Shane Paxton, 'You Are What You Digest', *Age, EG*, 3.4.98, p. 11.
61 Unknown member of audience, 'Issues of Regional Youth' conference, Central Queensland University (Mackay), 9.7.98.
62 Drew Williamson, private conversation, 11.10.98.
63 Bernard Cohen, 'Symposium: Are There Gangsters and Gatekeepers Dominating Public Space?', *ABR*, November 1997, p. 25.
64 Peter Craven, 'A Defence of the Critic's Right to Criticise', *Australian, HES*, 10.6.98.
65 Gerard Henderson, 'It's a Myth that the Media Made One Nation', *Age*, 14.7.98. Anne Henderson, 'Crawlies in the Crannies', *The Australian's Review of Books*, July 1998, vol. 3, no. 4, pp. 3–4.
66 Hage, *White Nation*.
67 Readings bookshop, panel discussion with Elisa Berg, Peter Craven, Helen Daniel, Mark Davis, Morag Fraser, Dean Kiley, chaired by Moira Rayner, 13.11.97.
68 Slattery, 'Far-fetched and Fallacious'. Guy Rundle, 'Gangbashed'.
69 Noel Pearson quoted in Debra Jopson, 'Help Us Solve it, says Pearson', *SMH*, 7.7.97

70 Natasha Stott Despoja, 'Surge in Youth Vote for Democrats', Australian Democrats: Online News Service: August 1998, http://www.democrats.org.au/media/1998/08/602nsd.html
71 Australian Democrats: Online News Service: August 1998, http://www.democrats.org.au/media/1998/08/598nsd.html
72 *Lateline*, 18.9.98.
73 Hugh Mackay, *Generations: Baby-boomers, Their Parents and Their Children*, Pan Macmillan, Sydney, 1997, pp. 138–9.
74 Murray Hogarth, 'Young, Organised and Out There', *SMH*, 11.7.98.
75 Christopher Dore, 'Child Protesters Given a Stern Scolding', *Weekend Australian*, 4–5.7.98.
76 Wendy Robertson, quoted in Susan Chenery, 'How Many Mines', *SMH*, 11.7.98.
77 Emily McPherson, 'White Girl in a Black Land: My Journey Across the Gulf', *Age*, 1.12.98. Chris Ryan, 'Youth Get Together to Work for Justice', *Age*, 16.7.98.
78 Annie Beck, quoted in Susan Chenery, 'How Many Mines'.
79 Natasha Stott Despoja, 'Surge in Youth Vote for Democrats'.
80 Richard Neville, 'The Business of Being Human', p. 50.
81 http://www.green.net.au/activism/

Chapter 14

1 Noel Pearson, 'Dreadful Experiment That Went Wrong', *Australian*, 19.6.98, p. 13.
2 Tan Le, 'A Nation Without Vision', *Age*, 3.1.99.
3 Caroline Overington, 'Talkback Bias: Laws Reads the Riot Act', *Sunday Age*, 25.10.98, p. 11.
4 Elisabeth Wynhausen, 'Ratbag King of Radio Ga-Ga', *Weekend Australian*, 31.10–1.11.98.
5 Pearson, 'Dreadful Experiment That Went Wrong'.
6 Ibid.
7 Barry Cohen, quoted in Philippa Hawker, 'Black, White and Grey', *Age, News Extra*, 6.3.99.
8 Quoted in Pearson, 'Dreadful Experiment That Went Wrong'.
9 Noel Pearson, quoted in Richard McGregor and Georgina Windsor, 'PM Rules Out Wik Compromise Veto', *Australian*, 1.7.98.
10 Unspecified ministerial spokesman in Sian Powell and Diana Thorp, 'PM Tries to Censor Coombs Eulogy', *Weekend Australian*, 15–16.11.97.
11 Laura Tingle and Claire Miller, 'Williams Tried to Gag Wik Report: Labor', *Age*, 30.9.97.
12 Quoted in Ben Mitchell, 'Council's Opinion on Wik "Suppressed"', *Age*, 21.8.97.
13 Elisabeth Wynhausen, 'Ratbag King of Radio Ga-Ga'.

Notes

14 Quoted in Paul Heinrichs, 'Yorta Yorta Elders Curse Elliot to "Rot and Decay"', *Age*, 18.3.99.
15 Robert Manne, speech to Melbourne Writers' Festival, 22.8.98.
16 See Robert Manne, 'The Stolen Generations', in *The Way We Live Now*, pp. 7–41.
17 Marcia Langton, interviewed in Robert Dessaix, *Speaking Their Minds: Intellectuals and the Public Culture in Australia*, ABC Books, Sydney, 1998, p. 233.
18 Langton in Dessaix, p. 239.
19 In private conversation, 1.9.98.
20 Interview, Jana Wendt with Toni Morrison, *Jana Wendt's Uncensored*, ABC Television, 9.7.98.
21 Jana Wendt, 'Ackland Needs a Watchdog', *SMH*, 15.8.98.
22 Jana Wendt, quoted in Brian Courtis, 'What's Wrong With Jana?', *Age*, *Green Guide*, 13.8.98.
23 *Two Nations: The Causes and Effects of the Rise of the One Nation Party in Australia*, Bookman, Melbourne, 1998.
24 Morag Fraser claimed her *Seams of Light: Best Antipodean Essays*, Allen & Unwin, St Leonard's, 1998, is 'a set of essays on Wik, although I doubt that word is ever mentioned', in Murray Waldren, 'Front-line Puritan', *Weekend Australian*, *Review*, 14–15.3.98. See also Peter Craven, 'Introduction', *The Best Australian Essays 1998*, especially pp. xiv–xv.
25 Anna Patty, '*Head On* Collision', *Sun-Herald*, 20.9.98
26 ABC Television news, Melbourne, Sunday 11.10.98.
27 Christopher Dore, 'Purge to End Dole for 25,000 Under-18s', *Australian*, 18.6.97.
28 Adele Horin, 'Another Blow to Youth as Lobby Group Hit', *SMH*, 20.6.98.
29 Anonymous delegate and Ryan Heath, in Stephanie Petaling, 'Seen But Not Heard: Young Australia Stifled', *SMH*, 12.6.99.
30 Nicole Brady, 'Teen Training Misses a Beat', *Sunday Age*, 8.6.98.
31 Carolyn Webb, 'Government Accused of Squeezing Out Program for Jobless Youth', *Sunday Age*, 6.9.98.
32 Andrew Darby, 'Drink Still the Bane of Youth', *Age*, 8.9.98.
33 Editorial, 'Tackling the Teenage Blues', *Age*, 8.8.98.
34 ABC Television News, Melbourne, 18.2.99.
35 Sushila Das, 'No Jobs Caused Rise in Dealing', *Age*, 15.5.97.
36 Adele Horin, 'Wanted: Jobs With Hope', *SMH*, 21.3.98.
37 Carolyn Jones, 'Warning on Nomad Homeless Children', *Age*, 8.4.98.
38 Gabrielle Costa, 'Allowance to Push Young Into Work', *Age*, 13.5.98.
39 In Misha Schubert, 'Fair Go Ethic and the Future', *Weekend Australian*, 9–10.5.98.
40 Adele Horin, 'The Betrayal of a Generation: How We Have Failed Our Youth', *SMH*, 21.3.98.

41 Shane Green, 'The Nation's Young Demand to be Counted', *Age*, 14.3.98.
42 Tim Pegler, 'Youth Housing Record Slammed', *Age*, 5.9.96.
43 Steve Dow, 'Cash Fears for Young Homeless', *Age*, 25.5.98.
44 Tim Pegler, 'States Fail to Protect Children, Report Says', *Age*, 20.11.97.
45 Stephanie Peatling, 'Politicians Ignoring Children', *SMH*, 5.12.98.
46 Chris Ryan, 'NT Looks at Night "Tags" for Children', *Age*, 10.9.97.
47 Maria Ceresa, 'Territory Law Puts $2191 Tag on a Beer', *Age*, 19.8.98.
48 Georgina Safe, 'Race Against Disadvantage', *Australian*, 9.12.98.
49 Paul Tabar, quoted in Damien Murphy, 'Gangs Outcry "Based on Class"', *SMH*, 5.12.98.
50 Chris Sidoti, quoted in Debra Jopson, 'Surge in Number of Blacks in Custody', *SMH*, 7.11.98.
51 Wendy Bacon and Bonita Mason, 'Aboriginal Deaths in Custody A Dead Issue?', *Reportage Media Magazine*, Issue 5, Autumn 1995. http://jsa-44.hum.uts.edu.au/acij/reportage5/R5DIC.html
52 Ruby Langford Ginibi quoted in Debra Jopson, 'Surge in Number of Blacks in Custody'.
53 Michael Gliksman, 'Crucifying Youth for Our Failure', *Australian*, 10.6.98.
54 AAP, 'Homeless Risk for Students', *Age*, 6.9.96.
55 Steve Dow, 'Cash Fears for Young Homeless'.
56 JJJ news report, 28.1.99.
57 Sue Cant, 'Believe It or Not, Students Revolt', *SMH*, 6.9.97.
58 Linda Grant, 'Sorry Teenagers, the Power Game is Up', *Age*, 17.6.98.
59 Giroux, 'Nymphet Fantasies', p. 34.
60 Ibid., p. 46.
61 Ibid.
62 For a more detailed version of this argument, see Mark Davis, 'Sick, Wicked Culture'.

Chapter 15

1 John Docker, in 'Symposium: Are There Gangsters and Gatekeepers Dominating Public Space?', *ABR*, November 1997, p. 24.
2 Rosi Braidotti, 'Remembering Fitzroy High', in Jenna Mead (ed.) *Bodyjamming: Sexual Harassment, Feminism and Public Life*, Vintage, Milson's Point, 1997, pp. 142–3.
3 Anne Manne, 'Pillars of Predictability', *Weekend Australian*, 2–3.1.98.
4 Anne Neumann, 'Men Are People Too', *Weekend Australian, Review*, 7–8.3.98.
5 See Kerryn Phelps, 'Why Must Teachers Remain Closeted', *Age*, 15.5.98, p. 15.
6 Giles Auty, 'Battles with Unreason', *Weekend Australian, Review*, 3–4.1.98, p. 19.

Notes

7 McKenzie Wark, *Celebrities, Culture and Cyberspace: The Light on the Hill in the Postmodern World*, Pluto Press, Annandale, 1999, p. 226.
8 Katherine Wilson, 'Naughty Auty', *Weekend Australian*, 7–8.3.98, p. 27. Giles Auty, 'Parochialism Rears Its Ugly Head', *Weekend Australian*, 7–8.3.98, p. 27.
9 Peter Timms, 'Competitive, but Light on Winners', *Age*, 25.3.98.
10 Giles Auty, 'A Brace of Farewells', *Weekend Australian, Review*, 15–16.5.99. Peter Timms, 'Feathers Fly Over New Art Curator', *Age*, 9.6.99.
11 Peter Craven, 'Why All the Fuss About Hughes?', *Age*, 10.11.98.
12 Luke Slattery, '"Unconscious Cannibal" Says Sorry', *Weekend Australian*, 7–8.11.98.
13 Luke Slattery, '"Cannibal" Eats His Own Words', *Weekend Australian, Focus*, 7–8.11.98.
14 See Peter Craven, 'Stuck in the Middle with Hughes', *Age, Saturday Extra*, 8.5.93, p. 7. Luke Slattery, 'I Think, Therefore I Think', *Weekend Australian, Focus*, 15–16.5.93, p. 20. Peter Craven, 'Hughes Jumps the Net of Cultural Politics', *Weekend Australian*, 29–30.5.93, p. 5. Luke Slattery, 'Expatriates on a Pedestal', *Weekend Australian, Focus*, 30.11–1.12.96, p. 24. Luke Slattery, 'The Art of Being Robert Hughes', *Australian Magazine*, 12–13.8.95, pp. 16–23. Peter Craven, 'American Stars and Bars', *Age, Saturday Extra*, 14.6.97, p. 10.
15 Robert Dessaix, 'Plays Well with Others', *Age, Saturday Extra*, 9.5.97, p. 8.
16 Helen Garner, 'Still Angry After All These Years', *Age, Saturday Extra*, 6.3.99.
17 Stephen Knight, untitled review, private copy in my possession.
18 Don Anderson, 'A Doctorate in Disillusion', *SMH, Spectrum*, 20.6.98.
19 Janet Malcolm, 'Women at War', *New Yorker*, 7.7.97, pp. 73–5. Andrew Clark, 'Garner's Book Slated in US', *Age*, 10.7.97.
20 Peter Craven, 'She Who Miscasts Garner's Stone', *Australian, HES*, 16.7.97.
21 Malcolm, pp. 74–5.
22 Andrew Clark, 'Author Sparks War of Words', *Age*, 25.8.98.
23 Gideon Haigh, 'Bryce Shows Off the Power of Whinge', *Australian*, 26.8.98. Jane Sullivan was one of the few journalists to show an interest in the basic questions at the heart of the session, in 'No Prophets at Home', *Age, Saturday Extra*, 19.12.98.
24 Peter Craven, 'Inside and Out at a Literary Talkfest', *Australian, HES*, 22.10.97.
25 Nuala O'faolain, 'My Week', *Age*, 29.8.98, p. 8.
26 Rosi Braidotti, 'Remembering Fitzroy High', p. 132.
27 Kate Legge, 'Come Out Fighting', *Weekend Australian, Review*, 15–16.11.97.
28 Robert Manne, 'The Second Stone', in *The Way We Live Now*, p. 243.

29 See, Peter Craven, 'Gang Warfare', p. 7. Andrew Riemer, 'The Cultural War Has Broken Out Again. Which Gang Are You In?', *SMH*, 18.10.97. Guy Rundle, 'Gangbashed', *Arena Magazine*, no. 31, October–November 1997, pp. 46–8. Luke Slattery, 'Far-fetched and Fallacious'. Virginia Trioli, 'Curse of the Old Farts'.

30 Virginia Trioli, 'Curse of the Old Farts'. 'Baby Boomers Leave Behind an Empty Wake', *Age*, 17.9.97. 'Symposium: Are There Gangsters and Gatekeepers Dominating Public Space?', *ABR*, November 1997, p. 25.

31 Peter Craven, 'Gang Warfare', *ABR*, no. 195, October 1997. *Australian, HES*, 24.9.97, 5.11.97, 3.3.98 and 14.10.98.

32 Robert Manne, 'A Generational Divide Defines Cultural Debate', *Age*, 22.9.97. Robert Manne, 'Old Gang has Something to Offer', *SMH*, 22.9.97. Robert Manne, Editorial, 'Gang Warfare', *Quadrant*, October 1997, pp. 3–4. Robert Manne, *The Way We Live Now*, pp. 262–6.

33 Rundle's original review contained misleading errors of fact, for which he has subsequently apologised. Kerryn Goldsworthy, 'Essaying the Essay', p. 10. Guy Rundle, 'Gangbashed', in Peter Craven, *Best Australian Essays 1998*, pp. 157–61. Mark Davis, 'Not the New Generationalism', *Arena Magazine*, no. 32, December 1997–January 1998, pp. 12–13. Guy Rundle, 'Vested Interest', *Arena Magazine*, no. 32, December 1997–January 1998, p. 13.

34 Les Carlyon, 'Shooting the Thought Police', *SMH*, 6.6.98. Les Carlyon, 'The Politics of Confusion', *Age, Saturday Extra*, 6.6.98.

35 Michael Duffy, 'Against the Grain', *Weekend Australian, Review*, 6–7.6.98.

36 Michael Duffy, 'Multiculturalism is Divisible — and Divisive', *Weekend Australian*, 3–4.1.98.

37 Anne Henderson, 'Crawlies in the Crannies'. See also Jenny Lee, 'The New Grievance Industry', *Overland*, no. 153, Summer 1998, pp. 85–7.

38 In Matthew Condon, *Weekend Australian, Review*, 3–4.4.99.

39 See 'The ALP's Race to Power', *Age*, 30.5.98.

40 P. P. McGuinness, in 'The ALP's Race to Power'.

41 Christopher Koch, quoted in Errol Simper, 'What's Right, Who's Left?', *Weekend Australian*, 7–8.3.98, p. 33.

42 Les Murray, quoted in Simper, 'What's Right'.

43 Shelley Gare, 'Windbag Thrives on Indulgence', *Weekend Australian*, 8–9.5.99.

44 Andrew Denton in Simon Pristel, 'Acting His Age', *Herald-Sun, Weekend*, 22.5.99.

45 Many thanks to Marcus Westbury for the conversation out of which these questions emerged.

Index

Abbott, Margaret 342
Abbott, Tony 53, 72, 328, 342
Aboriginal and Torres Strait Islander Commission (ATSIC) 46, 68, 70
Aboriginal: activists 305; children 15, 235–42, 252; activism 110; incarceration 15, 240, 241, 320; land rights 304; remains 176; representation 292, 303; representation in publishing industry 149, 209; *terra nullius* 297; writers and hoaxes 209, 222–3; youths and crime 235–41, 252; *see also* Royal Commission into Aboriginal Deaths in Custody; stolen generations
Absolutely Fabulous 178
Abstudy 321
academics 37, 76, 84, 95, 97, 98, 118, 136, 157, 158, 159, 164, 168, 170–4, 176, 178–83, 187–207, 210, 216, 224, 226, 261
Accordion Crimes 178
Acker, Kathy 155, 157
Ackland, Richard 342
activism 35, 182, 202, 267, 299–300
A Current Affair 13, 104, 106, 342
Adams, Phillip 24, 58, 64, 70, 170, 217, 280, 281

Adelaide Review 30, 61, 72, 215
Adler, Jacques 219
Adler, Louise 25, 36, 218, 219, 220
affirmative action 33, 67, 69, 71, 88, 96, 103, 198, 215
Age 23, 24, 47, 64, 97, 120, 124–7, 133, 211, 219–21, 229, 252, 277, 329, 330, 332, 337, 339
AIDS/HIV 3, 14, 16, 57, 244
Akerman, Piers 25
Alder, Christine 277
Allen & Unwin 148
Allinson, Mark 156, 170
American Psycho 14, 199
American Visions 185, 204
Amis, Kingsley 126, 270
Amis, Martin 270
Amnesty International 57, 241
Among the Barbarians 295, 307, 339–40; *see also* Sheehan, Paul
A Mother's Disgrace 135
Anderson, Don 30, 61, 157, 169, 170, 191, 192, 281, 330
Anderson, John 59
Ang, Ien 312
Angus & Robertson 148
anti-discrimination 33, 243
anti-intellectualism 49, 95, 97, 98, 118, 136, 157–9, 164, 168, 170–4, 176, 178–83, 187–207, 210, 216, 224, 226, 261, 288

Gangland

Antonious, Zita 312
Arcade, Penny 81
Archibald, J. F. 185
Arena Magazine 219
Armstrong, David 59, 341
Arndt, Bettina 24, 75, 82, 92, 327
Arnold, Matthew 177, 282
assimilation 275, 297
Attitude 104
Ausmusic 9
Austen, Jane 123, 124
Australia All Over 106
Australia Council 29, 70, 112, 118, 133, 134, 186, 209, 215
'Australia's Youth: Reality and Risk' 316, 317
Australian 24, 40, 47–9, 66, 67, 102, 120–7, 133, 166, 174, 210, 211, 212, 216, 219, 220, 221, 224, 229, 234, 247, 252, 289, 329, 333, 338, 339
Australian Art Collector 329
Australian Book Review 120, 122, 123, 125, 126, 131, 138, 218, 219, 220, 277, 331
Australian Broadcasting Authority 9, 104, 106, 182, 221
Australian Broadcasting Corporation (ABC) 24, 104, 221, 303, 313, 342; *see also* JJJ; *7.30 Report*; *This Day Tonight*
Australian Centre for Equity through Education 316
Australian Democrats 298; Youth Poll 300
Australian Jewish News 219
Australian Law Reform Commission 306, 318
Australian Society 125
Australian Women's Forum 12
Australian Youth Policy and Action Coalition (AYPAC) 314, 318
Australian's Review of Books, The 128–9, 339
Auty, Giles 327, 328

baby-boomers x, xi, 1, 3, 4, 6, 7, 9, 16, 44, 99, 100, 134, 229, 245, 248, 254, 255–69, 278; boomer-whinge xii, 3, 44, 45–74; generation of '68 140–54, 174
Bach, Johann Sebastian 126
Bacon, Wendy 85, 320
Bad Manners xv, 30
Bail, Kathy 27, 38, 42, 211
Baker, Candida 21
Barnard, Marjorie 118
Barnard, Michael 47
Barthes, Roland 263
Basic Instinct 89
Baudrillard, Jean 263
Baum, Caroline 186
Beatles 100, 101, 229, 265
Beavis and Butthead 199
Beazley, Kim 302
Beck, Annie 300
Before Sunrise 256
Bell Curve, The 193, 196
Bennett, David 66, 177
Bennett, William 192, 206
Bernstein, David 219
Berridge, Edward 130
Best Australian Essays, 1998 313, 338
Beverly Hills 90210 256
Big Chill, The 101
Biological Diversity Advisory Council 306
Bird, Carmel 115
Birmingham, John 26
Birthday Party 345
Blainey, Geoffrey 34, 49, 50, 62
Blake, William 124
Blankety Blanks 101
Bloom, Allan 187–200, 206
Bly, Robert 100
Bob Roberts 21
Bodyjamming 335–6
Bone, Pamela 219
book reviewing 117–39, 285
Bookmark 14

Index

Borbidge, Rob 107
Boyd, Brian 126
Boyer Lectures 30, 172
Bragg, Melvyn 102
Braidotti, Rosi 326, 335–6
Breaking the Cycle 315
Brennan, Christopher 121
Bridges of Madison County 100–1, 112
Bridging Education and Training Service (Beat) 315
Brilliant Lies 30, 36, 89, 103, 200
Bringing Them Home: The Stolen Generations Report 309
Brooks, David 116
Brown, Bob 298
Buchanan, Pat 206
Bulletin 59, 60, 185, 236
Burchill, Julie 105
Bush, George 196
Butler, Judith 160
Button, John 120

Cabin Fever 124
Campbell, Graeme 46
canon 31, 118–27, 132, 135, 136, 137, 164–7, 174–7, 185–9, 194–6, 199, 202, 211–13, 267
Capp, Fiona 137
Cappiello, Rosa 130, 136
Carey, Peter 331, 333
Carleton, Richard 24
Carlton, Mike 272, 275, 276, 277
Carlyon, Les 48, 339, 340
Carmen, Leon 209, 222
Carney, Shaun 109
Carr, Bob 232, 238, 239
Carroll, John 167
Carver, Raymond 123, 132, 211
Casey, Ron 25, 105
Castro, Brian 140, 162, 175, 312, 313
censorship viii, xii, 9, 11, 32, 34, 58, 109, 187, 199, 207, 217
Centre for Adolescent Health 316

Centre for Independent Studies 67
Chamberlain, Chris 316
Chan, Jackie 157, 295, 296
Chekhov, Anton 123, 124
Christoff, Peter 219, 220, 221
Churchill, Caryl 111
Citizens' Electoral Council 19
Clark, Andrew 332–3
Clark, Manning 119, 174, 209, 217
Clarke, John 344
classic rock 75, 76
Classification of Films and Publications Act (1990) 12
Clinton, Bill 233
Clinton, Hillary 109
Closing of the American Mind, The 187–200
Clueless 156
Cobain, Kurt 2–3, 7
Cohen, Barry 33, 48, 216, 220, 305
Cohen, Bernard 162, 294
Coalition government 9, 13, 15, 46–7, 65, 67, 69–71, 109–10, 242, 253, 302, 303, 304
Cold War 17, 59, 194, 195
Coleman, Peter 30, 32, 34, 37, 59, 60–3, 83, 339, 341
Collits, Terry 122
columnists (newspaper) 8, 80, 98, 102, 112, 119, 185, 187, 191, 192, 193, 214, 222, 242, 247, 266
Common Youth Allowance 314, 317
Commonwealth Employment Service 315
Commonwealth Games 313
Coombs, Anne 60
Coombs, H. C. (Nugget) 306
Cosmo Cosmolino 123, 135
Costello, Peter 67, 328, 342
Costello, Tanya 342
Coupland, Douglas 45, 100, 112, 255–6
Courier-Mail 209
Court, Richard 15, 233

385

Courtenay, Bryce 143–4, 328, 331–4
Cox, Eva 61, 85
Craven, Peter 30, 40, 119–27, 132–3, 167–8, 212, 218–19, 220, 223, 228, 277, 281, 285, 290, 295, 313, 329–32, 338
Crean, Simon 12
Credo 102
Crime (Serious and Repeat Offenders) Sentencing Act (1992) 15, 237
Crimes Amendment Act (1993) 238
Crystal Ballroom 345
cultural cringe 118, 184–207
cultural elites ix, 28, 31, 35, 36, 69, 141, 145, 179, 183, 185, 188, 193, 194, 199, 204, 207, 227, 232, 252, 253, 261, 336
cultural establishment xii, 87, 164, 182, 186, 207, 217, 261, 265, 274, 282, 289, 326, 345
cultural monopoly xi
cultural policy 119
cultural primacy 295
cultural relativists 31, 162, 163, 264
cultural renewal 283, 284, 288, 289
cultural studies 156, 157, 161, 166, 169, 170, 199
cultural value 282–3; print culture vs electronic media 282–3
culture, high vs low 31, 144, 146–7, 154, 172, 199, 200, 215, 224, 273, 274, 281; official viii; popular 24, 144, 146, 177, 181, 187, 189, 197, 199, 200, 229, 258, 262, 281–3; renegade viii
Culture of Complaint 30, 42, 185, 187, 200–7
Culture of Forgetting, The ix, 30, 37, 54, 121, 156–61, 168, 170, 194, 195, 197, 216, 221, 222, 224, 225, 288
culture industry xiii, 141, 149
culture racket 113–39

culture wars viii, ix, xii, 16, 31, 84, 184–207, 210, 308, 345, 348
Cunneen, Chris 241
current affairs 24, 25, 104, 109, 292, 324
Currey O'Neil 148
Currey, John 148

Daily Telegraph Mirror 10, 11
Dale, Leigh 187
Damned Whores and God's Police 30, 98
Daniel, Helen 116, 122, 123, 124, 125, 208, 218, 220, 331
Dartmouth Review 197
Darville-Demidenko, Helen x, 26, 37, 39, 40, 43, 54, 122, 156, 158, 160–1, 175, 181, 195, 200, 208–31, 328; 'affair' 25, 26, 28, 30, 116–17, 122, 158, 174, 187, 214–28, 251
date rape 76 *see also Morning After, The*; Roiphe, Katie
Dead White Males ix, 30, 32, 36, 37, 55, 57, 60, 95, 156, 165, 176–8, 181, 186, 190, 197, 200, 209, 262, 288
Deane, Kirsten 108
Death of Marat 136
Death of Napoleon, The 178
deconstruction 131, 136, 162; courses in 47, 162, 170; deconstructionists 35, 37, 131, 136, 156, 157, 161, 162, 163, 165, 170, 192, 196; *see also* theory
Delahunty, Mary 207
Demidenko Debate, The 216, 220
Demidenko Diary, The 216
Demidenko File, The 216, 220
Democrats (US) 303
Denfeld, Rene 26, 76, 81, 88
Denton, Andrew 344
Department of Education, Training and Youth Affairs 315
Derrida, Jacques 163, 165, 201

Index

Dessaix, Robert 25, 30, 36, 37, 39, 135–7, 173, 177, 186, 275, 281, 285, 310–11, 330
Devine, Frank 339
Devine, Miranda 340, 341
DiCaprio, Leonardo 323
Didion, Joan 116, 123
Dillon, Paul 11
Ding Xiaoqi 312
Dingo, Ernie 313
Dirt and Other Stories 132
dirty realism 131–2
DIY Feminism 27, 38
Docker, John 59, 119, 326
Dodson, Pat 306
Don's Party 31
Don't Take Your Love to Town 136
Dostoyevsky 123, 124, 126, 136
Doubletake 30, 34, 60, 61, 83
Downer, Alexander 62
Drewe, Robert 102, 135
Drowner, The 102
drug use 10, 107, 111, 234, 236, 238, 244, 251, 258, 267; Ecstasy 10, 37, 193, 230
D'Souza, Dinesh 47, 49, 55, 66, 70, 71, 187–90, 192–3, 196–8, 204, 206
Duffy, Michael 305, 339, 340
'dumbing-down' 95, 99–112
During, Simon 125, 126, 167, 173, 209
Dusseldorp Skills Forum 316
Dutton, Geoffrey 126, 148
Dworkin, Andrea 87–8
Dylan, Bob 229
The Devils 136

E is for Ecstasy 230
Easton Ellis, Bret 14, 199
Eastwood, Clint 100
Eccleston, Roy 62–3
economic rationalism xii, 96–7, 105, 115, 118, 131, 140, 153, 249, 271, 308, 309; impact on youth 66, 97, 140–54, 242, 246–52; policy 65, 71, 118; *see also* youth
Economist 247
Ecstasy 10, 37, 193, 230
Ellingsen, Peter 47
Elliott, Helen 289
Elliott, John 306
Ellis, Bob 27, 61, 62, 215, 328, 342
Ellmann, Richard 126
Emery, Ted 290
employment viii, 16, 171, 232, 242–7, 271
End of Certainty, The 193
End of Racism, The 71
Epanomitis, Fotini 312
Equal Opportunity Commission 77
Equal Rights Amendment 67, 206
'Eros' 89–90, 95
Essentials, The 111
Ettler, Justine 14, 130
Essays, 'revival' of 285–8
Eureka Street 80, 115, 123, 211, 218, 285
Evans, Gareth 193

Face, The 262
Fairfax Press 24
Fairfax, George 133
Falconer, Delia 178
Fallon, Mary 135
Fatal Attraction 89
Fatal Shore, The 176, 185
Faust, Beatrice 25, 29, 30, 38, 41, 54, 61, 75, 82–4, 95, 180
fees, university, introduced 13; increased 13, 243
Female Eunuch, The 98, 174
feminism 19, 29, 32, 34, 36–8, 42–3, 51, 56, 69, 75–96, 97, 156–7, 161, 168, 176, 181, 187, 191, 197, 201, 211, 228, 247, 252, 260, 261, 278, 288, 303, 339, 341, 347; academicisation of 50, 79, 97, 168; as threat to

387

Western civilisation 61, 156; decline of 22, 97, 102; equity 91, 94; 'femi-nazis' 46, 64, 106; feminist courses 47, 50, 168, 176; feminist hoax 38; libertarian 326, 347; media-feminist 83–8; 'victim feminism' viii, xii, xiii, 22, 36, 37, 75–98, 190, 194, 234, 265, 291, 346; 'wimp' 75; 'young feminists' vii, 31, 37, 39, 64, 75–96, 127, 168, 181, 268

femme fatale 89

Fire with Fire 81, 90

First Stone, The viii, x, xiv, 4, 12, 21, 22, 26, 30, 34, 37–8, 41, 53, 55, 60, 75–98, 114, 124, 126–7, 135, 138, 156–61, 168, 178, 181, 190, 197, 208–31, 273, 288, 291, 327, 330, 335–7

Fischer, Tim 47, 50, 110, 253

Fitzgerald, F. Scott 124

Fitzpatrick, Michael 248

Flaubert 136

Fogarty, Lionel 312

Footy Show, The 33

Forbes, John 220

Ford, Catherine 132

Ford, Richard 132

Forrest Gump 107–9, 112

Foster, David 275

Foucault, Michel 73, 90, 162

Fox FM 9

Frankfurt School 282

Fraser, Malcolm 304

Fraser, Morag 25, 80, 115, 123, 124, 126, 138, 211, 218, 281, 285, 286, 296, 308, 312

Freedman, Tim 303, 342

Freedom of Information Act 64

freedom of speech 49, 64

Freeman, Jane 148

From Dusk to Dawn 24

Frontline 157, 177

Fukuyama, Francis 193, 194

Gaita, Raimond 332–4

Games, The 344

Gare, Shelley 128–9

Garner, Helen viii, 4, 21, 26, 29–34, 36, 38, 41, 53, 60, 75–98, 113–14, 116, 119–27, 132–3, 135, 138, 156–61, 168, 170, 174, 181, 190, 197, 208–31, 273, 276, 281, 283, 285, 327, 328, 330, 335–6; *see also First Stone, The*

Gawenda, Michael 23–4, 99, 221

Gecko, Gordon 5, 99

Gelder, Ken 289

generation of '68 *see* baby-boomers

Generation F 27, 211

Generation X 45, 255

generation X viii, x, 3, 6–7, 15, 255–6, 270–1, 272, 300

generational divide ix, x, 6, 15, 132, 276; discourse of 16; generationalism 16, 19, 20, 26, 38, 232, 243, 255–69, 276, 278

Generations 299

Genet, Jean 123

GenX Reader, The 256

George's Wife, The 124

Gide, André 123, 136

Gingrich, Newt 189, 192, 198

Giroux, Henry A. 323

globalisation, of markets 17, 42, 43

Goethe 124

Golding, William 126

Goldsworthy, Kerryn 212, 285, 338

Goodbye Jerusalem 342

Good News Week 343

Gorbachev 270

Göring, Hermann 157

Gough, Austin 176

Graham, John 313

Graham, Mary 313

Grant, Jamie 130

Grass Sister, The 111

Green (party) 298

Green Day 229

Greene, Graham 126

Index

Greenhouse 148
Greenpeace 57
Greer, Germaine 27, 29, 61, 105, 174, 184, 186, 211, 286, 330, 337
Grenville, Kate 115
Gribble, Di 120, 148
Groom, Ray 233
Gross Misconduct 89
Grosz, Elizabeth 85, 188
grunge viii, 6, 115, 129, 131, 132, 138, 234; writers 14, 37, 39, 130
Gude, Phil 243
Guernica 136
Gunew, Sneja 85, 188
Gurganus, Allan 329

Hage, Ghassan 275, 296
Haigh, Gideon 120, 220, 333
Hall, Rodney 135
Hand that Signed the Paper, The x, 159, 160, 174, 187, 197, 208–31, 291
Hanson, Pauline 46, 55–6, 68–9, 70–3, 107–9, 241, 246–7, 296, 297, 299, 304, 305, 307, 308, 309, 310, 312
Happy Days 101
HarperCollins 148, 149
Harris, Max 148
Hartley, John 251, 252
Hasluck versus Coombs 68
Hawke, Bob 270
Hayden, Bill 33, 341
He Died With a Felafel in His Hand 26
Head On 313
Heartbeat 101
Heat 118, 218
Heath, Ryan 315
Henderson, Anne 295, 339
Henderson, Gerard 24, 25, 64, 117, 217–20, 225, 228, 280, 281, 295
Hendrix, Jimi xii, 2, 229
Herald-Sun 289

Herbert, Xavier 118
Heretic 30, 36, 58, 60
Heritage Foundation 206
Hernstein, Richard 193
Herron, John 60, 68
Hewett, Dorothy 288
Heyward, Michael 116, 121, 122, 147, 208–9, 212, 220, 332–4
Hibberd, Jack 133
higher education *see* universities
Hill, Anita 87–8, 95, 97
Hill, Barry 135
Hill, Benny 48
Hindmarsh Island 61, 230
Hippie Hippie Shake 101
History of Australia, A 174
HITZ FM 8, 9
Hobbyhorses 30, 32
Hobsbawm, Eric 200
Holocaust 156, 160, 161, 166–7, 170, 195, 227–8
homelessness viii, xii, 74, 233, 234, 260, 318
Honour and Other People's Children 133
hooks, bell 78, 85
Hope, A.D. 118
Horne, Donald 59
Howard, John 46, 52, 56, 60–1, 64–6, 68, 69, 70, 109–10, 241–2, 253, 298, 302, 305, 306, 307, 309, 318, 321
H. R. Nicholls Society 67
Huggins, Jackie 312, 313
Hughes, Robert 29, 30, 39, 42, 61, 76, 88, 110, 119, 120, 137, 164, 176, 184–6, 200–7, 286, 310, 328–9; *see also American Visions*; *Culture of Complaint*; *Fatal Shore, The*; *Shock of the New, The*
Hughes, Ted 161
humanism 21, 135–6, 168, 176, 177, 180, 197, 201; liberal humanism 119, 156, 165–6, 176, 266, 294

human rights 303; Human Rights and Equal Opportunity Commission 318
Humphries, Barry 124
Hyde, John 48, 67
Hyland House 147

Idol, Billy 255
Illiberal Education 55, 66, 187–90, 196
immigration 42, 52, 56, 68, 252, 304, 347
In Melbourne Tonight 101, 343
Independent Monthly 26, 83, 102, 218
Indyk, Ivor 218–20
Institute for Educational Affairs 66
Institute of Public Affairs (IPA) 48, 67, 68
intellectual property 18
International Convention on the Rights of the Child 128
Internet xii, 18, 315
Internet Resources for Australian Activists 300
INXS 345

Jabiluka 298, 299
Jack Maggs 331, 333
Jagger, Mick 3, 101
Jaivin, Linda 120, 147
James, Clive 61, 184, 186
Jennings, Kate xv, 30, 34, 60, 113, 136, 168
JFK 39
JJJ 25, 303
Jobs Network 314, 315
Jolley, Elizabeth 119, 123, 124, 125, 135
Jones, Alan 12, 25, 62, 63, 105, 302, 304, 306, 307, 328, 339, 350
Jones, Margaret 218
Jones, Peter 166
Joplin, Janis 2

Jost, John 216, 220
journalists vii, 29; current affair 22
Joyce, James 120, 126

Kalantzis, Mary 47, 72, 312
Kalinowska, Monica 45
Kangaroo Palace 101
Katter, Bob 46
Keating, Paul 270, 273
Keats 126
Kee, Thuan Chye 314
Kelly, Paul (journalist) 29, 193
Kelly, Paul (musician) 277
Kemp, David 243, 315
Kemp, Rod 67
Keneally, Thomas 133
Kennedy, John F. (JFK) 7, 39, 208
Kennerley, Kerri-Anne 343
Kennett, Jeff 11, 56
Kenny, Chris 61
Kerr, Duncan 306
Kiley, Dean 331
Killing of History, The 30, 171, 181, 187, 191, 192
Kimball, Roger 187, 188, 191, 192, 196, 197, 198, 206
King, Poppy 23
King, Richard 140
Kinsley, Michael 1
Knight, Stephen 330
Ko Un 138
Koch, Christopher 30, 34–6, 162, 171, 178–9, 209, 341
Kokkinos, Ana 313
Kokokiris, Maria 45
Koolmatrie, Wanda 209
Kosky, Barrie 21, 34, 141
Kotz, Dorothy 233
Kramer, Leonie 48
Kristol, Irving 65
Kroger, Michael 302, 303
Kruger, Barbara 11
Kulcha 8
Kureishi, Hanif 51
Kurosawa, Susan 6

Index

Labor (government) 9, 10, 12, 13, 15, 47, 65, 70, 144, 302
Lacan, Jacques 162
Lane, Terry 30, 31, 32, 54, 80, 102, 108, 216
lang, k.d. 81
Langford Ginibi, Ruby 136, 312, 320
Langton, Marcia 309, 310–11, 312
Lansdowne Press 126
Lapham, Lewis 189, 192, 194, 198
Last Days of Chez Nous 122
Laster, Kathy 108
Lau, Siew Mei 314
Lavarch, Michael 240
Lawrence, Carmen 15, 230
Lawrence, D.H. 124, 126
Laws, John (2UE) 12, 13, 25, 30, 32, 62–3, 105, 108–11, 280, 328
Lawson, Henry 53
Lawson, Sylvia 85, 185, 186, 188
Le Pen, Jean-Marie 186
Leave it to Beaver 157
Leavis, F.R. 164, 177, 282, 297
Legge, Kate 336, 339
Less Than Zero 14
Leys, Simon 178, 285
Liberal government *see* Coalition government
liberal: coterie 286; liberalism 270–301, 313, 346, 348–9
libertarianism 35; *see also* Anderson, John; Sydney Push
Life 7
Limbaugh, Rush 67, 192, 304
Linklater, Richard 256
literary theory *see* theory
literature, death of 21; high 332; wars 346
Littlemore, Stuart 24, 217
Lives of the Saints 130
Livin' Large 45
Loaded 39, 130, 135, 288
Lohrey, Amanda 162, 285
London Review of Books 190

Loukakis, Angelo 312
Love, Courtney 208, 263
LSD 3
Luck, Peter 24
Luckman, Sue 280
Ludbrook, Robert 238
Luhrmann, Baz 23–4
Lumby, Catharine 85
Lyneham, Paul 24

McAuley, James 59, 119
McCarthy, Joe 206
McDermott, Paul 344
McDonald, Donald 303
McDonald, John 328
Macdonald, Patricia 329
McGahan, Andrew 130–1
McGough, Roger 111
McGregor, Andrew 316
McGregor, Malcolm 25, 304
McGuinness, P.P. 24, 29, 30, 49, 50, 60, 61, 71, 80, 99, 102, 217, 242, 246, 247, 305, 328, 340–1
Macintyre, Stuart 175
Mackay, Hugh 52, 299
MacKenzie, David 316
MacKinnon, Catharine 87–8
McLaren, John 39
McLaren, Malcolm 263
McNiven, Ian 72
McPhee Gribble 120, 148
McPhee, Hilary 120, 133–4, 148, 209, 215
McQueen, Humphrey 164–5, 217
Mabo judgment 68, 73, 107, 223
Macken, Deirdre 3
Madison Centre 66
Madonna 81, 199
Magabala Books 209
Major, John 177, 233
Malcolm, Janet 123, 127, 160, 161, 330
Malouf, David 119, 120, 123–5, 135, 215
Mamet, David 89

391

Manne, Anne 327
Manne, Robert ix, 24, 30, 36, 37, 49, 50, 53, 59, 69, 70, 73, 116, 120–2, 158–61, 170, 172, 176, 177, 181, 184, 187, 194, 195, 197, 200, 216–28, 276, 280, 281, 282–3, 295, 308, 309, 332, 334–5, 336–8, 341; see also *Culture of Forgetting, The*; *Way We Live Now, The*
Mansfield, Katherine 122, 123, 136
Mapplethorpe, Robert 199
marketing 17, 19, 153, 255–61
Marketing to Generation X 255
Marr, David 125, 126, 219, 227, 328
Martin, Adrian 49, 183, 308
Martin, Ray 24, 52, 105, 217, 342, 343
Martin, Tony 8, 109
marxism 261
Mason, Bonita 320
Matthews, David 318
Matthews, Gordon 43
Mead, Jenna 135, 210, 212, 335–8, 339
Meanjin 118, 120, 218, 219
Mears, Gillian 111
media: alternative 324; demographic targeting 292; mainstream 350; power 291
Media Watch 342
Medicare 13
Melrose Place 256, 257, 260
'Metropolis' 194–207
Mickey Mouse 156, 199; Mickey Mouse Club 7
Mickler, Steve 252
Mighty Morphin Power Rangers 256
Miles Franklin Award 30, 35, 122, 159, 162, 187, 209, 215, 218, 219, 220, 222, 226
Milperra, Doug 61
Minogue, Kenneth 61
minority rights 33

Mitchell, Susan 30, 40–2, 84
Modjeska, Drusilla 58, 87, 120, 123–5, 135, 281, 285
Moi, Toril 50
Moller, Jerry 244
Monkey Grip 132, 135, 174
Monkey's Mask, The 147
Moore, Suzanne 105
Moore, Tony 282
Moorhouse, Frank 25, 29, 30, 36, 115, 225, 270–5, 277
moral panic 15, 36–7, 45–74, 240, 246–9, 252, 346; see also youth
Morgan, Hugh 67
Morgan, Roy 292
Morning After, The 26, 76, 78, 81, 89, 90, 94
Morris, Dick 233
Morris, Meaghan ix, 30, 85, 168, 172–3, 181, 188, 308
Morrison, Jim 2, 3, 260
Morrison, Toni 75, 95, 311–12
Mr Scobie's Riddle 125
Mudrooroo 43, 209
Muller, Laurie 151
multiculturalism 22, 29, 32–3, 35–7, 43, 48, 52, 67–9, 73, 102–3, 136, 187, 190, 201–2, 204, 215, 222–3, 227, 275, 291, 296, 303, 304, 309, 310, 339–40, 349; 'multicultural industry' 295, 327
Munro, Mike 24
Murdoch, Lachlan 289
Murdoch, Rupert 24, 148, 289
Murnane, Gerald 162
Murphy, Paul 24
Murray, Charles 193
Murray, Les 29, 30, 33, 34, 53, 61, 102, 108, 133, 171, 209, 215, 285, 341
Murray-Smith, Stephen 120
Mushroom Records 343
Musil, Robert 120
My Father's Moon 124

Index

My Own Sweet Time 209
Myth of Political Correctness, The 55

1968 101, 260
1988 130
Nabokov 126
Naher, Gaby 130
National Children's Summit 319
National Children's and Youth Law Centre 238
National Drug and Alcohol Research Centre 316
National Gallery of Australia 328
National Homeless Children's Report 318
National Party 47
National Youth Media Awards 293
National Youth Reconciliation Convention 300
Native Title Act (1993) 46, 305
Nature Strip 135
Naylor, Brian 343
Negus, George 24, 272, 275, 276, 277
Neill, Rosemary 42, 211, 216
Nelson, H. G. 344
Nelson, Penelope 343
Neumann, Anne 327
Neville, Richard 27, 30, 31, 32, 61, 101, 184, 186, 271–3, 276–7, 281–2, 300
New Criterion 192
New Establishment 21–44, 172
New Left 274
New Right 287, 296, 304, 305, 325, 345, 347, 348, 351
New Victorians, The 26, 81, 90
New Yorker 330
Newman, Jocelyn 321
Newsweek 3
Night Letters 186
Nine Inch Nails 229
Nirvana 2

O'Brien, Kerry 24, 182

O'Chee, Bill 64
O'faolain, Nuala 334
O'Hara, Frank 255
O'Keeffe, Georgia 204
O'Neil, Lloyd 126, 148
O'Neill, John 83
O'Shane, Pat 62, 72
Oakes, Laurie 27
Oakley, Barry 30, 156, 165, 170, 175, 192, 285
Observer 59
Octapod 287
Of Grammatology 165
Office of the Status of Women 71
Official Slacker Handbook, The 256
Oh Lucky Country 130, 136
Oldfield, David 304
Oleanna 89
Olin Foundation 66, 189, 197, 206
Olney, Justice 308
One Nation Party 107, 297, 307, 308
Optimist, The 121
Orchard, The 87, 135
Orchard Thieves, The 124
Ormond College 12, 119, 126, 181; 'affair' 26, 27, 37, 42, 55, 75–98, 156, 158, 160, 161; *see also First Stone, The;* Garner, Helen
Orr, Sydney Sparkes 89
Overland 39, 118, 120, 219
Oz 31, 32, 101
Oz rock ix

Packer, Kerry 304
Paglia, Camille 76, 84–8, 90, 94, 105, 190, 197
Painter, George 126
Palmer, Nettie 119
Pan Macmillan 148, 149
Panel, The 343, 344
Papaellinas, George 218, 312
Partington, Geoffrey 68
Pauline Hanson: The Truth 107

Paxton family vii, 13, 66, 230, 251, 303; Shane Paxton 293, 342
Peace Corps 57
Pearson, Christopher 30, 61, 62, 68, 121, 215, 340, 341
Pearson, Noel 46, 297, 298, 302, 303, 304, 305, 312
Penguin Books 143, 148
Penny Dreadful 343
Perkin, Graham 64
Petkovic, Daniella 45
Pharmakon 165
Phillips, A.A. *see* cultural cringe
Picasso 136
Pierce, Peter 133, 331–2
Pinter, Harold 123
Plato 164–5
Plays Well with Others 330
political correctness viii, xii, xiii, 19, 30, 33, 36–7, 40, 43, 45–74, 69, 177, 181, 202, 206, 217, 222, 234, 246, 248, 278, 291, 295, 303, 304, 305, 307, 309, 338–9, 346, 349; and economic rationalism 66, 308; attack on 66, 194; demise of 102; hoax 38
Poppy 135
Porritt, Don 1
Port Arthur 9, 10, 72
Port Hedland 64
Porter, Dorothy 147
postcolonialism 108, 162
postmodernism 36, 136, 156–7, 159, 160, 161–2, 177–8, 180, 195, 216, 221, 224, 261, 263–4, 341
poststructuralism 156, 162, 166–7, 177, 202–3, 261–2
Potato Factory, The 333
Prior, Natalie Jane 216
Priscilla, Queen of the Desert 310
Proulx, E. Annie 126, 178
Proust, Marcel 126
public culture 17, 279, 309
public debate xi

public intellectuals 173, 310
public space xi, xii, 28, 173, 181, 264, 313
public sphere 35, 324, 347, 351
publishing industry 17, 114–15, 140–54
Pulp Fiction 15, 157, 199
punk 345–6
Pusey, Michael 97
Push, The *see* Sydney Push
Pybus, Cassandra 212

Quadrant 59, 60, 70, 118, 156, 218, 285, 328, 341
Queen 229

Rabelais 12
Race Discrimination Commission 47
race 35, 296; and authenticity 43; race politics 31, 27, 203; racism 33
radio hosts 8, 12 *see also* Jones, Alan; Laws, John; Limbaugh, Rush; Sattler, Howard; shock jocks; talkback radio; Zemanek, Stan
Radley, Paul 133, 209
Ramsey, Alan 70
Rand Corporation 320
Random House 148, 149, 343
Rayner, Moira 249
Reagan, Ronald 66, 110, 303
Real Opinions 30
Reality Bites 256
Reed Books 148–9
Regurgitator 12
Rehame 302
RePublica 210, 218, 288
Republican Party (US) 97, 110, 198, 206, 303, 304
republicans 29
Resistance 299
Revolution X 256
Reynolds, Henry 47, 69, 108–9

Index

Richardson, Owen 120, 121, 123, 132
Riders, The 135
Riemer, Andrew 61, 170, 187, 216–20, 330
Rimmer, Stephen 62, 215
Ritchie, Karen 256
River Ophelia, The 14, 130
Robb, Andrew 303, 304
Robbins, Tim 21
Robertson, Wendy 299
Roiphe, Katie 26, 76, 78, 81, 82, 85, 88, 94, 95, 190, 191
Rolling Stones 229
Romper Stomper 32
Roseanne 157
Roundtable 314, 315
Rowley, Hazel 125
Royal Commission into Aboriginal Deaths in Custody 238, 240, 252, 320
Rundle, Guy 219, 290, 291, 338
RuPaul 208, 223
Rush Hour 296
Rutherford, Andrew 120–1, 126, 221
Ruxton, Bruce 62
Ryan, Rebekah 8
Ryckmans, Pierre 30, 172–3, 177–8, 281, 285
Ryder, Winona 256

7.30 Report 24, 72, 182, 290
60 Minutes 55, 104, 230
Sabto, Michelle 289
Safran, John 342
Saints, The 345
Salusinszky, Imre 285, 286, 341
Salvation Army 315
Sandstone Gothic 330
Sang Ye 312
Santamaria, B. A. 19
Sattler, Howard 237
Savage Garden 9
Sayer, Mandy 131

Schofield, Leo 137
scrapheap 21
Scripsi 119, 122, 123, 124, 125, 147
Seams of Light 312, 313
Segal, David 47
Sessions, Bob 332
Sex Pistols 345
Sex and Text 30
Sexual Personae 90
sexual harassment 41, 42, 75–98
Shakespeare 31, 57, 121, 138, 155, 156, 177, 181, 186, 190, 199, 200, 329
Shapcott, Thomas 133, 170
She 12
Sheehan, Paul 275, 295, 305, 306, 327, 339, 340–1
Sheiner, Paul 237
Shirvington, Matt 305, 313
Shock of the New, The 185
shock jocks 12, 62, 67, 72, 112 *see also* Jones, Alan; Laws, John; Sattler, Howard; talkback radio; Zemanek, Stan
Sidoti, Chris 238–9, 244, 318, 320
Silent Woman, The 160–1
silverchair 9, 229
Simpsons, The 157
Slattery, Luke 30, 47, 49, 53, 120–2, 126, 156–57, 163, 173–4, 201, 210, 277, 285, 286, 289, 290, 292, 329
Slaven, Roy 344
Smallwood, John 235
Soapbox 287
Sommers, Christina Hoff 81, 189
Sontag, Susan 119, 123
Sorensen, Rosemary 120, 131–2
South Park 281
Southerly 118
speaking position 42, 43, 178
Speaking Their Minds 310
speech codes 37, 45
Spiderbait 9
Sprinkle, Annie 81

St Vincent de Paul 19
Star, Darren 257
Stead, Christina 125, 132, 184
Steele, Peter 285
Stendhal 124, 126, 136
Stephenson, John 121
Stevens, Leonie 135
stolen generations 298, 309, 341
Stone, John 25, 62, 67
Stone, Oliver 39
Stonier, Brian 148
Stork 31
Stott Despoja, Natasha 298
Stove, David 34
Stretton, Andrea 14
Students Against Racism 299
Students Who Action Reconciliation Seriously (STARS) 299
suicide rates (young) viii, xii, 14, 244
Summers, Anne 25, 27, 30, 38, 84, 88, 97, 281
Sun Books 148
Sun-Herald 313
Sunday Age 6, 120, 121, 125, 126, 132, 221, 229, 235, 236
Sydney Institute 64, 209–10
Sydney Morning Herald 6, 23, 24, 27, 80, 125, 211, 215, 218, 252, 328, 330, 338, 339
Sydney Push 9, 29, 59, 60, 61
Syson, Ian 219–20

Tabar, Paul 319
talkback radio 8, 12, 22, 62, 67, 72, 106–7, 110–12, 221, 289, 292, 305, 324; *see also* Jones, Alan; Laws, John; Sattler, Howard; shock jocks; Zemanek, Stan
Tall Poppies 40
Tan, Le 302, 317
Tarantino, Quentin 14, 24, 199
Tasman Institute 67
technology 17; link with culture 18, 273

teen gangs *see* youth gangs
Tennant, Kylie 119
Ten-Point Plan 305
Tenured Radicals 187, 191
Tertiary Education Amendment Act 11
Text Publishing 120–1, 148, 334; *see also* Gribble, Di; Heyward, Michael
Thatcherism 97
The Cook, the Thief, His Wife and Her Lover 32
The Last Shout 25
theory viii, 43, 163–70, 172, 187; and moral panic 37; anti- 36–8; teaching of 36, 182, 202; 'theory wars' 180; *see also* cultural studies; deconstruction; feminism: postcolonialism; postmodernism; poststructuralism
think-tanks 66, 68
This Day Tonight 22, 24, 25, 27, 103–4
This Is Your Life 101
Thomas, Clarence 87–8, 95, 97
Thomas, Dylan 126
Thompson, Christina 120
Thoughts of Chairman Stan, The 306
Threesome 256, 259
Throsby, Margaret 126
Time 125, 291, 329
Timms, Peter 327, 328
Today Tonight 106, 293
Tolstoy 124, 136
Top Girls 111
Total Recall 262
Totaro, Gianna 216
Trainspotting 131
Tranter, John 128, 140
Trilling, Lionel 282
Trioli, Virginia 27, 42, 152, 211, 278–9, 280, 338
True Stories 126, 138, 212
Tsiolkas, Christos 14, 39, 51, 115, 130, 135, 288, 312
Tucker, Chris 296

Index

Tuckey, Wilson 46
Turgenev 124
Two Nations 312–13
Tyshing, Christine 216

Underwharf, The 130
unemployment viii, xii, 2, 14, 309, 317; *see also* youth
United Nations Convention on the Rights of the Child 318
Universities ix, xii, xv, 4, 11–14, 36, 41, 48–50, 53–4, 55, 57–9, 66, 70, 77, 79, 80, 83, 94–5, 97, 118–9, 122, 125, 149, 151, 156–7, 159, 168–70, 172, 176, 178, 180–3, 188–92, 196–200, 216, 260, 288
University of Queensland Press 151

Vanstone, Amanda 4, 13, 273
Veitch, Kate 130–1
Victorian Domestic Violence Act 75
Victorian Premier's Literary Awards 30, 136
Victory, The 303
Vietnam (war) x, xii, 32, 74, 102, 260
'victim cults' 33, 202
'victim feminism' *see* feminism
'victim-panic' 75–98
Vincent, Frank 235
Virtual Artists 287
Vogel award 133, 140, 209
volunteer rates 57

Wade, Jan 12
Walpole, Sue 71
Walsh, Peter 33, 62
Walter, James 193, 249
Wark, McKenzie 36, 155, 172, 188, 327
Warren Commission 39
Watson, Sam 312, 313
Waugh, Evelyn 126
Way We Live Now, The 338

Wayne's World 259
Weatherburn, Don 319
Webby, Elizabeth 124
'wedge politics' 303, 304, 305, 348
welfare 303, 315
Welsh, Irvine 131
Weller, Archie 314
Wendt, Jana 311–12
West Australian 237, 251–2
Westbury, Marcus 270, 274–5
Western Mining 67
Whitaker, Bob 101
White Australia Policy 108
White Nation 296
White, Patrick 118, 124–6, 137, 156, 167, 184, 209
White, Rob 249–50, 277
Whiteley, Brett 184–5
Whitlams 303
Whitlam's coalition 29, 42; government 343
Who Stole Feminism? 81, 189
Whole Woman, The 330
Wik 107, 109, 110, 296, 306, 307
Willessee, Mike 24
William Shakespeare's Romeo and Juliet 23
Wiliams, Daryl 306
Williams, Pamela 303
Williamson, David ix, 29, 30, 32, 36, 53, 55, 57–8, 62, 73, 89, 95, 103, 108–9, 133, 156, 165, 171–2, 181, 197, 209, 215, 262, 278, 281; *see also Brilliant Lies, Dead White Males, Heretic*
Williamson, Drew 294
Williamson, Kristin 126
Wilson, John 55, 196
Windschuttle, Keith 30, 156–57, 162–3, 169, 172, 181, 187–8, 191–2, 232
Winton, Tim 121, 135
Wolf, Naomi 76, 81, 85
Wolfe, Tom 287
Wonder Years 101

Wood, Anna 10, 193, 230
Woodstock x, 65, 229
Woodward, C. Vann 196–7
Woodward, Roger 133
Woolf, Virginia 123, 124, 136, 211
Work for the Dole programme 317, 321
Working Hot 135
World Wide Web 199
Wright, Judith 119
writers' festivals 116–17; Brisbane Writers' Festival 36, 313; 'Grunge' panel 115; Melbourne Writers' Festival 113–17, 121–2, 125, 137–8, 286, 308, 331–5; National Young Writers' Festival 287; Sydney Writers' Festival 138, 218; Warana Writers' Week 36
Wynbyne, Margaret Nalyirri 319
Wyndham, Bill 2
Wynhausen, Elizabeth 239

Yahp, Beth 312
Yang, Lian 312
Yellow Pages 1
Yock, Daniel 241

Yorta Yorta 307, 308
youth vii, 159, 199, 216, 349; affairs reporting 40; and drugs 236; crime viii, 15, 194, 233–54, 268, 319, 320, 322; cult of 27; culture 5, 200, 232–54, 344; demonisation in media 322; employment 2, 14, 171, 192, 242–4, 246–7, 271–2, 314, 316–17; gangs viii, xii, 37, 78, 232–54; 'ghetto' 27; homelessness 314; magazine 4; mandatory sentencing 15, 239–40; migrant 319; and moral panic 15; policy xii, 192, 232–54; regional 293; reporting 292; rights 314; suicide 2, 14, 244, 309, 314, 327; tribes 5; wage xiii, 242, 314
Youth Homelessness, Early Intervention and Prevention 316
Youth Predators Act 233
Yuson, Alfred 314

Zeitgeist x, 208, 231, 232
Zemanek, Stan 62, 63, 105, 306
zero-tolerance policing 193

pamphleteering', John McLaren, *Australian Book Review* ¶ 'His chapter on *The First Stone* is one of the best pieces of writing on feminism by a man that I've read . . . Davis is a lively writer, unafraid to name names and chart networks and his book takes on and assiduously demolishes several icons of public intellectual life', Anne Coombs, *The Australian's Review of Books* ¶ 'I've been reading newspapers, listening to the radio and watching television with different eyes since I read *Gangland*', Mary-Rose MacColl, *Independent Monthly* ¶ 'A book that will strike fear — and loathing — into most of the arts establishment', Helen Elliott, *Herald-Sun* ¶ 'I enjoyed this book immensely . . . its message is long overdue', Ken Gelder, *Sunday Age* ¶ 'Accessible . . . spirited and provocative', Philippa Hawker, *Elle* ¶ 'An exhilarating discussion of Australian literary culture', Leigh Dale, *Australian Literary Studies* ¶ 'Much o'